A Budgeting Guide for Local Government

Fourth Edition

Robert L. Bland
and Michael R. Overton

ICMA

INTERNATIONAL CITY/COUNTY
MANAGEMENT ASSOCIATION

ICMA, the International City/County Management Association, advances professional local government through leadership, management, innovation, and ethics. ICMA provides member support; publications; data and information; peer and results-oriented assistance; and training and professional development to more than 12,000 city, town, and county experts and other individuals and organizations throughout the world. The management decisions made by ICMA's members affect millions of individuals living in thousands of communities, from small villages and towns to large metropolitan areas.

Library of Congress Cataloging-in-Publication Data

Bland, Robert L. and Overton, Michael R.
A budgeting guide for local government / by Robert L. Bland and Michael R. Overton – Fourth edition.
pages cm
Includes index.
978-0-87326-435-8 (alk. paper)
1. Local budgets–United States–Handbooks, manuals, etc. I. Title.
HJ9147.B55 2014
352.4'82140973–dc23
2013021354

978-0-87326-435-8

Design: Erika White and Kirie Samuels
Composition: Ecoprint

Printed in the United States of America

2020 2019 2018 2017 2016 2015 2014 2013
54321

About the Authors

Robert L. (Bob) Bland is professor of public administration at the University of North Texas, where he has been on the faculty since 1982 and teaches graduate courses in public finance, governmental accounting, and budgeting. He is the author of *A Revenue Guide for Local Government* (2nd ed., 2005) and *A Budgeting Guide for Local Government* (3rd ed., 2013), both published by ICMA, as well as of several articles on the municipal bond market, property taxation, and municipal budgeting. In 2007 he was the first recipient of the Terrell Blodgett Academician Award presented by the Texas City Management Association; he also received ICMA's Stephen B. Sweeney Academic Award in October 2007. In 2012, Professor Bland was elected as a fellow in the National Academy of Public Administration. He received his BS from Pepperdine University, his MPA and MBA from the University of Tennessee, and his PhD from the Graduate School of Public and International Affairs at the University of Pittsburgh. He can be reached at bbland@unt.edu.

Michael R. Overton is an assistant professor of public administration at the University of Idaho. His research explores the intersection of local government management and fiscal policy, specifically focusing on local government competition, economic development, and transportation financing issues. His research into these areas has been funded by the U.S. Department of Housing and Urban Development, the Lincoln Institute of Land Policy, SMART Transit, and the North Central Texas Council of Governments. In 2015, he received the University of North Texas's Toulouse Dissertation Award in Social Science. In 2016 he was selected for the Emerging Scholars Award by the Lincoln Institute of Land Policy, and in 2017 he was selected as a Founders Fellow by the American Society of Public Administration.

This book is dedicated to Jane Cotnoir (1948–2019), editor extraordinaire.

Green Books—Authoritative source books on local government management

ICMA's "Green Books" (a designation derived from the original bright green cloth covers) have a long history as the authoritative source on local government management. They are used by local government managers in cities and counties worldwide, by university professors and students as textbooks for undergraduate and graduate courses, and by public safety professionals in preparation for promotional exams. The Green Books cover the range of local government functions, linking the latest theories and research to specific examples of day-to-day decision making and the nuts and bolts of management. Current titles in the Green Book series include

Local Planning: Contemporary Principles and Practice
Management Policies in Local Government Finance, 6th edition
Managing Fire and Emergency Services
Managing Fire and Emergency Services Study Guide

Other recent titles

Capital Budgeting and Finance: A Guide for Local Governments, 2nd edition
Economic Development: Strategies for State and Local Practice, 2nd edition
The Effective Local Government Manager, 3rd edition
Effective Supervisory Practices, 5th edition
Effective Supervisory Skill Building Study Guide
Ethics Matter! Advice for Public Managers
Getting Started: Performance for Local Government
Leading Performance Management in Local Government
Leading Your Community: A Guide for Local Elected Leaders
Managing Local Government: Cases in Effectiveness
Managing Local Government Services: A Practical Guide
Service Contracting: A Local Government Guide
Statistics for Public Administration: Practical Uses for Better Decision Making, 2nd edition

Learn about these and other titles at icma.org/publications.

Contents

PART II: Preparing and Approving the Local Budget

Sidebars

Figures

Tables

Acknowledgments

This edition of *A Budgeting Guide* and its predecessors have benefited from a superb editorial team at ICMA. At the outset to preparing the revisions for this edition, Ann Mahoney led the publication team. Her creative touch is evident in the appearance and content of the book. With Ann's retirement, ICMA turned to Cory Fleming, Senior Technical Specialist, Global Program Management, to press forward with the project. She has done so graciously and has kept the project on schedule and doubtless within budget.

We have benefited from the students at the University of North Texas and the University of Idaho who have challenged us to refine our explanations of theories and their implications for policy and management. We also owe a debt of gratitude to users of the book in other universities and in local government who have made thoughtful suggestions for additions to the book. To our friends and colleagues in the Association for Budgeting and Financial Management (ABFM), thank you for providing opportunities for testing our ideas and learning from your insights.

As part of its commitment to excellence, ICMA provides exceptional editorial support to its authors. From the earliest iterations of this book, the editorial support has added substantially to the clarity and coherency of the text. For the past 25 years, Jane Cotnoir tirelessly reworded, honed, trimmed, and prodded us to achieve what we thought impossible. She was intolerant of sloppiness, unforgiving of carelessness, and insistent on clarity. Jane loved her job; she loved ICMA; and she loved the local government management profession. Her valiant two-decade battle with cancer as well as her wish to complete the edits for this edition ended on January 3, 2019. In appreciation for her devotion to our profession, we dedicate this 4th edition to her.

Anne Phelan graciously and ably stepped in to complete the editorial duties. She was backed by a team of ICMA professionals who carry forward the standard of excellence that has become the hallmark of ICMA publications.

With this edition, Michael Overton assumes co-authorship and as such brings a younger voice and passion to future editions. For both of us, our greatest debt of appreciation is to our best friends with whom we share our hopes and dreams and love and life.

Bob Bland
Endowed Professor of Local Government
University of North Texas
bbland@unt.edu

Michael Overton
Assistant Professor
University of Idaho
moverton@uidaho.edu

Foreword

In the six years since publication of the 3rd edition of *A Budgeting Guide for Local Government*, social, political, and financial evolutions have reshaped the way local governments deliver and pay for public services. Written with managers, budget directors, and students of the profession in mind, Professors Bob Bland and Michael Overton offer a fresh and forward-looking examination of local government budgeting.

Building on the success of the past editions, Bland and Overton forge into new arenas that shape the "warp and woof" of budgets and the policies and processes managers use to craft spending decisions. This edition introduces several new topics. Bland and Overton highlight recent innovations in the ways that budget practices are used to allocate resources and to increase the productive use of those resources. Smart communities, or what the authors prefer to call technology-enhanced communities (TEC), are reshaping how governments work and consequently how they prepare their budgets. Given that over 84 percent of the cities in the United States have populations under 10,000, this edition has added a discussion of how smaller cities and counties adapt their budget practices to their institutional constraints. The authors also examine the evolution in the relationship between citizens and their local government and speculate that, in the near future, local governments will enter a private government era in which citizens become subscribers to public services.

This 4th edition expands on themes introduced in previous editions. As the public sector's equivalent of a broker, the budget analyst brings together producers and consumers of local services, thereby transforming the budget process into a commodity exchange for those services. Although local governments have adopted more entrepreneurial methods of management, Bland and Overton provide the reasons why budgeting processes in the private sector cannot (and should not) be replicated in the public arena. They go further and call on local managers to embrace truth-in-budgeting—creating an organizational culture that ensures the budget office is a dependable source of credible analyses. Good budgeting effectively links inputs (capital and labor) with outcomes. As the authors note, divining the linkage between inputs and their impact on the community is the key budget problem that managers must wrestle with. They offer practical guidance on how managers can effectively communicate budget information with their stakeholders and elevate the legitimacy of local government. Fiscal crises precipitated by natural or human actions impact budgets differently depending on their severity and duration. The authors offer specific strategies for responding to and mitigating the range of crises that can potentially strike a local government.

The greatest challenge for balancing local budgets remains finding sufficient revenues to fund the services communities expect. Bland and Overton skillfully navigate the complex terrain of revenue policy and administration. They provide an intriguing assessment of the impact of property tax exemptions on local budgets and the strategies used to compensate for the lost revenue. The authors provide an updated assessment of the general and excise sales taxes and the limited applicability of a local income tax. One of the bright spots for local revenues has been the steady shift toward charges on users of services. The authors introduce a typology of strategies for structuring prices that give managers a clear understanding of the tradeoffs that must be made when designing a price structure.

The 4th edition also has an updated appearance. Each chapter begins with a sidebar highlighting its takeaways—specific learning outcomes that the reader can expect to obtain. The exercises and discussion questions that were at the end of each chapter in the 3rd edition have now been moved to ICMA's website (icma.org), giving users easier access and allowing the authors to quickly update and expand the inventory of questions. The text retains the popular Excel exercises but they, too, have been moved to the ICMA website.

ICMA is pleased to introduce this 4th edition of what has become one of the classics in its repertoire of publications for students and managers of local government. We are grateful to Professors Bob Bland and Michael Overton for their contributions to the study and practice of local government management.

Marc A. Ott
Executive Director
International City/County Management Association
Washington, D.C.

CHAPTER 1

The context of local government finance

Economics is the fate of all politicians.

—*Unknown*

This chapter provides the following takeaways:

- Know why local governments provide not only basic public services but also a variety of other not-so-public services.
- Distinguish among four types of public-private partnerships and how each leverages a local government's resources.
- Understand how the current budget environment and the citizens it serves have been shaped by past budget eras.
- Know what managers should anticipate in the coming private government era.
- Know the three external forces that affect the financial health of local governments and how managers can mitigate those effects now.

Navigating the increasingly complex crosscurrents of local government finance has become an essential skill for today's public administrator. The convergence of rising expectations from citizens and council members, anemic growth in revenue sources, and unfunded pensions now coming due has complicated the local manager's task of preparing a budget that balances revenues with expenditures. More fundamentally, today's managers must deliver services at a time when public confidence in government and its ability to perform have reached unparalleled lows.

This book examines the issues that a local manager confronts in developing a budget—both the choice of public services and projects to provide, and the choice of revenue sources used to pay for them. When formulating a budget, the manager must balance what is economically best, politically expedient, and administratively possible. Because the manager must also respond to citizens' perceptions of an issue, whatever their accuracy, this book also examines budgets in those terms. In a more general sense, effective leadership requires that the public administrator shape as well as follow public opinion. The recommendations made throughout this book are designed to enhance citizens' confidence in the responsiveness and competence of local government leaders.

The budget document, in its arduous journey from preparation to adoption, expresses the basic political values of a government. It reflects the compromises negotiated in the contentious process of budget adoption. It guides public administrators, defining government's economic and political roles in the community and sanctioning, as well as limiting, administrative action. It not only operationalizes a community's plans for its future but also molds that future by the policies it contains. A good budget brings order to an uncertain world.

The budget document is foremost a tool for maintaining financial accountability. Yet as its preparation has evolved into a forum for establishing strategic goals and performance expectations, the resulting document has become the public record of a community dialogue for improving organizational performance and management oversight. Thus, the budget is also a tool for holding administrators accountable for performance expectations.

The economic nature of government services

A recurring aspect of government reform in the United States has been efforts to imbue the public sector with the values of efficiency and effectiveness found in the private sector. Economic theory holds that the competitive marketplace compels the private sector to give top priority to increasing productive efficiency, customer satisfaction, and innovation. Governments, which operate as monopolies within their service areas, are presumed by economic theory to be less efficient, less innovative, and less sensitive to customer needs. Many chief executives have asked the age-old question: Why can't government be run like a business? And many advisory commissions have been convened to try to provide an answer.

But a satisfactory answer remains frustratingly elusive. Government and business, as public administration scholar Wallace Sayre is said to have observed, "are alike only in all unimportant respects."[1] The most essential difference is economic, a function of the kinds of goods and services each produces. Governments produce public goods and, under certain conditions, private goods, whereas the private sector produces only private goods.

Private goods versus public goods

Private goods and services are rivalrous and excludable: their consumption by one person precludes others from consuming them and their benefits are limited to those who are willing to pay for them. Consumer goods commonly sold in the private sector possess these attributes. The price affixed to a good or service reflects the competition (rivalry) for that item. A sales receipt (or title or contract) gives the buyer exclusive access to the good or service and precludes others from its benefits. An attorney sells his or her services usually on an hourly basis; a physician may charge a set price for each procedure. Because they possess these properties, private goods and services are traded in a competitive marketplace with multiple buyers and sellers. Other things being equal, the producer that provides the good at the lowest unit cost will garner the greatest market share.

By contrast, public goods and services are neither rivalrous nor excludable. For example, public safety cannot be restricted to one person and one person's use of the service does not preclude others from its benefits. The benefits of a mosquito eradication program accrue to all citizens, even those who live outside the jurisdiction. Often the benefits of public services, such as emergency preparedness, emanate more from what the services prevent than from what they provide. A city with an emergency management unit will likely incur fewer fatalities, injuries, and property losses from a disaster than one that lacks such a unit. The benefit from increased police surveillance accrues to all residents, yet it becomes most apparent when a household or business is a victim of crime.

Because public goods cannot be traded in a marketplace, governments collectively finance and provide them. The funding decision is separated from the spending decision, and the amount of taxes imposed on a household or business bears little correlation to the amount of service each receives. The absence of a competitive marketplace for public goods means that, unlike what occurs in the private sector, the level of spending for a public service (supply) determines the amount that will be consumed. If a city chooses to increase its **appropriation** for police protection, more security will be "consumed."

Enter politics. The separation of payment made from services received creates an incentive for individuals and organized interest groups to influence the budget process so as to maximize their benefits from the service while minimizing their share of the cost. During budget deliberations, interest groups express their preferences for public services. In a sense, the budget process is a surrogate for the private marketplace, where the levels of demand and supply are established. The budget process does for citizens what the marketplace does for consumers—or, as a logical statement,

budget process : citizens :: market : consumers.

Public provision of private goods

While the private sector limits its activity to producing private goods, the public sector, especially state and local governments, produces both public and private goods. For example, public transit, water and sewer service, sanitation, and even education can be sold in units and the benefits excluded from nonpayers. Why does government produce these services?

Market failure One reason is market failure—the inability of a competitive market to efficiently produce a good or service. The private sector has no incentive to provide a service that does not yield profits. Private businesses either may choose not to provide an unprofitable service or may "cream" the market by providing the service only in those sectors that are profitable. Before World War II, public transit was largely an investor-owned business: a city would grant a franchise to a trolley car company, giving it a monopoly within the city. (Franchise agreements would specify the level of service to be provided and the fare to be charged.) When interstate highways and suburbanization made mass transit unprofitable, the trolley companies stopped operating. Yet the need for public transit persisted, especially in the more congested urban centers. Thus, cities assumed the financing and provision of public transit because of market failure. The Tennessee Valley Authority and Amtrak are also examples of government services provided because of market failure.

Natural monopolies A second reason that government assumes production of private goods is natural monopolies. Some services, such as utilities, are capital-intensive: much of the cost of the service arises from the investment in equipment and pipelines needed to produce it. Because of these costs and the limited opportunities for product diversification, unit costs to customers are minimized if only one producer provides the service. Government may choose to regulate producers through a state utility commission, as is often the case for natural gas, electricity, and local telephone exchange services, or it may choose to produce the service itself, as is often the case with water, sewer, and solid-waste services. As a monopolist, government may choose to produce these services at cost, produce them below cost and subsidize them with tax revenues, or produce them at a profit and subsidize otherwise tax-supported services.

Merit goods and services A third reason that government assumes responsibility for producing private goods is that some private goods are **merit goods and services**. An otherwise rivalrous and excludable service may have such widespread benefits to a community that government provides it free or at a greatly subsidized price with the difference financed from general tax revenues. Education is a classic example: it possesses the essential characteristics of a private good, yet because an educated workforce and electorate provide benefits to the entire community, governments finance this service with general taxes. States provide sizeable subsidies to public universities and colleges, and they subsidize local school districts with grants-in-aid, which, when combined with the district's own property tax revenue, make possible a system of virtually "free" public schools.

Historical precedent A final reason for government production of private services is historical precedent. For example, the state of North Dakota owns and operates the Bank of North Dakota, a commercial bank that provides all the depository and loan services of an investor-owned bank. Yet the bank's profits accrue to the state treasury. In the early twentieth century, members of the Grange Movement, an influential agricultural group, convinced the state to establish a central bank to promote agricultural and industrial development.[2] At about the same time, the state legislature also established the nation's only state-owned grain mill, the North Dakota Mill and Elevator Association. For historical reasons, the state maintains ownership of both the bank and the grain elevator, although the private sector is fully capable of managing each. State-owned liquor stores are another example of government provision of a private service that lingers largely as a result of precedent and the profit that these stores provide to the general fund.

The importance of local budget decisions

No other policy area evokes such strong opinions so quickly as a discussion of government spending, particularly as it relates to the revenue needed to finance it. Many citizens believe they pay too much in taxes. Yet when they consider the options, few are willing to sacrifice reduced public services for lower taxes, especially when they realize the minuscule impact that even sweeping reductions in city or county property taxes will have on their monthly household budgets. A local budget—and its revenue structure (taking into consideration nontax sources such as service charges and intergovernmental aid)—evolves from a complex mingling of past decisions and chance economic and political events, blended with shifts in community attitudes. Why, then, would a manager ever wade into a politically charged discussion of how a city or county finances its operations and what mix of public services it should provide?

Implications for the local economy

Occasionally local leaders mistakenly assume that all that is needed to achieve economic prosperity is new business investment in the community. But no amount of economic development effort can compensate for poor budget decisions. A city can "give away the farm" in tax incentives and never reap the benefits if it maintains the same tax structure that it had in the nineteenth century—and, in reality, a good many tax structures have not been overhauled since then.

A well-designed revenue structure—one that promotes fairness and market **neutrality** and is administratively cost-effective—is a local government's most effective tool for attracting and retaining business investment. In fact, tax incentives may be unnecessary if a community's leadership has focused its efforts on building a sound tax structure. Businesses, like citizens, are not averse to paying taxes if they see that local government operates efficiently and that value is added between the taxes they pay and the quality of public services they and their employees receive, such as increased public safety or greater mobility on city streets.

It is axiomatic that the stronger the local economy, the stronger the local government's revenue base. Investment in prudent budget choices leads to a stronger economy, which leads to more stable, sustainable revenue yields and thus to less budget volatility. Good tax policy is good economics and provides long-term benefits to the manager willing to invest time and political capital in tackling the sacred cows. Conversely, an inefficient, cluttered tax structure creates a drag on local economic growth. In a real sense, economic prosperity begins with carefully crafted budget policies. This book is about articulating such policies.

Implications for leadership

Budget discussions are politically costly because they realign winners and losers in the distribution of the benefits and costs of public services. Yet such discussions cannot be avoided—at least not indefinitely. Delaying difficult decisions pushes local leaders into a crisis mode, seeking ad hoc resolutions rather than long-term, comprehensive solutions. It narrows the choices that leaders are willing to consider because their attention is focused on the crisis. Local government leaders' inability to take timely action leads to more drastic actions later, further affirming a cynical citizenry's perception of ineffective government. One distinct, although unexplored, advantage of the council-manager form of government is the appointed career executive's greater political capacity to bring to the table a timely discussion of difficult budget choices.

Allowing a dysfunctional budget process to struggle along heightens citizen cynicism. Everyone knows the process is broken, yet no one has the political courage to engage citizens in a meaningful dialogue on solutions. Unfortunately, the important discussions emerge only in the crisis that is precipitated by a court ruling or a significant bond downgrading. The most productive reforms in local finance (1) occur in small increments over a long period of time, (2) are guided by a clear set of criteria that are widely shared by the community, and (3) choose economic prudence over political expediency on the general assumption that a strong economy will benefit all stakeholders rather than just the well connected (and then only temporarily).

Trends in local government finance

Ongoing changes in state and national economies have had a significant impact on local budget deliberations. The shift from a manufacturing to a service-based economy has prompted widespread efforts by both state and local governments to revamp their tax policies in order to capture more of the benefits from growth in the service sector. The influence of these external forces has created the following five trends in local government finances:

1. Greater dependence on own revenue sources
2. Increased use of public-private-nonprofit agreements for service delivery
3. Increased intergovernmental competition for new business investment
4. Citizen distrust of government
5. Increased economic uncertainty.

Greater dependence on own revenue sources

The decline in federal aid has ushered in what Robert Kleine and John Shannon, two noted public finance experts, called the "finance-it-yourself" fiscal era.[3] At its peak in 1979, federal aid represented about 17.6 percent of own-source revenue for local governments.[4] By 2015, however, federal aid had declined to 4.2 percent of general revenues.[5] This has imposed a significant realignment in local government budgets.

State aid has not replaced lost federal aid but has declined along with it. The combined loss of federal and state aid has required local officials to choose between curtailing services and increasing their own revenue. It has also exacerbated local officials' traditional mistrust of state and federal aid policy. In retrospect, those governments that shunned almost all federal aid may have taken a more politically prudent—although, in the short term, financially costly—course of action.

But declines in state and federal aid have not been accompanied by reduced constraints on local governments. In fact, state restrictions on local financial discretion—particularly in the choices of revenue sources used to fund local operations—have increased as the federal government has reduced its financial support for local affairs. For example, nearly every state now places a limit on the property tax rate or levy that local governments may impose. As a result, city and county officials have found themselves caught between the standardized revenue policies imposed by state law and the preferences of their citizens, which vary from community to community.

Paradoxically, as local governments have become more dependent on their own revenue sources, they have also become more prominent partners in the federal system. Since the federal government began turning more responsibility back to subnational governments, municipalities and counties have assumed greater responsibility for providing public services, such as for terrorism preparedness and highway construction.

Increased use of public-private-nonprofit agreements for service delivery

One of the most pervasive developments across all sectors of the American economy has been the partnering with other local governments, nonprofit organizations, and for-profit firms to produce and deliver services. Partnerships offer the possibility of providing better-quality services at a lower cost. But their success does not ensure either improved quality or a lower cost, let alone both objectives concurrently.

Governments have always contracted with other governments, private firms, and nonprofits for various services. The military depends on private vendors to supply equipment and materiel. Local governments bid out contracts to vendors for office supplies, vehicles, and technical support. Professional service agreements, such as for engineering design or executive searches, typically involve retaining a qualified firm to assist with the decision-making process.

In recent years, governments have greatly expanded their use of public-private-nonprofit agreements—generically known as **public-private partnerships** (PPPs, or P3)—to produce and deliver public services. Some local governments, such as Weston, Florida, rely on such agreements to provide all their services.[6] With this expansion has come a wide variety of experimentation in the methods used to select contractors, compensate them, and share the financial risk. And with this experimentation has come a new vocabulary that lacks consistency in its use and connotations.

Two dimensions of joint agreements A useful way of discussing the various kinds of joint agreements is in terms of their two main dimensions: *the end customer being served* (the unit of government versus citizens, businesses, or investors) and the *bearer of financial risk* (unshared versus shared by the partners). When a local government contracts with another government, a private firm, or a nonprofit organization to provide a service, the final customer is either the government itself (as in a contract with a law firm for the collection of delinquent property taxes on behalf of the city) or citizens or businesses outside the government (as in a contract with a private firm to collect solid waste on behalf of residents or businesses).

Joint ventures also have financial risk.[7] That risk may be borne exclusively by one party (unshared) or partially by both parties (shared) as a condition of the agreement. In the case of a **tax increment financing (TIF)** district, for example, if private investment meets expectations, the benefits from the shared financial risk in the redevelopment district are lower start-up costs for businesses that locate there and higher tax revenues from increased property values for the local government. However, if private investment lags expectations, neither the local government that provided financial backing nor the private firms that invested in the district realize the anticipated benefits of the venture. Financial risk is shared.

Typology of public-private ventures These two dimensions provide a typology, depicted in Figure 1–1, for characterizing four generic categories of partnerships and standardizing the terminology that has emerged concurrent with the growth in public-private-nonprofit agreements. Historically, those partnerships involved unshared financial risk: typically, the private or nonprofit firm bore the financial risk. The rapid expansion of partnerships in the past three decades, while including **contracting** and **outsourcing**, has moved more broadly into agreements that share the financial risk—**mixed delivery** and **collaboration**. Such partnerships, all of which require a contractual agreement among the participants, have forced local managers to be more entrepreneurial as they evaluate the risks of these more complex agreements.

Figure 1–1 Typology of public-private agreements

		Customer or owner	
		Government itself	**Citizens or businesses**
Risk of financial failure	Unshared	Contracting	Outsourcing
	Shared	Mixed delivery	Collaboration

Contracting In this typology, contracting is narrowly defined as a partnership in which the unit of government itself is the end customer and the financial risks are borne by the contractor; if the contractor fails to deliver on the agreement, the local government bears no financial risk other than that it must now find a new vendor. A contract for the construction of a new city facility, for example, will involve the city government as final customer when it takes possession of the building and leave the city bearing no financial risk of failure. Most construction contracts fit into this category. Construction contracts usually include a performance bond: typically, up to 10 percent of the value of the contract is withheld until the completed project is inspected and the terms of the contract certified as having been satisfied. Once the project is accepted by the local government, the performance bond is released as the final payment to the contractor.

Open-bid contracts with vendors for various operating supplies also fit into this category. So, too, does a state's partnership with a management consulting firm to operate a state lottery: the lottery commission is the customer, and the consulting firm assists the commission in its mission.

Outsourcing Outsourcing typically involves a unit of government selecting a vendor to provide a service that the unit of government normally could provide to its residents. In this case, the customers are persons or organizations other than the unit of government itself, and again financial risk is not shared. For example, a local government will retain a private or nonprofit vendor to operate a toll road, collect solid waste, operate a transit system, provide school bus service to children, respond to burglar alarm calls, provide insurance for municipal bonds, or supply and maintain red-light cameras. The direct customers of these outsourced services are citizens or businesses or investors. As in the case of contracting, the financial risk of failure is borne by the vendor. Failure to perform according to the terms of the agreement results in nonpayment and cancellation of the agreement by the unit of government. If a government **defaults** on its insured bonds, the private insurer bears financial responsibility for meeting the debt service obligation per the terms of the insurance policy. Outsourcing also opens up opportunities for an infusion of new capital. In 2009, the City of Dallas entered into a partnership with the Dallas Zoological Society (DZS), a nonprofit organization, to manage the city zoo. The result was a capital campaign to raise $53 million in public and charitable donations to the DZS to upgrade the zoo and add a new exhibit area.[8]

Mixed delivery As per the typology in Figure 1–1, as financial risks increase, local governments may use joint ventures as a way to share the risk of financial loss. In their research on the growing use of collaborative approaches to service delivery, Mildred Warner and Amir Hefetz introduced the term mixed delivery.[9] Mixed delivery occurs when the local government itself is the end customer but the financial risk (or return) is shared with the partner to the agreement. A **tax abatement** to attract private investment constitutes a mixed-delivery strategy. The city gains taxable property if the partnership is successful but shares in the financial risk through lost tax revenue should the business venture fail to meet expectations. To attract start-up industries as partners in developing new products, a university may use a mixed-delivery strategy by establishing a research park with which it shares profits from the sale of the patented innovations.

Collaboration When the final customers are outside the local government and the partnership involves shared financial risk, the relationship is a true collaboration in which risks and rewards are shared. For example, in a partnership between a city and a university to develop a conference center, the anticipated customers are conference hosts and their conferees, but they share the financial risk from the venture. An agreement between a city and a professional athletic franchise or symphony orchestra to construct and maintain a facility also constitutes such a collaboration. Similarly, in a collaboration between a city (or county) and a local chapter of a Humane Society to build an animal shelter, the local government retains ownership of the facility, and the staff, particularly the licensed personnel, are public employees. But fund-raising, adoption programs, and engaging citizens in adopting abandoned pets are duties of the nonprofit group. Collaboration with other organizations is particularly common in the fledgling smart-cities initiative. For example, the City of Toronto is collaborating with Sidewalk Labs, a subsidiary of Google's parent company Alphabet Inc., to develop a fully integrated technology community in the city's waterfront neighborhood.[10] Such technology-driven projects, however, have languished as a workable business model has yet to emerge for the corporate partners.

Noticeably missing from this typology is **privatization,** a term that has taken on innumerable meanings. Phillip J. Cooper characterizes "real privatization" as occurring when government is completely removed from the production and delivery of a service.[11] For example, seventeen states have an exclusive monopoly on the distribution and sale of some or all types of alcoholic beverages through state-owned stores. If a state were to sell its monopoly, as the State of Washington did in 2013, and completely remove itself from the distribution and sale of one or all types of alcohol, that would constitute privatization.

Methods for awarding contracts to third parties

Governments have always used agreements to achieve results beneficial to both or all parties. International treaties represent a special case of intergovernmental agreements in which the parties agree to actions that are seen as mutually beneficial. Governments use a variety of methods to select outside service providers, but all these methods are variations on two basic approaches: **competitive bidding** and **negotiation**.

Competitive bidding

In competitive bidding, the local government may issue a **request for proposals (RFP)** or other type of announcement in which it invites prospective providers to submit bids. This method works best where the service or product is provided by multiple vendors. For example, local governments often competitively bid the sale of their bonds. Banks and investment companies form syndicates that diversify their risk and increase their potential to resell the bonds to investors should they win the bid. Each competing syndicate submits a bid offering an interest rate for the purchase of the bonds. The syndicate with the lowest overall net interest cost wins the sale.

In cases where the product or service is complex or where the qualifications of potential bidders vary, a local government may initiate the process by issuing a **request for qualifications (RFQ)**, through which it can identify qualified prospective vendors and then invite them to submit a bid. Once qualified bidders are identified and the terms of the transaction are established by the government seeking a vendor, a call for bids is issued as either an RFP or another public notification. The invitation includes a date, time, and location to submit bids. Prior to that date, the government making the call may host a pre-bid conference, at which time prospective bidders may ask questions in a public forum to get further clarification of the terms of the proposed agreement.

Managed competition is a special case of competitive bidding in which units within a local government compete with other vendors for a contract to provide the desired services or products. For example, a municipal solid-waste department may be invited to compete, along with vendors from the private sector, for a contract to outsource the collection of residential solid waste.

Bidders then submit their best offers on a form or in a format specified in the RFP or other call for bids. Each bidder must also submit a good faith deposit (e.g., 10 percent of the bid) when submitting a bid. Once the deadline for bids passes, the host government opens the sealed bids and awards the contract to the best qualified bid, which is not always the lowest bid. State laws typically provide extensive guidance on how local governments must conduct their purchasing activities, including the selection of vendors through competitive bidding.

Negotiation

Professional service providers, such as management consultants, architects, and legal counsel, are often selected through a negotiation process. In such cases, state or local law may specify the circumstances in which a local government or state agency can identify a qualified provider and negotiate directly with that vendor on the terms of the agreement. At other times, governments seek a sole-source agreement (or no-bid contract) because there is only one qualified supplier or, owing to the urgency of the situation, because selecting a vendor through competitive bidding is not feasible.

A number of analyses have been made of the relative effectiveness of negotiated versus competitively bid contracts in providing the best price to local governments. Several studies have compared the interest cost of municipal bonds sold through competitive bidding with that of municipal bonds sold through negotiation.[1] Competitive bidding more often assures public administrators that they are getting the best terms when awarding third-party agreements. But negotiation can be done effectively, especially when government representatives are knowledgeable and can negotiate with more than one prospective vendor concurrently.

The figure below displays the range of methods used to engage outside vendors in the delivery of services.

In-house delivery (no outside provider)	**Managed competition**	**Public-private-nonprofit agreement** (contracting, outsourcing, mixed delivery, collaboration)	**Privatization of service** (shift to private sector of a previously publicly provided service)

1 Dwight V. Dennison, "Debt Management," in *Management Policies in Local Government Finance*, 6th ed., ed. John R. Bartle, W. Bartley Hildreth, and Justin Marlowe (Washington, D.C.: ICMA Press, 2013), 279–295.

Increased intergovernmental competition for new business investment

Although local governments have always formulated budget decisions with an eye toward other jurisdictions, taxpayer resistance and declining federal aid have created an unprecedented level of interlocal competition. **Tax competition** occurs on three fronts: (1) tax revenues, (2) the **tax base**, and (3) exportation of the tax burden.

Cities, counties, and independent school districts may have the authority to tax the same parcel of property. When overlapping governments levy a tax on the same tax base, as in the case of the real property tax, competition for revenue inevitably follows. Each government considers its budget needs to be more pressing than those of the overlapping governments, and each sets its tax rate independently, without regard for the aggregate impact on the property owner. The result is an overburdened taxpayer. Tax competition is also in evidence when a local government tries to lock in voter approval for a **general obligation (GO)** bond issue before other overlapping jurisdictions have an opportunity to seek voter approval for competing bond issues. Christopher Berry found compelling evidence to support what he terms "overfishing" by overlapping local governments: the more overlapping special districts there are, the higher the taxes and spending by general-purpose governments.[12]

Competition for business investment has also assumed unparalleled proportions. As state and local governments cultivate reputations for providing favorable business environments, interlocal competition undoubtedly lowers tax burdens on businesses. Intensified interlocal competition has spurred public officials' efforts to shift more of the local revenue burden to nonresidents—a sort of "beggar thy neighbor" strategy. **Tax exportation** has become particularly commonplace at the state and local levels through such measures as hotel and motel taxes, entertainment taxes, taxes on the income or purchases of commuters, and taxes on businesses selling their products or services to customers outside the taxing jurisdiction.

To what extent should a local government export its tax burden? The principles of social equity would say that it should do so only until it recovers the cost of serving nonresidents. Political reality dictates a more aggressive response. Regrettably, the current environment compels local officials to maximize opportunities for tax exportation. Most local governments have at least one economic strength—tourism, natural resources, a cultural or commercial center—that can be used to budgetary advantage. Those local governments with opportunities for tax exportation will tailor their tax policies to maximize their competitive advantage.

Citizen distrust of government

Tax revolts are nothing new in the United States. After all, hatred for the Crown's taxes precipitated the Revolutionary War. Like previous revolts, the **tax and expenditure limitation (TEL)** movement of the past three decades has been motivated in part by the public's perception that it has no control over government spending decisions. Often, this frustration is directed at the state and especially federal levels, but local government provides the most easily accessible target. While public opinion polls consistently indicate that citizens regard local government as giving them the most for their money, the polls also reveal a long-standing dislike for the property tax. Local governments have responded by investing more heavily in economic development initiatives to attract more commercial and industrial taxpayers.

Increased economic uncertainty

Three principal economic events at the regional, national, and international levels affect local budgets:

- Cyclical shifts in the economy brought on by recession, inflation, and expansion
- Sectoral shifts brought on by changes in technology and economic development (principally, in the United States, the movement away from manufacturing and toward an information- and service-based economy)

- Population movement across regions or national borders brought on by changes in job markets and technology.

The most obvious factor affecting local government budgets is the business cycle in the regional and national economies: economic growth followed by decline, price stability followed by inflation, low unemployment followed by high unemployment, and low interest rates followed by rising rates. The ability of local government budgets to withstand these cycles depends in part on the degree of diversification in the property tax base and revenue sources and on the flexibility in spending. Cities and counties with more diversified property tax bases, more diversified revenue sources, and higher levels of spending flexibility will generally have more stable **operating budgets** over the business cycle.

As a result of sectoral shifts in the U.S. economy, local governments luring high-growth industries will achieve stronger revenue positions, the qualification being that not all high-growth industries affect local budgets the same way. Clearly, some areas win as a result of this shift while others lose. The success stories have received extensive press coverage: California's Silicon Valley, Route 128 around Boston, North Carolina's Research Triangle, and Austin, Texas, are just a few of the more notable examples in the computer industry.

Population shifts—from central city to inner-ring to outer-ring suburbs back to central city, from the Frost Belt to the Sun Belt and back to the Frost Belt, or across national borders—are the third major influence on local budgets. When urban areas lose population, revenues and expenditures also decline, but declines in revenues are more rapid. This is because expenditures—especially for pensions, debt service, and contracted services—tend to be fixed, at least in the short run.

These three external forces—cyclical, sectoral, and population shifts—create continuous strains on local budgets that require prudent action by managers. No quick and easy solutions exist. The remainder of this chapter provides the historical development of budget practices as local managers have searched for ways to legitimize their spending recommendations with citizens and their elected representatives.

The evolution of budgeting innovations

Since the birth of modern public administration with the publication of Woodrow Wilson's call for a professional administration,[13] the budget process has provided the forum that reformers use to introduce better ways to deliver services at the lowest possible cost. If governments, through their budget processes, can successfully reduce costs, those resources can be reallocated for other spending priorities or for reductions in taxes and fees.

However, public budgeting also provides the forum where governments decide what services to provide and at what level of funding to provide them. In 1940, V. O. Key posed his oft-quoted rhetorical question, "On what basis shall it be decided to allocate x dollars to activity A instead of activity B?"[14] As the demand for public services has outpaced the resources available to meet those needs, the allocation function has risen in prominence.

In sum, the budget process fulfills three key purposes:

1. To decide what services to provide (allocative efficiency). This aspect concerns the "ends" of government: who gets how much of what. These matters of allocative efficiency seek to produce just enough goods and services to meet consumer demand and allocate those goods and services to those who value them the most—in other words, the Pareto optimum.
2. To promote greater productivity in the delivery of those services (productive efficiency). This aspect concerns the "means" of government: producing goods and services at the lowest possible cost.
3. To connect local government actions with the expectations of citizens (legitimization purpose). Over the past century, the quest for budgeting methods that would legitimize

government actions with citizens has steadily expanded in response to changing citizen expectations for both the ends of public services and the means for their delivery.

The process that produces the final budget provides the forum where public problems are identified, prioritized, and resolved or at least deferred.

The evolving role of citizens

The impetus underlying the progression of budget reforms has been the evolving role of citizens in shaping the public discourse on budget decisions (see Figure 1–2). The quest for allocative and productive efficiency in public budgeting occurs within a political context—specifically, a quest for processes and data that legitimizes budget choices with citizens and their elected representatives.

Through the first half of the twentieth century, citizens were clients of government who received public services that were largely the choice of those in power. Yet changes at the outset of that century, such as the direct election of senators and women's suffrage, signaled the opening of the good government era and awakened citizens to their role as constituents. Citizens had gained a direct voice in public matters, at least through their elected representatives. Depictions of organizational pyramids now had citizens at the top. By midcentury, budget deliberations routinely included more involvement by constituents through public hearings and a federally mandated "maximum feasible participation" in how grant awards were allocated.

Figure 1–2 The evolving role of citizens in budget innovations

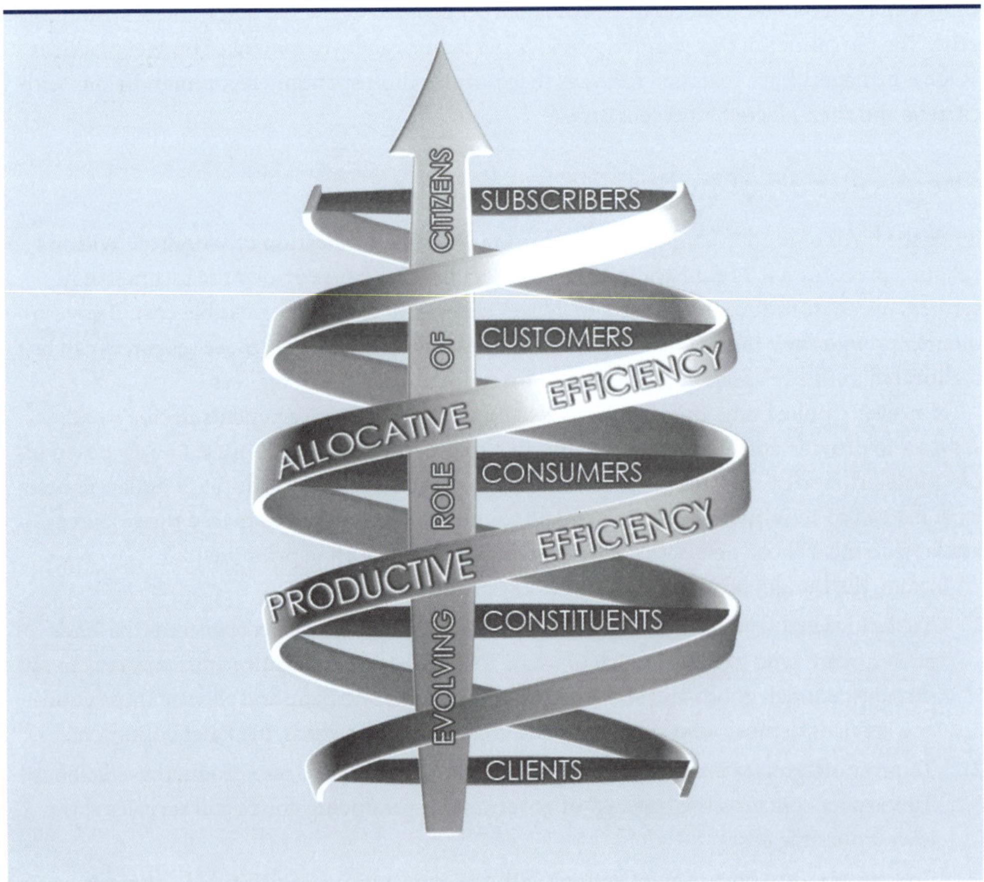

Then in 1978, the landslide approval of Proposition 13 by California voters kindled latent antipathy for what some believed was the unchecked expansion of government. The presumption was that, if controls could be placed on the revenue side of the budget, the inevitable outcome would be a reduction in the cost of public services. The property tax was an easy target for citizens who were transitioning from being merely passive constituents to being watchful consumers of public services. Those services were now less distinguishable from the plethora of private goods and services available to consumers.

By the end of the twentieth century, the relationship between the governed and those governing was undergoing yet another major change. Restive citizens had found their voice and were now pressing for more choices in public services. No longer just consumers of public services, citizens were now customers who expected choices in the quantity and quality of public services,[15] and public administrators were now public entrepreneurs who provided customers with choices. **Entrepreneurial budgeting** gained traction as managers experimented with a host of innovations to introduce surrogates for market processes into the production and delivery of public services.[16]

So what role for citizens will likely emerge in the coming decades, and what are the ramifications for the budget process? The integration of more technology into the delivery of services opens a new relationship in which citizen-customers can become subscribers deciding when and how much of a public service they desire. Smart communities are now emerging that enable local governments to customize services to neighborhood and even individual household demands. The future interaction of citizens and local governments will likely involve much more customization of public goods and services.

The progression of budget reforms

Building on the work of Allen Schick[17] and Irene Rubin,[18] four eras of budget reform can be identified: the administrative engagement era (1900–1949), the legislative engagement era (1950–1978), the leadership accountability era (1979–2000), and the public market era (2001–present). A fifth era—the private government era—looms on the horizon as technology reshapes the delivery of services and citizens transition into subscribers to those services (see Figure 1–3).

Administrative engagement era The earliest era began with Woodrow Wilson's 1887 call for a politically neutral administrative branch outside the political arena. The period saw initiatives to strengthen productive efficiency through spending controls and increasing the administrative capacity of the executive branch. It was an era when citizens as clients entrusted those in power to make budget decisions in the public interest. Legitimacy with citizens was achieved by building the administrative capacity of the executive branch and its control over the budget.

The early twentieth century was a fertile period for innovation in government, and central to the plethora of innovations was the introduction of an **executive budget**. Reformers sought to empower the executive branch at all levels of government with the responsibility for preparing a spending plan and ensuring that there were adequate revenues to pay for it.

As executive budgeting gained acceptance, the need emerged for generalist professionals with knowledge of public policy and financial management to staff newly organized budget offices. Budget manuals became tools for guiding the preparation of the budget and standardizing the data used in deliberations. By the 1930s, governments experimented with separating out capital spending into its own budget to better track the use of bond proceeds and document the cost of big-ticket projects.[19]

Figure 1–3 Eras of budget innovations

Budget eras	Predominant values	Focus of budget/ management innovations
Administrative Engagement Era (1900–1949)	Efficiency through control of spending Executive centered Citizens as clients	Building budget capacity in the executive branch through • executive budget, line-item detail, fund accounting • separate capital budget, budget manual, long-range forecasts • emergence of budget office in executive branch.
Legislative Engagement Era (1950–1978)	Efficiency through strategic use of resources Politics-administration inseparable Citizens as constituents	Building budget capacity in the legislative branch through • PPBS, budgeting toward planned goals • citizen input, public hearings, public choice • 1974 Congressional Budget and Impoundment Control Act • cost/benefit, cost-effectiveness analysis • ZBB; MBO; target-base budgeting.
Leadership Accountability Era (1979–2000)	Efficiency through working smarter Citizens as consumers	Building budget capacity by holding executives and legislators accountable through • restricting discretion (TELs) • balanced budget • sequestration, truth-in-taxation, TABOR • National Performance Review.
Public Market Era (2001–present)	Efficiency through competition Citizens as customers	Building budget capacity by revealing customer preferences through • public choice, vouchers, pricing public services, deregulation; managed competition • entrepreneurial budgeting • Bounded benefits (TIF, PIDs, HOAs, crime control districts).
Private Government Era (Future)	Efficiency through customized services Quasi-market processes to reveal citizen preferences Citizens as subscribers	Building budget capacity by applying quasi-market processes to budget choices through • subscription for premium services • direct contracting with subscribers for services • growth of smart communities.

Notes: PPBS = planning, programming, budgeting system; ZBB = zero-base budgeting; MBO = management by objectives; TELs = tax and expenditure limitations; TABOR = Taxpayer Bill of Rights; TIF = tax increment financing; PID = public improvement district; HOA = homeowners association.

Concurrent with the introduction of the executive budget was the adoption of line-item classification of spending, a mainstay in budgets to this day. Ratification of the Sixteenth Amendment in 1913 meant a new and increasingly important source of revenue to the federal budget—the individual income tax—and with it an expectation for greater accountability in the use of those funds. Revenue forecasting became integral to the budget office's duties as state and local governments extended their revenue sources to consumption- and income-based taxes.

The era saw the introduction of purchasing systems and, in 1936, the promulgation of the first accounting guidelines by the National Committee on Municipal Accounting.[20] The emergence of **fund accounting**, charts of accounts, financial reporting, and independent auditing added levels of accountability that could not be achieved with **line-item budgeting**. These added levels freed up budgets for broader purposes, including tracking the productivity of public programs.[21]

The era culminated with the Hoover Commission's 1949 report calling for the development of performance budgeting that, in turn, launched the quest for methods to measure, manage, and evaluate performance. But **performance measures** do not provide the data that policy makers need to make allocative judgments. They link **inputs** to **outputs** and, only weakly, to **outcomes**. V. O. Key's famous appeal anticipated the emergence of the next era: legislative engagement.

Legislative engagement era With the emergence of professional budget analysts and improved tools for analysis, budget innovations shifted to providing information that would better legitimize the allocative choices made by legislators. The era began in the 1950s with local and then state governments experimenting with **planning, programming, budgeting systems (PPBS)**. The era was shaped by the belief that politics and administration were inseparable and that economic growth could be achieved through strategic allocative choices.

In the early 1960s, PPBS was a relatively new budget methodology that caught the attention of the secretary of defense. Here, at last, was a method that provided policy leaders in the Department of Defense with information on the relative value of options for the budget and with a budget process that, on the surface, answered Key's question.

By the 1960s, the era had transitioned to the pursuit of bold public policy goals: placing a man on the moon by the end of the decade, ensuring a decent and affordable home for every American family, fighting a war on poverty, and protecting American interests in a global cold war. The federal budget was used to prepare analyses of the costs and benefits of options for meeting a goal, and then using those analyses to identify the option that maximized social benefits.

The early 1960s also saw the emergence of another movement to promote allocative efficiency in budgeting: **public choice**. Political economists James Buchanan and Gordon Tullock called for relying on market choices to more efficiently allocate resources to and within the public sector.[22] They saw government monopolies as inherently inefficient. The solution was to expand the use of quasi-market mechanisms, such as toll roads, vouchers for public education, the contracting out of public services, and increased privatization of government-provided services. Public choice's impact on budget innovations continued into successive budget eras and has been the genesis for the emergence of entrepreneurial budgeting in the twenty-first century.

Citizens were now legitimate stakeholders in the choices of services they would receive and pay for. They had transitioned from clients into constituents: they were at the top of the organizational chart and were, in principle, the ultimate source of authority for budget choices.

Citizen participation meant developing methods to ensure that citizens' voices were heard. State governments mandated public hearings as a step in the process of local budget adoption. Citizen surveys grew in popularity as legislators wanted to know the spending preferences of their constituents. State legislatures adopted open meeting laws, compelling their agencies and local governments to conduct more of the public's business in view of that public. At the federal level, Congress passed the Economic Opportunity Act of 1964 calling for "maximum feasible participation" by stakeholders in the creation and funding of community action programs.

The culminating event of the legislative engagement era was played out in Washington, D.C., with passage of the 1974 Congressional Budget and Impoundment Control Act. This legislation superimposed a process, along with the institutional support in a new Congressional Budget Office (CBO), to analyze the economic impact of and set targets for federal spending, revenue, deficits, and debt before deliberating on specific appropriation bills. The act significantly limited the president's previously unchecked prerogative to impound **budget authority** without congressional approval. Allocation decisions were firmly lodged with Congress.

By the late 1970s, the legislative engagement era was fading into a new era brought on by a grassroots tax revolt that began in California and quickly spread across the nation.

Leadership accountability era The leadership accountability era began in 1979 following ratification of Proposition 13 by California voters. Productive efficiency once again took center stage as tax limitations forced governments to work smarter and decentralize decision making. TELs, outsourcing, privatization, and performance management sought to shift decision making away from both the executive and legislature and to the public.

Consumerism was embraced by citizens, and public goods were now viewed as part of the larger pool of consumables available in the marketplace. With tax limitations, citizen-consumers had found a powerful tool to hold both executive and legislative leaders accountable: restricting the resources available for spending. Their expectation was that by restricting resources, the cost of production could be lowered without reducing either the quantity or quality of public services.

Citizens aimed to redefine efficiency by forcing government to work smarter. Working smarter meant improving the productive efficiency of government by constraining the options of its leaders and holding those leaders more accountable for the cost of producing its services. A smarter government meant an increase in the discretionary income available for consumption. At its root, budget reform meant reinventing government.[23]

The zenith of the leadership accountability era came in 1993 with the launching of the National Performance Review (NPR) by President Bill Clinton. NPR sought to create a new culture in the federal workforce that valued customer service, innovation, and interagency and intergovernmental cooperation and that streamlined the central administration of agencies. The NPR staff issued a series of reports subtitled "Creating a Government That Works Better and Costs Less," a phrase that captures the underlying values of the era.

Productive efficiency was front and center in this era as public administrators searched for innovations to contain the cost of providing public services. For example, a few cities were using cost accounting to build budgets; Sunnyvale, California, continues as an exemplar in this approach to budget preparation. Total quality management had been used in the private sector for several decades, but in the 1980s it captured the attention of some city and county executives. Benchmarking of public services was another innovation that some public managers believed could provide an effective tool for demonstrating their government's success at containing costs and maintaining a competitive position in the quest for business investment.

Outsourcing the provision of public services gained increased acceptance among consumers, public administrators, and even public employees. The role of outside providers expanded to include outsourcing of direct services to citizens, mixed delivery for more risky ventures, and partnerships with private (or nonprofit) vendors in which financial risks were shared. Governments even took the rare step of privatizing services that had previously been publicly provided; for example, the State of Washington sold its liquor stores. Since then, state and local governments have outsourced management and even ownership of their toll roads, prisons, and public assistance programs.

An interesting variation of this quest for productive efficiency is managed competition. Initially introduced into the public sector by the City of Phoenix in the late 1970s, the City of Indianapolis used it effectively to demonstrate the merits of empowering public employees to participate in the development of a bid for vehicle maintenance services.

But performance-based innovations proved incapable of providing the information that policy leaders need for making value-laden allocation decisions. Performance budgeting was unable to provide the justification for allocating more (or less) for agencies that were performing well above a benchmark level, which raises several questions: How should above- or below-benchmark performance be treated? What inherently justifies giving a successful agency even more money and reducing funding to the underperformer? Would such a rationale hold for police or fire service? A library? By the end of the twentieth century, with the shift rightward in the American politic, allocative efficiency had yet again moved to the forefront of budget reforms.

Public market era The current era—the public market era—emerged at the outset of the twenty-first century as citizen expectations migrated from those of consumers, who use what is provided, to those of customers, who choose among options for purchase. Allocative decisions in public services increasingly shifted from legislatures as providers of services for consumers to customers who make their choices using vouchers, institutional arrangements offering **bounded benefits**,[24] and tiered levels of services. **Budgeting for outcomes (BFO)** is designed to reveal customers' preferences through competition. The culmination of this era likely will be the customization of the quantity and quality of public services to satisfy the preferences of individuals or small geographic areas.

The research shows mixed results for the tax revolt in limiting growth in state and local budgets;[25] however, the entrenchment of consumerism among citizens during the leadership accountability era shaped both the study and the practice of public administration. While consumers rely on competition to contain costs, customers expect choices in the quantity and quality of services available to them. They have an array of services from which to choose, and public managers have added "entrepreneurial" to their job descriptions.

Rather than relying on analyses to identify the policy options that maximize social benefits, reformers of this era have picked up the mantle of public choice and reinventing government and look to the tools of competition to guide budget deliberations. Public administrators, especially in local government, have been at the forefront in experimenting with innovations that provide a market signal as to customers' preferences for public services.

Budget innovations seek to reveal customer preferences. Entrepreneurial budgeting broadly describes a variety of innovations designed to introduce quasi-market mechanisms into the discourse on spending priorities. Many of these innovations have the added benefit of increasing productive efficiency by providing public managers with an incentive to contain production costs.

BFO, also called **priority-based budgeting**, embraces entrepreneurial solutions to budget allocation. A statement on the website for Fort Collins, Colorado, which has been at the forefront in implementing BFO for its **biennial budget**, captures the values of the public market era: "Final output is a budget that reflects citizen priorities and delivers service efficiently."[26]

Public-private partnerships have expanded in popularity and creativity. So, too, has the use of special districts that provide premium benefits while restricting those benefits to those within its borders; such districts may take the form of crime control districts, public improvement districts, TIF districts, charter schools, municipal utility districts, and managed toll lanes.

The world of public budgeting continues to undergo transformation as policy leaders search for measures that provide the information they need to better match the allocation of public funds to the preferences of customers. The emerging economy is one in which public service delivery is more segmented geographically and socioeconomically and citizens, individually or in clusters, can opt to contract for the quantity of services needed at the time they are needed.

The coming private government era The combination of advances in technology applications and new institutional arrangements portends a new era of citizen-government relations in which citizens are not just customers of public services but subscribers who can customize packages of services. Public service provision will increasingly look like that of the private sector with the allocation of choices made directly by customers and less by legislative bodies. Several trends portend the emergence of the private government era.[27]

First, the public sector offers a tantalizing arena for the application of information and communication technology (ICT). ICT will enable governments to provide premium subscription for some public services. In some cities, neighborhoods may contract for supplemental police patrol. Smart public transit is being tested in some European cities to better meet commuters' needs during **peak periods** of demand. Charter schools offer educational options that target the preferences of parents. CareFlight ambulance service is available in some metropolitan areas as a subscription service. Premium subscription services will likely emerge for other public services, such as parks, recreation, energy, communications, Internet, and public safety. Subscriptions also raise significant issues of equity and affordability that fundamentally change the nature of public goods. One study found evidence that the emergence of private governments, such as HOAs, has a substitution effect resulting in a reduction in local government expenditures.[28]

Second, institutionally governments will expand their creative use of PPPs. As governments and their partners gain experience at collaborating, new applications will emerge and existing partnerships will be refined. PPPs can lead to dramatic improvements in productive efficiency when partners leverage various **economies of scale**, improved task specialization, and mutual learning opportunities.[29] Unfortunately, preliminary studies on budgeting in PPPs suggest that current budgeting processes lag behind the actual development of PPPs.[30]

Third, technology and new institutional arrangements will allow disaggregation of public services into more discrete packages that citizens can choose to purchase as needed. Public services, especially premium-level services, will increasingly be provided only on demand and in preferred quantities. The marginal cost of premium services will be shifted to the marginal customer who subscribes to a preferred package of public services.

The emergence of the smart community initiative offers a glimpse into the future of public services. In its background paper on smart cities, the British Department for Business Innovation & Skills notes that "the concept of a Smart City goes way beyond the transactional relationships between citizen and service provider. It is essentially enabling and encouraging the citizen to become a more active and participative member of the community."[31]

Smart communities rely on big data sets to develop models capable of tracking demand and adapting public services to strategically target their resources. The role of the budget office will change accordingly. Budget analysts will be the point of reference in using these data and in allocating resources to meet changing customer preferences. The private government era likely will usher in a greater acceptance of experiments to gauge the impact of funding changes on programmatic outcomes. Citizen-subscribers who contract with governments for a package of services likely will be accepting of an expanded role for budget offices to better link how changes in funding affect the outcomes of programs.

Issues of **equity** and availability across neighborhoods, regions, and economic enclaves will become even more contentious. What constitutes a fair distribution of funding for public services? How much redistribution of wealth should occur on the expenditure side of the local budget?

While representative government will remain the mainstay of American society, ICT will bring a resurgence of direct democracy. It will fall to those in professional leadership roles to protect the public interest in this new era of private government. Those of us in public administration carry a particularly heavy responsibility for protecting the credibility of public interest in this emerging era of government-by-subscription.

Factors influencing local financial decisions

Local budgets are extremely sensitive to their political, economic, social, and legal environments (see Figure 1–4). Politically, the proximity of local governments to citizens means that public opinion plays a key role in shaping spending decisions.

Economically, both the revenue and expenditure sides of a budget are sensitive to cycles of boom and bust, as well as to competition for residents and business investment. Local governments are primarily concerned with using their budget decisions to stimulate economic growth by attracting new industries or keeping large employers from leaving the area. Changes in inflation and interest rates can tear apart the best-laid financial plans. Socially, budgets are sensitive to factors such as in- and out-migration; the age distribution of the population; and problems such as drug use, homelessness, and crime. Legally, governments have to work within laws that limit debt; require a **balanced budget**; specify legal revenue sources; mandate particular activities, procedures, or spending levels; and forbid certain activities.

Citizen involvement

Involvement in local government has been a hallmark of democracies since Greek city-states invented the form of government; the Athenian Oath is a classic expression of a citizen's obligation. With the advent of locally regulated cable television, citizens can now watch council hearings live on the public access channel. Cities and some counties have long relied on citizen surveys to gauge local opinion on the quality and quantity of public services.

Figure 1–4 The political, economic, social, and legal environments of public budgeting

The political environment is affected by	The economic environment is affected by	The social environment is affected by	The legal environment is affected by
• Feedback from citizens • Citizen involvement	• Recessions and expansions • Inflation and changes in interest rates • Competition for business investment and residents	• Population change • Age distribution • Personal income	• Requirements for budgetary balance • Mandates

Some major cities have experimented with the use of focus groups. For example, New York City's Center on Municipal Government Performance (CMGP) undertook a citywide evaluation of citizen perspectives using focus groups. The most compelling discovery from this initiative was that "people use different measures, want different information and wanted it presented in different ways" than what local governments typically use and want.[32] Interestingly, the CMGP's model has been replicated in a number of other communities across the United States, a growing recognition of the importance of citizen participation in shaping the local budget and of the long-term impact of that participation on the quality of life in all communities.

Neighborhood forums and even town hall meetings have been used since antiquity to obtain citizen input on local budget priorities and funding choices. Today, local governments are also using interactive websites to obtain citizen feedback on policy issues confronting the community. Comparable citizen participation is impossible to achieve in a large state or at the federal level.

What appears to be occurring at the local level is that city and county managers and their legislative boards are increasingly using the budget to better understand how citizens, rather than internal participants, see government.[33] Such a transformation will have a major effect on budget allocations and the relative size of city and county agencies. In fact, we should anticipate greater diversity among local governments in the type and quality of services provided, particularly as communities develop reputations for having strengths in particular services. And given the powerful differences in service preferences that have been documented among age groups, we should also anticipate further segmentation of communities along generational lines.

Economic influences

A number of factors can affect the economic environment of local government budgeting: economic cycles, inflation, interest rates, and competition among local governments.

Economic cycles Economic downturns affect local budgets in two main ways. First, revenues may decline, especially such revenues as sales or income taxes, which are more sensitive to economic cycles. Second, during a recession, state and federal revenues are often hit hard, which means that intergovernmental aid to local governments may decline.

The onset, severity, and duration of economic slowdowns are nearly impossible to predict. Any revenue projection, no matter how carefully prepared, is likely to be off if the economy takes an unexpected turn. Because of this irreducible source of uncertainty and the widespread requirement for a balanced budget at the state and local levels, budget planners must build in some flexibility, some way of adjusting during the year if revenues fall below expectations or expenditures are greater than predicted. The budget office accommodates unexpected changes by prohibiting departments from spending all their allocations, holding back on permission to hire new staff or make other contractual commitments, building reserves or **rainy day funds**, and authorizing the chief executive to make small cuts in existing allocations without council approval.

Inflation Inflation creates uncertainty in local government revenue and expenditure forecasts. When the cost of living increases rapidly, organized labor exerts pressure to keep wages current with inflation. Because local government is more labor-intensive than the private sector, increases in labor expenditures outpace inflation-driven increases in revenues. This is called the **relative price effect**, and it leaves local governments with the difficult task of reducing public services when demand for those services is on the rise. Tax limitations may further exacerbate the disparity between income and outflow.

Interest rates Changes in interest rates can also affect the budget, although their effects are not as great at the local level as they are at the national level, where the federal deficit requires continual borrowing. Because they are required to balance their budgets every year, most local governments can usually time the sale of long-term bonds to take advantage of lower interest rates; however, higher interest rates may still adversely affect the budgets of local governments that depend on short-term notes (tax anticipation notes) to meet cash flow needs. When interest rates remain high for long periods, local governments may be forced to borrow at high interest rates rather than delay needed projects indefinitely.

Competition among local governments Because it affects taxation decisions, competition among local governments for new residents or business investment also exerts an economic influence on local budgeting. One way to obtain a competitive advantage over other jurisdictions is to export the tax burden, shifting it from residents to nonresidents. Such action reduces taxes on residents while allowing service levels to be maintained; the combination of low taxes and high service levels thereby improves the community's competitive advantage for new businesses and residents. One example of tax exportation is a levy on hotel and motel occupancy, which is paid by visitors rather than by residents. In a community that is home to a regional mall, the general sales tax also serves as a form of tax exportation.

Intergovernmental competition seems to influence expenditure levels as well as taxation decisions. Local governments are aware of their neighbors' service levels. Thus, improvements in the quality and range of library services in one jurisdiction, for example, often induce surrounding municipalities to follow suit.

Critics of government often argue that competition forces inefficient businesses into bankruptcy but that there is no comparable mechanism for weeding out inefficiency in government. Competition among governments, however, helps improve management and keeps taxes down without resulting in bankruptcy. Moreover, while businesses are unlikely to share the secrets of their success, governments regularly share innovations and improvements. Local governments do not benefit from the financial failures of other jurisdictions; in the eyes of the public, one city's failure is likely to redound to the disadvantage of all. Thus, competition among local governments is not zero-sum.

Social and demographic change

Changes in three social and demographic factors—population, age distribution, and **personal income**—have significant and lasting effects on local budgets.

Population Basic economic principles suggest that as population increases and fixed costs are divided among more households, the resulting economies of scale will mean lower per-unit costs. Because financial obligations do not decline in proportion to population loss, communities with declining populations have difficulty reducing spending. The same amount of infrastructure (roads, streets, lights, traffic signals, storm drainage) must be maintained, while pension commitments and debt service payments (the annual payment of principal and interest on borrowed funds) must now be borne by fewer taxpayers. Similarly, in communities experiencing inordinate population increases, excess capacity in public services will be quickly exhausted. Streets, recreational facilities, and public school classrooms will become congested; and demand for water, sewer services, and waste disposal may exceed capacity, requiring major investment in expanding the physical plant. This suggests that the cost curve with respect to population changes for local governments is U-shaped: highest for those experiencing rapid declines or increases in population, but lowest for those with more moderate rates of change in population.

The cost of local services appears to be affected not only by the rate of population growth but also by absolute size of population. Studies have repeatedly found that as jurisdictions grow beyond some minimum threshold, the same services cost more per capita. There are many possible explanations for this phenomenon, including the greater likelihood of crime in large cities; increased fire risks associated with greater population density; the greater power of unions when the workforce is large; and the difficulty of maintaining adequate oversight in multiple locations, such as garages, lockups, and housing facilities. The level of complexity of operations may also increase as the population grows.

The age of the city may also explain budget variations. Older housing stock and aging infrastructure add to the cost of older urban areas. Communities experiencing rapid growth will, at some future point, face the daunting task of replacing their infrastructure all at once, by which time the tax base (property values) will most likely have peaked and started to decline.

Age distribution Spending for public education, public safety, and recreational services are the budget categories most likely to be affected by the age distribution of the population. Younger families with children push up the costs of schooling and the likelihood of crime; crime, particularly violent crime, is concentrated among persons between the ages of twelve and twenty.[34] The number and proportion of elderly residents may also be relevant, not only in terms of service needs but also in terms of residents' ability and willingness to pay property taxes. Many states provide **circuit breakers** or freeze property tax liability for elderly citizens. Despite these tax breaks, however, local governments that have large concentrations of retirees on fixed incomes may have difficulty gaining support for programs that benefit younger families.

Personal income Research consistently shows that growth in personal income significantly affects the size of local government budgets. Higher-income households often demand more and better services from government, although these same households are more likely to advocate limited government, especially at the state and federal levels. The answer to this apparent contradiction may lie in the relative homogeneity of wealthier communities, where community preferences are easier to identify and satisfy. Charles Tiebout, a noted public finance scholar, conjectured that people vote with their feet by gravitating to communities that offer a package of public services that fits their preferences, a phenomenon known as the Tiebout hypothesis.[35] Finding acceptable budget solutions seems to be more complex in heterogeneous communities, possibly because it is more difficult to negotiate the level of agreement required to decide on spending levels, budget allocations, and tax rates. The aging of the population has further complicated local budgets as preferences for public services have shifted. In addition, technology has changed the way we work, while growing income inequality leads to political dissatisfaction and slower economic growth.

Legal and intergovernmental matters

Legal and intergovernmental factors shape local budgets in three principal ways: through balanced budget requirements, TELs, and mandates.

Budgetary balance The legal environment in which state and local budgeting operates typically requires that budgets be balanced, that is, current revenues must equal current expenditures (CR = CE).

On the one hand, this requirement shapes the entire budget process: it makes budget deliberations, especially at the local level, revenue driven, meaning that available revenues determine the level of spending. In economic downturns, however, state and federal spending—and, to a lesser extent, local spending—tends to be countercyclical as demands for unemployment compensation, food stamps, and even subsidized student loans rise. **Budget deficits** (CR < CE) become more commonplace, and governments scrounge around for additional revenues. At such times, TELs reduce governments' ability to deal with recessions; they may also exacerbate the intensity and length of economic downturns, much as the ill-advised price controls of the 1970s exacerbated inflationary effects.

On the other hand, the definition of balance is less clear in practice than it may appear. The most current tally of state practices shows that twenty-seven states have constitutional requirements and eighteen have statutory requirements that the legislature adopt a balanced budget.[36] The remaining states either have no restrictions (North Dakota) or have less strict balanced budget requirements (Vermont and Wyoming have vague references to budget balances). The definition of a balanced budget, moreover, is highly variable, much looser in some states than in others. For example, in forty-four states the governor must submit a balanced budget, but only thirty-five states have controls in place to avoid a deficit at the end of the fiscal year[37] Fewer than half the states apply the balanced budget test to all funds. Although no current tally exists of the practices among cities, past studies suggest that the requirements for balance widely vary in stringency, with most requiring a balanced budget at submission but fewer requiring a balance at year-end.[38]

Requirements for budgetary balance are further complicated by a technical question: Is the budget balanced on a **cash basis** (i.e., revenues are recorded when cash is received, and expenditures are recorded when disbursed) or on a **modified accrual basis** (i.e., liabilities are recognized at the time they are incurred, and revenues are recognized when they are available for budgeted purposes)? This question is important because cash balances can be easily manipulated: to make the budget look more balanced than it is, payments can be delayed until the following fiscal year, and revenue collections can be accelerated for credit to the current year.

Tax and expenditure limitations States have always imposed limitations on the taxing capabilities of local governments—for example, by capping the property tax rate. Since 1978, however, when Californians ratified Proposition 13 to roll back property tax rates, local governments have seen a groundswell of measures limiting their revenue-raising capacity. TELs have drawn on the California approach, and while each limitation has its own unique set of constraints and targets, they all fall into two groups: those that are broad based and those more targeted.

Four states—Colorado (1992), Missouri (1996), Nevada (1996), and Oklahoma (1992)—forbid increases in local tax rates without voter approval. Colorado's Taxpayer Bill of Rights (TABOR) not only requires voter approval for any increases in local tax rates but also restricts revenue growth in local governments to inflation plus population growth, unless voters approve otherwise. In 2005, because of the adverse effects of the law, Coloradoans voted to relax the terms of TABOR for five years to allow the state to use a surplus from existing taxes—revenue that would otherwise be returned to the taxpayers—to increase funding of public services. In 2010, TABOR's limits on the state's capacity to raise revenue went back into effect.

Several states cap tax rates, particularly for the property tax. Although many states set constitutional limits on the maximum rates that particular types of local governments can impose, Proposition 13 unleashed citizen efforts to limit the combined tax rates of overlapping local governments. Thirteen states use some variation of **truth-in-taxation** to hold local lawmakers more accountable for increases in local property tax rates. Two states, Kentucky and Texas, empower voters to overrule their local lawmakers if those lawmakers approve an extraordinary increase in the tax rate.

Several states have also pursued tax relief measures targeted to specific classes of citizens, particularly senior citizens. For example, Pennsylvania's Act 77 freezes property assessments of senior citizens in counties that levy a sales tax. As part of a sweeping tax reform initiative, Michigan adopted a two-tiered rate structure for school property taxes that was designed to reduce the burden on homeowners. Still other states, such as Texas, freeze the school taxes of senior citizens at the amount they pay in the year that either spouse turns 65. In 2003, Texas voters amended the state constitution to give cities and counties the option to extend the senior **tax freeze** to their levies. City councils and county commissioner courts have been slow to adopt the freeze, however, because of the long-term adverse impact it would have on local budgets.

Mandates A mandate involves one level of government requiring another level to provide particular services or follow certain procedures, as well as specifying the quality or frequency of service provision. Both the federal and state governments impose mandates on local governments. The problem is that unless the federal or state government also provides full funding to implement the mandates, local officials may have to cut other services to comply. Federal and state priorities thus preempt local ones.

As long as the level of federal and state funding to local governments continued to grow, mandates did not impose a severe problem. But as reliance on property taxes has moderated and reliance on more economically sensitive revenue sources has increased, local governments have become more vulnerable to recessions, exacerbating the difficulty of complying with mandates. Communities suffering the effects of recessions have sometimes been hit simultaneously by unfunded mandates and cutbacks in state spending.

In response to pleas from local governments, states have tried to curtail unfunded mandates. Their most common response has been to require that proposed mandating legislation include a **fiscal note** that estimates the cost of the mandate to local governments. By forcing state policy makers to calculate the costs imposed on local governments, fiscal noting exposes the real cost of mandates. However, noting has not been particularly successful in curtailing state mandates. The requirement is too easy to bypass, and costs to local governments are difficult to measure accurately, especially before the legislation is implemented.

A combined effect To summarize, the legal and intergovernmental environment of budgeting has been highly restrictive—forbidding particular revenue sources, constraining tax increases, requiring balance, and mandating some services and service levels. Moreover, the unpopularity of the property tax has led to increasing dependence on the general sales tax, but the sales tax is more **income elastic** (i.e., sensitive to growth or decline in the economy) than the property tax. In fact, because sales tax revenue fluctuates more widely than the growth or decline in the economy, it tends to exaggerate the impact of recessions on local spending. This combination of factors has created enormous fiscal stress at the local level over the past four decades.

Conclusion

Budgeting in the United States provides local governments with the equivalent of a marketplace where they can decide on the quantity of goods and services that will be produced and on how they will pay for them. Budgeting fulfills a legal function by giving legitimacy to budget decisions, and it provides a mechanism for holding administrators accountable for providing the services authorized by lawmakers.

Governments produce public goods, but they are also major producers of private goods—often because those goods lack a profit incentive to attract private investors. Given the nature of public and private goods and services produced by local governments, public budgeting is more complex and is subject to more constraints than private sector budgeting. Budget processes must provide for public accountability: the budget document must be comprehensible to citizens as well as to elected officials; and the budget must comply with a variety of laws, including those that specify the basis of fund accounting and the definition of budgetary balance. Moreover, local governments face a battery of legal limitations that affect spending decisions: TELs, balanced budget requirements, and state and federal mandates.

The budget process fulfills the basic functions of (1) determining the spending priorities to which funds will be allocated, (2) devising ways to reduce the cost through improved efficiency in providing those services, and (3) seeking to legitimize those two goals with citizens. For over a century, local budgeting has undergone numerous transformations and innovations in the pursuit of these three goals. The current public market era and its emphasis on using competition to gauge both allocative and productive efficiency may be morphing into a new private government era in which citizens become subscribers to the quantity, quality, and timing of the services they want.

So that governmental budgeting can take public interests into account, budget processes must also provide for public participation. Social transformations, such as shifts in population, changes in age distribution, and growth rates in personal income, shape community values and citizens' preferences and expectations for local services. Thus, budgeting at the local level is distinguished by citizen involvement through public hearings, focus groups, and citizen surveys. Recent budget innovations have emphasized "customer satisfaction" as a key measure of good budgeting.

Not surprisingly, economic conditions have profound effects on local budgets as well. Recessions and inflation alter revenues coming in and the cost of providing services. Changes in interest rates directly affect the annual operating budget through debt service requirements, and increased debt service squeezes out funding for other local services. Finally, interlocal competition for business investment influences the tax incentives that local governments offer and thereby alters the revenue available for other services.

Notes

1 Wallace Sayre, "The Unhappy Bureaucrats: Views Ironic, Helpful, Indignant," *Public Administration Review* 10 (1958): 245.

2 Bank of North Dakota, "The BND Story," https://bnd.nd.gov/the-bnd-story/ (accessed December 30, 2018).

3 Robert J. Kleine and John Shannon, "Characteristics of a Balanced and Moderate State-Local Revenue System," in *Reforming State Tax Systems,* ed. Steven D. Gold (Denver, Colo.: National Conference of State Legislatures, 1986), 33–34.

4 U.S. Bureau of the Census, *Statistical Abstract of the United States,* 1982–83 (Washington, D.C.: U.S. Government Printing Office, 1983), Table No. 470.

5 U.S. Bureau of the Census, *2015 State and Local Government Finance,* "Table 1. State and Local Government Finances by Level of Government and by State: 2014–2015."

6 The City of Weston, Florida, "Employees/Contract Services," https://www.westonfl.org/government/city-manager/employees-contract-services (accessed December 30, 2018).

7 Peter V. Schaeffer and Scott Loveridge, "Toward an Understanding of Types of Public-Private Cooperation," *Public Performance & Management Review* 26 (December 2002): 169–189, www.researchgate.net/publication/247885699_Toward_An_Understanding_Of_Types_Of_Public-Private_Cooperation.

8 "History of the Dallas Zoo," n.d., https://www.dallaszoo.com/about-us/history-of-the-dallas-zoo/.

9 Mildred E. Warner and Amir Hefetz, "Managing Markets for Public Service: The Role of Mixed Public-Private Delivery of City Services," *Public Administration Review* 68 (January/February 2008): 155–166.

10 WATERFRONToronto, 2017/18 Annual Report, June 28, 2018.

11 Phillip J. Cooper, *Governing by Contract: Challenges and Opportunities for Public Managers* (Washington, D.C.: CQ Press, 2003), 71.

12 Christopher Berry, "Piling On: Multilevel Government and the Fiscal Common-Pool," *American Journal of Political Science* 52 (October 2008): 802–820.

13 Woodrow Wilson, "The Study of Administration," *Political Science Quarterly* 2 (June 1887): 197-222.

14 V. O. Key, "The Lack of a Budgetary Theory," The *American Political Science Review* 34 (December 1940): 1137-1144.

15 David Osborne and Ted Gaebler, *Reinventing Government, How the Entrepreneurial Spirit is Transforming the Public Sector* (Reading, Mass.: Addison-Wesley Publishing Co., 1992).

16 Dan A. Cothran, "Entrepreneurial Budgeting: An Emerging Reform?" *Public Administration Review* 53 September/October 1993): 445-454.

17 Allen Schick, "The Road to PPB: The Stages of Budget Reform." *Public Administration Review* 26 (December 1966): 243-258.

18 Irene Rubin, "Past and Future Budget Classics: A Research Agenda." *Public Administration Review* 75 (January/February 2015): 25-35.

19 Jesse Burkhead, *Government Budgeting* (New York: John Wiley & Sons, Inc., 1956), 183.

20 Stephen Gauthier, *Governmental Accounting, Auditing, and Financial Reporting (GAAFR)* (Chicago: Government Finance Officers Association, 2012), 24.

21 Schick, "The Road to PPB," 249.

22 James Buchanan and Gordon Tullock, *The Calculus of Consent: Logical Foundations of Constitutional Democracy* (Indianapolis, Ind.: Liberty Fund, 1962).

23 Osborne and Gaebler, *Reinventing Government.*

24 Robert L. Bland and Michael Overton, "Assessing the Contributions of Collaborators in Public-Private Partnerships: Evidence from Tax Increment Financing," *The American Review of Public Administration* 46 (July 2016): 418-435.

25 Ellen C. Seljan, "The Limits of Tax and Expenditure Limits: TEL Implementation as a Principal-Agent Problem," *Public Choice* 159 (June 2014): 485-501. Ryu Sun, "Reevaluating the Effect of Tax and Expenditure Limitations: An Instrumental Variable Approach," *Public Finance Review* 42 (January 2014): 92-116.

26 City of Fort Collins, "Budgeting for Outcomes," https://www.fcgov.com/bfo/ (accessed December 30, 2018).

27 Robert W. Helsley and William C. Strange, "Private Government," *Journal of Public Economics* 69 (1998): 281-304.

28 Ron Cheung, "The Interaction Between Public and Private Governments: An Empirical Analysis," *Journal of Urban Economics* 63 (2008): 885-901.

29 Tony Bovaird, "Public–Private Partnerships: From Contested Concepts to Prevalent Practice," *International Review of Administrative Sciences* 70 (June 2004): 199-215.

30 David Mitchell and Kurt Thurmaier, "(Re)Defining the Disarticulated Municipality: Budget Accountability for Networked Governance," *Public Budgeting & Finance* 36 (Spring 2016): 47-67.

31 Department for Business Innovation & Skills, *Smart Cities: Background Paper* (London: Department for Business Innovation and Skills, 2013), 7.

32 Barbara J. Cohn Berman, *When Governments Listen: Moving Toward Publicly Engaged Governing* (New York: National Center for Civic Innovation, 2012), 14.

33 James H. Svara and Janet Denhardt, eds., *Connected Communities: Local Governments as a Partner in Citizen Engagement and Community Building* (Phoenix, Ariz.: Alliance for Innovation, October 15, 2010).

34 National Institute of Justice, Office of Justice Programs, *From Juvenile Delinquency to Young Adult Offending,* March 2014. https://www.nij.gov/topics/crime/Pages/delinquency-to-adult-offending.aspx

35 Charles M. Tiebout, "A Pure Theory of Local Expenditures," *Journal of Political Economy* 64 (October 1956): 416–424.

36 Yilin Hou and Daniel L. Smith, "A Framework for Understanding State Balanced Budget Requirement Systems: Re-examining Distinctive Features and an Operational Definition," *Public Budgeting & Finance* 26 (Fall 2006): 22–45.

37 Ibid., 34–35.

38 Carol W. Lewis, "Budgetary Balance: The Norm, Concept, and Practice in Large U.S. Cities," *Public Administration Review* 54 (November-December 1994): 515–524.

PART I:

REVENUE SOURCES TO FINANCE THE LOCAL BUDGET

CHAPTER 2

Revenue choices: Principles to guide the manager

Our plans miscarry because they have no aim. When a man does not know what harbor he is making for, no wind is the right wind.

—Seneca

This chapter provides the following takeaways:

- Recognize the three basic powers that governments use to impose taxes, charges for services, or fees and fines.
- Apply the three pillars of good revenue policy: fairness, neutrality, and effective administration.
- Identify the measures that managers can take to create a more resilient local economy.

Strengthening a community's economy begins with an assessment of the taxes and fees currently in use. Are they consistent with the community's economic goals? Do they promote a diverse tax base, encourage the development of countercyclical industries, and bring greater revenue stability to the budget? Are there opportunities for increased use of benefits-based levies and for reducing or even eliminating nuisance taxes? Do certain groups receive unjustified tax favors?

Managers need specific criteria to guide their planning and deliberations toward policies that strengthen the local economy. This chapter begins with a discussion of the legal foundations for the various taxes, service charges, fees, and fines that local governments collect. It then synthesizes public finance research addressing the criteria that should guide local revenue policy making and that form the pillars supporting a sound local economy: equity, neutrality, and effective administration.

The legal basis for local revenues

In Western democracies, governments derive their revenues using one of three legal powers: taxing, proprietary, or regulatory. These powers are most typically granted in constitutions or charters but may also come from statutory authority or, infrequently, through court orders.

Taxing powers

Governments levy taxes on any of three tax bases—income, consumption, and wealth (or property)—to pay for the cost of their operations.

Income-based taxes Income-based taxes, such as the personal and corporate income tax, rely on a sophisticated process to determine liability. The tax base may extend only to wages and salaries (earned income), as is the case of the widely used local wage tax in Pennsylvania or the federal Social Security tax (the Federal Insurance Contributions Tax, or FICA); however, state and federal governments usually use a broader definition for their personal income tax bases that includes unearned income, such as interest and dividends, realized capital gains, royalties and rents, and alimony.

Consumption-based taxes Consumption-based taxes include an array of taxes usually collected as part of a sales transaction. The general sales tax is the broadest-based consumption levy, and it typically includes most consumer goods; food consumed in restaurants; and selected services such as telecommunications, lodging, and amusements. On the other hand, **excise (or selective sales) taxes** are levied on specific types of transactions at a separate rate from that of the general sales tax and under separate statutory authority. For example, cigarette and alcoholic beverage taxes are nearly universal among the states, and in a few cases, local levies are added. In the case of these "sin taxes," which are designed to discourage consumption, a general sales tax may be levied on top of the excise tax. Other widely used excise tax bases include motor fuels, hotel/motel occupancy, and natural resources at the point of extraction (severance taxes). Frequently, revenue from excise taxes is earmarked for a particular purpose. For example, motor fuels taxes are almost universally dedicated to highway and street construction or repair.

Wealth-based taxes Wealth-based (or property) taxes constitute a class of levies that fall on the value of assets. For example, an estate tax requires determining the value of the deceased person's remaining property. The more familiar **property tax** (or *ad valorem* = "according to the value" tax) is actually levied on several tax bases. Real property represents the largest component and includes land and any improvements (houses, shopping malls, landscaping) to the land. Personal property represents more mobile assets (vehicles, equipment, inventories of raw or finished goods) in the tax base. In some cases, the base may include intangible personal property (stocks, bonds, insurance policies), which poses particularly difficult administrative challenges.

Tax bases may be distinguished by whether the tax is levied on the value *(ad valorem)* or on a quantity (*in rem* = "against a thing"), such as the motor fuels tax, which is levied per gallon. *Ad valorem* taxes require more effort, usually by government, to establish the tax base's value and thus the taxpayer's liability. Unfortunately, taxable value bears only a partial connection to the taxpayer's ability to pay, as in the case of a "property-rich but cash-poor" farmer. On the other hand, *in rem*–based taxes are more easily administered and thus less open to dispute as to the basis of the tax liability.

Proprietary powers

Governments also possess broad constitutional powers to own and operate—even at a profit—various enterprises. The list of such activities is quite astounding: North Dakota owns and operates a state bank; Dallas, Texas, owns and operates a popular FM radio station (WRR); a number of states own liquor stores; and Glasgow, Kentucky, operates a fiber-optic network that provides cable television and Internet access to city residents and parts of the surrounding county. Locally owned utilities and transit systems are quite common and, in some cases, profitable. San Antonio, Texas, owns and operates all of the city's major utility services (water, wastewater, natural gas, and electricity), which collectively provide a substantial subsidy to the city's general fund through interfund reimbursements. Of growing interest among larger cities is the installation of WiFi (wireless fidelity) technology, a citywide broadband wireless network that provides high-speed Internet service to citizens at a fraction of the cost of other modes of service. Several European cities now provide this low-cost technology to their citizens as well.

Proprietary activities give rise to **fees-for-service** as opposed to taxes. Whereas taxes represent involuntary conscriptions, service fees culminate in a quid pro quo in which government provides a good or service in exchange for the fee. For example, cities charge private utilities for the use of their rights-of-way; this is often called a street rental fee. In this case, the utility company gains access to public rights-of-way to lay its lines or cables and pays rent in exchange. It is interesting to observe how the use of proprietary powers varies among state and local (and even the federal) governments. In the Southwest, for instance, solid-waste collection is usually funded with a monthly service fee paid by households and businesses; in the Northeast, such service is more often funded with general taxes.

The accounting and financial reporting requirements for proprietary activities differ from those for tax-supported services. The Governmental Accounting Standards Board (GASB) requires the use of **enterprise funds** to account for services that are self-supporting and derive most of their income from user charges. Typically, water and wastewater service is accounted for in an enterprise fund, as are other utilities or quasi-business activities of government, including toll roads, airports, public transit systems, docks, golf courses, and even government-owned radio and television stations. Inflows to the fund include the fees charged to users of the service. Outflows include the labor and operating costs incurred in providing the service. Even if a service is not fully self-supporting, maintaining it in a separate enterprise fund provides managers with information on the amount of subsidy required to support the service. The GASB now requires that an activity be accounted for in an enterprise fund if it is financed with debt that is backed by fees generated by that activity.

Regulatory powers

The third broad class of constitutionally derived powers comprises those that empower governments to promote the health, safety, and general well-being of a community or state. Sometimes called police powers, this class enables local governments to regulate land use through zoning ordinances, to license various professions and activities, and to inspect and certify the safety of food establishments; the list of state and locally regulated activities is long. In exchange for the cost of regulating an activity, state laws usually permit governments to collect a fee not to exceed that cost.

Although not a large source of revenue for cities and counties, regulatory fees do augment more general revenues. From an accounting perspective, regulatory fees are typically treated as general revenue and thus are accounted for like unrestricted taxes. No effort is made, nor should be made, to fund the building inspection department from its inspection fees or to fund the police department from its traffic citations.

Raising revenue: Proprietary versus regulatory powers

A gray line exists between a service charge levied under a government's proprietary powers and a license or permit fee levied under its regulatory powers. Both involve an exchange (quid pro quo). In the case of proprietary activities, the exchange involves a good or service: a service charge for water, tuition for credit hours, etc. In the case of regulatory activities, the exchange grants a privilege: a fishing license, driver's license, or building permit.

But there are a couple of important differences. A proprietary transaction involves goods or services being provided in exchange for the charge. Each month city residents receive a water bill for the amount of water they consumed in the preceding month. Each semester students receive a tuition bill for the forthcoming semester. By contrast, a regulatory exchange involves an intermediary step in which eligibility for engaging in the regulated activity is first established. Issuance of a license or permit (or other form of approval such as a visa) provides evidence of that eligibility (or conversely, a fine being assessed for violating the boundaries of the regulated activity).

Another difference is that the proprietary activity involves governments providing a private good or service. A regulatory activity involves granting access to a privilege that is created by statute (laws passed by legislative bodies) and can be taken away (driver's license revoked; admission denied). Governments usually issue a license to engage in the privilege (fishing, hunting, owning a dog, building a house). Without a license or permit, a person cannot legally engage in the regulated activity.

Occasionally, governments also may regulate rights, such as speech, assembly, or gun ownership. Rights are granted by constitutions (e.g., the Bill of Rights). In the case of the basic rights granted by the First Amendment to the U.S. Constitution (speech, religion, petition, assembly, and press), the U.S. Supreme Court has ruled that governments may regulate the time, place, and manner in which the right is used but cannot regulate the content of the constitutionally protected right.

The three pillars of support

Not only does a revenue structure reflect a community's values, but citizen attitudes toward local government are shaped largely by the perceived fairness of the revenue structure. Fairness, or equity—the fair distribution of both the tax burden and the benefits from public services—is the first pillar.

Neutrality of tax policies is the second pillar. Taxes alter the way markets function by prompting producers, consumers, workers, and investors to find ways to reduce or eliminate their tax liability. Economists refer to these tax avoidance behaviors collectively as deadweight losses to the economy. The goal is to minimize interference from tax policies in the private marketplace where consumers, producers, investors, and workers are making their choices, thereby maximizing the efficiency of these markets. The less interference by taxes in the marketplace, the more neutral the tax policies and, by implication, the more productive the market's operation—up to a point. No economy operates perfectly—that is, with perfect competition, free flow of information, and freedom of entry or exit by participants. Tax neutrality requires placing the long-term economic health of a community above any short-term political advantages.

The third pillar is effective administration. Not all revenue options that have economic or political merit are feasible for local use when the cost to government to administer the tax, or the cost to taxpayers to comply with the tax, is taken into account. For example, charging a fee for the use of municipal parks has economic merit but lacks administrative feasibility, given the high cost of collecting the fee. Moreover, municipal parks, like other public services, provide benefits that spill over well beyond individual users, making their financing solely from benefits-based sources less attractive.

Equity, neutrality, and effective administration are principles to guide local managers in formulating revenue policies for their communities. But as will become evident, even with the aid of these principles, local leaders are left with the unsavory task of making trade-offs among them. Gains in equity often come at the expense of lost neutrality and increased administrative complexity. In the political context in which local managers operate, much of their time is devoted to resolving the conflicts that arise. The formulation of revenue policy occurs in an imperfect world with incomplete knowledge; the prudent manager takes full advantage of those occasional opportunities when balance can be achieved in the trade-offs made among these three pillars of tax policy.

Choices that promote fairness

Few issues rankle taxpayers more quickly than the conviction that they bear an unfair share of the tax burden relative to the share borne by others. Especially at the local level where the linkage between tax burden and public services is the closest, managers have a particular obligation to constantly monitor the fairness of the tax burden. But how can fairness be measured or otherwise gauged?

Equity in theory

From a theoretical perspective, equity is measured along two dimensions that are often at odds with one another. **Horizontal equity** refers to the distribution of the tax burden among persons or businesses in comparable circumstances. For example, households that live in comparably valued housing should incur the same property tax liability, assuming that housing value is the basis for establishing comparability. [1]

Horizontal equity is a deeply held value in the United States. "No taxation without representation" implicitly appeals for fair treatment for persons in similar circumstances. But on what basis should tax burdens be measured? Current annual income provides the most commonly used indicator of the relative impact of taxes on a household's available resources (effective tax rate = tax liability/current income). Some economists argue, however, that a broader measure, such as lifetime income, is justified because many decisions with tax consequences (e.g., the purchase of a home or vehicle) are made from a long-term perspective.[2] But since most tax policies focus on current income, that is the more appropriate measure of relative tax burdens.

Many of the deductions allowed in determining federal taxable income seek to establish horizontal fairness for the current tax year. Adjustments are made for extraordinary medical expenses, state and local taxes, mortgage interest, gifts to charities, and property losses due to federally declared casualties or theft. However, several state constitutions include a **uniformity clause** that, in varying degrees, compels even treatment of all citizens, or at least of those in comparable situations, and precludes state and local governments from making adjustments for individual circumstances. The Pennsylvania Supreme Court has ruled, for example, that the state's uniformity clause prohibits the extension of personal exemptions (a fixed dollar amount deducted for each dependent) or deductions and requires that personal income be taxed at a flat tax rate rather than a progressive one and with no adjustments for family size or other socially justified reasons.

Whereas horizontal equity considers the burden for each cross section of the income spectrum, comparable to the balance sheet in financial reporting, **vertical equity** takes a more dynamic look at how that burden varies across the spectrum of income, comparable to the income statement. Vertical equity refers to the variation in tax burden among taxpayers in different circumstances. As circumstances change, how much should a taxpayer's burden change? Three possibilities exist: regressive distribution, proportional distribution, or progressive distribution.

In a **regressive distribution**, the effective tax burden declines as income increases. For example, in the case of the sales tax, it is well known that while higher-income households buy goods and services that cost more and thus pay more in sales taxes, their effective tax burden as a percentage of their household income is less than that of low-income households. Accordingly, sales taxes are generally acknowledged to be regressive.

On the other hand, a **progressive distribution** means that the effective tax burden increases across the income spectrum, resulting in both absolute and relatively higher tax burdens for higher-income households. Progressivity can be achieved through incrementally higher tax rates, which is the case with the federal and most state income taxes. Alternatively, it can be achieved by targeting the sources of income and consumption of higher-income households, as New Hampshire and Tennessee have done by taxing only the unearned income of households, or by imposing a luxury excise tax that targets the purchases of the wealthy.

Lying between regressive and progressive taxes is a **proportional distribution**, in which the effective tax rate remains flat across the income spectrum. On the surface, a flat-rate income tax should exhibit proportionality, but because of the federal tax's progressive rate structure, the value of the deductibility of certain state and local income taxes increases with income, making an otherwise proportional state or local tax effectively regressive.

Equity in practice

Theories of equity provide valuable benchmarks for evaluating taxes, but they do not offer prescriptive guidelines for designing an equitable tax structure. Two basic principles in public finance offer a more prescriptive basis for tax policy: the benefits-received principle and the ability-to-pay principle.

At the local level, the **benefits-received principle** offers the most defensible basis for tax equity: those who benefit from a public service should bear a pro rata share of its cost. The simplicity of this principle largely explains its appeal. Even in the case of goods and services with some public benefits, to the extent that beneficiaries enjoy private benefits, they should bear part of the cost. Charges for services or utilities and fees for licenses find their justification in the benefits-received principle and, much like their counterparts in the private marketplace, these services are available for a price to consumers.

Taxes administered in accordance with this principle are called benefits-based taxes. Gasoline and hotel/motel occupancy taxes, for example, possess benefits-received properties to the extent that they are dedicated to funding activities that benefit the taxpayers who pay them. In the case of gasoline taxes, revenue is typically dedicated to highway, street, and bridge construction. In the case of occupancy taxes, revenues may be dedicated to promoting tourism, hospitality services, or convention services. Even the property tax has some benefits-received properties. For example, as crime declines or the quality of parks and recreational services improves, property values rise. This rise is particularly evident in neighborhoods known to have better schools. Increased property values represent a return (benefit) from investment in public services that can then be recaptured through the property tax. In fact, as property values increase, tax rates may decline and still generate the same amount of revenue. This feature represents one of the greatest advantages of the property tax over other types of taxes.

The **ability-to-pay principle** resonates deeply with Americans: those with the greater ability to pay—usually measured in terms of annual income or wealth—should bear a greater share of the burden for financing government. The progressive rate structure of the federal and several state income taxes is predicated on this principle, which implicitly recognizes that "from those to whom much is given, much shall be required." Since its inception in 1913, the federal income tax has always had a progressive rate structure, and calls for a flat rate structure must overcome more than a century of precedent. Yet, as a practical matter, presidents and congresses struggle with finding the right degree of progressivity, and marginal rates have generally converged since the Tax Reform Act of 1986 and, more recently, the Tax Cuts and Jobs Act of 2017.

Moreover, local and even state taxes based on the ability-to-pay principle encounter significant difficulty when higher-income households avoid the burden by "voting with their feet" and moving next door to a lower-tax jurisdiction.[3] The ability-to-pay principle brings into stark reality the complexity of tax policy and the inevitable trade-offs that must be made. As discussed later, equitable tax policies often lack economic neutrality, making them unwise for local governments. The general sense among public finance experts is that taxes predicated on the ability-to-pay principle are better left to the states and even better left to the national government. Redistribution of income, if done at the local level, is best accomplished through expenditure decisions.

Equity in action: The good, the bad, and the really ugly

Ultimately, defining a fair revenue structure is a political decision. Yet there is general agreement on the fundamental elements:

- Benefits-based levies are the most defensible in terms of fairness.
- Tax favors to particularly vocal or well-connected groups undermine the perceived equity of the revenue structure.
- Revenue policies should ease the burden on the poorest and not punish the wealthiest.
- Tax fairness varies among local communities, depending on their age, income distribution, and preference for public services.

When in doubt, use benefits-based levies Local governments have numerous opportunities to expand their use of benefits-based charges and fees. With the notable exception of landfills, the full costs—direct and indirect—of all utility services should be funded from service charges. Managers should look carefully at using **block-rate** and peak-period pricing structures for utility services. (Chapter 5 contains a full discussion of these and other issues managers must address in developing prices for public services.) Charges for the use of public rights-of-way provide another benefits-based levy that can generate significant amounts of revenue. Despite the political difficulty, recreational services should be partially financed from user charges—at the very least to minimize a wasteful use of the service, such as registering for a free recreational program and then failing to participate.

On the tax side, greater use of gasoline taxes should be encouraged at the local level through more lenient state enabling legislation. These taxes not only provide a viable revenue source for funding local streets and highways, but also make good equity sense for financing public transit. Commuters benefit from public transit through reduced highway congestion and greater convenience, and short of levying tolls for road and bridge use, gasoline taxes provide the local government with the most appropriate mechanism for capturing the individual benefits from the enhanced convenience. To discourage motorists from purchasing gasoline in neighboring cities with lower tax rates (a reduction in tax neutrality), gasoline taxes must be levied regionally—and preferably as an added levy to the state tax that is allocated to the county of origin and distributed among the county's municipalities on a population basis.

Cities and counties should also have access to the hotel/motel occupancy tax, with the revenue dedicated to promoting tourism, conventions, and the like. Some states allow local governments to use the revenue for historic preservation, county fairs, and the arts, both visual and performing. And it is reasonable for local governments to receive a portion of the hotel/motel tax for truly public goods and services, such as police and fire protection, general management, planning, and other property-based services, because nonresident guests also benefit from these services and should therefore share in paying for their costs.

Everybody is a special case when it comes to taxes Managers know the truth of this axiom and, unfortunately, so do politicians—especially those looking for a cheap strategy for securing voter support. The problem is that such favors undermine the tax system's horizontal equity and contribute to the public's cynicism about government. As discussed in the next section, special tax relief also undermines the tax system's neutrality and introduces significant incentives for unproductive or even counterproductive market behavior. Once Pandora's box of special tax favors is opened, there is no closing it. And new opportunities for granting such favors appear regularly, including

- Classifying property by type of use (residential, commercial, industrial, agricultural) and then applying a separate assessment ratio or tax rate to each class, with those classes that are perceived to have a greater ability to pay incurring the more punitive ratios or rates.
- Freezing tax liability for certain classes of property owners, usually senior citizens, again on the misguided assumption that ability to pay is linked to age of household.
- Granting partial or full exemptions from the tax base or from tax liability for certain classes of consumers, producers, types of property, property owners, or income sources. State and local tax codes, not to mention the federal code, are riddled with such exemptions, known as **tax expenditures**. Often these exemptions are permanent, although some are temporary. One special privilege that has gained popularity is the **sales tax holiday** (see sidebar in Chapter 4): On the assumption that the sales tax imposes an unfair burden on families buying clothes and essential supplies for their school-age children, several state legislatures have implemented a sales tax holiday of two or three days preceding the beginning of the school year, during which time such purchases are temporarily exempted from the sales tax base.

While tax favors should generally be avoided, they have a legitimate place in the local manager's toolbox, particularly for economic development purposes. The key is whether the tax favor (tax expenditure) is part of an overall plan for achieving certain economic goals or an attempt to garner political favor with a particularly vocal group of voters. The latter undermines the long-term economic health of the community and inevitably leads to woeful ends. Cities such as Detroit, Newark, Philadelphia, and Pittsburgh, once economically robust, now must face the consequences of special favors granted in past years.[4] Their experience should serve as a clarion call to local governments everywhere that the long-term cost of special tax favors far exceeds the lost revenue. Fairness in tax policy makes good sense not only politically but also economically.

Revenue policy should be humane While local governments are ill-suited to pursue the redistribution of income on the tax side, they have a responsibility to protect their most vulnerable citizens by finding innovative mechanisms for targeting relief to the poorest households. For example, while it is administratively awkward to attach a means test to the property tax, tax relief can be targeted through a circuit breaker program, which is a state-funded income tax credit for extraordinarily burdensome property taxes, or through a partial **homestead exemption** (less preferable because it less effectively targets relief to those who need it).

Figure 2–1 Relationship of political environment to revenue structure

		Revenue effort	
		Low	High
Revenue capacity	Low	**Caretaker community** Keeps cost of government down	**Arbiter community** More public services are expected, but resources are limited
	High	**Growth community** Creates favorable business climate	**Consumption community** Maintains quality public services that preserve community appeal

Local governments should maintain a utility relief fund, paid for by donations from users, to target utility fee subsidies to qualifying households. Some governments offer free or significantly reduced admission charges to recreational programs during off-peak periods. Conversely, local tax policies should not single out the wealthier households for discriminatory taxation. The openness of local economies means that people and their wealth will move to lower-tax areas that offer adequate public services. As discussed in the next section, pursuing good tax policy is a tightrope walk that balances fairness with neutrality.

Fairness is a community-based standard A politically acceptable revenue policy reflects the political environment of the community—and changes with it. For the public manager, the challenge is to assess the political environment and then design a budget that complements it.

Figure 2–1 combines revenue effort and capacity to depict four types of communities according to their political environment.[5] Revenue *capacity* indicates the local government's ability to raise revenue, and it is usually measured in terms of per capita income or per capita wealth of the property tax base. In other words, if residents have low personal income or low property wealth, the local government's revenue capacity is limited. Revenue *effort,* or the actual amount of revenue the local government raises, is measured in terms of revenue per capita. A high revenue effort indicates a comparatively high tax or service charge burden.

A caretaker community has a low revenue capacity and a low revenue effort. Expenditures are for basic services only. Citizens expect and want nothing more. Caretaker communities generally obtain their revenues from a modest property tax, a limited number of license and permit fees, and possibly some service charges. Smaller, more rural communities often fall into this category.

A growth community also maintains a low revenue effort but has the capacity for more. Typically, growth communities pursue laissez-faire economic policies on the assumption that such policies will create a more favorable business environment and thus more economic development. While per capita property wealth and personal income levels could support a much larger public sector, growth communities prefer a modest revenue effort and modest level of locally provided public services. Rapidly growing suburban towns at the edge of metropolitan areas and inner-ring suburban communities experiencing slower business investment often fit this profile.

By contrast, an arbiter community has a relatively high per capita revenue effort but a low capacity to provide the required revenues. Therefore, the manager must arbitrate among competing interest groups who want a share of an already stretched local budget. Citizens expect a diverse and significant number of services, but available resources are limited, possibly because the local tax base has eroded. This type of community makes heavy use of the property tax, but because intergovernmental competition keeps dependence on that tax in check, other broad-based taxes, such as income or sales taxes, may be used. Arbiter communities also pressure state legislatures to pass enabling legislation giving them access to tax revenues from nonresidents who use local services. Older central cities and counties dominated by manufacturing may fall into this category.

A consumption community, which is usually an upper-middle-income area, values locally produced public services and is willing and able to pay for good services. Consumption communities rely primarily on the property tax and possibly the sales tax but also make extensive use of service charges and regulatory fees. Older suburban communities dominated by higher-valued residential properties often fit this profile.

Like households, communities age. They evolve as their populations change, but it is difficult for the revenue structure to keep pace with demographic-driven changes. Young families, which are the most mobile households, seek growth-oriented communities where public services are plentiful and affordable. Consumption and borrowing characterize these households and thus shape their communities. As these families reach middle age, however, they find less satisfaction in the consumption of goods and more satisfaction in the consumption of services—namely, those services that enhance their quality of life, providing security, stability, and even serenity. Community services begin to reflect these new caretaker values, as typified by communities—especially those organized as homeowners associations—that exclusively serve active senior citizens.

But aging rarely proceeds gracefully or uniformly. Some communities become more diverse socially, ethnically, and economically. Arbitration among competing interests becomes the norm and brings a unique set of revenue and expenditure challenges for the public manager.

Choices that strengthen the local economy

Every bit as important as the more frequently debated issue of fairness is neutrality, the second pillar of sound public finance. Neutrality addresses the impact of tax and revenue policies on the local economy. Achieving neutral tax policies requires extraordinary care that cannot be found on the cutting-room floor of political compromise. Tax neutrality is intentional. It places the community's long-term economic viability ahead of short-term political accommodation. Unfortunately, the nation's current political environment does not bode well for tax neutrality. However, the unique vantage point of professional managers enables them to push the neutrality question onto the public agenda and shape the debate to ensure that important questions get addressed.

Why is neutrality important? Taxes affect the way we behave. Some consequences are intended and positive. Consider the effects of individual retirement accounts on Americans' willingness to save; of cigarette taxes on the consumption of tobacco, especially by younger consumers; or of "business-friendly" tax policies on economic development. On the other hand, some consequences are unintended and negative. For example, taxes on improvements discourage inner-city property owners from upgrading their properties, while taxes on property at the urban fringe, where property values are rapidly increasing, encourage speculators to convert farmland to housing development. California's Proposition 13, discussed more fully in the accompanying sidebar, is a poster child for the consequences of ignoring the effects of tax policy on the economy, as it has penalized new arrivals to the state, discouraged long-term owners from selling their property unless they plan to move out of state, and discouraged investment in new construction. [6]

Tax reform requires a careful assessment of the short- and long-term consequences for the economy. Every tax has economic consequences, some more obvious than others. The public manager's task is to ensure that those consequences are understood and that, where possible, negative consequences are mitigated in order to strengthen, rather than weaken, the community's economy.

California's nonneutral property tax

The budget crisis that routinely grips local and state governments in California has a connection to the state's fateful decision in 1978 to implement a major retooling of the property tax. When Californians passed Proposition 13 by almost a two-to-one margin, no one fully anticipated the economic consequences. But the Golden State has become the beholden state—to creditors and suppliers—periodically issuing IOUs to cover its obligations. Normally, the state would turn to the short-term credit market to finance its cash flow needs, but even that market has been closed at times to the one-time economic powerhouse.

The California economy is a poignant case study in how the cumulative effects of nonneutral tax policies can eventually undermine even the most vibrant marketplace. Such is the case with Proposition 13. This citizen-initiated tax reform introduced acquisition-based valuation as the basis for determining property tax liability (the selling price determines the taxable value), and then shielded annual increases in that value to no more than 2 percent per year, regardless of changes in the marketplace. The longer Californians hold onto their property, the more they benefit from this property tax break. Buying and selling real estate in California is now driven not only by market considerations but also by property tax considerations, a distortion of the market that causes buyers and sellers to make less than optimum decisions.

Those adverse effects have accumulated over time and become most apparent in recessions. During the decades since Proposition 13, the multiple budget-related initiatives passed by Californians have limited the ability of the state's political leadership to effectively pursue countercyclical policies. As a result, recessions have become steeper and more protracted in California. That reality is not lost on investors as they assess the state's business climate.

Although not the intent of its proponents, Proposition 13 gradually shifted more of the responsibility for funding California's local governments to the state. But no state's revenue structure has the capacity to support both state and local operations. According to data from the California Department of Finance, in fiscal year (FY) 1978, the state spent $1.90 on local assistance for every $1 spent on state operations; by FY 2018, that ratio had inched up to almost $2.7 on local assistance for each $1 spent on state operations.[1] California dedicates 72 percent of its state spending to local assistance.

California's revenue structure has shifted increasingly to dependence on the personal income tax, a revenue source that is typically more income elastic (i.e., sensitive to growth or decline in the economy) than the general sales or property tax. In 1978, the state derived 31 percent of its tax revenue from the personal income tax and 34 percent from the general sales tax; forty years later those proportions had changed to 51 percent and 20 percent, respectively.[2] These proportions make the state's budget much more vulnerable to cyclical shifts, especially in the absence of a budget surplus.

In sum, Proposition 13 has significantly altered the economic fortunes of Californians by making their local governments more dependent on state funding; introducing nonneutrality into the real estate market, in which its adverse effects have accumulated over time; shifting the state's revenue structure to greater dependence on more volatile revenue sources; limiting state leaders' ability to take countercyclical actions in their taxing and spending decisions; and increasing the severity and length of recessions in California.

What lessons can public administrators take from the misfortunes of the Golden State? And what recourse do Californians have to restore budget stability?

- First and foremost, states are well served by promoting the financial autonomy of their local governments, particularly cities and counties. Municipalities with access to their own sources of revenue can provide greater continuity and sustainability in the delivery of essential public services over the business cycle.
- Tax policies shape state and local economies. Taxes that interfere excessively in the competitive market create a drag on the state's economy that eventually leads to stagnant growth and disinvestment by business.
- The design of tax policy is a complex political process that requires the utmost care so as to generate adequate revenues with minimal inequities and market distortions. At the state and local levels, particular attention must be given to the effect that tax policies have on the investment decisions of businesses.
- State and local governments need to take into consideration the effect of their revenue decisions on budget stability over the business cycle.

California's experiment in direct democracy shows that the most carefully crafted decisions by the governor and legislature can be undone by a relatively small group of aggrieved citizens through a statewide initiative. That threat casts a pall over all major policy debates, undercuts the efforts of elected representatives to craft compromises, and has thus made governing the state problematic. Finally, and most telling, the budget instability that has rocked the California state government has had a chilling effect on business investment in that state.

1 California Department of Finance, *2017–18 State Budget, Statewide Financial Information, Schedule 9*, 16. www.ebudget.ca.gov/2017-18/pdf/Enacted/BudgetSummary/BS_SCH9.pdf.

2 California Department of Finance, *2017–18 State Budget, Summary Charts* (Figure SUM-05), 10. www.ebudget.ca.gov/2017-18/pdf/Enacted/BudgetSummary/SummaryCharts.pdf.

Tax neutrality in theory

From a public finance perspective, taxes introduce inefficiencies into a perfectly competitive market. Welfare economics holds that consumer satisfaction is maximized when markets are left to operate without outside interference. They produce just enough goods and services to meet consumer demand, and they allocate those goods and services to those who value them the most. This is the familiar Pareto optimum.[7] Any interference in this ideal state, from taxation or regulation, diminishes this optimality and results in economic losses—fewer goods and services available at less-than-optimum prices. Consumer welfare is less than optimal.

But the ideal state does not exist and doubtless never will. Consumer goods and services produced through competitive markets represent only some of the products that communities and societies need. For example, citizens demand a whole range of public goods and services, from national security to land use controls. Because these services lack marketplace properties (as they are nondivisible and nonexcludable), they must be produced through nonmarket mechanisms. Most Western democracies have chosen a representative government with majority rule to produce and allocate such goods and services.

Public goods make up only a portion of the services and products that governments produce. For varying reasons but mostly because of the lack of a profit incentive, local governments also provide an array of private goods and services (as they are divisible and the benefits are excludable): utilities, recreation, parks, public transit, and even education. Sometimes a government provides services, such as libraries, that could be provided by the private sector if their social and cultural benefits to the community did not make profiting from their sale inappropriate. Most citizens regard such services as merit goods—that is, goods that merit subsidization by the community. The mix of public, private, and merit goods varies widely among cities, counties, and states—each the product of an admixture of history, local preferences, and necessity.

But the production of these nonmarket goods and services requires that governments, through some collective decision process, collect the resources needed for their production. In theory, taxes provide governments with the funding needed for public and merit services and goods, whereas service charges and fees more typically finance the private services and goods produced by government. Of course, such a tidy distribution of funding is not the case in reality.

While all taxes diminish the market's efficiency—their very presence affects the market and are therefore not neutral—some taxes create more inefficiencies than others. The challenge is to design a tax structure in which unintended interference is minimized (keeping in mind that some changes caused by tax policies, such as increased business investment from a tax abatement, are intended).

One final observation. Markets are affected not only by the choice of the type of tax (the tax base) but also by the tax rates themselves. Arthur Laffer, widely regarded as the father of supply-side economics, conjectured that as tax rates increase, tax yields increase at a decreasing rate and at some point begin to decrease[8] (see Figure 2–2). The implication of the Laffer curve, or what is now called the "revenue hill," is that for governments with tax rates beyond the peak, any reduction in rates results in increased yields, in which case tax reductions will pay for themselves.

One study of the revenue hills for four major cities found that Houston, New York City, and Philadelphia were at or just beyond the peak of the hill and that reductions, especially in the property tax rates for Houston and New York City, would result in increased revenues. Only in Minneapolis was the property tax rate below the peak of the revenue hill.[9]

Figure 2–2 The Laffer curve

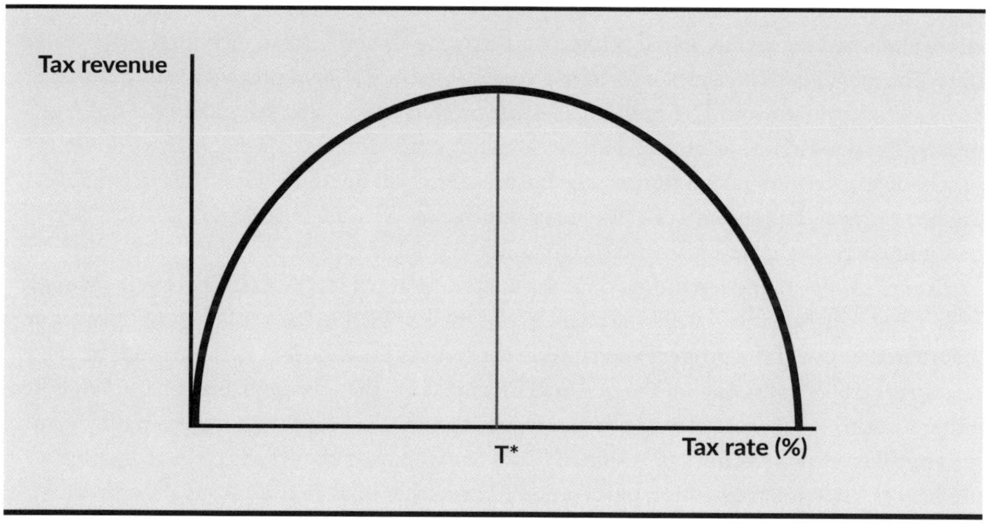

Source: Reprinted with permission from "Laffer Curve," Will Kenton, https://www.investopedia.com/terms/l/laffercurve.asp ©2003 Investopedia.com.

* The tax rate that yields the greatest amount of revenue.

Tax neutrality in practice

The pragmatic question then arises: how can the adverse market effects of taxes be identified and then minimized? Four principles for strengthening the local economy may provide useful guidance to public managers as they grapple with difficult trade-offs:

- The broader the base and the flatter the tax rate, the more neutral a tax will be.
- Given their quasi-market character, benefits-based taxes and charges interfere the least in the economy.
- Neutrality is more adversely affected by tax rate differentials than by the absolute level of the tax rate.
- Particular care is required in the design of local business taxes.

The broad, flat expanse of neutrality One of the axioms of tax policy holds that broad-based taxes are more neutral than narrow-based taxes, and that a flat rate is more neutral than progressive or multiple rates. Obviously, this rule runs counter to the equity-maximizing principles of ability to pay and progressive rate structures. Where neutrality is the goal, however, communities are best served by taxes that fall broadly on the tax base at moderate, but flat, rates.

Of course, exemptions and exclusions are usually offered—some for administrative reasons, others for social and political reasons. Whenever such tax expenditures are introduced, the subsidized activity will be encouraged, shifting economic activity toward the favored sector or activity. Thus, seniors whose property assessments or property tax liabilities are frozen will stay in their larger homes for a longer period of time; nonprofits that are exempted from local property taxes will gravitate toward more expensive property that otherwise would be used for taxable purposes. Market participants are drawn to locations where their costs are minimized, assuming that quality remains constant.

The property tax that pays for education in most states poses an interesting case in point. Prior to 1993, Michigan's school districts set their own tax rates, creating a patchwork of varying tax rates and revenue yields.[10] In the summer of 1993, in response to the disparities in funding levels between property-rich and property-poor school districts, the Michigan legislature abolished the locally levied property tax for schools and instead instituted a two-tiered statewide rate of 6 mills (a mill is 1/10 of a cent; for each $1,000 in property value, the tax is $6) on primary homes and 24 mills on all other property, including second homes and businesses. The two-tiered structure significantly reduces rate differentials and makes differences in school property tax rates a nonissue in business location decisions. This reform enhances the neutrality of the property tax. The downside, however, is the local school districts' loss of autonomy, a price that many would regard as not worth the gain in neutrality.

Complicating an understanding of how a tax proposal affects the market is **tax incidence**. Who ultimately bears the burden of a tax? While the law establishes tax liability—owners of record in the case of the property tax, buyers (or sometimes vendors) in the case of the sales tax, wage earners in the case of the personal income tax—the economic burden can be shifted either forward to consumers in the form of higher prices or backward to owners in the form of lower profits. How a tax burden is shifted depends on (1) whether the tax falls at an intermediary point in the transaction process and (2) whether market conditions allow shifting forward or backward.

Sin taxes, otherwise known as **sumptuary taxes**, such as taxes on tobacco and alcohol products, are largely shifted forward to the final consumer because demand remains fairly price inelastic, particularly among long-term consumers. By contrast, when Texas tripled the fee for vanity license plates, thinking that the revenue yield would increase commensurately, demand for the license plates plummeted and increased yields never materialized. A substitute product—nonpersonalized plates—was available, and consumers showed their price sensitivity by shifting to the lower-priced alternative.

The tax on business property poses a more complex situation. While the owner bears **legal liability** for the tax, the owner can shift the burden forward in the form of higher rents if the market allows it. But in the case of rental property, if comparable housing is available at a lower price in a nearby jurisdiction, renters will move there if the difference justifies it, so the landlord must either lower rents or risk losing tenants. If the landlord cannot shift the cost of the tax forward, the only other direction is backward as lower profits. But a lower profit, or even loss, on the rental property means that it is a less valuable business enterprise; that is, it has lost value. Consequently, changes in the property tax are **capitalized** into values: the cost of a tax increase is borne as a reduction in property value and vice versa for a tax reduction. In competitive markets, a property tax increase results in property values declining by a commensurate amount, and a tax decrease results in property values rising. One of the consequences of Californians' ratification of Proposition 13 in 1978 was a reduction in the cost of owning property in the state and thus a rapid increase in the value of property there, resulting in an immediate windfall to everyone who owned a home or business in California at the time.

Still the best for the money: Benefits-based levies Because they function like prices in the marketplace, benefits-based levies are as valuable a tool for achieving neutrality as they are for achieving equity. In addition, tying expenditures to service charges in particular, or even to benefits-based taxes, reduces the pressure on government to expand public services beyond the real demand for them.

When it comes to tax rates, keep an eye on the Joneses Interjurisdictional differences in tax rates, particularly highly visible rates like those of the property tax, are factors in the locational decisions of industries and, to a lesser extent, of commercial and residential owners. Small rate differences, when compared in present value terms, can have significant cumulative effects on the corporate bottom line. As implied by the Tiebout hypothesis, interlocal tax competition imposes a quasi-market discipline on local budgets and, if ignored, can result in the erosion of a community's tax base. Thus, city and county leaders must constantly scrutinize their rates to ensure that they are competitive. In some cases, higher tax rates may be a strategy, intentional or otherwise, to bar commercial and particularly industrial development and preserve the "residential" flavor of a town. Every business has a critical point at which differences in tax rates among local governments in a metropolitan area become significant to its locational decision. However, sensitivity to those differences increases in areas with higher tax rates. That is, in metropolitan areas characterized by high property tax rates, small differences in rates across municipalities can have significant implications for where businesses choose to locate.

Consumption and income-based taxes pose special challenges for local governments because of the potential for **border-city** and **border-county effects**. For example, two cities that share a border or are within commuting distance from each other will experience such effects if one has a significantly lower sales tax rate than the other. Retail stores will prefer to locate in the lower tax jurisdiction, where they can draw consumers from neighboring communities. Similar effects occur with local income and, to a lesser extent, property taxes. The greater the disparity in tax rates, the more sensitive workers and consumers become to the effects of the tax. Towns around Tucson, Arizona, use billboards to advertise their lower sales tax rates for shoppers. In its final report, published in 2003, the Philadelphia Tax Reform Commission estimated that 172,889 jobs left the city between 1971 and 2001 because of increases in the wage tax rate relative to the rates levied by surrounding municipalities.[11]

Some states have designed local enabling legislation that precludes border-city effects. As noted above, North Carolina has taken a particularly laudable approach toward the local sales tax, as has Maryland in the case of the local income tax. Counties in North Carolina levy a uniform sales tax and share the revenue with municipalities on the basis of either the municipalities' pro rata share of the county's population or the municipality's share of the total property value in the county. Similarly, counties in Maryland levy a personal income tax, collected by the state, with limited discretion in the range of local rates that may be levied. By placing limits on local discretion over taxes, these states have eliminated the inefficiencies of border-city effects without compromising local autonomy.

With the popularity of Internet sales, another set of tax issues has arisen. In 1998, Congress imposed a moratorium, which it renewed several times over the next twenty years, on local and state taxes on the fees that subscribers pay for various Internet services. In 2016, Congress permanently banned state and local taxes on Internet access (but not sales taxes on online purchases). It did, however, allow the seven states that already collect taxes on Internet access to continue doing so until 2020. That year, the Congressional Research Service estimated the annual loss in state and local sales tax revenues on Internet access at $6.5 billion.[12]

A separate issue concerns state and local sales taxes on purchases made online. In 1967 the U.S. Supreme Court ruled that retailers without a taxable nexus in a state could not be required to collect state or local sales taxes. In terms of tax neutrality, this prohibition created the e-commerce equivalent of a border-city effect by making online purchases tax-exempt but on-site purchases of the same products taxable. In 2018, the Court took the unusual action of agreeing to hear an appeal from the states to reconsider its 1992 ruling prohibiting states from collecting their sales tax from out-of-state vendors. In its ruling in *South Dakota v. Wayfair*, the Court lifted its ban and allowed state and local governments to compel remote vendors to collect the sales tax. Credible analyses placed the lost revenue for state and local governments from uncollected sales taxes at $8.5 billion to $13 billion in 2017.[13] If such nonneutral disparities had persisted, a disproportionate share of the retail market would have shifted to the Internet and further undermined the sales tax bases of state and local governments.

For two special types of communities, tax competition is less of an issue. The first type is communities with established **agglomeration economies**, businesses in the same industry that locate near each other to take advantage of savings from shared services and a shared labor pool. These communities have a competitive niche, which allows them to attract additional economic activity and, with it, a lower tax rate to sustain the same level of public services. Most cities have some degree of agglomeration economies.

The second type is communities that are able to shift taxes to nonresidents through tax exportation. Some taxes are specifically intended to maximize this practice by shifting the tax burden either to nonresident consumers as higher prices, as in the case of hotel/motel taxes, or to nonresident owners as lower profits, as in the case of taxes on stock transactions; however, more of the local tax burden is borne externally than is commonly realized. For example, in 2018 the Texas state comptroller estimated that 21 percent of that state's general sales tax, 20 percent of its property tax, and 65 percent of its oil production tax are exported to nonresident consumers or producers.[14] Some communities have extraordinary opportunities for tax exportation either as a result of natural advantages, as in the case of Maui County, Hawaii, or through agglomeration economies, as in the case of Branson, Missouri. No rules, in theory or in law, set the appropriate amount of tax exportation.

When it comes to local taxes on business, go with the Joneses Businesses represent tempting targets for revenue-pressed governments, particularly those experiencing a fiscal crisis or crush. Since businesses are able to pass their tax liability on to consumers (forward shifting) or investors (backward shifting), it becomes politically expedient for these governments to shift more of the tax burden on to businesses. And since businesses don't vote, they represent to the imprudent political leader the perfect candidates for discriminatory tax treatment. But businesses do "vote"—by moving their investment to more favorable tax jurisdictions. Unless a community has unique resources—Alaska's oil, Colorado's ski slopes, Florida's beaches, for example—virtually all business investment is mobile, and in an era when technology is the coin of the realm, that mobility has only increased.

Where businesses are concerned, local governments should avoid imposing two types of taxes: corporate income taxes and gross receipts taxes on sales. Corporate income taxes introduce serious equity and neutrality problems. Only a few cities still attempt to collect a true corporate income tax, and when they do, it is on declining tax bases. Gross receipts taxes are more prevalent because of their relative ease of collection. Unfortunately, they can have a **tax pyramiding** effect, which occurs when a production process has multiple stages (raw materials are converted into intermediary goods, which in turn become finished goods that are sold to wholesalers and then, finally, to retailers). The problem occurs because, unlike the general sales tax, the gross receipts tax is applied at each stage of the production process. The portion of the tax that is shifted forward creates a cascading (or pyramiding) effect, with taxes falling on top of taxes. To avoid such tax effects and gain a competitive advantage in the market, businesses have an incentive to vertically integrate the production process by consolidating all stages of production into one company, which may not be the most efficient means of operation. Because of these effects, gross receipts taxes have nonneutral consequences and so compromise the efficiency of business production.

For business taxation, the following guidelines should be considered:

- Any tax on business should be widely used in that state or region. If a city or county is the only jurisdiction in the area to impose a particular tax on business, the tax almost certainly will have a detrimental effect on that community's long-term economic growth.
- Taxes on the less mobile components of production—land, buildings, and equipment—have the least detrimental effect on markets. Statewide taxation of such property, while undermining local autonomy, greatly enhances tax neutrality through the imposition of a

Tips for would-be tax reformers

Initiatives to reform the local tax structure always begin with the highest aspirations and noblest intentions but frequently end in disappointment. As discussions for tax reform progress, participants come to realize the complex trade-offs that must be made, and too often they conclude that the political costs are not worth the economic gains. The following tips, while lowering aspirations, may elevate results:

- The more heavily a tax is used, the more apparent its economic and political defects become. Increasing the rates of existing taxes without correcting the deficiencies of the existing tax structure exacerbates hidden flaws.
- Because of their visibility, higher tax rates on a relatively narrower tax base have a more detrimental effect on economic growth than more moderate rates on a broader tax base. Tax reformers should look first to broadening the existing tax base before raising tax rates.
- An axiom of public finance is "an old tax is a good tax" because the marketplace has adjusted to accommodate the tax. In general, improving the equity and neutrality of existing taxes is preferable to introducing a new tax unless the inequities and inefficiencies of the existing taxes are greater than those of a proposed new tax.
- Tax reforms that occur incrementally over time generally have a better chance of succeeding politically than sweeping tax reforms introduced over a short period.
- One of the easiest reforms is the elimination of nuisance taxes that have low revenue yields and high administrative and/or compliance costs. Taxes targeted to incidentals, such as fireworks or soft drinks, or that are largely evaded because of lax and costly enforcement, have low revenue yields, and they impose unfair burdens, especially on lower-income households.
- Excise taxes, especially sin taxes and those borne by nonresidents, usually arouse the least political opposition.
- Because tax reform almost always comes with considerable political costs to leaders, successful tax reforms require strong political support from elected officials who have an abundance of credibility with voters. The key is to clearly and convincingly articulate the benefits from the reforms, whether through improved public services on the expenditure side or reduced inequities and inefficiencies on the revenue side.
- Low tax rates do not guarantee economic growth, as a number of states are discovering. On the other hand, nonneutral tax policies do guarantee that a state or local government's economy will never grow to its fullest potential. For the tax reformer the lesson is this: In the long term, the greatest gains toward economic prosperity come from increasing tax neutrality rather than from reducing tax rates, all other things being equal.
- A well-designed tax structure can make tax incentives unnecessary. An equitable tax structure that minimizes adverse economic effects, such as border-city/county effects, is a government's most effective tool for creating a favorable business environment.

uniform tax rate. As an alternative, regional **tax-base sharing**, such as in Minneapolis/St. Paul, Minnesota, and Racine County, Wisconsin, offers an approach to reducing interlocal tax competition and enhancing regional tax neutrality.[15]

- Sales taxes on business purchases will be less detrimental to local economies if the tax base is defined by the state rather than by local governments.

- Because business investment benefits more than just the jurisdiction in which the new development occurs, business taxation seems a prime candidate for greater cooperation between a state government and its cities and counties. The state-local partnership required to attract and retain business investment could also design more equitable and neutral tax policies.

Tax neutrality in action: The good, the bad, and the still ugly

This chapter has thus far considered two key components to tax policy: equity and neutrality. Much to the frustration of tax analysts and legislators, these two components often exist in tension with one another. Gains in equity come at the expense of reduced neutrality, and vice versa. And both often create additional administrative costs and compliance complexity for taxpayers. For example, considering family size or inordinate casualty losses may promote horizontal equity, but it may also reduce neutrality by narrowing the tax base, and it adds significantly to compliance costs by requiring the taxpayer to provide supporting documentation. Flat-rate, broad-based taxes are regressive. Progressive income taxes produce nonneutral effects by discouraging work and penalizing investment in income-producing ventures, which adversely affects economic well-being. What should local managers do?

- First, there is no perfect tax source. Each suffers from its own set of deficiencies, some more than others.
- Second, at the local level, primary consideration must be given to tax neutrality—that is, to tax and revenue policies that minimize market distortions and maximize economic growth. Failure to give neutrality priority condemns a community to lackluster growth or even decline, in which case any efforts to promote fairness are doomed as well.
- Third, special tax favors that are not part of a comprehensive economic development plan, while gaining political favors in the short term, increase inequities and lessen neutrality—a double negative. A written, formally adopted plan for promoting economic growth can prove particularly helpful in managing persistent demands for tax favors.
- Fourth, policies that promote horizontal equity merit priority over those that promote vertical equity at the local level. Redistribution of income is part of a civilized society, but because of the openness of state and particularly local economies, those efforts result in economic decline as production capabilities shift to more favorable tax environments.
- Finally, benefits-based levies offer the best option for promoting horizontal equity and tax neutrality. They reduce overconsumption of an otherwise "free" good or service by providing consumers and public managers with an awareness of the true cost of its production.

Choices that facilitate effective administration

The new reality in local public finance dictates that jurisdictions channel more funds into service delivery by minimizing overhead costs in tax administration. The third pillar of sound economic policy considers both the government's cost to administer taxes and the taxpayers' cost to comply with them.

Figure 2–3 depicts the phases that governments typically go through when collecting taxes and service charges. The specific issues involved in collecting each type of revenue are

Figure 2–3 Information flow in the tax administration process

Notification → **Collection** → **Enforcement**

discussed more fully in the following chapters. The sections below discuss the general principles that guide revenue administration.

Notification

Notification of tax liability comes either indirectly through self-reporting by taxpayers, as in the case of most state and federal income taxes, or directly as an invoice from the governing jurisdiction, as in the case of property taxes and utility service charges. Notification includes a due date (or dates, if payments may be split over several periods) and the **penalty and interest** for late payments. Late payment of tax liability always involves a penalty in addition to interest for the elapsed time since it was due. Failure to receive notification of a tax liability does not absolve the taxpayer of liability. Governments operate on the assumption that its citizens are responsible for knowing their obligations and fulfilling those obligations faithfully.

Even before notification can be made, legal liability for the tax or charge must be established. For example, in the case of a property that was sold during the year, is it the current owner or the previous owner who is liable for the tax? This issue becomes particularly problematic with more mobile property such as vehicles and manufactured housing. Utility charges for service to rental properties pose their own set of challenges. Local governments typically require a larger **security deposit** for service to such properties until the user establishes a record of timely payments.

Establishing legal liability also poses challenges where tax overlapping exists—that is, where multiple jurisdictions tax the same property, consumption spending, or household income. If the overlapping governments use somewhat different tax bases, taxpayers can easily become confused as to their liability.

Political boundaries add to the complexity of tax liability. For example, some properties straddle two or more taxing jurisdictions. **Apportionment** becomes an issue in the case of an income tax on a wage earner who works in one state (or county) but lives in another. Taxes on business activity (e.g., locally levied sales and excise taxes), especially for businesses with a **taxable nexus**, or connection, in multiple jurisdictions and in jurisdictions where income is the base, pose significant apportionment issues—particularly when those taxes are allocated on the basis of the consumer's point of residence and not the more typical **point of sale.**

The final general issue in notification of liability involves the attachment of a **tax lien.** State laws typically impose a blanket lien on **fixed assets**, usually real property, as collateral for pending tax liability. Such a lien is usually automatic, which is to say that it affixes to each property title as of a particular date and does not require specific action by the taxing jurisdiction. The lien remains attached until the liability is paid in full. Usually the asset cannot be sold with an outstanding lien attached to the title. In some cases, such as with special assessments, governments must formally file documentation affixing a lien for an obligation. As discussed below, a lien becomes particularly useful when taxes or charges for services become delinquent and payment is not likely to be forthcoming.

Collection

The process of levying taxes or service charges creates accounts or taxes receivable for the local government. The goal is to collect all **receivables** by their due date. Unfortunately, as in business, governments encounter bad accounts, some that result from bankruptcy and others from evasion. Although the collection rate can vary with the business cycle, governments should normally achieve rates of at least 95 percent of the current liability of each revenue source. Lower rates risk undermining taxpayer confidence in the tax system and, more generally, in the management capabilities of that jurisdiction.

The cost of administering a tax or any revenue source should never exceed 5 percent of the revenue collected. A key to reducing collection costs is to share notification, collection, and enforcement of tax liabilities with overlapping governments: centralized tax collection and enforcement programs provide economies of scale. For example, state governments should collect local sales and income taxes in tandem with state taxes, funneling local taxes back to the local government of origin. (The exception is the truly rare case in which the state does not collect the tax on its own, as in Alaska, where local sales taxes are levied but not a state sales tax.) Cooperative arrangements for revenue administration almost always result in lower unit costs and more uniform enforcement of the law.

From a local government perspective, the most obvious problem with state administration is the perceived loss of political autonomy, although local autonomy rests on powers far more fundamental than tax collection. In fact, the reduced costs of centralized revenue administration greatly outweigh any political costs from perceived reductions in local autonomy. Centralized administration also lowers taxpayers' compliance costs by making it possible to complete only one tax return for two or more taxing jurisdictions.

From a state perspective, the primary concern with centralized administration is whether taxpayers differentiate state from local tax liability. If they do not, the state tax burden appears much greater, placing the state government in an undesirable political position. Whether such blurring of liability occurs depends on the clarity with which the tax return differentiates between state and local liability. Several states—most notably Maryland—have successfully overcome potential problems by designing exemplary tax returns.

An alternative is outsourcing collection and/or enforcement. For example, Pennsylvania local governments rely on third-party firms to collect and enforce payment of the earned income tax levied by municipalities and school districts. In Texas, local governments generally contract with law firms that specialize in collecting delinquent property taxes. As in all types of outsourcing, there is the danger that contractors will focus on easier accounts—a practice that is often referred to as "creaming"—unless the contract is structured to prevent this from occurring.

Finally, each revenue source responds differently to the business cycle, resulting in income elasticities that can vary significantly over time. Tax yields that increase at rates greater than growth in the economy, which is usually measured as changes in personal income, have income elasticities greater than 1.0, whereas yields that do not keep pace with economic growth have income elasticities of less than 1.0.

An income-elastic revenue source performs well during upswings in the economy but leaves governments short of revenue in the downswings. A diversified tax base and multiple tax sources can help offset these cycles in tax collections, producing a more stable stream of income for budget purposes.

Enforcement

The integrity of a tax system ultimately depends on enforcement. Vigilance in auditing and collecting delinquent receivables conveys a government's commitment to fairness and the uniform application of the law, whereas cutting corners on revenue enforcement undermines the community's confidence in its leaders' management capabilities. As with collections, enforcement offers some opportunities for coordination with overlapping jurisdictions, thereby reducing administrative costs to all participating governments and compliance costs to taxpayers.

Tax liens represent powerful enforcement tools, enabling local governments to foreclose on delinquent taxpayers. State laws specify the procedures, but they typically require that the taxpayer (assuming his or her whereabouts are known) be duly notified of the delinquent tax liability. If the taxpayer fails to settle the claim within a reasonable period, the taxing jurisdiction petitions a court to give it title to the property on which the lien is attached. If the order is granted, the jurisdiction then sells the property for the outstanding taxes. In recent years, a number of states have adopted provisions giving the previous property owner a grace period following foreclosure in which he or she can reclaim the property. Some states also grant special protection to homesteads (i.e., primary residences), a practice rooted in the principles of frontier justice.

One controversial enforcement measure is the widespread practice among local governments of offering **amnesty** to delinquent taxpayers (and, more commonly, for traffic fines). Amnesties, which states and the federal government have not used very much, usually proliferate during tight budget periods when local governments are looking for additional revenue at little political cost. Often the penalty portion of the delinquent charge is reduced or eliminated as a reward for payment during the amnesty period, after which threats are made to redouble enforcement. If the threat is credible, such strategies produce an infusion of delinquent payments. Scofflaws, of course, weigh the probability of being caught against the cost of paying the delinquent tax or fee. Investment in a professional, dedicated team of enforcement officers obviates the need for amnesty programs and minimizes the incentives for the gamesmanship they encourage.

Putting it all together: Creating a more resilient local economy

A strong revenue structure begins and ends with a strong local economy. Adopting and tenaciously pursuing prudent revenue policies is the key to strengthening the local economy. In other words, a perpetual feedback loop exists between a local government's revenue policies and its economy.

Where should local leaders begin to build a resilient economy? The answer depends on the severity and duration of the fiscal problems confronting the jurisdiction. Noted public administration scholar Charles Levine developed a typology for understanding the various strategies that governments use to cope with fiscal stress.[16] Levine's presentation, represented by a 2 x 2 table, focuses on the spending side for strategies to redress the budget problem; however, the revenue side cannot be ignored if a more resilient local economy is to emerge. Assuming that local governments will take appropriate actions on the spending side to mitigate the adverse budget trends, Figure 2–4 adapts Levine's table to the revenue side and recommends different strategies depending on the severity of the problem. The following discussion elaborates on those recommendations.

Develop a strategic plan

Revenue problems do not develop suddenly, so it follows that their resolution requires a long-term plan, a carefully crafted strategy, and continuous attention. Neglecting to assess objectively the impact of local taxes and fees on the economy is an invitation to a revenue crisis in the future. The first task, then, is to undertake a strategic planning process to assess the local government's economy. What are its strengths and weaknesses? Does it already support agglomeration economies, or is there the potential to build clusters of related businesses? What other opportunities exist for strengthening the economy? What threats exist to undermine it? How do current tax and fee policies affect the economy?

On the basis of this analysis, local leaders can develop a multiphased plan for building on the community's economic strengths and ameliorating its weaknesses, and for capitalizing on opportunities while mitigating threats. Part of the plan may incorporate the principles of good revenue policy. For example, one consequence of agglomeration economies is that a local

Figure 2–4 Strategies for strengthening local economies through prudent revenue policies

		Duration of fiscal stress	
		Short term	**Long term**
Severity of fiscal stress	**Low**	**I. Fiscal crunch** – Increase service charges – Grant amnesty for delinquent taxes and fees – Move up due dates for taxes or fees – Automate tax/fee collections – Identify possible piggybacking of tax and fee collections with other governments	**III. Fiscal squeeze** ***All of II plus*** – Undertake strategic review of the city/county's strengths and design revenue policies that augment agglomeration economies – Examine tax-exempt policies for citizen groups, nonprofits, and businesses – Eliminate minor taxes and fees that are costly to administer
	High	**II. Fiscal crisis** ***All of I plus*** – Impose temporary increase in property tax rate – Impose temporary increase in fees	**IV. Fiscal crush** ***All of III plus*** – Aggressively target tax incentives only to business investment that strengthens agglomeration economies – Reduce rates on taxes/fees that are excessively high (by regional standards) – Eliminate property tax exemptions for targeted citizen groups – Increase service charges or convert more tax-supported services to a fee base and account for as self-supporting enterprises.

Source: Adapted from Charles H. Levine, "Police Management in the 1980s: From Decrementalism to Strategic Thinking," *Public Administration Review* 45 (November 1985): 695. Published by Wiley. © American Society for Public Administration.

government, especially a smaller one, may become more vulnerable to economic cycles in that particular industry or business sector. A rural community that builds its economy around the farm implement industry will experience large swings in its tax and fee bases. Such a community's plan should include economic development measures that diversify the tax base, ideally introducing countercyclical industries to offset the adverse effects from downturns in its preeminent business sector.

Local governments facing a fiscal crunch or crisis may focus on longer-term strategies to sustain the viability of their economies, such as revenue policies that support an adequate supply of public services while encouraging reinvestment in the local economy. Or they may need to take more intentional and immediate measures to attract business investment, diversify the tax base, and sustain an adequate level of public services.

Once a plan has been formally adopted by the council and is in place, local leaders have a reference point for legislators, managers, and citizens evaluating the merits of revenue proposals, and a standard for discarding economically imprudent ideas. For example, how will freezing tax liabilities for senior citizens help accomplish the community's economic goals?

Of course, local governments are "creatures of the state" and do not hold complete sway over their destinies, as Californians demonstrated with Proposition 13. Our world is interdependent, and policies in one jurisdiction ripple through to affect other jurisdictions. But even in this environment, Torrance, California, took swift and aggressive action to mitigate the effects of economically imprudent state actions. After the passage of Proposition 13, it added a utility user's tax, increased service charges, and pursued an aggressive economic development plan using tax increment financing to attract new commercial and industrial development.[17] The result has been a more stable revenue structure for the city over the long term.

Avoid tax favors

As politicians know, everyone is a special case, and the quickest way to win political support is to provide tax relief to one's constituency. But one of the most destructive actions any government can take is to extend permanent tax favors to a particular sector, industry, or segment of the population. Besides the blatant inequity it introduces, such action also interferes in the market by skewing decisions to benefit from the tax treatment and not necessarily to achieve greater productivity. In short, governments that feel compelled to hand out tax favors invite increasing inefficiencies into their local economies—inefficiencies that eventually stifle new economic initiatives and emerge as chronic revenue shortfalls.

Yet tax incentives are essential tools that local governments use to shape their economies, and if local leaders enter into economic development without a well-articulated plan, these tools will not be used constructively. The key is to use tax favors to strengthen the long-term economic viability of the community, and that requires careful, thoughtful, and thorough planning and the political discipline to stay the course.

Pursue tax diversification

Tax diversification has two targets: tax sources and the tax base. In addition to the property tax, local governments should have one other broad-based tax source available, such as a general sales tax or a personal income tax. Both sources have greater income elasticity than the property tax, which means that they yield greater amounts of revenue as the local economy grows. (The property tax is generally income inelastic, which means that its revenue yield does not keep pace with economic growth—the result of assessment practices that fail to keep pace with market values.) Balancing an income-inelastic source with a more elastic source results in a more stable overall revenue yield.

A diversified property tax base maintains a balance among residential, commercial, industrial, and vacant properties. When a tax base is weighted too heavily toward one type of property, revenue yield becomes more vulnerable to economic cycles. Similarly, the local sales tax base should be diversified among a variety of retail and service industries. A city or county that strategically plans its economic development will identify new investment opportunities that simultaneously complement its unique strengths while diversifying its residential, commercial, and retail tax bases. For example, San Antonio, Texas, has attracted tourism and financial services to build on its strengths and diversify its large military tax base. Although diversifying revenue sources almost always requires legislative approval, an existing tax base can be diversified through local initiative.

Increase use of service charges

Service charges promote revenue stability by reaching beneficiaries of local services who would otherwise escape taxation (e.g., owners of tax-exempt property), and by reducing the need to expand local government staff and facilities to levels beyond citizens' preferences and needs. Service charges promote economic efficiency by ensuring that public services are used by those who value them the most.

Economists are fond of noting that the pricing system is a far more precise measure of citizens' preferences than the ballot box. Financing public services solely from general tax revenues results in wasteful consumption because the service is effectively "free" to any one user, and local governments must expand staffing levels and facility capacity to meet a potentially wasteful level of demand. User charges serve to limit the use of public services, thereby reducing the need to expand government staff and facilities beyond what consumers are willing to pay for them. For example, customers who are charged for the amount of water they consume will use less than they would if water were financed with general revenues. Other local services that could be effectively financed through user charges include solid-waste services, utilities, highways, parks and recreation, planning and land use, information services, transportation, and public health.

One final note on the productivity gains from service charges. Public managers tend to overemphasize productivity gains on the supply side—improving worker performance to reduce cost—and underemphasize gains on the demand side—reducing wasteful consumption of local services. Even if a manager succeeds in improving production efficiency, the demand for the service is not thereby reduced: the pressure remains to provide higher levels of service than what citizens would be willing to pay if the service were provided on a fee basis. The significant productivity gains in local government are on the demand side. Only by eliminating wasteful use of public services will a local government realize significant savings, and services provided on a fee basis are less likely to be wastefully used than services financed through general tax revenues.

Limit nuisance taxes

One common consequence of patchwork tax reform is the adoption of narrowly based taxes, particularly excise taxes, such as on admission to entertainment events, on specific products (e.g., cigarettes and tires), or on employees for the privilege of working (occupation privilege taxes). These taxes are generally costly to administer and have small revenue yields. Yet local governments find it difficult to abandon them because narrowly based taxes provide just enough revenue to make a difference in the local budget. Local governments needing extra revenue should develop a plan to gradually eliminate these taxes, replacing them with broader-based taxes or service charges.

Promote revenue self-sufficiency

Accepting state or federal aid places a local government at risk of becoming too dependent on those funds. One drawback of dependency is the local government's increased vulnerability to changes in funding policies—changes in either the amount of funding or the formulae used to allocate grant funds.

Another drawback is the distortion of local budget priorities. Most local governments find the inducements of a grant too great to pass up; once the grant is in place, however, the federal or state government's priorities move to the top of the local agenda, and local priorities are supplanted or delayed. This centralization of policy making and priority setting undermines the diversity of spending patterns that has been a hallmark of local government. Grants also increase local government spending by typically requiring a local match.

A policy of self-sufficiency does not mean that local governments should shun all grants-in-aid; grants serve an economically efficient function by compensating recipients for locally produced services that benefit the region or nation. Such a policy does mean, however, that local governments should minimize their dependency on grants, and one way they can do this is by linking grants to specific programs or projects and then varying service levels in the targeted areas according to the availability of grant funds. Another recommendation is to account for grants in separate funds or, at the least, in restricted accounts within a fund. Linking available money in the fund to particular activities provides a defensible basis for terminating the program once grant funds are exhausted.

Develop a revenue policy to guide decisions

Local government managers are finding formal revenue policies valuable as guides both for themselves and for local governing boards. Maureen Godsey has identified some of the benefits from such statements:[18]

- By making explicit the important assumptions underlying revenue practices, a policy statement helps management and members of council achieve congruent expectations about how the government finances its operations. If annual tax increases are not to exceed 5 percent, the statement should make that explicit.
- A revenue policy provides continuity in the procedures used to fund services. Management and members of the governing board may move on to other positions, but the policy remains to familiarize incoming officials with the practices deemed to be in the public interest by previous administrations.
- A policy statement saves time for executives and legislators. For example, once agreement is reached on the fraction of costs to be recovered in service charges for park and recreation services, setting a fee for new services becomes relatively simple. A policy statement also brings a second, related benefit: those seeking an exception to the policy bear the burden of demonstrating why such an exception should be granted. A general policy statement on fees also makes it politically easier to adjust individual fees annually to bring them into compliance with the policy.

Conclusion

As Chapter 1 made clear, local governments rely on three types of legal powers to collect revenue that pays for the services they provide: taxing powers, proprietary powers, and regulatory powers. Every revenue source derives its legal foundation from one of these types of powers.

The three pillars of tax policy—fairness, neutrality, and effective administration—require that the manager continuously make trade-offs in order to keep local budgets stable and economies resilient. In the quest for good tax policy, fairness ranks high with taxpayers and ratepayers. Unless taxes and user charges are perceived as imposing a fair burden, citizens' dissatisfaction with local government will persist.

Issues of tax neutrality bring to the fore a discussion of the policy choices that strengthen the local economy. Failure to consider these choices or their adverse effects on an economy inevitably leads to economic stagnation and even decline. Every tax has economic consequences, some more disruptive than others. The public manager's task is to make sure that those consequences are understood and, if at all possible, mitigated through careful design of the policy. A well-designed revenue structure is a local government's most effective business recruitment and retention tool. No amount of tax favors for new business investment can compensate for tax policies that interfere excessively in the local market.

The third pillar of sound public finance is administratively effective policies—that is, policies that limit the cost of administration (notification, collection, and enforcement) to no more than 5 percent of the revenue yield and that minimize costs for taxpayers to comply with the law.

Local governments will continue to assume more responsibility for raising the revenues needed to finance their services. In order to create a more stable revenue structure and, by extension, a more resilient economy, local governments must begin with a strategic plan and then use that plan to guide their revenue decisions. They must diversify their tax sources and tax bases, increase the use of service charges, limit the use of nuisance taxes, avoid extending tax favors indiscriminately, evade budget distortions that come from being overly dependent on intergovernmental aid, and adopt a revenue policy that guides budget deliberations. Those local governments in the strongest financial position will be able to export a greater share of their tax burden.

Notes

1 In fact, Californians, when they ratified Proposition 13 in 1978, introduced a new measure of comparability called acquisition-based value. Under the amendment's bizarre rules for property taxation, horizontal equity exists only for homes purchased in the same year and for the same price. Otherwise, two houses standing side by side with equal market value may have markedly different tax liabilities, especially if one house was purchased before 1975, the base year for establishing value under Proposition 13, and the other was purchased during one of California's housing booms. The acquisition value and thus tax liability for the more recent buyer could be many times greater.

2 Gilbert E. Metcalf, "The Lifetime Incidence of State and Local Taxes: Measuring Changes during the 1980s," in *Tax Progressivity and Income Inequality*, ed. Joel Slemrod (Cambridge, UK, and New York: Cambridge University Press, 1994), 59-88.

3 Charles M. Tiebout, "A Pure Theory of Local Expenditures," *Journal of Political Economy* 64 (October 1956): 416–424.

4 Philadelphia Tax Reform Commission, *Final Report* (November 15, 2003), www.philadelphiataxreform.org. One widespread practice among older cities is the ad hoc practice of fractional assessments (discussed in Chapter 3): the more favorable valuation of residential property relative to commercial and industrial property, which thereby shifts the tax burden to the latter types of property.

5 The four types of communities used in Figure 2–1 were first proposed by Oliver P. Williams. He did not use them in the context they are used here—namely, to demonstrate the types of linkages between revenue structure and political environment—although his typology has been adapted for this purpose. See Oliver P. Williams, "A Typology for Comparative Local Government," *Midwest Journal of Political Science* 5 (May 1961): 150–164.

6 Lenny Goldberg and David Kersten, "Huge Disparities Found in California Commercial Property Taxes," *State Tax Notes* 31 (May 10, 2004): 437–457; Gregory D. Saxton, Christopher W. Hoene, and Steven P. Erie, "Fiscal Constraints and the Loss of Home Rule: The Long-Term Impacts of California's Post–Proposition 13 Fiscal Regime," *American Review of Public Administration* 32 (December 2002): 423–454; Carol Douglas, "Proposition 13—25 Years Later," *State Tax Notes* 30 (October 20, 2003): 222–226.

7 Ronald C. Fisher, *State & Local Public Finance,* 4th ed. (New York: Routledge, 2016), 32–35.

8 Victor A. Canto, Douglas H. Joines, and Arthur B. Laffer, eds., *Foundations of Supply-Side Economics: Theory and Evidence* (New York: Academic Press, 1982).

9 Andrew F. Haughwout et al., "Local Revenue Hills: Evidence from Four U.S. Cities," National Bureau of Economic Research (NBER) Working Paper 9686 (Cambridge, Mass.: NBER, May 2003), nber.org/papers/w9686.

10 Paul D. Ballew, Richard H. Mattoon, and William A. Testa, "School Reform and Tax Reform: A Successful Marriage?" *Government Finance Review* 10 (August 1994): 32–35.

11 Philadelphia Tax Reform Commission, *Final Report,* 33.

12 Jeffrey M. Stupak, "The Internet Tax Freedom Act: In Brief," Congressional Research Service, April 13, 2016, fas.org/sgp/crs/misc/R43772.pdf.

13 U.S. Government Accountability Office, "Sales Taxes: States Could Gain Revenue from Expanded Authority, but Businesses Are Likely to Experience Compliance Costs," November 2017 (GAO-18-114), www.gao.gov/products/GAO-18-114.

14 Glenn Hegar, *Tax Exemptions and Tax Incidence* (Austin: Texas Comptroller of Public Accounts, November 2018), 47, 67, 71.

15 TischlerBise Consultants, *Study of the Metropolitan Area Fiscal Disparities Program* (St. Paul: Minnesota Department of Revenue, February 13, 2012). https://www.revenue.state.mn.us/propertytax/reports/fiscal-disparities-study-executive-summary.pdf.

16 Charles H. Levine, "Police Management in the 1980s: From Decrementalism to Strategic Thinking," *Public Administration Review* 45 (November 1985): 691-700.

17 Saxton, Hoene, and Erie, "Fiscal Constraints and the Loss of Home Rule."

18 W. Maureen Godsey, "Establishing Financial Policies: What, Why, and How," in *Practical Financial Management: New Techniques for Local Government,* ed. John Matzer Jr. (Washington, D.C.: International City/County Management Association, 1984) 27-33.

CHAPTER
3

The property tax

> Every advantage has its tax.
>
> *—Ralph Waldo Emerson*

This chapter provides the following takeaways:

- Two reasons for the continuing shift of the property tax onto single-family homeowners.
- Four factors that alter the relative share of property taxes between residential and nonresidential property owners.
- Five benefits of the property tax to local governments and their budgets.
- Three phases of the property tax cycle and strategies for improving the tax's fairness.
- Four ways that local governments give tax relief to homeowners, and the special case of tax relief following a disaster.

Although the taxpayer revolt that began in the late 1970s has moderated its importance in local government budgets, the property tax remains the mainstay of most municipal and county revenue structures. It is the only major tax common to all fifty states, and it is the oldest tax levied in the United States. Why does the tax persist as an important source of revenue in local budgets?

The property tax provides local governments with a powerful financial and economic tool. In addition to its utility in balancing operating (and sometimes capital) budgets, the tax is often used to assure creditors that the borrower has a stream of income to repay its general

Portions of this chapter were adapted from previous publications of the author, including "The Property Tax," Chapter 9 in *Management Policies in Local Government Finance*, 6th ed. (Washington, D.C.: ICMA Press, 2013).

debt obligations. Economically, it is used as a tool to attract and retain business investment. Local governments may use property tax relief to target certain categories of households (such as senior citizens and veterans) or attract businesses to shape their economies. Yet the property tax remains intensely disliked by taxpayers and, consequently, by state and local lawmakers. This creates a quandary for the local manager who may have no recourse but to use the tax to meet the local government's financial obligations.

This chapter, which examines issues associated with the property tax, is designed to help city and county managers answer questions about the tax posed by citizen groups, business leaders, and elected representatives.[1]

The changing role of the property tax

Although the property tax is largely the domain of local governments, especially for funding public education, a few states still collect a property tax statewide for their operating and debt service purposes. Heaviest users include New Hampshire and New Jersey, followed by several other New England states.[2] In order to promote funding equity and provide tax relief to homeowners, a few states, such as Michigan and Washington, use a statewide property tax to assume substantial responsibility for funding K–12 public education. Nevada's statewide tax of 17 cents per $100 assessed value provides the funds to service the state's general obligation debt.

Historically, county governments have depended on the property tax much more heavily than cities because counties generally have less access to alternative taxes. But while the tax declined in its relative importance to both municipalities and counties during the 1980s and 1990s, it has seen a resurgence in the twenty-first century (Table 3–1). Whether it continues to grow in importance depends on several factors. If federal and state aid continues its precipitous decline, local governments will probably increase their use of the tax. Alternatively, if

Table 3–1 Local government revenue as a percentage of general revenues, FY 2007 and 2012

Revenue source	FY 2007		FY 2012	
	Counties	Municipalities	Counties	Municipalities
Property taxes	**40.1**	**27.8**	**42.7**	**29.8**
All other taxes	18.1	24.0	16.8	22.3
Current charges	28.3	19.1	30.1	20.8
Utility charges	2.1	18.6	2.3	19.6
Other nontaxes	11.4	10.6	8.1	7.5
Total	100.0	100.0	100.0	100.0
Total general revenue (in millions)[a]	$223,246	$395,046	$243,140	$439,100

Source: U.S. Census Bureau, "2012 Census of Governments: State & Local Government Finance," 2012 Local Government Table 2, https://www.census.gov//govs/local/historical_data_2012.html and "State & Local Government Finance, Historical Data: 2007," Table 2, https://www.census.gov//govs/local/historical_data_2007.html.

a Total general revenue includes utility charges but excludes intergovernmental aid, liquor store income, and insurance trust revenue.

state legislatures continue to allow municipalities and counties greater access to sales and, to a lesser extent, income taxes, local governments will have revenue sources to replace lost federal and state aid and will thus be able to reduce their dependence on the property tax.

Do municipalities and counties rely too heavily on the property tax? As shown in Table 3–1, the combined annual yield from that tax for all local governments—cities, counties, townships, special districts, and school districts—is now over $470 billion. Although school districts depend most heavily on it, their dependence has grown in recent years, too. The evidence in Table 3–1 indicates that taxpayers' resentment against the property tax is probably motivated, in part, by local governments' growing reliance on it.

Changes in the property tax base

The property tax is really a collection of taxes on several different types of property, which can be grouped into two broad categories: real and personal (Figure 3–1). **Real property** is immobile and includes land, natural resources, and fixed improvements to the land. **Personal property** is mobile and includes **tangible property** (furniture, equipment, inventory, and vehicles) and **intangible property** (stocks, taxable bonds, and bank accounts). Because of the difficulty of establishing ownership, only a few states still include intangible property in the tax base. A third, smaller category is state-assessed property (railroads and other public utilities), which spans several local jurisdictions and whose specialized use makes appraisal by state government more cost-effective and equitable.

Figure 3–1 Types of property

Real property	Personal property
Land	Tangible
Farmland	Inventory
Open spaces	Equipment
Timberland	Vehicles
Minerals	Jewelry
	Artwork
Improvements	Furniture
Buildings (residential, commercial, industrial)	
Infrastructure	Intangible
Underground improvements	Stocks
	Taxable bonds and notes
	Insurance policies
	Bank deposits (CDs, time deposits)
	Patents, copyrights, trademarks

The property tax base (TB) comprises the assessed (or taxable) value of all property subject by law to taxation. Tax liability (TL) is the product of the tax base and a tax rate (TR) that is usually determined locally. Thus, TB x TR = TL. The **effective property tax burden** measures the ratio of property tax liability to the market value of a property or, in the aggregate, the ratio of total property tax revenue to the sum of the market values of all taxable property in a taxing jurisdiction. Bond rating firms use the effective property tax burden to gauge the capacity of the property tax base to support additional tax-supported debt, and budget analysts use it to assess the revenue capacity for new initiatives being considered by a local government.

Shift from personal to real property Over the past five decades, the property tax base has shifted away from personal property and toward real property. This shift is attributable to the complexity of discovering and valuing personal property and to the much greater growth in the value of real property. Although the exact proportion is difficult to know, at least 85 percent of the tax base is now real property.

Twelve states exempt all machinery, equipment, and business personal property from state or local taxation.[3] Forty-two states exempt business inventories from the property tax.[4] A few states set the taxable value of business inventory at less than 100 percent of its true value. In some cases, the exemption—sometimes called a **freeport exemption**—applies only to finished goods destined for out-of-state markets. In the case of agricultural personal property (farm equipment and inventories), most Midwestern states exempt these items from the property tax base. In general, the trend toward state exemption of personal property has benefited the business sector far more than it has the residential sector because a far greater proportion of business fixed assets is in equipment, vehicles, and inventory.

Shift from business to residential real property Significant shifts have also occurred within the real property component of the tax base. Residential real property, especially single-family homes, represents a rapidly growing share of the tax base, while business real property continues to decline in relative importance. Although nationally aggregated data are not available, the trend in Texas is likely indicative of what is happening across the nation. In 1981, real residential property (single and multifamily) represented 31.5 percent of the tax base in the state, increasing to 41.3 percent in 1990 and peaking at 52.8 percent in 2008 before the housing market collapsed. By 2015, it had resumed its upward climb to 48.6 percent of the total tax base.[5] In other words, in this thirty-five-year span, real residential property increased from one-third to about half of Texas's tax base.

By contrast, real commercial and industrial property in Texas (including utilities and minerals) declined from 41.5 percent in 1981 to 25.8 percent in 2009, rising to 31.5 percent in 2015.[6] The principal cause of this change was the rapid appreciation in residential real property values relative to business real property values that occurred from 1981 until the housing bubble burst in 2007.

The 2007–2008 crash in the housing market exposed just how vulnerable local budgets are to the value of housing. Researchers at the Lincoln Institute of Land Policy found that property tax yields have about a three-year lag, on average, behind changes in the housing market.[7] They also found that cities offset about three-quarters of their lost property values by increasing their property tax rates.

In short, the property tax is no longer a general tax on all types of property but is instead increasingly limited to property—real property and especially single-family residences—that is easiest to discover and appraise and has the greatest potential for appreciation in value. As a result, pressure continues to build on state legislatures for property tax relief for property owners. But the limited revenue options available to local governments to balance their budgets, especially for school districts, make for an increasingly precarious balance between tapped-out state funding and restive local property taxpayers.

Economic growth and the property tax base

The relationship between property taxes and business investment is a primary concern for local government managers. Research indicates that taxes increase in importance as a relocating business narrows its choice from a regional to a local level.

For example, several studies have examined the effect of property taxes on employment growth and the property tax base, and have concluded that higher property tax rates diminish economic growth and encourage the out-migration of households and businesses.[8] Over the long term, cities with higher-than-average property tax burdens have lower property values. For cities experiencing declining property values, an even higher tax rate must be imposed if a comparable level of services is to be provided. For businesses (and households) seeking to maximize after-tax profits, the greater the differentials in regional property tax rates, the more important the tax becomes to their locational decisions—although some of these differences may be offset by higher-quality public services, such as a better-educated workforce and improved transportation networks. Conversely, cities and counties experiencing rising property values can levy a lower effective tax rate and still provide the same level of services.

Capital-intensive industries, such as manufacturing and wholesale trade, are likely to weigh property taxes more heavily in their locational decisions than are less capital-intensive firms, such as those in the construction, retail, finance, real estate, insurance, and service industries. This difference is mostly attributable to the fact that the latter industries follow consumer markets, whereas manufacturing and wholesale trade firms are more conscious of the cost of production, which includes local taxes.

Of the three types of tax bases—property (wealth), consumption (sales), and income—the property tax base is the most sensitive to population changes. Such changes can have profound effects on a community's dependence on property tax revenues.[9] A population increase usually creates higher property values as households and businesses bid for the limited supply of desirable land and buildings. Similarly, property values usually drop with declines in population as the demand for property, especially residential property, declines; at that point, other things being equal, the remaining property owners incur a higher property tax burden to sustain public services. For communities that rely heavily on the property tax, population losses can have highly destabilizing effects on local budgets, especially if appraisals are kept current with property values.

Balancing residential and nonresidential property taxes

Governments have considerable discretion in distributing the property tax burden among owners. Using such devices as homestead exemptions, circuit-breaker programs, classification of property, use-value appraisals, tax abatements, tax freezes for certain classes of property owners, and preferential assessment practices, a local government allocates its property tax between residential and nonresidential sectors. This gives rise to four questions:

- How does the proportion of commercial and industrial property to residential property affect the tax burden of homeowners?
- Do local governments tend to shift the tax burden to business property?
- How does the partial or full exemption of property affect the tax burden of the remaining owners of taxable property?
- Does the shift from a manufacturing to a service-based economy affect the property taxes borne by the business sector?

Taxing commercial and industrial property A widely held assumption is that the revenue from property taxes on the business sector generally exceeds the cost of providing public services to that sector. Other things being equal, expanding the commercial and industrial share of the tax base reduces the property tax burden on the residential sector. For this reason, property tax rates tend to be highest in cities and towns that are mostly residential.

A corollary is that jurisdictions experiencing rapid increases in business activity, as measured by the number of private sector jobs, will generally tax business property more heavily than they tax residential property. Conversely, where job growth is slow, property tax relief favors business owners over residential owners. Apparently, cities that wish to attract business investment tend to impose a relatively lower property tax burden on that sector.

A 1997 study that examined the ninety-three largest cities in Texas found that those with greater concentrations of industrial property had comparatively higher per capita property tax burdens, specifically for operating purposes, apparently in recognition of industry's greater ability to export its tax burden forward to nonresident consumers or backward to stock owners.[10] By contrast, cities with higher concentrations of commercial property (shopping malls, retail stores, business offices) had relatively lower property tax burdens than other cities in the study, controlling for all other effects. These cities relied on a local option sales tax, which provides a mechanism for tax exportation, especially in the case of regional shopping centers.

Allocating the property tax burden In many communities, the relative political strength of homeowners compared with business property owners, many of whom are absentee, creates pressure that effectively shifts the tax burden to business. A 2016 analysis of fifty-three large cities in the United States found that, on average, the effective tax rate on homes was 1.50 percent. In other words, each $100,000 in a home's value would, on average, add $1,500 in property tax liability.[11] By contrast, the average effective tax rate for commercial property was $2.10, industrial property was $1.55, and apartment property was $1.87.[12] This annual study of each state's largest metropolitan area consistently shows that business property—industrial and especially commercial—incurs a relatively higher share of the property tax.

Some states permit local governments to classify property by use and then apply a different tax rate or level of assessment to each class, a practice commonly known as a **split tax roll**. Such classification schemes generally favor residential property over income-producing property, with the exception of agricultural property, which typically uses a more favorable appraisal standard of use (or production) value, as discussed in the accompanying sidebar.

Local governments may also use the frequency and methods of appraisal to shift the tax burden. In the absence of state regulation of assessment practices, the tendency is for local governments to under-assess residential property and over-assess commercial and industrial property.

These findings suggest that local governments use discretionary measures to strategically allocate the property tax burden between the residential and nonresidential sectors to maximize the competitive position of the jurisdiction. Informally, this shift of the property tax burden to commercial and multifamily (and less to industrial) property occurs, in part, because of the de facto classification system created by differential assessment practices among the different types of property.

The impact of tax exemptions[13] The property tax has never been universally applied to all property. Throughout the twentieth century, state and local governments expanded the use of exemptions to ease public dissatisfaction with the tax. Economically, exemptions are tax expenditures that, once adopted, constitute a form of "spending" through forgiven tax liability but go unreported as part of that local government's approved budget. After the market value of a property is appraised, a tax exemption lowers its assessed (or taxable) value, thereby narrowing the tax base available to local governments. Two general types of exemptions are applied to determine assessed value: (1) absolute exemptions that exclude the full value of qualifying property from the tax base, and (2) partial exemptions that reduce, but do not necessarily eliminate, the taxable value of qualifying properties or property owners.

Absolute exemptions Absolute exemptions have their origin in Elizabethan England, where only one level of government existed, making it pointless for that government to levy a property tax on itself.[14] In the United States, the absolute exemption of federal property from state and local taxation was institutionalized in the landmark opinion by Chief Justice

John Marshall in *McCulloch v. Maryland* (17 U.S. 316, 1819). According to the doctrine of tax immunity, Marshall, who held that "the power to tax is the power to destroy," ruled that state and local governments do not have the powers to tax federal establishments.

Going beyond federal property, absolute exemptions typically originate in state law as a mandate on local governments with usually no compensation from the state for the lost revenue. The usual justification for fully exempting the taxable value of a qualifying nonprofit's property is that it provides public services that otherwise would be the responsibility of local governments: education, health care, post-incarceration rehabilitation, shelter and food for the homeless, and recreation, among other services. As for property owned by charitable nonprofits, the exemption has an even more convoluted history among the states, resulting in greater variation in state law as to what constitutes an exempted nonprofit organization. In the case of religious institutions, the exemption is also premised on the separation of church and state.

All fifty states have extended Marshall's doctrine of tax immunity to include the property of state and local governments themselves. As a result, substantial amounts of property—state and national forests; state and national parks; military bases; universities and colleges; schools; courthouses; and federal, state, and local office complexes—remain off the tax rolls and incur no tax liability. One study has concluded that the largest loss of property tax revenues came from the exemption of government property, which has the greatest impact in state capitals.[15] Some local governments particularly affected by such exemptions have begun negotiating with the exempt nonprofit organizations for **payments in lieu of taxes (PILOTs)**.[16] The U.S. Department of Interior annually makes PILOTs to approximately 1,900 local governments, mostly in the western states, with large concentrations of tax-exempt lands set aside as national forests, national parks, military bases, and waterways. A few states also compensate their local governments with PILOTs for tax-exempt state property.

Partial exemptions Partial exemptions, by contrast, exclude a portion of a property's value from the tax base. These exemptions may use a mixture of local and state authority. State law may set a minimum level of exemption with a local option for increases above the state-mandated threshold. Or it may give local governments discretionary authority to grant partial exemptions for specific purposes or categories of property owners.

States use two types of partial exemptions: tax relief generally benefiting the primary residence of homeowners, and tax incentives designed to attract business investment. The most common tax relief measure is the homestead exemption used by thirty-seven states.[17] A homestead exemption excludes a portion of a property's value, up to its full value, from taxation. After the appraised value of a home is established, the homestead exemption is deducted, resulting in a property's assessed or taxable value. This exemption has its origins in Spanish law, which protected a person's homestead from foreclosure by creditors. Former Spanish colonies, such as Texas, continue to provide this protection. Over time, states extended this protection to taxes on the primary residence of homeowners.

While granting a general exemption on the primary homes of taxpayers, some states have expanded partial exemptions to authorize local options above the general exemption or partial exemptions that benefit specific groups of homeowners, such as those sixty-five and older, veterans, and disabled persons. In some cases, homeowners may qualify for more than one homestead exemption for their property. These exemptions further reduce a property's taxable value and increase the horizontal inequities among property taxpayers.

The other type of partial exemptions—those used as tax incentives—have grown rapidly in popularity over the past four decades as have the measures used by cities to attract new business investment. One of the first tax incentives was tax increment financing, introduced in California in 1952.[18] In the intervening decades, local governments have added an array of tax incentives to attract businesses, including tax abatement, freeport exemption, tax credits, and partial exemptions for such purposes as equipment for renewable energy and pollution control.

The variety of incentives has expanded beyond those that alter the property tax to involve other revenue sources and nonrevenue inducements. State governments often collaborate with cities and counties, especially on politically or financially high-impact projects, to provide financial packages as inducements for larger business investment.

Budgetary effects of tax exemptions The long-term impact of exemptions is not fully understood by public finance scholars. At a minimum, however, exemptions erode a government's property tax base, forcing those responsible for budget preparation to search for ways to compensate for the lost revenue. Budget preparers have three options, or combinations thereof, with which to address the cost of exemptions: (1) shift the cost to other property owners, (2) shift the cost to other revenue sources, or (3) absorb the cost by reducing expenditures, especially for capital improvements. How local budgets adapt to the impact of exemptions likely depends on the composition of the tax base and its competitiveness with surrounding communities. Local governments with higher-than-average exemptions but robust economies, such as state capitals, can likely shift a portion of the cost of exemptions to other taxpayers as a higher effective tax rate. Those with less robust economies can likely maximize revenue from non-property tax sources and postpone capital improvements for longer periods. Those local governments with the least robust economies have the fewest options; they are likely to absorb the cost of exemptions by reducing spending not only for capital improvements but also for general operations.

Exemptions have another adverse effect on local economies that has not been studied. These preclude a local government from fully benefiting from the capitalized benefits of its investment in higher-quality public services. As explained in a later section, the property tax constitutes a benefits-received levy: the investment in higher-quality public services is capitalized into property values, thereby benefitting current property owners with increased value for their property. A good example is investment in better-quality schools, which accrues as higher property values for surrounding homeowners. Exemptions, however, erode that connection by creating free riders who benefit from the higher quality of public services without bearing the cost. Conceivably, local governments with above-average exemptions may have relatively higher spending because of the political influence of free riders. Unfortunately, public finance scholars have not thoroughly studied the impact of exemptions on local budgets largely because of the difficulty in obtaining credible parcel-level data on exemptions.

Impact of growth in the service sector The growth in the service sector over the past four decades relative to that of manufacturing has decreased the share of property taxes borne by the business sector. This is because service firms have a lower investment in property-intensive facilities for manufacturing, warehousing, and transporting finished goods. Service-oriented businesses may also receive favorable tax treatment because they are generally more mobile than manufacturing firms, so local governments must make efforts to stem their emigration to jurisdictions with lower taxes.

In sum, the tax burden on residential owners does decline significantly as the per capita amount of commercial and industrial property increases. However, tremendous diversity exists among local governments in how they allocate the burden between the residential and business sectors. Local governments seem to allocate this burden so as to maximize their competitive position relative to other governments.

Getting to value

One of the most confusing aspects of the property tax is the process for establishing taxable value. The following terms should be understood:

Market value: The price that a knowledgeable and prudent buyer would agree to pay a willing seller in a competitive and open market. True market value is unknown and can only be estimated.

Sales price: The amount of money (or other goods or services) exchanged for a property. In legal parlance, sales price is often referred to as the consideration given for a property.

Appraised value: An estimate of market value made by a knowledgeable person using appropriate methods. Appraisers rely on three basic methods to estimate market value:

1. The *sales comparison method* uses data from recent sales as an indicator of what buyers are asking and sellers are negotiating for settlement prices.
2. The *cost method* determines property values, especially for such unique properties or intermediary facilities as warehouses, by using the cost of materials and labor, less depreciation, for replicating the structure, plus the value of the land associated with the structure.
3. The *income method* uses the capitalization formula [value = (revenues–expenses) / rate of return] to determine the value of income-producing property such as a retail or wholesale outlet or industrial plant.

Use (or production) value: An alternative basis for establishing appraised value that considers the property's worth given its current use (such as a farm) rather than its highest and best use (such as a housing development).

Mass appraisal: A variation of the sales comparison method. Sometimes referred to as computer-assisted mass appraisal, this method uses statistical modeling and geographic information systems to replicate the market and provide a basis for establishing appraised value, especially for single-family residential properties.

Assessed value: The adjusted value for limits on increases in appraised value or for the application of a fractional rate of valuation. If a state or local government has a cap on increases in appraised value or if it uses fractional assessments, the adjusted value is a property's assessed value. For example, if state law caps increases in appraised value at 10 percent, any increase in a property's appraised value greater than 10 percent, then the property's assessed value is capped *at* the 10 percent level. For any increase that is 10 percent or less, the assessed value is the same as the appraised value. If state law authorizes a fractional assessment of 50 percent for single-family residences, the applicable ratio is applied to a property's appraised value to determine its assessed value.

Taxable value (TB): The tax base for the property tax. Any partial exemptions (such as a homestead exemption) are applied to the property's assessed value to determine the final taxable value of the property. This value is then used by budget offices to determine the expected amount of revenue by multiplying taxable value by the tax rate to determine tax liability (TB × TR = TL). The sum of all tax liabilities in the jurisdiction is the expected tax yield.

Acquisition value: A valuation standard, introduced by Proposition 13, in which appraised and assessed values are set by the purchase price and recalibrated only when a real property sells. Florida and New Mexico limit the use of this valuation standard to single-family residences; the standard sets appraised value at a property's selling price and then benchmarks the capped annual increases in assessed value to this new appraised value: for example, California at 2 percent; Florida, New Mexico, and Oregon at 3 percent; and Michigan and Oklahoma at 5 percent.[1]

Equalized value: An adjustment to assessed value, often made by a state agency, to bring assessments into closer conformance with a common statewide assessment ratio. In states where the formula for allocating funding for public education includes a factor for the taxable value of property in the school district, equalized values ensure equity in the allocation of that aid.

The following flow chart summarizes the steps taken to get to tax base:

Market value

→ **Appraised value:** estimate of market value

→ **Assessed value:** capped increase or fractional rate applied to appraised value

→ **Taxable value (or tax base):** assessed value less exemptions

Two special cases of taxable value:

(1) Productivity (or use) value (for agriculture and timberland)

(2) Acquisition value (initial assessed value is the purchase price)

1 Terri A. Sexton, "The Property Tax Base in the United States: Exemptions, Incentives, and Relief," *Assessment Journal* 10 (Fall 2003): 6.

Benefits of the property tax to the budget process

Despite a lengthy list of disadvantages, the property tax continues as a mainstay in the revenue structures of most local governments, probably because of its capacity to adapt to the preferences and needs of different interest groups. For example, local governments can target tax relief to groups considered deserving while they shift more of the tax burden to sectors with a greater ability to bear it. On the other hand, the property tax abatement provides a discretionary incentive that local governments can use to attract or retain business investment.

From a strictly fiscal perspective, the property tax has many advantages that make it a likely permanent fixture in local revenue structures. Among these advantages, it

- Provides a stable source of revenue
- Reaches nonresident property owners who benefit from local services
- Finances property-related services, such as police and fire protection, and the construction of publicly owned infrastructure, such as streets, curbs and sidewalks, and storm drainage systems
- Is difficult to evade, making collection and enforcement easier for local governments
- Enables local governments in the United States to achieve their unique form of autonomy from state and federal control, thereby forestalling centralization of power at higher levels of government.

Provides a stable source of revenue

The primary reason for the property tax's continued importance to local government is the reliable flow of revenue it provides during the budget period, although that revenue will vary from one budget period to another, depending on the frequency with which property is reevaluated and on changes in the local real estate market. Other taxes, such as the sales and income taxes and even nontax revenues, have greater income elasticity, causing their yields to fluctuate more dramatically with changes in the local and national economies. Governments that depend more heavily on the property tax are less vulnerable to midyear revenue shortfalls precipitated by changing economic conditions.

Reaches nonresident property owners

A related merit of the property tax, from a local government perspective, is its exportability to nonresidents who benefit from local services yet escape the local sales or income tax. Exportability depends primarily on the nature of the demand for a product or service. When there are few substitutes for a good or service and consumers' purchases are relatively unaffected by price fluctuations, the tax burden shifts forward. The more sensitive consumers are to price changes, or the more available substitutes are that are not subject to the tax, the more the burden shifts backward to owners. The property tax can shift the tax burden (especially on income-producing property) forward to nonresident consumers through higher prices or backward to nonresident owners, such as stockholders, through lower profits. In a 2017 study, the Texas state comptroller estimated that 19 percent of the property taxes levied by that state's school districts was exported to out-of-state taxpayers, with the remainder borne by in-state property owners.[19]

Finances property-related services

The property tax recaptures for the community some of the increase in property value created by government-provided services. For example, assume that two towns have exactly the same population characteristics and spending levels, but one spends twice as much on police protection as the other and has half the crime rate. Other things being equal, property values will be higher in the town with the lower crime rate. Through the property tax, property owners return to the local government some of the value that its services have created, giving the tax a benefits-received component. A familiar example of this phenomenon is seen in the variations in housing values created by the differences in the quality of public schools. The property tax is unique among the major taxes in its capacity to recoup government-created increases in property value.

Is difficult to evade

Tax levies on real property, which are now estimated to make up 85 percent of the property tax base, are secured in most states by an automatic tax lien on the property. If the owner fails to make timely payment, the local government can seek a court judgment foreclosing on the lien and then sell the property for back taxes, penalties, and interest. Compared with collection rates for other taxes, those for the tax on real property remain high—usually 92 to 96 percent of the current levy. Although collection is still legally complex, the automatic lien and the impossibility of obtaining a mortgage without its removal greatly simplify the eventual recovery of the 4 to 8 percent of the levy that is delinquent.

Promotes local autonomy

The property tax is the only tax levied in all fifty states. (Five states levy no sales tax, and seven states have no personal income tax.) At the local level, the fact that the tax is on relatively immobile assets means that more than one government can tax the same property while maintaining political autonomy from overlapping local governments. Counties, cities, school districts, and a host of special districts all coexist as overlapping governments, and each taps into the property tax base.

More important, the property tax has effectively become the domain of local governments, which strengthens their autonomy from state control. David Brunori and Michael Bell note that "no other source of revenue can ensure local government autonomy. And such autonomy has been a critical factor in American government since the beginning of the republic."[20] According to Glenn Fisher, one of the foremost authorities on the property tax,

> It is clear that the tax had one feature that was of great importance in explaining its development and growth: it was ideally suited to financing local government in a large, developing, diverse country populated by people with a very strong sense of independence and a very great distrust of centralized bureaucracy. . . . Local government, as it developed in the United States, could not survive without the property tax.[21]

Analyses of the impact of Proposition 13 on local government autonomy in California provide the most compelling evidence of the property tax's role in intergovernmental relations. These studies show that Proposition 13 (1) shifted power from local governments to the state, (2) slowed but did not halt increases in spending, and (3) limited the mobility of homeowners, especially owners of higher-priced residences, as a result of the assessment provisions in state law.[22] Because property taxes provide a much smaller share of total state and local revenues, California now subsidizes its local governments using revenue from the more volatile income and sales taxes, giving rise to an endless cycle of booms and busts in its budget.

In summary, the property tax has proven remarkably resilient and capable of being tailored to local interests, and it survives as the most prominent source of revenue in local government primarily because of its stability and the ease with which it can be enforced.

Figure 3–2 Phases of the property tax cycle

Appraisal determines the value of property for tax purposes, using legally specified standards of valuation.

- Taxable and tax-exempt property are discovered.
- Legal owners and taxable site of property are identified.
- Property is appraised on the basis of use and estimated value as of the appraisal date.
- Property owners are notified of changes in appraised value.
- Appeals from property owners are heard by independent board of review.
- Adjustments to appraisals are reviewed and approved by board and appraiser.
- Final certified appraisal roll is prepared.

Assessment adjusts appraised value to determine the taxable value of property.

- Appraised value is multiplied by assessment rate (or ratio) to determine assessed value.[a]
- Assessments are equalized by state agency to the same percentage of full value across jurisdictions.[a]
- Assessed value is adjusted for partial exemptions, such as homesteads.[a]
- Truth-in-taxation notices are prepared and published.[a]
- Public hearing is held on proposed tax rate and/or budget.
- Tax rate(s) is(are) set by governing board.
- Rate(s) is(are) certified as being within legal limits.[a]
- Tax roll is prepared and certified.

Collection involves the preparation and distribution of tax notices to both current and delinquent taxpayers.

- Tax bills are prepared and mailed to owners of record.
- Lien is attached to property to secure payment of taxes, penalties, and interest.
- Current tax payments are received, credited, and distributed.
- Unpaid taxes become delinquent after due date.
- Delinquent-tax roll is prepared.
- Delinquent-tax notices are prepared and property owners are notified.
- Court order is sought to foreclose on lien on outstanding delinquencies.
- Property is sold at a public auction for payment of back taxes, penalties, and interest.

a Not performed in all states.

The property tax cycle

Because the property tax, unlike most other taxes, falls on the value of wealth, the government must determine the taxable value of that wealth—a task that greatly complicates administration of the tax. Figure 3–2 depicts the three phases of the property tax cycle: appraisal, assessment, and collection.

Appraisal

The appraisal phase begins with the identification and valuation of all taxable property in a jurisdiction and ends with the preparation of an appraisal roll, which lists the owner of each property, along with the property's legal description and appraised value. State law specifies a date, such as January 1, to which all appraisals are pegged and on which legal ownership is established. The owner of the property on the appraisal date is legally liable for the tax, regardless of whether the property is subsequently sold.

State law usually defines the basis for appraising property for tax purposes. In most states that basis is an estimate of the property's fair market value. However, there are significant deviations from this standard. For example, in California, the post–Proposition 13 basis is either the selling price (acquisition value) of the property or its 1975–1976 appraised value if the property has not sold since ratification of the amendment. Starting from this basis, county assessors may annually increase real property appraisals by no more than 2 percent or the consumer price index, whichever is less. Whenever a property sells, the purchase price becomes its new appraised (and assessed) value, creating a higher tax liability for home buyers, including first-time buyers, and for businesses moving into or relocating within the state. Curiously, property transferred within a family across generations retains its original value plus, of course, the annual 2-percent adjustment. A number of studies have documented the significant inequities and adverse economic effects over the long term that such a valuation scheme introduces.[23]

Both Florida and Michigan have adopted this acquisition basis of appraised value, capping annual increases in assessments at the rate of inflation or at 3 percent in Florida and 5 percent in Michigan, whichever is less. Unlike California, however, Florida and Michigan apply caps only to the principal residences of homeowners.

As might be expected, state laws vary considerably in defining how appraisals are done; variations include (1) the level of local government responsible for appraisal administration, (2) the frequency of reappraisal, and (3) the state's role in ensuring professional standards of appraisal. Because it directly affects allocation of the tax burden in a jurisdiction, property appraisal is a politically charged task. However, as it is a matter of expert judgment, it should be removed from the political arena.

Administration of appraisals County governments are the ones most frequently assigned the task of administering appraisals, although New England states tend to give the task to cities and towns. Maryland is the only state that places that responsibility in a state department of assessments and taxation.[24] In Montana, the county assessor is a state employee, and the state provides all the funding for the assessor's office.

Texas has made the greatest effort to remove appraisal from the political arena: it created 253 countywide appraisal districts charged with the responsibility for valuing property in the district. While their boundaries are coterminous with counties, central appraisal districts (or CADs) are politically and administratively self-governing. Each CAD is governed by a board of directors appointed by local governments levying a property tax in the district, and each annually prepares an appraisal roll for its taxing jurisdictions. Local governments in the CAD then use this roll to develop their certified tax rolls. Appraisal districts receive their funding through service charges on the local governments they serve.

Property tax experts recommend that appraisal administration be centralized at least at the county level, with state oversight to ensure consistency in assessment administration. Centralization provides greater economies of scale and more efficient use of limited professional staff.[25] Only one appraisal for tax purposes should be done for each property. A few states still permit overlapping taxing jurisdictions to prepare separate appraisals, which confuse taxpayers and are an inefficient use of administrative resources.

Frequency of reappraisal Reappraisal poses a major political problem for state and local legislators because taxpayers anticipate that their tax burden will increase. An increase in taxable value, without a concomitant reduction in the tax rate, leads to a higher tax liability. However, frequent reappraisal prevents large shifts in the tax burden across classes of property and, depending on the frequency, also prevents large increases in individual appraisals. The result is increased equity in the allocation of the property tax burden.

Out-of-date appraisal records, such as land maps and property descriptions, increase the cost of reappraisal, so more frequent reappraisals are generally less costly to administer. Local governments are advised to reappraise all property at regular intervals and real property at least once every three years. Most states require reappraisal of property at least once every five years; however, eight states have no frequency requirements.[26]

Most states also require that property owners be notified by mail of any changes in appraised and assessed values and be given an opportunity to appeal the revaluation. States usually assign the task of hearing appeals to an independent board of review. North Carolina assigns it to the county board of commissioners; Illinois creates a separate board of review in each county. In addition, taxpayers should have access to appraisal information on comparable properties. Illinois requires each county assessor to list in a newspaper the appraised value of each property in the county.

State involvement in appraisal With the exception of Delaware and Hawaii, all state governments assume some role in overseeing local appraisal practices. State involvement, which is critical to the long-term improvement of appraisal quality, must begin with state-provided in-service training and certification of local appraisers. At least twenty-eight states require certification of the chief local appraiser, and twenty-five require certification of all local appraisal staff.[27] States should also provide local tax offices with technical assistance, such as manuals on appraisal law and practice, maps, computer software, forms, and readily accessible technical or legal advice. For railroad and utility properties, which are difficult to appraise, the task of valuation is almost always assigned to a state agency, with the taxable value then allocated among local governments.

State governments must enforce a professional standard of quality, either indirectly through interjurisdictional equalization or more directly through challenging valuations, adjusting local appraisals, or assuming responsibility when inequities exceed acceptable limits. State involvement in promoting more professional appraisal practices is critical to improving the quality and equity of local appraisals.

Assessment

Assessment involves making adjustments, such as partial or full exemptions or **fractional assessments**, to a property's appraised value to determine its assessed value and ultimately its taxable value. A property's assessed value provides the basis on which the tax burden is distributed among property owners. Variations among state practices are greatest in this phase.

The assessment phase begins with the appraised value of each property being multiplied by the statutory assessment ratio, which is the principal adjustment in this phase. At least twenty-one states and the District of Columbia nominally require **full-value assessments**; that is, assessments cannot be set at a fraction of appraised value. The remaining states generally sanction fractional assessments. For example, if property is assessed at 33 percent of its value, a property with an appraised value of $100,000 has an assessed value of $33,000. Additional adjustments, such as a homestead exemption, are applied after the adjustment for fractional assessment, resulting in the property's taxable value.

Fractional assessment is generally introduced when a long-delayed reappraisal would otherwise result in a sudden jump in appraised values and when a shift to full-value assessments would prompt considerable anger among taxpayers. However, evidence and experience show that appraisal equity improves significantly when governments use the full-value standard. In their review of assessment practices, John Bowman and John Mikesell conclude that property tax administration is most uniform when assessment ratios are high—that is, at or near 100 percent—and done with regularity.[28]

Texas's experience is instructive. In 1981, the state implemented a previously ratified constitutional amendment abolishing fractional assessments and empowering the State

Property Tax Board to monitor the progress of CADs toward achieving full-value and more uniform assessments. Within a decade thereafter, the 253 CADs had achieved a statewide median assessment ratio near 1.0 and coefficients of dispersion around 14.0. (The greater the coefficient of dispersion, the less uniform the assessments are relative to value. Values of 10.0 are considered evidence of high-quality appraisals.) Anecdotal evidence suggests that CADs continue to achieve a high level of appraisal accuracy. CADs serving the more populous cities and counties rely on mass appraisal technology that uses statistical methods combined with geographic information systems (GIS) to derive high-quality appraisals with minimal staff. Additionally, Texas state law requires CADs to reappraise real property at least once every three years and personal property annually through a rendition process that requires property owners to self-report taxable inventory, equipment, and other property used in the business.

In addition to Texas, North Carolina and Kentucky, among other states, provide evidence that full-value assessment can be achieved without creating a taxpayer uprising. The keys to success include preventing local governments from reaping revenue windfalls from reappraisal (through **full disclosure**), keeping taxpayers fully informed of the reappraisal process, sustaining a regular cycle of reappraisal, and compelling local governments to move toward a full-value standard.

Another tax relief measure benefiting homeowners is **assessment caps**. As a way of cushioning the impact of rising market values, at least nineteen states now limit increases, following reappraisal, in the assessed value of residences.[29] Such caps benefit property owners in real estate markets where property values are rising rapidly. Unfortunately, higher-valued properties tend to increase more rapidly in value, and any cap on assessed values differentially favors these property owners over other taxpayers. Assessment caps not only introduce horizontal unfairness but also create vertical inequity to the extent that a household's financial ability to pay its taxes is correlated with property value.[30]

Collection

Collection focuses on two sources of revenue: current taxes and delinquent taxes. The more successful a government is at collecting the first source, the less need there is for collecting

Strategies for improving property tax collection

Current taxes

- Use well-designed tax statements
- Mail reminder notices two to three weeks before taxes are due
- Keep taxpayer records current, especially mailing addresses
- Build taxpayer goodwill through more convenient collection points and office hours
- Apply penalties and interest rates that discourage delinquent payment

Delinquent taxes

- Pursue delinquencies immediately and aggressively
- Increase the intensity and urgency of each successive notice to delinquent taxpayers
- Use discretionary powers, such as setoff provisions
- Contract out delinquent collections to a law firm or collection agency
- Publish in a newspaper names of delinquent taxpayers and the amount owed
- Use small-claims court for minor delinquency cases

the second. As a general rule, local governments responsible for collecting property taxes should achieve at least a 95-percent collection rate on the current levy. That is, no more than 5 percent of the current levy should become delinquent.

Level of compliance depends primarily on local economic conditions, especially the unemployment level, and on the aggressiveness of the collection effort. The role of the tax collector requires professionalism and a balance of fairness and firmness. The accompanying sidebar lists strategies for improving current and delinquent tax collections.

Collecting current taxes The design of the tax statement is a key factor in improving the current collection rate. A well-designed statement clearly identifies the amount due, the basis for determining tax liability, and the penalties and interest charges for late payment. Some governments send tax invoices electronically to reduce printing and mailing costs and to provide more timely notice to taxpayers. State laws usually define the information that must be provided on the statement, but within those guidelines, governments can exercise discretion in bringing taxpayers' attention to the amount due and the due date.

Figure 3-3 provides an example of a typical tax statement. It begins by listing the market values of the improvement (the house itself in this case) and the raw land, or more accurately the appraised value of each component of the property. The following section of the statement provides details on each taxing jurisdiction, a column reporting the partial exemptions offered by each, the application of an appraisal cap of 10 percent (included in the exemptions), and a column on the taxable value of the property. The next column reports the nominal tax rate adopted by each overlapping local government. The final column reports the tax levy or liability. At the bottom, the invoice reports the total tax liability and the date that it is due. Although not evident in the invoice, the tax liability for the school district is frozen at the amount in the year that the owner turned sixty-five. Without that freeze, the liability for the current year would have been $3,953.

Some governments offer discounts for early payment, but the effectiveness of this approach is doubtful given the unattractive discount rates that local governments are able to offer. A more effective measure is to mail or e-mail a reminder notice to taxpayers two to three weeks before the due date. While this increases collection costs, governments generally find the improved collection rates well worth the effort.

Another means of improving current collections is to build goodwill through more convenient collection methods, such as an online payment option and extended office hours during peak collection periods. If it is legally possible, the tax collector should accept partial payment, with the unpaid balance subject to penalties and interest. Formal provisions should also be developed for hardship cases.

Collecting delinquent taxes The collection of delinquent taxes begins with the preparation of a delinquent taxpayer roll. Some states, such as Kansas, require the tax collector to publish in a newspaper the names of delinquent taxpayers and the amount owed.

Convincing taxpayers that they will eventually have to pay back taxes is critical to a successful delinquent-tax collection program. Once the due date passes, the tax collector should immediately send delinquent individuals a reminder that taxes are past due. Governments may use the same form as is used for the current tax statement but with penalties and interest added. Each successive contact with the taxpayer should increase in intensity and urgency. For example, if there is no response to a letter asking the taxpayer to contact the tax collection office, a letter should be sent by certified mail specifying the legal measures that will follow to collect overdue taxes. A payment plan can usually be worked out except in cases of bankruptcy, cases in which a taxpayer cannot be located, and cases in which taxable assets have been removed from the jurisdiction.

Figure 3–3 A sample tax statement for the overlapping taxes of a city, school district, and county

2018 ORIGINAL TAX STATEMENT

MICHELLE FRENCH
DENTON COUNTY
TAX ASSESSOR COLLECTOR
PO BOX 90223
DENTON, TEXAS 76202
940-349-3500

PROPERTY ACCOUNT NUMBER
22543DEN

PROPERTY OWNER	PROPERTY LEGAL DESCRIPTION
	AVONDALE 3 BLK H LOT 24
	SITUS: 0001613 VICTORIA DR
	EXEMPTIONS: General Homestead Over 65 Cap Adjustment, XT
	ASSESSMENT RATIO: 0%

PROPERTY VALUES			
IMPROVEMENT VALUE	247,132	MINERAL VALUE	0
NON HOMESITE IMPROVEMENT	0	PERSONAL PROPERTY	0
LAND MARKET VALUE	58,869	AG VALUE	0
		TOTAL MARKET VALUE	306,001

JURISDICTION	EXEMPTIONS	TAXABLE VALUE	TAX RATE	BASE LEVY
CITY OF DENTON	69,339	236,662	0.620477	1,340.44
DENTON ISD	49,339	256,662	1.540000	2,528.82
DENTON COUNTY	69,339	236,662	0.225574	533.85

*ADDITIONAL CITY SALES TAX REDUCED YOUR CITY AD VALOREM TAX BY $ 300.11.

TOTAL AMOUNT DUE IF PAID ON OR BEFORE JANUARY 31, 2019	$4,403.11

Local governments often include a **setoff provision** in their contracts to withhold payment from contractors who owe delinquent property taxes or utility service charges. In addition, a growing number of local governments contract out the collection of delinquent taxes to law firms specializing in this service, thereby saving the valuable time of staff attorneys for other work. A law firm has the expertise to prepare the legal documents and undertake the necessary title search in cases where foreclosure on the lien is necessary. Contracting out to a law firm also sends a message to taxpayers that the government intends to collect all taxes it is owed. Some states permit an additional collection fee to be added to delinquent taxes as compensation for the law firm. And contracting out protects local government staff from appearing to strong-arm delinquent taxpayers.

The continued unpopularity of the tax

The property tax ranks, along with the federal income tax, as one of the most unpopular taxes with the public—even after the passage of Proposition 13, the nearly universal approval

Taxpayer dissatisfaction

Reasons for dissatisfaction	Measures to reduce dissatifaction
• Tax falls on unrealized capital gains, making it punitive for those who are property rich but cash poor	• Circuit-breaker program • Tax freeze • Tax rate caps or freeze • Homestead exemption • Tax deferral program • Split tax roll
• Tax is collected in large lump-sum payments	• Installment option
• Anxiety about reappraisal	• Full disclosure or truth-in-taxation • Fractional assessments • Cap on increase in assessments • Classification of property values • Use-value appraisals • Acquisition-based appraisals
• Inequitable assessments and appraisals	• Full-value assessments • More frequent reappraisal • Full-time appraiser • State oversight of local appraisal practices

by state legislatures of targeted relief (particularly to homeowners), and the nearly universal reduction in local dependence on the tax. Why does this dissatisfaction persist, and what can local governments do to alleviate it? The accompanying sidebar summarizes the sources of irritation with the property tax and some of the remedies for reducing taxpayer dissatisfaction.

Property tax relief and issues of fairness and neutrality

Because it is a tax on wealth rather than on income or consumption, the property tax is particularly onerous for those who are *property rich but cash poor*, such as elderly residents. And because it falls on capital assets (property) that have not been realized (i.e., sold in the market), the property tax is a prime candidate for relief under the "everybody is a special case" principle.

One of the goals of tax policy, as discussed in the preceding chapter, is neutrality: The less interference by tax policies in the marketplace, the more neutral those policies and, by implication, the more productive the market's operation. Why is neutrality important? Taxes, and in particular the property tax, have major implications for the way our economy functions. State and local tax reform efforts in recent years repeatedly appeal for more "business-friendly" tax policies to create more jobs. Although tax relief violates the neutrality principle by creating noneconomic incentives that alter market-based optimums, many state-initiated measures of the past decade have been aimed at enabling local governments to provide that relief.

Since 1978, when Proposition 13 launched the tax revolt, tax relief has assumed an increasingly wide array of modes beyond partial exemptions. Changes in traditional fair market standards of valuation have emerged, such as California's acquisition value basis of appraisal. In addition to limiting the increase in assessed values, several states limit the increase in property tax rates either through a constitutional cap or through truth-in-taxation.

A more recent iteration on tax relief has frozen liability for certain qualifying property owners. For example, since 1982 Texas has frozen the school property taxes of senior homeowners at the liability incurred when one spouse turns sixty-five. Cities in Texas have the option, by voter referendum, of freezing the liability of seniors. Circuit-breaker programs provide property tax relief as a credit on income tax returns. The ultimate safety valve on property liability is the deferral of tax liability to a homeowner's estate. Fairness also becomes an issue following a major natural or technological disaster or combinations of the two (dubbed natechs) such as the 2011 Tōhoku earthquake-triggered tsunami that resulted in a meltdown of the Fukushima Daiichi nuclear power plant.

Tax freeze, tax cap, and tax referendum

While the media often uses the terms interchangeably, it is useful to distinguish among a tax freeze, tax cap, and tax referendum. One way to think of their differences is in terms of the scope (statewide, restricted, or conditional) of the action taken (freeze, cap, or referendum) and the component of the tax equation affected by the action (TB, TR, or TL).

Application:	**statewide**	**restricted**	**conditional**
Action:	**freeze**	**cap**	**referendum**
	TB: acquisition value	TB: exemption by taxpayer category	TB: exemption by referendum
	TR: fixed statewide	TR: limit by taxpayer category	TR: rollback-rate referendum
	TL: fixed statewide	TL: limit by taxpayer category	TL: revenue-limit referendum

For all property owners in California, Proposition 13 froze statewide (universal) both the tax base and tax rate when it imposed an acquisition basis for property valuation and a limit of 1 percent on all overlapping local rates. Colorado's Taxpayer Bill of Rights represents a statewide limit on tax liability.

A cap, by contrast, is restricted to qualifying groups of property owners such as senior citizens and veterans. A cap may extend a senior homestead exemption to the tax base or separate fractional rate of assessment. Tax rates may be capped for selected categories of property owners. And liability may be capped for selected categories of property owners such as the cap in Texas on tax liability for homeowners age sixty-five or older.

Finally, the tax relief may be subject to voter approval, such as a referendum to extend a free-port exemption to business inventory in transit, or a rollback election for extraordinary increases in the tax rate or voter approval for a tax rate. For example, the operating budgets of all but five of the largest school districts in New York must annually be approved through a referendum by the district's voters. Over the past decade, voters in 95 percent of the state's districts have approved the recommended budgets.[1] The most restrictive limitation may be a voter referendum to allow an increase in the total amount of revenue collected by a local government.

1 New York State School Boards Association, School Budget Votes, 2018. http://www.nyssba.org/news-media/school-budget-votes/

Circuit-breaker programs Circuit-breaker programs provide property tax relief to low-income homeowners or renters through a state income tax credit or rebate. With circuit-breaker programs, unlike with other tax relief programs, the state rather than local government bears the financial cost of the tax expenditure. The drawbacks of these programs are their relatively high cost of administration; their adverse impact on state budgets through lost income tax revenue, especially during economic downturns; and the need for beneficiaries to file a state income tax return even if they have no taxable income. Thirty-five states currently have some type of circuit-breaker program.[31]

The amount of relief varies inversely with household income up to a maximum income level, after which point relief ceases. To limit the impact of this subsidy on their budgets, some states target their circuit-breaker benefits only to senior citizens, usually defined as homeowners over age sixty-five. Maryland, Michigan, Minnesota, Vermont, Wisconsin, and Wyoming extend benefits to all homeowners, regardless of age. Four other states—Maine, Montana, New Jersey, and New York—use a two-tiered benefit system, with more generous benefits going to seniors than to younger citizens. Of the sixteen states that extend the circuit-breaker credit to renters, eight limit tax relief to senior citizens.[32]

Tax freeze and tax cap As another approach to tax relief, states can freeze or cap the tax base, tax rate, or tax liability. (The accompanying sidebar proposes a way to distinguish these actions.) For example, Indiana caps property tax liability by using the county-levied income tax to provide a credit to property owners for their liability that exceeds the cap.[33] Several states freeze property assessments, or at least severely limit annual increases in those values, which limits the effects of appreciation in property value on tax liability. Ten states cap the tax liability, usually when homeowners reach age sixty-five.[34] Texas automatically caps the tax liability for school purposes once one spouse in the household reaches sixty-five, but it gives cities and counties the option, via a referendum, of extending the benefit to their senior homeowners.

Several states now require voter approval to increase property tax rates. Other limits restrict the amount of revenue to a percentage of the property tax base, such as the 1-percent limit in California (Proposition 13) and the 1.5-percent limit in Oregon. The most common form of limitation among the states is a statutorily or constitutionally set maximum tax rate for different types or population groupings of local government.

Homestead exemptions Homestead exemptions target tax relief to some or all homeowners by exempting from taxation a fixed dollar amount or percentage of a property's assessed value. Partial exemptions have the important advantage of being easily understood by taxpayers and easily administered by local governments. After a property's appraised value has been determined, its assessed (or taxable) value is obtained by deducting any partial exemptions, such as the homestead. For example, a $5,000 homestead exemption means that a house with an appraised value of $100,000 has an assessed value of $95,000. The owner's tax liability is then determined by multiplying the tax rate (usually in mills or dollars) by the property's assessed value.

Among the forty-nine states with homestead provisions for disabled veterans (only Delaware offers none), thirty-seven states grant this partial exemption to elderly as well as disabled homeowners.[35] The amount of exemption varies from the first $1,000 of value in Oklahoma to $150,000 in Alaska. Homestead programs are often instituted concurrently with statewide reappraisal programs to soften the effects of the reappraisal on the homeowners' tax liability.

The economic value of the homestead exemption depends on the level at which property is assessed. In states where property is assessed at less than its appraised value (i.e., where taxable value is set at some legally specified fraction of appraised value), the economic value of

A tax freeze for senior home owners[1]

Who could be opposed to capping a city's property tax for homeowners who are at least sixty-five? Tax relief has great appeal across demographic and political lines. After all, senior citizens have already paid a lot of property taxes and have lower expectations for public services. However, when examining the effects of a tax cap on other citizens, it becomes clear that it negatively impacts property owners who are not eligible for the cap (existing businesses and young families, for instance), adversely affects attracting new job-creating businesses, and compromises the future prosperity of a city.

A senior tax cap means higher property taxes for those homeowners who are less than sixty-five and for all business owners. A tax cap does not decrease total tax collections for a city; it simply shifts the tax burden onto other property owners. As households age, their demand for public services shifts to different types of services (health care, ambulance service, senior leisure activities) but the impact of seniors on city budgets does not diminish. While senior citizens continue to enjoy the benefits of city services, the cap shifts to other property owners a greater share of the cost of services.

That means that a senior tax cap shifts even more of the funding burden to a shrinking pool of property owners. A cap increases the cost of homeownership for those under sixty-five by increasing their tax burden. That discourages new housing construction, especially for young, first-time homebuyers who are drawn to neighboring cities without a cap.

Some may argue that equity justifies this additional tax relief for senior homeowners and enables them to stay in their homes. If fairness is the driving force behind property tax relief, horizontal equity says that such relief should benefit all property owners rather than a select demographic group.

Not only does a senior tax cap shift the property tax burden to other property owners, it also incentivizes seniors to pressure their city councils for more services since the cost is borne by others. In other words, a cap creates incentives for cities to spend more than they otherwise would.

Why is the senior tax cap bad for job creation? The narrowed tax base increases the cost of doing business in a city. The city must now up the ante even more to attract job-creating businesses. In order to be competitive with businesses in surrounding cities, the added tax is capitalized as a lower value for their property.

At the same time, the cap lowers the cost of homeownership for those sixty-five and older and makes neighborhoods serving them more attractive. The cap artificially alters the housing market and tips the balance to favor homeownership by seniors.

Some have advanced the bogus argument that the cap will benefit lower-income homeowners. In fact, the big winners in the tax cap are owners of higher-valued homes. These are the homes whose values appreciate the greatest, and their owners stand to benefit handsomely from a cap over the long term. In short, a cap widens the gap between wealthy and poor homeowners at the expense of all other property owners in a city.

Why is a senior tax cap a bad idea for the future prosperity of a city? It is bad for a city because it narrows the funding options available to its elected leaders. The inability of a city to fund its most basic services and maintain the assets that it has developed makes it even less attractive to new investment. A cap stagnates economic growth and ultimately leads to decline in the quality of life of a city.

1 Portions of this sidebar were taken from Robert L. Bland, "Guest editorial: Should seniors get tax break?" *Denton Record-Chronicle*, April 23, 2017. Courtesy of *Denton-Record Chronicle* and www.dentonrc.com.

the exemption increases. For example, New Mexico assesses property at 33.3 percent of value and applies the homestead exemption after application of the assessment ratio. Thus, for a house with an appraisal value of $100,000 and a $5,000 homestead exemption, the following computation applies:

Appraised value	$100,000
× Assessment ratio	0.333
	33,300
– Homestead exemption	5,000
Taxable value	$28,300

Organizations of veterans and the elderly are often the most vocal opponents of full-value assessments because such assessments reduce the value of the homestead exemption.

Tax deferral A fourth approach to relieving the tax burden on lower-income households is a **tax deferral**, which, when opted for by the homeowner, delays tax payments until the property is sold or the estate is settled. The deferred portion of the tax is essentially a loan from the local government, rather than a state or local subsidy, to the property owner. Deferred taxes usually incur an interest charge but less frequently a penalty. Currently, twenty-seven states and the District of Columbia offer a tax deferral program, and in all but three states—Florida, Iowa, and Pennsylvania—the program is limited to elderly homeowners.[36] Most states also impose a limit on the amount of taxes eligible for deferral; the limit is usually pegged to a percentage of the value of the property, which serves as collateral for the deferred taxes. Because deferred taxes become a lien on the estate, homeowners do not often choose this option.

Split tax roll A growing practice is the use of a split tax roll: taxing single-family residential property at one rate and all other property at a higher rate. In 1994 Michigan, as part of its sweeping education finance reform initiative, basically eliminated tax rates set by school districts and, in their place, introduced a two-tiered rate structure levied statewide: 6 mills on all primary residences and 24 mills on secondary homes and businesses.[37] Municipalities and counties continue to levy their own taxes. Although such a plan reduces interjurisdictional inequities, creating two classes of taxpayers has a high likelihood of spawning more classes as taxpayer groups jockey for preferential treatment under the state tax code. The plan also shifts control over school governance from locally elected boards to a more distant and centralized state authority.

In an older version of the split tax roll idea, nineteenth-century economist Henry George advocated imposing a higher property tax on land values than on improvements as a way to encourage more efficient urban development. Economists contend that the tax discourages landowners from making improvements on their property, a clarification that is particularly damaging to declining areas. For example, an absentee landlord has little incentive to improve an apartment complex if the result will be a higher tax liability and no increase in rental income. Vacant lots in developed urban areas go undeveloped because the expected increase in the land's value exceeds the cost of the property tax on the undeveloped land. Several local governments in Pennsylvania, including Pittsburgh and Scranton, have at various times implemented George's theories. Typically, tax rates on land values are twice those on improvements, which penalizes speculators for leaving vacant land undeveloped. Because of their heavy reliance on wage taxes, local governments in Pennsylvania make relatively moderate use of the property tax, so the use of split rates on land development patterns in Pennsylvania has probably had a moderate impact.

Property taxes and disasters Natural disasters, such as hurricanes, earthquakes, tornadoes, droughts, and floods, and technological disasters, such as hazardous spills and war-induced suffering, create a unique set of challenges for the local manager. In 1942, Joseph Schumpeter first described what he called the process of creative destruction, an increase in economic productivity following an external shock.[38] Disasters provide opportunities for creative destruction. New technology replaces older buildings and equipment. Cities upgrade their infrastructure to more productive technology. Consequently, in some types of disasters—notably tornadoes, earthquakes, and hurricanes—local governments experience economic growth, at least after the initial impact of the disaster passes.

The initial impact of a disaster, however, typically requires adjustments to the property tax. For example, Texas law allows local governments to request a reappraisal of property by the CAD following the declaration of a disaster by the governor. The reappraisal determines the fair market value of property following the disaster. Tax liability for the year is prorated as follows: for the portion of the year prior to the disaster, liability is based on the assessed value as of January 1; for the portion of the year following the disaster, liability is based on the revised assessed value. Local governments may adopt a revised budget following a disaster with a revised tax rate to reflect the changes in expenditures.

Payment methods

The general practice among local governments has been to collect the property tax annually in one lump-sum payment. This increases the tax's visibility and may partially explain its unpopularity with taxpayers relative to other taxes.

Depending on the turnover rate in a jurisdiction's housing market, anywhere from 40 percent to 80 percent of the property tax payments from residential owners are collected from mortgage lenders. Usually these lenders establish an **escrow account** into which each homeowner makes monthly payments against property tax liability. This both reduces the visibility of the property tax for these owners and effectively makes their tax liability payable in installments. The problem of lump-sum payments is greatest for owners who must pay their tax directly, either because they have no mortgage obligation or because the mortgagor does not require an escrow account.

Most states now permit local governments to collect the tax in smaller, more frequent installments. For example, Pennsylvania gives local governments the option of collecting the tax in quarterly installments. Some states, such as Arizona and Maryland, require semiannual payments. Local governments in Texas may, at their discretion, adopt the split payment plan.

In a recent study by the Lincoln Institute of Land Policy, over half of the nation's single-family homeowners must pay their property tax liability in a single or a few lump sums.[39] However, local governments are increasingly adopting more flexible payment options. Milwaukee, Wisconsin, for example, gives taxpayers the option of a lump sum payment or monthly installment. In the latter case, homeowners are automatically enrolled in the monthly option when they make their first payment.

One disadvantage of more frequent payments is that local governments lose interest income during the additional time that tax receivables remain outstanding. Other problems are the increased administrative cost of notifying taxpayers of payment dates and the additional accounting required for partial payments. But these disadvantages pale in comparison to the benefits in increased taxpayer compliance and goodwill from more frequent installments. Increasingly, local governments are giving taxpayers the option of paying via the Internet with a credit card, an option that taxpayers are accustomed to having in the retail market and that thereby gives local governments opportunities for creating goodwill and enhancing taxpayer compliance.

Reappraisal

In general, taxpayer concern about property reappraisal will be the greatest where reappraisal is done infrequently or at irregular intervals. The longer the intervals between revaluations, the greater the inequities that will develop during the intervals and the louder the complaints that will be heard from property owners who had benefited from undervaluation. However, frequent reappraisal increases the cost of administering the tax. Moreover, in a period of rapid appreciation in property values created by inflation or a population increase, frequent reappraisal may not reduce taxpayer concern, as was the case in California prior to Proposition 13.

Full disclosure Reappraisal usually leads to increases in taxable value. If the tax rate remains unchanged, taxpayers will incur higher tax liabilities. To protect taxpayers and prevent the local government from reaping a windfall that taxpayers have not approved, some states require a full-disclosure procedure, sometimes known as truth-in-taxation or **truth-in-millage (TRIM)**. Essentially, full disclosure does for the property tax what indexing of the marginal tax rates does for state and federal income taxes. Full disclosure shifts responsibility for increases in the tax levy away from reappraisal (and the appraiser) and onto the tax rate (and the legislative body responsible for setting it).

Full disclosure originated in Florida in 1971 and is now used in thirteen states.[40] Although state statutes vary widely in the specifics, full disclosure involves three steps:

1. Each taxing jurisdiction determines a tax rate that will yield the same tax levy produced in the preceding year. In a jurisdiction where taxable property values are increasing, this rate, called an effective or constant yield rate, will be lower than the preceding year's rate. (All states exclude voter-approved debt from the computations.)
2. The effective rate is published in a local newspaper. (In Florida and Utah, individual notices are mailed to property owners along with an estimate of the owner's tax liability.)
3. The taxing jurisdiction then adopts a tax rate that will generate sufficient tax revenues to balance the current operating budget, and it advertises or individually notifies property owners of the percentage difference between the final rate (or levy) and the effective rate. Kentucky and Texas authorize citizens to petition their local governments for an election to roll back extraordinarily large increases in tax rates (above 4 percent in Kentucky and above 8 percent in Texas).

Florida's local governments distribute a customized notice to each property owner before adoption of the final tax rate explaining how proposed property tax changes will affect the owner's liability and notifying them about the time and location of the public hearing where the proposed budget will be discussed.

Fractional assessments and assessment caps Two approaches aimed at constraining increases in assessments—fractional assessments and caps on increases—have provided momentary relief for taxpayers but almost always at the expense of horizontal equity in the property tax burden. Assessing property at less than 100 percent of appraised value, which often arises because of infrequent reappraisals, creates an illusion of constraining the tax, but in fact reduces the accountability of the assessment process with property owners.

Capping assessments, as previously noted, takes several forms. But, again, assessment caps both introduce horizontal inequity and create vertical inequity as a household's ability to pay is correlated with the value of its property.

Property classification Whereas a split tax roll always targets tax relief—often for homeowners—through the use of differential tax rates, **classification of property** is more closely associated with providing tax relief on the heels of a reassessment. Classification involves grouping real property by type (e.g., single-family, multifamily, commercial, industrial, vacant land) and then treating each type differently through the application of either a different assessment level, which is the case in nineteen states, or a different tax rate, which is the case in Hawaii, Kentucky, New Hampshire, South Dakota, and West Virginia.

Where revaluation is done infrequently or enforcement of a uniform assessment level is lax, residential property generally has lower assessment ratios than nonresidential property, and a reappraisal will shift the tax burden back onto owners of single-family homes. Some states use classification to legitimize the favorable level of assessment given de facto to residential property. In almost all cases, classification grandfathers a situation created by negligent appraisal practices.

When considering the adoption of a classification system, state legislatures must address two issues. The first is the number of classes to create. Of the twenty-four states and the District of Columbia that classify property, most designate from two to four classes. Missouri law specifies three classes of real property, each assessed at a different fraction of appraised market value: residential (19 percent), agricultural (12 percent), and income-producing property (32 percent). Because political rather than economic criteria are the basis of all state classification policies, residential and agricultural property are almost always the most favored classes. Unfortunately, once the practice of classification is introduced, political pressures build to create even more classes. For example, Minnesota began with just four classes in 1913 but now has possibly more than one hundred classes, creating an administrative nightmare for tax assessors and a patchwork of assessments of doubtful fairness to taxpayers.

The second issue concerns the degree of differentiation among the classes. Mississippi assesses residential property at 10 percent, all other real and personal property at 15 percent, and state-appraised utility property at 30 percent of its value. Montana has at least thirteen classes of property, with assessment ratios ranging from 3 percent to 100 percent of market value. (It assesses coal reserves at 100 percent of value as a way to export the tax burden.) No economic criteria guide these decisions, only the relative political power of affected groups.

Use value Like classification, use value (or production value) treats particular types of property more favorably, especially those that are adversely affected by a reappraisal. **Use-value appraisals**, first adopted by Maryland in 1960, give preferential treatment to farmland and open spaces by basing the value of the property on its current use rather than on its best possible use or market value. The intent of this approach, now used for some types of agricultural land in all fifty states, is to reduce the adverse impact of reappraisal on farmland surrounding urban areas, where the potential for future development causes land values to appreciate rapidly.

Most states impose penalties if the property's use is changed once it has been classified and valued as farmland. Some states enter into contracts with owners of agricultural property, restricting land use in return for appraising the property at its production value. While the intention is to protect farmers from the adverse effects of urban growth, owners can abuse the approach by holding their land for future development while keeping it in farm production to qualify for the tax break.

Acquisition-based appraisal As noted earlier, Proposition 13 ushered in acquisition-based appraisal, a new basis for valuing property now used in California, Oregon, and Georgia (local option). Not only are annual assessment increases capped in these states (3 percent in Oregon and the lesser of 2 percent or the consumer price index in California), but property is reappraised only when it sells. Such skewed valuation standards, as has also been noted earlier, interject significant and economically destructive inequities and inefficiencies that eventually drag down a state's economic growth and discourage new business investment.

Equity

Appraisal equity within a taxing jurisdiction is gauged by the intra-area coefficient of dispersion (CD), which measures the average deviation in assessment levels from the median level of assessment. Higher CDs imply greater dispersion and thus greater levels of inequity in appraisal practices. A CD equal to zero implies perfect appraisal equity; that is, all properties within each appraisal class, if applicable, in a jurisdiction are appraised at the same percentage of market value of that class.

Inequitable tax appraisals most commonly arise from (1) state laws that permit assessments at a fraction of appraised value (less than full-value assessments), (2) infrequent and irregular revaluations, (3) the absence of qualified personnel to perform appraisals, and (4) the absence of state oversight to enforce uniform professional practices. Research confirms that these factors, especially the first three, are associated with poor-quality appraisals.[41] Because they are more easily understood and scrutinized by property owners than fractional assessments, full-value assessments provide assessors with less opportunity to "bury their mistakes." The same study also found that local governments in Virginia that undertook more frequent reappraisals had lower appraisal errors (CDs) than governments that undertook reappraisals less frequently. Similarly, governments with full-time appraisers had lower CDs, which implies that a full-time professional staff devoted solely to property valuation contributes significantly to reducing appraisal inequities.

Although not addressed by research, it would seem that state oversight of local valuation practices should lead to greater uniformity in assessment levels.

Conclusion

Several significant trends are now apparent in the role and character of the property tax:

- During the last three decades of the previous century, the property tax increased in importance as federal and state aid declined, and that trend has continued in the first two decades of the current century. The property tax base is increasingly dependent on real property, and residential property represents a growing share of the real tax base. That base is increasingly a tax on property that is easiest to discover and appraise and has the greatest potential for appreciating in value.
- Growth in the property tax base has been greatest in cities with higher levels of economic activity.
- The decline in manufacturing and the growth in service industries have not reduced the amount of potential business property subject to taxation. Local governments exercise wide discretion in how they allocate their property tax burden between residential and business property owners, and they appear to do so to maximize their competitive position with respect to other local governments.

The property tax survives despite its unpopularity with taxpayers because (1) it provides a stable source of revenue for local governments; (2) it is exportable to absentee property owners; (3) it is equitable to the extent that the benefits from the public services funded by the tax are rolled into higher property values and thus higher tax liability; (4) it has several administrative advantages, including the difficulty of evading the tax, especially on real property; and (5) it is largely a locally levied tax in the United States, which helps promote the political autonomy of local governments. One fact remains clear: the property tax is remarkably adaptive to the political machinations of the day. It is because of that adaptability that the tax survives—and even thrives in some states.

Notes

1 The Lincoln Institute of Land Policy, in collaboration with the George Washington University Institute of Public Policy, maintains a website titled "Significant Features of the Property Tax," which provides information on a state-by-state basis as well as summarized across all states. See http://datatoolkits.lincolninst.edu/subcenters/significant-features-property-tax/.

2 Urban Institute, *State and Local Finance Initiative, Property Tax Revenue,2015, Percentage of State and Local General Revenue.* https://www.urban.org/policy-centers/cross-center-initiatives/state-local-finance-initiative/projects/state-and-local-backgrounders/property-taxes.

3 Alan S. Dornfest et al., "State and Provincial Property Tax Policies and Administrative Practices: Compilation and Report," *Journal of Property Tax Assessment & Administration* 7 (July 2014): Table 6, p. 26.

4 Ibid.

5 Texas Comptroller of Public Accounts, *Annual Property Tax Report,* Tax Years 1982, 1990, 2009, and 2015, https://comptroller.texas.gov/taxes/property-tax/reports/index.php.

6 Ibid.

7 Howard Chernick, Adam H. Langley, and Andrew Reschovsky, "Central City Revenues after the Great Recession," *Land Lines* (July 2012): 6.

8 Therese J. McGuire, "Do Taxes Matter? Yes, No, Maybe So," *State Tax Today* (June 9, 2003): 22; Yan Song and Yves Zenou, "How Do Differences in Property Taxes within Cities Affect Urban Sprawl?" *Journal of Regional Science* 49 (2009): 801–831; John Deskins and William F. Fox, "Measuring Behavioral Responses to the Property Tax," in *Challenging the Conventional Wisdom on the Property Tax,* ed. Roy Bahl, Jorge Martinez-Vazquez, and Joan Youngman (Cambridge, Mass: Lincoln Institute of Land Policy, 2010): 47–66.

9 J. Edwin Benton, "Trends in Local Government Revenues: The Old, the New, and the Future," in *Municipal Revenues and Land Policies*, ed. Gregory K. Ingram and Yu-Hung Hong (Cambridge, Mass: Lincoln Institute of Land Policy, 2010): 81–112.

10 Robert L. Bland and Phanit Laosirirat, "Tax Limitations to Reduce Municipal Property Taxes: Truth in Taxation in Texas," *Journal of Urban Affairs* 19 (Spring 1997): 45–58.

11 Minnesota Taxpayers Association, *50-State Property Tax Comparison Study for Taxes Paid in 2016* (Cambridge, Mass: Lincoln Institute of Land Policy, May 2017): 13.

12 Ibid., 19, 24, 29.

13 Portions of this section are taken from Robert L. Bland and Jingran Sun, "Do Property Tax Exemptions Increase the Tax Liability of Other Property Owners and Shift Budgetary Dependence to Other Revenues?" Unpublished monograph, May 2017.

14 H. Woods Bowman, "Reexamining the Property Tax Exemption," *Land Lines* (July 2003): 3.

15 Jennifer Gravelle and Sally Wallace, "Overview of the Trends in Property Tax Base Erosion," in *Erosion of the Property Tax Base, Trends, Causes, and Consequences,* ed. Nancy Y. Augustine et al. (Cambridge, Mass: Lincoln Institute of Land Policy, 2009), 17–46.

16 Kellie McGiverin-Bohan et al., "Local Officials' Support for PILOTs/SILOTs: Nonprofit Engagement, Economic Stress, and Politics," *Public Administration Review* (November/December 2016): 951-963.

17 Dornfest et al., "State and Provincial Property Tax Policies," 30.

18 Sherri Farris and John Horbas, "Creation vs. Capture: Evaluating the True Costs of Tax Increment Financing," *Journal of Property Tax Assessment & Administration* (October 2009): 5-28.

19 Texas Comptroller of Public Accounts, *Tax Exemptions and Tax Incidence* (Austin, Tex.: Texas Comptroller of Public Accounts, February 2017), 67, https://comptroller.texas.gov/transparency/reports/tax-exemptions-and-incidence/.

20 David Brunori and Michael E. Bell, "Property Taxes and Local Autonomy, An Overview," in *The Property Tax and Local Autonomy,* ed. Michael E. Bell, David Brunori, and Joan Youngman (Cambridge, Mass: Lincoln Institute of Land Policy, 2010), 8.

21 Glenn W. Fisher, "The Changing Role of Property Taxation," in *Financing State and Local Governments in the 1980s: Issues and Trends,* ed. Norman Walzer and David L. Chicoine (Cambridge, Mass.: Oelgeschlager, Gunn & Hain, 1981), 45.

22 Jack Citrin, "Proposition 13 and the Transformation of California Government," *California Journal of Politics & Policy* 1, no. 1 (January 2009); Nada Wasi and Michelle J. White, "Property Tax Limitations and Mobility: Lock-in Effect of California's Proposition 13," *Brookings-Wharton Papers on Urban Affairs* (2005): 59–97; Keith R. Ihlanfeldt, "Do Caps on Increases in Assessed Values Create a Lock-in Effect? Evidence from Florida's Amendment One," *National Tax Journal* 64 (March 2011): 7–26.

23 Gregory D. Saxton, Christopher W. Hoene, and Steven P. Erie, "Fiscal Constraints and the Loss of Home Rule: The Long-Term Impacts of California's Post–Proposition 13 Fiscal Regime," *American Review of Public Administration* 32 (December 2002): 423–454; Carol Douglas, "Proposition 13—25 Years Later," *State Tax Notes* 30 (October 20, 2003): 222–226; Lenny Goldberg and David Kersten, "Huge Disparities Found in California Commercial Property Taxes," *State Tax Notes* 31 (May 10, 2004): 437–457; Randall G. Holcombe, "Tax and Expenditure Limitations: Issues for Florida," James Madison Institute Policy Report no. 932 (April 2001); Terri A. Sexton, Steve M. Sheffrin, and Arthur O'Sullivan, "Proposition 13: Unintended Effects and Feasible Reforms," *National Tax Journal* 52 (March 1999): 99–111.

24 Dornfest et al., "State and Provincial Property Tax Policies," 33.

25 David L. Sjoquist and Mary Beth Walker, "Economies of Scale in Property Tax Assessment," *National Tax Journal* 52 (June 1999): 207–220.

26 Dornfest et al., "State and Provincial Property Tax Policies," 33.

27 Ibid., 33.

28 John H. Bowman and John L. Mikesell, "Improving Administration of the Property Tax: A Review of Prescriptions and Their Impact," *Public Budgeting and Financial Management* 2 (November 2, 1990): 151–176.

29 Dornfest et al., "State and Provincial Property Tax Policies," 30.

30 Mark Haveman and Terri A. Sexton, *Property Tax Assessment Limits, Lessons from Thirty Years of Experience* (Cambridge, Mass.: Lincoln Institute of Land Policy, 2008.

31 Dornfest et al., "State and Provincial Property Tax Policies," 30.

32 Ibid.

33 Indiana Legislative Services Agency, *Indiana Handbook of Taxes, Revenues, and Appropriations* (Office of Fiscal and Management Analysis, 2017): 61-80, iga.in.gov/documents/85254c11.

34 Dornfest et al., "State and Provincial Property Tax Policies," 30.

35 Samantha Reeves, "Full List of Property Tax Exemptions by State," Veterans United Network, July 27, 2017, https://www.veteransunited.com/futurehomeowners/veteran-property-tax-exemptions-by-state/.

36 Dornfest et al., "State and Provincial Property Tax Policies," 30.

37 Paul D. Ballew, Richard H. Mattoon, and William A. Testa, "School Reform and Tax Reform: A Successful Marriage?" *Government Finance Review* 10 (August 1994): 32–35.

38 Joseph Schumpeter, *Capitalism, Socialism and Democracy* (New York: Harper & Row, 1942).

39 Adam H. Langley, "Improving the Property Tax by Expanding Options for Monthly Payments," Working Paper WP18AL1 (Cambridge, Mass.: Lincoln Institute of Land Policy, January 2018).

40 Bland and Laosirirat, "Tax Limitations to Reduce Municipal Property Taxes," 47.

41 Timothy Schiller, "What's It Worth? Property Taxes and Assessment Practices," *Business Review* (2011): 21–30.

CHAPTER 4

Other tax revenue

An invasion of armies can be resisted, but not an idea whose time has come.

—*Victor Hugo*

This chapter provides the following takeaways:

- How states can design the general sales tax to promote equity and economic neutrality among local governments.
- Policy choices that complicate the administration of the sales tax.
- Those excise taxes that local governments could use to help balance their budgets and those that are more of a nuisance than they are worth.
- How a few local governments are able to successfully levy an income tax but the unlikelihood that the tax will achieve a broader usage at the local level.

In addition to the property tax, other sources of revenue available to local governments are consumption taxes and income-based taxes. Consumption taxes are of two types: the general sales tax, which is levied on a broad range of goods and services sold at the retail level, and excise taxes, each of which is levied on a specific product or service usually under separate statutory authority that establishes the base and rate. Some excise taxes, such as those on gasoline and other motor fuels, are earmarked for uses that benefit the consumers of the good or service being taxed, making them a benefits-received tax. It is not uncommon for some goods, such as tobacco products, to be subject to both an excise tax and the general sales tax.

Consumption taxes distribute the cost of local government services according to spending levels of individuals and businesses. In most cases, vendors merely collect the tax from consumers on behalf of the state or local government. However, the actual legal relationship is more complex in state law depending on whether the tax is on vendors as a business privilege levy, on consumers as a consumption levy, or on some combination of the two.

Income-based taxes differ depending on who is legally liable for the tax. The personal or corporate income tax is a liability of the person or business receiving the income whereas the **payroll tax**—for example, the employer's portion of the federal tax that supports Social Security (i.e., the FICA tax)—is liability of the employer prior to distribution of income to employees.

Consumption taxes: The sales tax

Next to the property tax, the general sales tax has become the most important tax source for local governments, and it remains the option of first choice for tax diversification. Over 10,000 local governments in thirty-eight states now levy a general sales tax;[1] its use is most widespread in the Midwest. Counties have also increased their use of the tax, with more than 1,500 jurisdictions now collecting it. The general sales tax is levied on retail transactions, as opposed to transactions further back in the production chain, on a broad range of goods and services that state or local law classify as taxable.

The most important reason for its relative popularity is that the sales tax is collected in small increments over a large number of transactions. Another reason is that legislative authorization is now almost always couched in terms of providing property tax relief, especially to residential property owners. Some states go to unusual lengths to ensure that local sales tax revenues will be used for this purpose. For example, the Texas legislature authorizes counties not served by a public transit district to levy a 0.5-percent optional sales tax but specifies that such revenue be held in escrow and used only to replace revenue lost through a reduction in those counties' property tax levies.

Along with enabling governments to tax a broad range of consumer goods and services, the local sales tax expands the number of persons and businesses subject to local taxation by reaching nonresidential shoppers who do not pay a property tax but who benefit from local services. By reducing dependence on federal and state aid, it also increases local government autonomy, giving local managers added flexibility in financing their operating and capital budgets.

A sales tax is almost always adopted in tandem with a **use tax**. A jurisdiction levies a use tax on items purchased in another jurisdiction but brought back or delivered to the taxing jurisdiction. Payment of the use tax falls on the buyer, not the seller. In theory, use taxes protect retailers in the taxing jurisdiction by discouraging consumers from making their purchases online or outside the jurisdiction simply to avoid its sales tax. Enforcement of use taxes, however, is effective only in cases where governments maintain records of ownership, such as when a vehicle's registration is transferred from one state to another. The issue of enforcement

Figure 4-1 Variations of local control over the general sales tax

No local control (15)	Local discretion over base (4)	Local discretion over rates (22)	Local discretion over liability (3)	Local administration (7[a])

Note: Figures in parentheses indicate the number of states.

a Local administration is available in seven states. In Alaska, which has no state sales tax, and Louisiana, local governments must collect their own sales tax. Most smaller local governments in the other five states opt for state administration while the more populous cities and counties prefer to collect and enforce the tax themselves.

has assumed greater attention nationally with the advent of Internet purchases and the trend toward national and even international marketing by vendors through online sales.

The evolving role of the local sales tax

Several characteristics affect the role of the general sales tax in local government revenue structures:

- Once one level of local government gains access to the tax, political pressure builds to extend authority to other levels. Typically cities are the first to receive such authorization, followed by counties and then special districts, especially public transit, fire, and hospital districts.
- The growth of online sales has complicated the ability to determine liability for the sales (or use) tax and collection of that tax from vendors located in another state or even outside the United States.
- Tax rates tend to migrate upward as local governments face growing expectations for services and limitations on other revenue sources, particularly the property tax.
- Because the sales tax base is more responsive to economic growth, at least in the short term, than the property tax, local governments have become increasingly dependent on it.
- Revenue yields from the sales tax are procyclical (i.e., they are income elastic, expanding and contracting with the business cycle), increasing the likelihood of midyear budget shortfalls for local governments whenever the business cycle turns downward. The more dependent a local government is on the tax, the more vulnerable its operating budget is to the ups and downs of the business cycle.

Local government access to the general sales tax In most cases, state-enabling legislation is required to levy a local sales tax, although municipalities in Colorado, Illinois, and North Dakota rely on their home rule powers while those in Alabama and Arizona derive their authority from business licensing powers.[2] When first authorizing the adoption of local sales taxes, states tend to begin with only one level of local government—often, selected cities or counties. With time, as the tax gains acceptance politically and administratively, states expand authorization to all cities and/or counties; some states even authorize that revenues be shared locally among cities and counties and sometimes special districts.

Of the thirty-eight states that authorize a local sales tax, thirty grant their municipalities (cities and/or towns) authority to levy or otherwise share in revenue from the tax, and twenty-eight authorize their counties to do so.[3] Two states—Nebraska and South Dakota—still give municipalities exclusive access to the tax; four states—Georgia, Ohio, Wisconsin, and Wyoming—give counties virtually exclusive access.[4] Local sales taxes are virtually nonexistent, however, in the Northeast with the notable exception of New York.

Ten states authorize their transit authorities to levy the tax. Four states—Florida, Georgia, Iowa, and Louisiana—allow school districts to levy the tax, although several states now link their county levies to school funding. Florida school districts may levy a voter-approved sales tax for capital improvements, including technology; most Georgia counties redistribute the revenue to their schools; Iowa also makes extensive use of a voter-approved countywide tax for infrastructure improvements in school districts. North Carolina, which has designed one of the most equitable and economically neutral local sales tax policies, requires that revenue from the county tax be allocated to cities on a pro rata share of population or assessed value, a formula that greatly reduces intergovernmental competition for the tax base.

Since local option sales taxes were first introduced in the 1930s, their popularity has spread and their use has increased. Cities now derive almost 8 percent of their revenue from the tax

Table 4–1 The general sales tax, excise taxes, and income tax as a percentage of general revenues, FY 2007 and 2012

Revenue source	FY 2007		FY 2012	
	Counties	Municipalities	Counties	Municipalities
Property taxes	40.1	27.8	42.7	29.8
General sales tax	**9.8**	**7.6**	**9.7**	**7.8**
Selective sales taxes	**2.6**	**4.8**	**2.7**	**4.9**
Income tax	**2.0**	**6.4**	**2.1**	**6.1**
All other taxes	3.7	5.0	2.2	3.5
All other nontaxes	41.6	48.4	40.6	47.9
	100.0	100.0	100.0	100.0
Total general revenue (in millions)[a]	$223,246	$395,046	$243,140	$439,100

Sources: U.S. Census Bureau, *2012 Census of Governments: State & Local Government Finance*, Local Government Table 2, https://www.census.gov//govs/local/historical_data_2012.html, and *State & Local Government Finance, Historical Data: 2007*, Table 2, https://www.census.gov//govs/local/historical_data_2007.html.

a Total general revenue includes utility charges but excludes intergovernmental aid, liquor store income, and insurance trust revenue.

(Table 4–1), down from a peak of 8.4 percent in FY 2002, and counties derive 9.7 percent of their revenue from the tax, essentially the same as in FY 2002. Several factors may account for a decline in municipalities' rate of dependence on the tax—particularly, the contraction caused by the Great Recession, online sales, and the significant expansion of the service sector, which generally lies outside the tax base. Nevertheless, the general sales tax remains the tax of choice by state and local governments seeking to diversify their revenue sources.

Several states give their local governments limited control over their own tax bases. Twenty-two states sanction local discretion over tax rates, an option that allows local governments to better match revenue yields to budget needs but that also greatly increases border-city effects. A few states also allow local governments to abate or remit part of sales tax revenues, particularly for large commercial projects such as regional shopping centers, as a tool for economic development.

Adoption of a local option sales tax is more universal in states where voter approval is not required; however, the need for voter approval has not significantly deterred its spread. States generally specify the maximum sales tax rate that local governments can levy, or the maximum overlapping (combined state, county, city, and special districts) tax rate that can be levied in any one jurisdiction. Some states, especially those in the South, Midwest, and West, have given municipalities and counties access to the tax with rates usually in the 1–3 percent range.

Defining the general sales tax base In most cases, the sales tax base consists of purchases of goods or services by households and businesses for final (retail) consumption. The tax rate is assessed as a percentage of the retail value of the goods and services purchased. State laws vary as to the types of transactions included in the tax base. Hawaii, New Mexico, and South Dakota tax virtually all transactions, including many services.[5] By contrast, Connecticut, Massachusetts, and Rhode Island exempt all prescriptions, food purchased for home consumption, consumer utilities, some clothing, and professional services.

Inclusion of services In the past two decades, state legislatures have expanded their tax bases by adding services—personal, business, professional, repair, computer, and amusement admissions. This rapidly expanding sector of the economy—45 percent of gross domestic product in 2017 compared with 30 percent fifty years earlier—represents a politically tantalizing source of revenue for states and their local governments.[6] However, states have been somewhat selective in bringing services under the tax umbrella: the general conclusion is that adding professional and business services, in particular, to the tax base is ill-advised because of the opportunities for tax avoidance (e.g., consumers can use an out-of-state law firm) and tax pyramiding (as taxing business inputs increases the cost of outputs to the consumer, who in most cases bears the cumulative incidence of the tax).[7]

Population changes Like the property tax base, the sales tax base is sensitive to population changes. At least in the short term, it is less sensitive to population declines than the property tax base because it draws on the spending of consumers from outside the area and thus is not as closely linked to changes in a particular city's population. Over the long term, however, changes in population—growth or decline—will affect the sales tax base and ultimately sales tax yields.

Internet sales A high-stakes national debate continues over how to extend state and local sales taxes to online sales. The issue has its origins in the case of *National Bellas Hess, Inc. v. Department of Revenue of the State of Illinois* (1967), in which the U.S. Supreme Court ruled that states could not compel a mail order firm to collect sales taxes if the firm had no taxable nexus in the state.[8] Such a nexus exists if a firm has any physical presence in the state, such as a warehouse, sales representatives, or a retail outlet; however, merely mailing a catalog to potential buyers did not, in the Court's pre-Internet opinion, constitute a taxable nexus. In 1992, the U.S. Supreme Court reaffirmed and clarified its ruling in *Quill Corp. v. North Dakota* by blocking North Dakota from compelling Quill Corp., an online office supplier with no nexus in the state, from collecting the use tax from remote sales. Without a mechanism for collecting taxes from retailers, states are left to compel compliance from consumers for payment of the use tax, which is impossible except in cases where licensing or title transfer occurs, such as with vehicles.

As a result, online purchases were free of a sales tax although technically liable for the use tax, giving these vendors a competitive advantage over a comparable purchase made from a local vendor. As remote retailing gained popularity with consumers, it has created horizontal inequities between online and brick-and-mortar retailers and eroded the sales tax bases of state and local governments. Recent estimates place the revenue loss from online sales between $8 and $13 billion for state and local governments.[9] The revenue hemorrhage has been slowed as states have taken a more aggressive position with e-marketplaces, such as Amazon and eBay, which provide a platform for third-party retailers. All forty-five states with a general sales tax now have agreements with Amazon to collect state and local sales taxes. But a sizeable portion of online sales on e-marketplaces went untaxed under the protection of *Quill*.

Recognizing this transformation in retailing and the adverse and inequitable effect of Quill on located retailers, the U.S. Supreme Court agreed in 2017 to reconsider its ruling in *South Dakota v. Wayfair, Inc.* In June 2018, the Court reversed its decision in *Quill*, a rare course of action for the Court, and ruled that states had the authority to require online vendors to collect state and local sales taxes even if they lacked a taxable nexus. The *Wayfair* ruling levels the playing field with brick-and-mortar retailers who have always had to withhold sales taxes for state and local governments. In the long term, *Wayfair* likely benefits consumers who will see more competitive pricing by online retailers. When pricing their products, online retailers will not have the benefit of using the absence of a sales tax to price their products higher.

In addition to a judicial remedy, the National Governors Association and the National Conference of State Legislatures have collaborated to create the Streamlined Sales and Use Tax Agreement. This coalition seeks to encourage retailers to collect sales taxes on all sales—especially those from retailers doing business in multiple states—by simplifying state and local sales tax reporting and remittance. The agreement focuses on improving sales and use tax administration systems by (1) centralizing the administration of sales and use tax collections at the state level, (2) making local tax bases uniform with those of the states, (3) increasing uniformity of major tax bases across the states, (4) simplifying tax returns for retailers, and (5) simplifying state and local sales tax rates.[10]

Food exemptions Evidence shows that the general sales tax is regressive with respect to household income. Exempting food purchased for home consumption, which thirty-four states now do, reduces but does not eliminate the tax's regressivity.[11] Several states complicate tax equity, neutrality, and administration by giving local governments the option of including food in their tax base. Six states—Arkansas, Illinois, Missouri, Tennessee, Utah, and Virginia—have a two-tiered tax structure and tax food at a lower rate. Illinois, for example, levies a 1-percent tax on food but a 6.25-percent tax on all other purchases. All states include food consumed in restaurants in their sales tax base.

An alternative to exempting food is to provide an **income tax credit** for lower-income households to offset the tax paid on food purchases. Currently five states—Hawaii, Idaho, Kansas, Oklahoma, and South Dakota—provide such a credit.[12] Although this approach reduces the sales tax's regressivity more effectively than a blanket exemption or a two-tiered rate structure, it has not found favor with most state legislatures because of the compliance cost to taxpayers and the lost income tax revenue for the state.

Tax base conformance Sales tax experts strongly recommend tax base conformance—that is, that the state and local bases be the same. Wherever local bases vary, border-city/county effects follow. Consumers have an incentive to shop in areas where particular transactions are exempt or taxed at lower rates, which reduces the tax's neutrality and thereby creates an economic drag on the local economy. Tax base conformance also simplifies compliance for retailers since only one set of rules governs the definition of taxable items as well as the auditing of tax returns and the verification of tax liability by the tax enforcement unit. But despite the advantages of conformance, the trend among states has been to increase local government discretion in the definition of their sales tax bases.

Local government dependence on the tax Expected revenue yield is of paramount concern to local managers and elected officials contemplating adoption of a sales tax. Revenue from a sales tax is income elastic; its yields grow or decline at rates greater than the growth or decline in the local economy. If the local economy is growing, revenue from the tax tends to increase in importance in a local government's revenue structure. The tax's elasticity becomes particularly problematic during recessions, however, when sales tax yields typically contract at a greater rate than the economy.

Because the tax is procyclical, local governments that depend heavily on it to finance their operating budgets risk incurring revenue shortfalls midyear and greater revenue volatility

Sales tax holidays

A tax relief measure, popular with taxpayers, is the sales tax holiday now used in seventeen states and the District of Columbia.[1] First introduced by New York in 1997, a sales tax holiday offers a temporary moratorium—usually two to four days long and usually in August—on state and usually local sales taxes most often for back-to-school items such as clothing and school supplies. A few states extend the temporary exemption to hurricane preparedness and hunting and fishing supplies. While the specifics vary among the states, the holiday has proven quite popular with legislators and consumers but unpopular with tax experts, who see it as a gimmick that reduces the tax's neutrality.

Part of the criticism arises because of the obvious inefficiencies that sales tax holidays introduce: a reduction in the tax's neutrality and an increase in its administrative complexity. From a local government's perspective, they represent further state-mandated erosion of the tax base and an unwelcome reduction in tax revenues. Local governments point out that while state legislatures fret about the revenue windfalls that local governments receive whenever the base is broadened, no such fretting seems to vex their deliberations when the base is narrowed—even temporarily—as in the case of sales tax holidays. Tax experts generally agree that sales tax holidays do not increase economic activity and thus do not increase sales tax yields. Rather, these holidays only spur consumers to shift their purchases to the tax-free days.[2]

The political reality remains that these temporary exemptions are popular with consumers who see them as a targeted relief for working families, particularly those with school-age children. In fact, it is one of the few tax relief measures targeted to this group, with most other measures favoring more politically active groups, such as senior citizens. These moratoriums are also popular with retailers who capitalize on the marketing opportunities from the temporary suspension of sales taxes on selected items.

1 Federation of Tax Administrators, "2018 State Sales Tax Holidays," August 9, 2018, https://www.taxadmin.org/2018-sales-tax-holidays.

2 Joseph Henchman and Scott Drenkard, "Sales Tax Holidays: Politically Expedient but Poor Tax Policy 2017," Tax Foundation Special Report no. 236 (July 2011), https://files.taxfoundation.org/20170725133940/Tax-Foundation-SR236.pdf.

from year to year. Managers in such communities will want to set aside a larger budget reserve to provide more continuity in service levels during economic slowdowns.

Budget issues and the local sales tax

Once a state legislature grants one or more levels of local government access to the local sales tax, policy makers must resolve several issues in the tax's design and implementation:

- Does the tax adversely affect local retail sales?
- Does the tax reduce the property tax burden, or does it merely encourage increased local government spending?
- Does the tax shift the overall tax burden away from business and onto households, which purchase most of the taxable items?
- How much of the tax, if any, should be exported to nonresident consumers and businesses?
- Should revenue from the tax be dedicated to funding particular services?

Effects on retail sales The most frequently expressed concern about a local sales tax is that it will hurt retail sales. This issue becomes especially significant when a local government has a range of rates to choose from and the proposed rate is higher than those in surrounding jurisdictions, creating a border-city/county effect.

Several studies suggest that the impact of rate differentials on a local economy increases as the difference in interjurisdictional tax rates increases, the driving distance to a lower tax jurisdiction decreases, and the cost of a good or service increases.[13] In other words, border-city/county effects occur whenever it is economically feasible for shoppers to travel to nearby lower-tax areas to purchase more costly items. Because differences in sales tax rates for large-ticket items, such as cars or major appliances, profoundly affect consumer behavior, several states exclude vehicle purchases—both new and used—from the sales tax base in order to increase the neutrality of the sales tax. For all other products and services, states should design legislation so that local rates are relatively uniform (varying by no more than 1 percent) and local adoption is widespread or, ideally, universal.

Tax rate differentials among local governments may also shift more consumers to the Internet to avoid local and state sales taxes. A recent study using eBay data found that for every 1-percent increase in the sales tax, online buyers reduced their purchases by 2 percent.[14] The study then analyzed the effect of state tax policies and found that "a one percentage point increase in a state's sales tax leads to a 3 to 6 percent decrease in online purchasing from home-state sellers."[15] The net effect is that sales tax differences do shift buyers to make purchases online and particularly to out-of-state sources.

Effects on the property tax and on government spending Although reducing the property tax is one common justification for adopting a local sales tax, some critics contend that the sales tax only increases local government spending. A study of Texas cities found that dependence on the sales tax has no effect on property tax burdens levied for operating purposes.[16] However, a study of Illinois municipalities found that those in nonmetropolitan areas in particular substituted increased revenue from their sales tax for the property tax.[17] Another study of the local-option sales tax available to Georgia counties resulted in a reduction in the property tax but also an increase in total spending.[18]

Impact on the distribution of tax burdens Another concern about the imposition of a local sales tax is that it shifts a greater share of the local tax burden onto households, especially renters, and reduces the burden borne by the business sector. While consumers perceive that they bear a major portion of state and local sales taxes, in fact most states impose the tax on a wide range of business purchases. One study on this issue found that, nationally, consumers' share of the sales tax was 59 percent, although state-by-state variations ranged from 28 percent in Hawaii to 89 percent in West Virginia, depending on the composition of a state's tax base and exemptions.[19] The remainder of the sales tax fell on business purchases.

However, the trend in the past two decades toward narrowing the sales tax base, especially by removing machinery, tools, and building materials, undoubtedly shifts a greater proportion of the sales tax to households. Even the portion paid by business may be shifted forward to consumers in the form of higher prices for finished goods and services. Firms in the same industry that incur the same tax burden can more easily shift that burden forward to the final buyer as a price increase. The concern that a local sales tax will increase the overall tax burden of households thus has some justification.

Exportability of the tax burden Exporting the sales tax to nonresident consumers—commuters, tourists, and nonlocal businesses—is one means of reducing the burden on local households. For example, local governments whose economies are based on recreational services or tourism can export a significant portion of their sales tax burden because consumer demand for their goods and services is inelastic; in other words, because tourists lack information on where to find the lowest prices, they typically pay higher prices than local residents. For this reason, Colorado resort cities such as Black Hawk, Crested Butte, Estes Park, Steamboat Springs, Telluride, and Vail levy the highest rates in the state: 4.0 to 5.5 percent. Utah authorizes an additional 1-percent levy for its resort cities, and Idaho limits local sales taxes to specific resort communities. Cities that have regional shopping centers or large retailers (Ikea, Nebraska Furniture) also export a greater portion of their sales tax to nonresidents, at least for the limited life of the retailer. A study of Fort Collins, Colorado, found that 30 percent of the sales tax revenue came from purchases by nonresident households and businesses.[20]

Where state law does not allow local governments to share sales tax revenue with each other, jurisdictions with sales tax authority have a strong incentive to pursue regional shopping centers that attract nonresident buyers. If they can export the tax burden to nonresident patrons, they can provide better public services without raising the cost to their residents. Local governments in some states try to lure mall developers by devoting a portion of the sales tax revenue to tax abatement incentives. But these "beggar-thy-neighbor" measures create sales tax winners and losers among local governments. The North Carolina approach, described in the next section, minimizes these economically costly maneuvers while preserving local autonomy and promoting interjurisdictional equity.

A study of county sales taxes in six states—Florida, Georgia, Indiana, Ohio, South Carolina, and Tennessee—offers a few useful insights into the implications of local sales tax policies for economic development.[21] First, the largest benefit in increased sales taxes for this sample of counties came from the relocation of construction firms. Second, the addition of jobs in the service, agricultural, and public utilities sectors also had a favorable impact on sales tax yields. However, virtually no tax benefits were derived from the relocation of manufacturing firms or the preservation of military bases, which, the study's authors speculate, was because of the extensive exemptions and abatements afforded manufacturers and their finished goods generally being sold in markets outside the local community. The study also found that commuters—both those working in the county but living outside (in-commuters) and those living in the county but working outside (out-commuters)—had significant but inverse effects on sales tax yields. For this sample of counties, in-commuters added an average of $2 to county sales tax receipts for every $1 lost by out-commuters. Urban counties experienced this impact more than rural ones.

Dedicated sales taxes The proliferation of local sales tax authority has been accompanied by more widespread dedication of tax revenues to particular purposes. The chronology of Ohio's county sales tax is illustrative. As is typical, the initial authorization in 1987 imposed no restrictions on the use of the revenue. Then in 1993, the legislature expanded county powers to levy an additional incremental tax with revenues earmarked for detention facilities. Sports facilities were added in 1995, and acquisition of agricultural easements was added in 2001.[22] The use of dedicated sales taxes for law enforcement/crime control is particularly popular among local governments in Illinois, Louisiana, Missouri, Ohio, and Texas.

In 1994, Allegheny County and Philadelphia, Pennsylvania, were granted authority to become the first—and thus far the only—local governments in Pennsylvania to levy a local 1-percent sales tax, piggybacked onto the state's sales tax. Allegheny County's revenue is dedicated to the preservation of regional assets: libraries, parks, zoos, sports arenas, museums, and performing arts facilities.[23] But while legislative dedication of revenue increases political support for rate increases, it complicates local budgeting. Because of the volatility of the tax, services benefiting from the dedication experience fluctuations in funding that typically vary inversely with their expenditure needs.

Coordination of local sales tax rates Locally levied general sales taxes assume many forms, particularly in terms of their coordination with a state sales tax (Figure 4–1). Five states—Alaska, Delaware, Montana, New Hampshire, and Oregon—levy no statewide sales tax. Alaska is unique within this group in permitting its boroughs and cities to levy a local general sales tax while not imposing a tax at the state level.

States that authorize local sales taxes usually make their adoption optional, and many provide a range of rates from which the local governments may choose; this creates the potential for significant disparities in interjurisdictional revenue capacities. A further complication occurs when more than one overlapping level of local government levies a sales tax. Within a city's borders, if the city, county (or parish), and transit authority all collect a sales tax, the three overlapping tax rates can have a significant impact on consumer behavior.[24] States have resolved interlocal rate disparities and overlapping tax rates in a number of different ways (Figure 4–2).

At one extreme is the approach used by North Carolina, where all one hundred counties levy a 2.00- or 2.25-percent state-mandated tax (four urban counties add a 0.50-percent tax for transit services)[25] but share it with their incorporated cities and, in a few cases, their transit authorities. Fifty-three counties share sales tax revenues with cities on a per capita basis, and the other forty-seven do so on a pro rata share of the property taxes levied. This approach reduces intercity competition for retail business because the sales tax revenue is distributed countywide rather than to the city where the sale occurred—a tax base–sharing plan at the county level. The North Carolina approach also effectively eliminates in-state border city and county effects by creating a nearly uniform tax rate for all taxing jurisdictions.

Several states resolve the problem of rate overlap by restricting the tax to only county or municipal governments. In Nebraska and South Dakota, the two states where only cities levy the tax, households and businesses have an incentive to shop in or relocate to unincorporated areas. However, this is not a serious problem where rates are kept low.

California uses still another approach to overcoming overlap while promoting uniformity in local rates. Cities may adopt a rate of up to 1 percent, which is credited against the county's rate of 1.25 percent. Revenue from the unused portion of the county rate within the city limits and from the entire 1.25-percent rate in unincorporated areas goes to the county's general fund. All counties and most of the cities have adopted the tax, making the local rate nearly uniform statewide. The exception occurs in areas served by a transit district, which may levy an additional 0.5 percent rate.[26] Tennessee uses a similar approach, but the county rate takes

Figure 4–2 Strategies for interlocal coordination of sales tax rates

Minimum overlap ←——→ **Maximum overlap**

Only counties levy tax, but cities receive a share of revenue	Only one level is given access, with no sharing of revenue	City rate takes precedence over county rate within city's boundaries	County rate takes precedence over city rate	Local rates are stacked on top of each other
North Carolina	South Dakota (cities) Wisconsin (counties)	California	Tennessee	Louisiana Texas

precedence over the municipal rate within city corporate limits, and the county redistributes a portion of the revenue back to cities according to the point-of-sale.

The least coordination occurs in states such as Texas and Louisiana, where local rates are stacked on top of each other, with a maximum combined rate usually imposed by state law. For example, Louisiana municipalities may generally levy a rate of up to 2.5 percent. Parishes and school districts may levy a combined tax of 6 percent within city borders, but the city rate takes precedence. This approach creates border-city effects that skew business development, and it complicates tax compliance for vendors with multiple outlets, who must keep records on the various tax rates levied in each jurisdiction.

Considerable variation exists in the way that states resolve the problem of tax rate overlap. North Carolina's approach offers the most benefits, including universal participation by local governments, more equitable distribution of sales tax revenue, and reduced interlocal rivalry for retail business.

Local discretion in sales tax administration

In granting local governments access to a sales tax, state legislatures must address three issues concerning the adoption and collection of the tax:

- How much discretion should local governments have in choosing a tax rate?
- Should tax liability be based on the point-of-sale or the point-of-delivery?
- Should the state collect and enforce the local tax?

Setting of tax rates Most states give their local governments a range of tax rates from which they may choose and then limit the combined overlapping rate of all local governments. For example, Nebraska limits the total state-city rate to 7.5 percent, with 5.5 percent claimed by the state and the remainder available to cities in 0.5 percent increments.[27] Arkansas imposes a somewhat different cap: it limits city and county levies to $2,500 per transaction.[28] Invoices over $2,500 are eligible for a refund for the local portion of the sales tax, but purchasers must file for the rebate with the state, which collects the tax on behalf of local governments. Florida limits the optional county tax of up to 2 percent to the first $5,000 of a single sale.

Alabama, Arizona, Arkansas, and Louisiana have the highest combined state-local rates, each exceeding 12 percent.[29] When only local rates are considered, combined *local* tax rates generally cluster around 2 to 3 percent, although there are several notable exceptions. For example, combined local rates in Alabama range as high as 8.5 percent and in Colorado up to 8.3 percent. Local governments in Alaska, Louisiana, Missouri, and Oklahoma follow with maximum combined local rates of more than 6 percent. In the remaining states, maximum local rates are substantially less.

Tax liability If sales tax revenue is not redistributed countywide on a basis like that used by North Carolina, the state legislature must determine whether sales tax receipts are credited to the jurisdiction where the sale occurred or to the jurisdiction where delivery is made. The benefits of the latter approach are that (1) taxpayers have no incentive to shop in lower-tax jurisdictions and (2) communities that have little or no commercial activity receive a share of the revenue. However, this approach greatly complicates tax compliance for retailers, who must maintain records on taxpayer residency, and it provides significant opportunities for tax evasion by taxpayers who claim residency in lower-tax areas. Furthermore, it complicates the auditing of tax returns and increases the chances of allocating revenue to the wrong jurisdiction. Because of these disadvantages, most all states now use the point-of-sale to establish tax liability.

State collection and enforcement A final set of issues concerns the collection, distribution, and enforcement of the local tax. Most states require state administration of the local sales tax. A few states, such as Arizona, Colorado, and Minnesota, allow local governments to choose state collection or administer the tax themselves. Most smaller governments opt for state administration by piggybacking their tax onto the state's. Larger local governments and those with home rule powers tend to administer their own tax. Arizona and Colorado encourage state collection and enforcement by providing their services free to local governments, but Colorado collects for only non–home rule cities and most counties.[30]

Piggybacking collection and enforcement of the local tax onto the state's tax is more cost-efficient than local administration. State collection makes it unnecessary for local governments to staff their own collection offices. It also simplifies compliance for vendors, who need to complete only one tax return.

Consumption taxes: Excise taxes

Excise, or selective sales, taxes are levies on specific products or services at rates specific to each type of taxable transaction. Although revenue yields from excise taxes trail those of the general sales tax, excise taxes are in more widespread use among local governments. Counties or cities in all states derive revenue from at least one type of excise tax.[31] Unlike the general sales tax, excise taxes are usually locally administered.

The legal authority for each local excise tax is usually state legislation separate from that for the general sales tax. In some cases, home rule powers provide the legal basis for an excise tax, especially in states such as Colorado and Illinois, where local governments have broad discretion under their home rule statutes. Local governments in Alabama and South Carolina derive their authority to levy utility taxes from their business licensing powers, and municipalities in Oklahoma rely on their general taxing powers to levy certain excise taxes.[32] Local governments usually do not obtain voter approval before adopting an excise tax. Among the notable exceptions are the transportation and road taxes levied by Arizona's counties[33] and the optional motor fuels tax levied by Florida's counties.[34]

Excise taxes lack the equity and neutrality features that characterize good tax policy. Except for those targeted to luxury goods, excise taxes are usually regressive, falling more heavily on those citizens who are less able to pay. On the other hand, a number of benefits-based excise taxes work like prices, making them more equitable to the extent that users who benefit from the public service bear a pro rata share of the cost of the service. Taxes on motor fuels that are earmarked for highway and street construction are an example of this type of benefits-received levy.

Moreover, because they are controlled locally, excise taxes are more likely than general sales taxes to create border-city/county effects. However, since they tend to fall on products

Figure 4–3 Types of excise tax bases

Type of tax	Examples (basis for determining liability)
Benefits-based	Hotel/motel occupancy *(ad valorem)*; motor fuels *(in rem)*
Sumptuary	Tobacco *(in rem)*; alcoholic beverages *(in rem)*; mixed drinks *(ad valorem)*
Privilege	Utility franchise tax *(ad valorem)*; occupation privilege tax *(in rem)*

and services with few substitutes or with inelastic demand, excise taxes have less adverse impact on the local economy. As a rule, these taxes persist because of their political appeal and the relative ease with which they can be administered locally, and not because of their economic benefits.

Classifying excise taxes

Excise taxes are of three types: benefits based, sumptuary, and privilege (see Figure 4–3). Benefits-based taxes recover at least part of the cost of a public service from those who benefit from it. These taxes include room taxes on hotel/motel occupancy, levies on gasoline and other motor fuels, and, to some extent, gross receipts taxes (or street rental fees) on utilities.

Sumptuary taxes, also known as sin taxes, are levied in part on the assumption they discourage consumption of certain classes of goods, such as alcohol or cigarettes, by rendering their cost prohibitive for many consumers. Taxes on gasoline and diesel fuel, although benefits based, also qualify as sumptuary taxes because they effectively raise the price of these fuels and thus reduce consumption over the long term.

Privilege taxes are levied on the privilege of conducting a particular type of business or transaction. Examples include occupational privilege taxes levied on particular professions or on individual employees. Other privilege taxes include levies on admissions, restaurant meals, deed transfers, and bank franchises. Even taxes on utilities constitute a levy on the privilege of having an exclusive franchise to provide service to local residents.

Sumptuary taxes, such as tobacco taxes, are usually levied on a per unit (*in rem*) basis, although **mixed drinks taxes** are based on the selling price (*ad valorem*). Some benefits-based taxes, such as those on hotel/motel occupancy, are levied as a percentage of the value (*ad valorem*) of the service, whereas gasoline taxes are levied on a per gallon basis. Finally, the tax base for excise taxes on privileges, such as those on utility franchises and entertainment, tend to be levied on gross receipts, such as total charges for cable service; however, occupation privilege taxes are a head tax, meaning that they are levied at a flat amount on the employee.

The role of excise taxes in local budgets

Like the discussion of the general sales tax above, this discussion is limited to locally levied excise taxes and excludes the dedication of a portion of state excise tax receipts to local governments. Many of the questions discussed in the preceding section on the general sales tax resurface with excise taxes, including

- What is the revenue potential of each?
- What effect do excise taxes have on the local economy?
- Which types of excise taxes are best for local governments?

Because of the variety of excise taxes levied by local governments and the difficulty in obtaining information on their use, few studies have looked into their role in local government. However, some trends can be discerned from data produced by the Census Bureau:

- Both cities and counties have moderately increased their dependence on the revenue from excise taxes (Table 4-1), although these taxes represent a relatively modest source of revenue in the aggregate.
- Large urban cities and resort communities make the greatest use of excise taxes. Both use excise taxes selectively to export their tax burden.
- The largest source of excise tax revenue for municipalities is the gross receipts tax on utilities. Counties make comparatively greater use of sumptuary taxes, although revenue from these taxes has declined in importance for both cities and counties.

- Local governments that make greater use of excise taxes with broader bases, such as gross receipts taxes on utilities, depend more heavily on excise tax revenue.

Like most large cities in the United States, Chicago makes extensive use of excise taxes. The twenty-nine excise taxes it levies, as listed on the city's website, include a 9-percent amusement tax on ticketed events, a payroll tax on employers of $2.00 per employee per month, and a 9-percent tax on soft drink syrup sales.[35] Also included on the list are a bottled water tax, liquor tax, parking tax, real property transfer tax, and restaurant tax, which collectively account for more than 30 percent of the city's total revenue.

The remaining sections consider specific excise taxes, giving particular attention to their desirability as revenue sources.

Gross receipts taxes on utilities Because they have a broader base than other excise taxes, gross receipts taxes on utility companies offer the greatest revenue potential for cities and towns and are in very common use. Many of these taxes trace their origins to the nineteenth century, when utility providers were regulated by city governments and before regulatory oversight was consolidated at the state level in public utility commissions.

Most states give cities the power to regulate the use of their streets, including access to public rights-of-way. Local governments impose a gross receipts tax, or street rental fee, on utilities as compensation for the utilities using those rights-of-way to locate their service lines. Often the tax is part of a broader contractual agreement granting a utility company an exclusive franchise to provide service to consumers in the jurisdiction, and it represents compensation for the cost of administering the franchise. Taxes are usually fixed at a percentage of the utility's gross receipts, although charges are sometimes based on a fixed annual fee, a percentage of the utility's net earnings or dividends declared, the number of miles (or feet) of street used, the number of utility poles erected, or the number of units of service sold.

In addition to the more conventional taxes on utility providers—such as providers of natural gas, electricity, telephone, water, and cable television services—gross receipts taxes are occasionally imposed on taxicab companies, private solid-waste collection services, and fiber-optic telephone service. Several municipalities have agreements with fiber-optic firms for access to the city's rights-of-way. Usually the fee is specified on a per foot basis, ranging from less than a dollar to significantly higher rates in more congested urban centers. Where permitted by state law, local governments should charge all telecommunications providers for the use of public rights-of-way or for the privilege of holding an exclusive franchise to provide service to local consumers.

The gross receipts tax is similar to the general sales tax in several ways. First, state and local regulatory bodies usually permit utility companies to pass the cost of such taxes forward to consumers. Thus, the tax is regressive, falling more heavily on lower-income households because they spend a greater proportion of their income on utility services. Second, revenue from the tax may be responsive to cycles in the local economy, making local budgets vulnerable to midyear revenue shortfalls. As is the case with the general sales tax, the stability of revenue yields depends on the composition of the gross receipts tax base; yields for local governments with a larger proportion of residential utility customers tend to be more stable.

Whenever utility taxes are imposed, local government managers and legislators must resolve three issues:

- Which receipts of the utility company are included in the tax base?
- What tax rate fairly compensates the local government for the utility's use of public rights-of-way or the privilege of holding an exclusive franchise?

- What conditions should be included in the contract or ordinance to ensure more effective collection and compliance with the tax?

Hotel and motel occupancy taxes Although revenue from the occupancy tax on hotel and motel rooms is considerably less than that produced by gross receipts taxes on public utilities, lodging taxes have become much more commonplace among local governments. The occupancy excise tax, which is borne almost entirely by nonresidents, exports the local tax burden. Virtually all states levy a separate excise tax or extend their sales tax to hotel lodging charges (but usually not to other hotel services), and according to hotel and motel industry sources, most of the largest U.S. cities also levy a separate tax on hotel lodging.[36] Most states authorize their local governments to piggyback it onto the state's tax. The combined rates average about 14 percent of the cost of the hotel or motel room, including reservations made through Airbnb.[37]

The tax is often shared with local convention and visitors' bureaus as a reinvestment in promoting tourism and conventions. While the general sales tax base may include the consideration paid for a hotel or motel room, an occupancy or room tax is an *additional* levy imposed in part to compensate the local government for expanded services, such as police and fire protection and highway and public transit capacity, needed to meet weekend or peak convention demand; in this sense, occupancy taxes are benefits based. The tax revenue may also be dedicated for historic preservation, the visual and performing arts, and sports stadiums and leisure services.

With the advent of online booking of motel and hotel rooms through third-party vendors such as Expedia.com and Priceline.com, a messy legal issue has arisen over whether the tax should be based on the wholesale rate that the online travel companies pay for the room or the retail rate that the companies charge hotel guests. State courts have generally ruled against states and cities, thereby limiting the tax to the wholesale cost of the room.[38]

State law usually specifies the maximum rate that local governments can impose. Combined state and local rates typically fall between 8 percent and 18 percent, with the local share usually at least half of the levy.[39] Some communities impose a complex array of overlapping taxes. For example, Las Vegas, Nevada, levies a 13.38-percent combined local tax rate, which is divided among the Convention and Visitors Bureau, the city of Las Vegas, Clark County transit, Clark County schools, and a new levy for construction of the NFL stadium for the Raiders. States prone to natural disasters typically have special provisions that allow the governor or a local official to suspend liability for the tax during the response phase as a way to support first responders and other relief workers.

When considering adopting or changing the tax, local government managers and legislators should consider the following questions:

- Does the occupancy tax adversely affect businesses dependent on tourism, especially hotels and motels?
- What effect does the tax have on local government budgets?
- Who should administer the tax?

Motor fuels taxes Local taxes on gasoline and other petroleum products are authorized in at least fifteen states but are levied in only nine: Alabama, Florida, Hawaii, Illinois (Chicago and Cook County only), Nevada, Oregon, South Dakota, Tennessee, and Virginia.[40] In all these states, the per gallon tax is levied at the county level with some formula for sharing revenue or the tax rate with cities as a way to minimize border-city effects. In addition, Virginia requires a 2.1-percent excise tax in counties and cities that participate in a regional transit district—one of the few cases of a local *ad valorem* tax on motor fuels.

Not only do counties make more widespread use of this tax but they also generally depend more heavily on it than do municipalities. According to the 2012 Census of Government Finances, counties derived about $933 million from motor fuels taxes compared with $379 million for cities, with Cook County, Illinois, and counties in Florida deriving the most.[41] Because these taxes are levied on a per gallon basis, their revenue yields generally decline in relative importance because they fail to keep pace with growth in the local economy. As a result, researchers have explored alternative tax strategies, including taxes or fees based on the vehicle miles traveled, taxes or fees based on the weight and age of vehicles, and higher tolls during peak periods (congestion pricing).[42]

Local motor fuels taxes are earmarked either for street and bridge maintenance or for public transit.[43] In either case, the benefits-received aspect is obvious: vehicle operators who purchase the fuel benefit from the locally maintained streets and highways, from the reduced congestion on highways during rush hour, and from the reduced need to expand highway capacity to meet peak demand. Chicago levies a motor fuels tax of $0.05 per gallon in its jurisdiction, and Cook County levies a $0.06 tax per gallon in its jurisdiction, and both use the revenue for streets and bridges.

Florida counties are the nation's greatest local users of the tax, deriving almost $657 million annually from it.[44] They may, with voter approval, impose a tax of 1 cent per gallon on all fuel to be dedicated for street improvements or public transit; this tax is now levied in two-thirds of the counties, which are required by Florida law to establish interlocal agreements to share fuel tax revenue with their cities.

The primary deterrent to making greater use of a local option fuels tax is the heavy use of the tax made by state and federal governments. Some legislators contend that granting local governments access to the tax will preempt state efforts to impose future rate increases. Furthermore, because most states already share a portion of their fuels tax revenue with municipalities and counties, some state legislators believe that a local option fuels tax is unnecessary. In the case of public transit subsidies, a motor fuels tax makes more sense on a benefits basis than a general sales tax, although the revenue yield is substantially less.

If a local fuels tax is under consideration, managers and state and local lawmakers must resolve the following issues:

- Will the tax adversely affect motor fuels sales in the jurisdiction?
- If both city and county governments levy the tax, how should the revenue collected within the city be allocated between the two levels of government?
- If the tax is adopted, should the state administer the local portion of the tax?

Other sumptuary taxes Six states permit a local levy on cigarette and tobacco sales, and sixteen states permit local taxes on alcoholic beverage sales, piggybacked onto the state's tax. Of these two sumptuary taxes, alcoholic beverage taxes produce more revenue.[45] Chicago and Cook County in Illinois along with cities and counties in Alabama, Missouri, Tennessee, and Virginia levy an excise tax on tobacco products. The highest local rate is levied by New York City: $1.50 per pack. Local levies are in addition to state (average of $1.60 per pack)[46] and federal ($1.01 per pack) excise taxes. Although the evidence is not consistent, cigarette taxes, in general, reduce tobacco consumption especially among teenagers, and discourage non-smokers from consuming tobacco, one of the purposes often cited for adopting a sumptuary tax on tobacco.[47]

Most governments still use tax stamps to certify payment and to prevent bootlegging of tobacco products from tax-exempt sources, such as Native American jurisdictions. One study from 2000 found that commercial smuggling accounted for 3 to 4 percent of sales, a percentage that has likely increased as tobacco taxes have increased and web-based sales have become more common.[48]

Of the sixteen states with local taxes on alcohol products, the heaviest use is made by cities and counties in southern states—Alabama, Georgia, North Carolina, and Tennessee. Chicago, Cook County, and New York City also generate worthwhile amounts of revenue from their alcoholic beverage taxes. As with tobacco, excise taxes on packaged alcohol create significant border-city/state effects.[49] For example, New Hampshire, one of seventeen states that sell wine and spirits through state-owned liquor stores, has long benefited from selling to consumers in bordering states and Canada; New Hampshire has no general sales tax or excise tax on alcohol, although it generates a handsome profit through its state stores.

A variation on the more traditional beverage tax, which is levied on a per unit or liquid volume basis, is an *ad valorem* mixed drinks tax levied on the retail value of drinks. For example, cities and counties in Texas levy a local-option mixed drinks tax that is piggybacked onto the state tax, with a combined rate of 14.95 percent of the retail value of the drink. The revenue is divided roughly two-thirds to the city and county in which the sale occurred and one-third to the state. Because alcohol consumption generally grows faster than the economy, so too does revenue from the beverage tax, providing local governments with a small but significant source of income. In Texas revenue yield from the tax has increased almost without interruption since its inception in 1971 owing to the *ad valorem* basis of the tax.

The past decade has seen a rapid growth in legalization and taxation of marijuana consumption. California's legalization of marijuana consumption for medicinal use in 1996 opened the door to broader availability by states in defiance of the federal government's prohibition. In 2012, Colorado and Washington became the first states to legalize marijuana use for leisure purposes. As of 2018, nine states and Washington, D.C. had legalized "weed" with more state legislatures discussing the possibility.

Colorado levies its 2.9-percent general sales tax only on medical consumption of marijuana. In the case of recreational marijuana consumption, however, two state taxes apply: a 15-percent excise tax on the producers of marijuana and a 15-percent retail sales tax on the final consumer, with 90 percent of the latter tax retained by the state and 10 percent of the revenue shared with local governments.[50] Additionally, local general sales taxes are added to the levy along with local excise taxes such as the 3.5-percent levy imposed by the city of Denver. Some evidence exists that the higher cost from multiple layers of taxes has not reduced the black market for weed.[51]

In terms of the budget impact from marijuana taxes, like all other excise taxes, revenue from the marijuana tax increases state and local revenues modestly, but is not a major revenue producer. In Colorado, revenue has steadily grown each year since FY 2015, the first full year the tax was collected. Marijuana revenue has grown from 1.3 to about 2.4 percent of the state's general fund revenue. Washington's experience is similar, with revenues totaling about 1.2 percent of the state's general fund.

Privilege and other excise taxes Local governments levy a host of other excise taxes, many of which are holdovers from the eighteenth and nineteenth centuries. Some of the more frequently used taxes include an admissions (or ticket) tax, a business gross receipts tax, an occupation privilege tax, a bank franchise tax, a parking tax, a deed transfer tax, and a bingo tax. For most local governments, these taxes represent minor sources of revenue with comparatively high administrative costs. The bank franchise tax is usually levied in lieu of a property tax on a bank's intangible assets, including federal securities, which are exempt from state and local taxation.

Local taxation of nonresident professional athletes' earnings

In recent years, state and local governments have begun extending their wage and personal income taxes to nonresident professional athletes. These so-called jock taxes occur because athletes earn a pro rata share of their income when they play in the taxing jurisdiction. Philadelphia, for example, extends its nonresident wage tax of 3.465 percent to football, basketball, baseball, and hockey players for the portion of time they work in one of the city's stadiums or arenas. Players have a taxable nexus for the time they are playing and earning income in the city. At least a half dozen cities now impose their income tax on athletes, and twenty states extend their state income tax to professional athletes.

Several intergovernmental issues arise because of the jock tax, which is usually extended to other high-dollar wage earners, including musicians and actors. Not all states or local governments give a credit for taxes already paid on that income, creating a double tax on those earnings. The jock tax also imposes significant compliance expenses on nonresident athletes, who must complete a tax return for each city and state in which they play. And it gives rise to the potential for discriminatory taxation. For example, Alberta, Canada, imposes an extra 2.5-percent income tax on top of its 10-percent tax on all resident players of its two hockey teams, but it does not tax visiting players.

Source: Most of this information is from David K. Hoffman and Scott A. Hodge, "Nonresident State and Local Income Taxes in the United States: The Continuing Spread of 'Jock Taxes,'" Tax Foundation Special Report no. 130 (July 2004), taxfoundation.org/sites/taxfoundation.org/files/docs/fe9737a23595921c41616df11dc3cd48.pdf.

Deed or real estate transfer taxes are levied by local governments in at least seventeen states, mostly in the northeast and upper Midwest, usually at a fixed percentage of the property's sale price.[52] Pennsylvania authorizes its cities, townships, and boroughs to levy a 0.5-percent tax; school districts and the state also levy the tax.

Although admissions taxes are in fairly wide use by older cities, their revenue significance is usually negligible. Many central cities in metropolitan areas levy the tax as a way of exporting their tax burden to nonresidents, especially suburbanites. A study of the 5-percent tax in Boulder, Colorado, on all public events, including movies, concerts, and theatrical performances, concluded that the tax was almost certainly shifted forward to consumers as a higher ticket price.[53] The actual shifting depends on the availability of substitutes that are not taxed and on consumers' elasticity of demand for the event.

Occasionally cities test the viability of a new excise tax as a way to quickly raise modest amounts of revenue. Recent examples include Philadelphia's soda tax, which is dedicated to pre-K and community schools as well as renovations to parks, libraries, and recreation centers. But the city has had to scale back spending as revenue yields from the tax failed to meet expectations. In 2016, voters in Boulder, Colorado, approved a 2 cents per ounce tax on sugar-sweetened beverages with the revenue used to promote healthy lifestyles, general wellness, and prevention of chronic diseases such as diabetes. Revenue from the tax, although modest, exceeded expectations and, under the state's Taxpayer Bill of Rights (TABOR), the city had to seek voter approval to retain the excess tax revenue, which was approved. In 2018, Seattle city government adopted a head tax on employees that was dedicated to providing affordable housing and services for the homeless, but after only one month, the city council repealed the tax because of the negative publicity on the city's business environment. Such nuisance taxes have high administrative costs, adversely affect economic development, and produce relatively minor amounts of revenue.

Income-based taxes

As with sales and excise taxes, local income taxes come in many varieties, the variations largely emanating from how the tax base is defined and the tax rates are applied. Whatever their form, however, local income taxes have never achieved the same political acceptance as general sales and excise taxes.

The income tax's role in local budgets

Many of the same policy issues that local government leaders encounter with a sales tax reappear with an income tax. Yet the local income tax has much less public support. Local governments in only six states—Indiana, Kentucky, Maryland, Michigan, Ohio, and Pennsylvania—make broad use of the tax,[54] and except for Iowa, Missouri, and Oregon, only states east of the Mississippi River use variations of it. Iowa authorizes school districts to levy a supplemental tax on the state income tax. Table 4–2 summarizes the practices in those states that make the heaviest use of local income taxes.

The most extensive use of local income taxes is in Pennsylvania, where most cities, boroughs, and townships levy a flat-rate tax on gross income from wages and the net profits of unincorporated businesses. In addition, school districts in the commonwealth levy a separate tax on earnings. Most municipalities in Ohio also levy the tax. Income taxes are levied by county governments in only three states: Indiana, Kentucky, and Maryland. Indiana became the last state to authorize it, giving counties the option to levy the local income tax in exchange for freezing their property tax *levies* (not to be confused with their property tax *rates*). Universal adoption exists in Maryland, where counties and the independent city of Baltimore are required by state law to levy the tax and in Indiana where all counties have adopted the optional income tax.[55]

One of the strengths of an income tax is its capacity to extend the tax reach of a city to commuters who work in the city but otherwise bear no cost for financing city services. As noted in Table 4–2, state laws vary on how they treat nonresident and commuter income. The accompanying sidebar discusses the special case of professional athletes' earnings.

The deduction for state and local sales or income taxes from federal income tax liability complicates the economics of these local tax options. Federal tax itemizers are currently limited to deducting up to $10,000 for state and local income, sales, and property taxes. The rationale for the federal deduction is to reduce the occurrence of double taxation—taxing the same income more than once. Higher-income individuals benefit the most from this itemized deduction because they are in higher marginal tax brackets. The federal deduction effectively lowers the cost of these state and local taxes.

The local income tax base

The local income tax is most easily distinguished from its state and federal counterparts by its generally narrower tax base. Figure 4–4 shows the different types of income potentially subject to taxation, and Table 4–2 shows the tax bases actually used by local governments in the six states granting municipalities and counties authority to levy the tax. As with other taxes, the same relationship holds:

Tax base x tax rate = tax liability.

The legal definition of the income tax base affects liability for the tax, which affects revenue yield (the sum of all liabilities). The broader the tax base, the lower the tax rate needed to produce a given level of revenue.

Table 4-2 States making the greatest use of local income taxes

State	Range in tax rates (%)	Most common rate (%)	Nonresident/ commuter rate (%)	Tax base	Administration
Indiana[a]					
Counties	0.35–3.38	1.50	Same	PI, NP	State
Kentucky[b]					
Counties	0.008–2.25	1.00	Same	Varies	Local
Cities	0.075–2.50	1.00	Same	Varies	Local
Maryland[c]					
Counties	1.75–3.20	3.20	None	PI, NP	State
Baltimore	3.20		None	PI, NP	State
Michigan[d]					
Municipalities	1.00–2.00	1.00	½ residential	PI, NP, CI	Local
Detroit	2.40		½ residential	PI, NP, CI	Local
Ohio[e]					
Municipalities	0.40–3.00	1.00	Same	EI, NP, CI	Local
Cincinnati	2.10		2.10	EI, NP, CI	Local
Cleveland	2.50		2.50	EI, NP, CI	Local
Pennsylvania[f]					
Municipalities	0.50–1.25	0.50	None	EI, NP	Local
Pittsburgh	1.00[g]		None	EI, NP	Local
Philadelphia	3.89[h]		3.465	EI, NP, CI[i]	Local

Sources: Websites of local revenue departments and telephone interviews with state officials.

Notes: EI—earned income; PI—personal income; NP—net profits; CI—corporate income.

a Counties have exclusive authority to levy an income tax. County may adjust rates annually. Liability determined by residence as of January 1 of each year.

b Kentucky cities and counties, at their choosing, tax wages, net profits, gross profits, or some combination. A few choose to tax wages at a separate rate from net profits, and one city, Caneyville, levies its occupational tax at the rate of $1 per week worked (www.kyola.org).

c Baltimore is an independent city; Baltimore County has no jurisdiction within the city.

d Detroit levies a tax of 1.0% on all corporate net income apportionable to the city, regardless of whether the corporation has an office or place of business in the city. Financial institutions and insurance companies are exempt from the tax.

e Voter approval is required on any tax over 1%.

f Currently, 50 cities, 833 boroughs, and 1,262 townships levy a tax on wages and on net profits of unincorporated businesses. School districts levy a separate tax on this income.

g Pittsburgh also levies a 2% wage tax for its school district. Nonresidents of Pennsylvania also pay the 1% city tax but not the school tax.

h This rate includes funding for the city of Philadelphia schools and, for school purposes, extends to residents' unearned income.

i Philadelphia also levies a 6.41% tax on net income or 0.1415% on gross receipts tax on all business activity in the city.

Earned and proprietary income States that authorized the income tax early on, most notably Pennsylvania, limited the local tax base to earned and proprietary income because of the relative ease of collecting the tax from employers (Figure 4–5). If the tax is based on gross income (no deductions or exemptions) and is withheld by the employer, wage earners usually do not file a tax return with the local government.

Figure 4-4 Types of income

Personal[a]	**Business**
Earned (EI)	Proprietary[b]
Wages	Net profits (NP)
Salaries	Gross income
Tips	
Commissions	Corporate (CI)
	Net income
Unearned (UI)	
Interest	
Dividents	
Capital gains	
Rent	
Royalties	
Inheritances	
Gifts[c]	

a Personal income is the sum of earned and unearned sources.
b Unincorporated businesses and professions.
c Normally taxed separately and not included in the income tax base.

The significance of the income tax in a local government's revenue structure depends on the breadth of the tax base. For example, local governments in Indiana, Maryland, and Michigan tax the personal income (earned and unearned) of individuals and the net profits of unincorporated businesses. In general, these governments experience more rapid growth in income tax revenue than do those with more narrowly based earned income taxes, such as in Ohio and Pennsylvania. This is primarily because components of the tax base change in value at different rates, and data from the Internal Revenue Service (IRS) indicate that the greatest rate of growth occurs with **unearned income** (interest, dividends, and realized capital gains).

Personal income Although an income tax limited to earned income is less costly to collect and enforce, modern techniques of tax administration, especially the sharing of tax information between state and local revenue departments and the IRS, now make taxation of personal income administratively feasible. Consequently, states that have adopted the income tax somewhat recently—most notably, Maryland—define the tax base more broadly to include both earned and unearned income. Since higher-income individuals receive a greater portion

Figure 4-5 Income tax bases used by local governments

Narrowest tax base				**Broadest tax base**
Earned only	Earned and proprietary	Personal and proprietary	Earned, proprietary, and corporate	Personal, proprietary, and corporate
Alabama	Ohio Pennsylvania	Indiana Maryland	Philadelphia Ohio	Michigan New York City

of their income from unearned sources, excluding this income places a greater portion of the tax burden on wage earners in the lower- and middle-income brackets. A broad-based tax on personal income distributes the tax burden more evenly across all income categories and is more equitable on the ability-to-pay basis. All versions of the income tax, other than payroll taxes, include the net profits of unincorporated businesses in their tax bases (Figure 4–5).

Gross income Locally administered income taxes differ from their state and federal counterparts in still another way: most are levied on gross income with no exemptions, deductions, or credits, which facilitates local collection and enforcement of the tax. Including adjustments to gross income increases the complexity and cost of administering the tax, especially if locally administered. On the other hand, itemized deductions for certain expenses and exemptions for dependents generally increase the tax's progressivity by reducing the effective tax burden on lower- and middle-income households.

Piggybacking the local tax onto the state's income tax is a cost-effective approach to integrating such adjustments into the local tax. For example, the Maryland Department of Revenue collects the counties' taxes along with the state liability. The local share is remitted to the taxpayers' counties of residence. This approach reduces taxpayer compliance costs because only one tax return is filed. It also increases the equity of the local tax because local adjustments to gross income are the same as the state's. On the down side, state administration makes the state tax liability appear larger because taxpayers may not distinguish between the state portion and the local portion.

Payroll taxes Social security taxes are the most familiar example of a payroll tax where the employer and employee pay a matching percentage (currently 7.65 percent) of wages. Interest at the state level in payroll taxes has resurfaced as a result of Nevada's 2003 adoption of a modified business tax, which is currently at 1.475 percent of an employer's payroll less the cost of employer-paid health benefits. Several local governments have levied such a tax for a number of years, but Nevada is the first state to do so. The most widespread use of the payroll tax is in Alabama, where twenty cities levy a municipal occupation tax ranging from 0.50 to 2.0 percent of an employer's payroll. Generally, liability for payroll taxes falls on the employer.

Because they usually have no deductions or other adjustments, payroll taxes can be particularly onerous on smaller businesses that have narrow profit margins, operate in a highly competitive environment, and depend on highly skilled labor—for example, computer software developers. To accommodate such entrepreneurs, some local governments exempt a portion of the payroll from taxation.

While employers are generally liable for the payroll tax, the tax burden is likely shifted to employees as lower wages, particularly in industries employing lower-skilled workers. However, this may not be true in businesses where the demand for workers is more competitive. In general, the tax does not rate well on horizontal or vertical equity, and it likely has a negative impact on economic growth in the long term, particularly in sectors that rely on highly skilled, higher-cost employees, such as those in engineering and technology development.

Local government dependence on the income tax

Of paramount interest to local government leaders is the revenue potential of a new tax or fee. Revenue yields from local income taxes have shown modest increases for counties (Table 4–1) but have declined overall for cities. In those few states where counties do levy the tax, however, it represents a substantial portion of their revenue. For example, income tax revenues for Maryland counties in 2012 amounted to 20 percent of their general revenues and 33 percent of their tax revenues, only slightly less than the revenue yield from the property tax.[56]

Getting to tax liability

Defining the income tax base involves more steps than are needed to define either the sales tax base or the property tax base. This is because of a number of adjustments designed to promote horizontal and vertical equity. The process involves the following steps:

1. Define **gross income.** This involves listing all income subject to taxation. Here states can provide targeted relief, such as excluding from the tax base the interest income on bonds sold by local governments as well as by the state.
2. Deduct **adjustments.** Adjustments are reductions in gross income designed to reduce or eliminate double taxation, such as with alimony payments, or the cost of earning income, such as job-related moving expenses.

   Result: **Adjusted gross income (AGI),** the beginning point for computing taxable income.
3. Deduct **personal exemptions.** Some local and state governments provide for a fixed dollar reduction in taxable income for each dependent in the household. These deductions promote horizontal and vertical equity. President Trump's tax reform law, the Tax Cut and Jobs Act of 2017, eliminated personal exemptions from the federal income tax. Some states retain the deduction in computing their state and local tax bases.
4. Deduct **standard** (or **itemized**) **deductions.** Usually individual income taxes provide for a standard deduction: a fixed dollar amount for each category of tax filers (single, married filing jointly, married filing separately). The standard deduction is designed to promote horizontal equity and reduce compliance costs by eliminating the need for retaining records on deductible expenses.

   Alternatively, tax filers may itemize qualifying deductions, particularly if they have incurred deductible expenses that exceed the standard deduction. Depending on the marginal tax bracket of the taxpayer, the deductions represent significant reductions in tax liability. Most state revenue departments prepare analyses of the cost of these tax expenditures to state treasuries.

   Result: **Taxable income**, the tax base to which the tax rate(s) is applied.
5. Multiply the taxable income by the appropriate tax rate to determine tax liability. In states and the few local governments that use **graduated tax rate** structures, each bracket of income is subject to a separate tax rate, with higher brackets subject to progressively higher tax rates. In recent decades, states and especially local governments have gravitated toward flatter rate structures because progressive income tax rates may encourage higher-income households to migrate to lower-tax jurisdictions.
6. Deduct **tax credits**. The final step is to apply any qualifying tax credits to tax liability. These dollar-for-dollar reductions in liability are particularly powerful tools for tax policy. A number of states offer **earned-income credits** to working families with moderate to low income. While most credits are capped at tax liability—that is, the credit cannot be greater than the tax liability—some states allow the credit to exceed liability, creating essentially a negative income tax by providing a cash subsidy to these families.

The income elasticity of the tax poses a serious problem for local government budgets. For example, a 10-percent decline in personal income in the local economy may result in a 15-percent decline in income tax revenues. The more dependent a local government is on the revenue from the income tax, the more vulnerable it is to midyear revenue shortfalls and budget instability. For this reason and others discussed in the following sections, local governments should avoid overdependence on the income tax.

Budgetary issues and the local income tax

The greatest source of controversy related to a proposed income tax concerns its potential effects on business and household locational decisions. The common assumption is that the tax will drive businesses and families out of the jurisdiction. Because of the greater visibility of the income tax, such fears will be especially strong, and a proposal to adopt the tax will likely evoke even greater opposition than a proposal to adopt either a general sales tax or an excise tax. Opposition will also develop because income is already taxed by forty-three states and the federal government.

A study of four major U.S. cities found that in the case of both New York City and Philadelphia, changes in income (New York) and wage (Philadelphia) tax rates adversely affect job creation.[57] Both cities rely heavily on income-based taxes, and both are surrounded by communities that do not levy the tax, creating border-city effects that give households and businesses powerful incentives to relocate to the suburban areas. According to the authors' analysis, between 1971 and 2001, New York City lost 331,000 jobs because of income tax increases, and Philadelphia lost 173,000 jobs because of increases in its wage tax rate. Both cities have taken steps to reduce their dependence on the tax.

As noted in Chapter 2 in the discussion of tax neutrality, taxes do affect business investment and job creation. It is also reasonable to expect households and businesses to be more sensitive to rate changes in the local income tax than in the property tax. While the property tax is nearly universally levied and thus unavoidable, taxpayers can more easily avoid the income tax by locating in neighboring jurisdictions where it is not levied. Regional adoption of the tax plays a critical part in building taxpayer tolerance. In sensitive policy areas such as the adoption of a local income tax, regional precedent in demonstrating a policy's viability is essential for its dissemination.

It is somewhat curious, however, that local income taxes have gained a level of acceptability in some of the more politically conservative areas of the nation, such as Indiana and Ohio. Whether this is the result of historical events or underlying social mores is debatable. The fact that these taxes have become accepted sources of local revenue in this part of the nation and that they seem to work effectively at providing revenue diversity makes them worth further analysis, particularly regarding their effects on local spending levels.

Conclusion

The most widely used alternative to the property tax is the general sales tax. The base for the sales tax is procyclical, meaning that tax revenue rises and falls with the business cycle, creating the potential for midyear revenue shortfalls whenever the local economy turns downward. The trend among states has been to narrow the sales tax base by exempting food purchased for home consumption and business purchases of machinery and building materials. This reduces the tax's regressivity (a gain on equity).

A fundamental requirement for an economically neutral sales tax is that state and local bases should be the same and tax rates should be uniform across the state. Studies indicate that a local sales tax lowers retail business activity somewhat, but the effect is insignificant when local rates are uniform or nearly so and adoption of the tax is nearly universal among local governments. When more than one level of local government levies the sales tax, one problem is how to divide the revenue (or rate) among the levels of government.

Excise taxes offer another alternative to reducing dependence on the property tax. These consumption taxes are levied on specific products—gasoline, tobacco, distilled spirits, hotel rooms, utilities—at separate rates. Revenue from these taxes tends to be dedicated to purposes that benefit the taxpayer, at least indirectly. Local governments with competitive advantages, such as hotel occupancy taxes in resort communities, rely more heavily on excise taxes because of the inelasticity of demand by consumers. Local governments may use excise taxes to discourage consumption of a product, such as tobacco, although the effectiveness of such a strategy is doubtful.

Use of the local income tax remains confined largely to states east of the Mississippi River, especially in large central cities with declining property tax bases. One of the strengths of an income tax is its capacity to extend the tax reach of a city to commuters who work in the city but otherwise bear no burden for financing its services.

Because the revenue from the tax is income elastic, local governments become more dependent on the tax over time as it displaces revenue from the less elastic property tax. As a result, local governments expose their operating budgets to greater instability whenever the local economic cycle turns downward and the income tax base contracts.

Another issue concerns the administration of the tax. The most cost-effective approach involves piggybacking the local levy onto the state income tax, thereby reducing taxpayer compliance costs with the filing of only one tax return to satisfy both state and local needs. Maryland is the only state that requires local adoption of the tax, which reduces the nonneutral effects of the tax created by taxpayers searching for nontax areas in which to locate.

Notes

1 U.S. Government Accountability Office, *Sales Taxes: States Could Gain Revenue from Expanded Authority, but Businesses Are Likely to Experience Compliance Costs* (GAO-18-114), November 2017, 3.

2 John H. Bowman and John L. Mikesell, *Local Government Tax Authority and Use* (Washington, D.C.: National League of Cities, 1987), 51–53.

3 U.S. Census Bureau, U.S. Census Bureau, 2012 *Census of Governments: State & Local Government Finance,* 2012 Local Government Table 2, https://www.census.gov//govs/local/historical_data_2012.html.

4 Ibid.

5 Federation of Tax Administrators, "Sales Taxation of Services: 2017 Update," Summary Table, August 2017, https://www.taxadmin.org/sales-taxation-of-services.

6 Bureau of Economic Analysis, "National Data, National Income and Product Accounts," Table 1.5.6, https://www.bea.gov/iTable/iTable.cfm?reqid=19&step=2#reqid=19&step=3&isuri=1&1910=x&0=-9&1921=survey&1903=36&1904=2000&1905=2018&1906=a&1911=0 (accessed January 6, 2019).

7 Kirk J. Stark, "The Uneasy Case for Extending the Sales Tax to Services," *State Tax Notes* 29 (July 21, 2003): 211–232.

8 Gary C. Cornia, David L. Sjoquist, and Lawrence C. Walters, "Sales and Use Tax Simplification and Voluntary Compliance," *Public Budgeting & Finance* 24 (Spring 2004): 2.

9 U.S. Government Accountability Office, *Sales Taxes: States Could Gain Revenue from Expanded Authority,* 11.

10 Streamlined Sales Tax Governing Board, Inc., *Streamlined Sales and Use Tax Agreement* (adopted November 12, 2002, and amended through May 3, 2018), https://www.streamlinedsalestax.org/docs/default-source/agreement/ssuta/ssuta-as-amended-2018-05-03.pdf?sfvrsn=c5876d7_1.1.

11 Federation of Tax Administrators, "State Sales Tax Rates and Food and Drug Exemptions," January 1, 2018, https://www.taxadmin.org/assets/docs/Research/Rates/sales.pdf.

12 Ibid.

13 Gary C. Cornia et al., "The Effect of Local Option Sales Taxes on Local Sales," *Public Finance Review* 38 (2010): 659–681; Gregory Burge and Cynthia Rogers, "Local Option Sales Taxes and Consumer Spending Patterns: Fiscal Interdependence under Multi-tiered Local Taxation," *Regional Science and Urban Economics* 41 (2011): 46–58; David R. Agrawal, "Games Within Borders: Are Geographically Differentiated Taxes Optimal?" *International Tax and Public Finance* 19 (August 2012): 574-597.

14 Liran Einav, et al., "Sales Taxes and Internet Commerce," *American Economic Review* 104 (January 2014): 1-26.

15 Ibid., 24.

16 Robert L. Bland and Phanit Laosirirat, "Tax Limitations to Reduce Municipal Property Taxes: Truth in Taxation in Texas," *Journal of Urban Affairs* 19 (Spring 1997): 45–58.

17 Andrew J. Krmenec, "Sales Tax as Property Tax Relief? The Shifting Onus of Local Revenue Generation," *Professional Geographer* 43 (February 1991): 60–67.

18 Changhoon Jung, "Does the Local-Opton Sales Tax Provide Property Tax Relief? The Georgia Case," *Public Budgeting & Finance* 21 (Spring 2001): 73-86.

19 Raymond J. Ring, "Consumers' Share and Producers' Share of the General Sales Tax," *National Tax Journal* 52 (March 1999): 81–92.

20 Harvey Cutler and Irina Strelnikova, "The Impact of the U.S. Sales Tax Rate on City Size and Economic Activity: A CGE Approach," *Urban Studies* 41 (April 2004): 875–885.

21 Richard Hawkins and Matthew N. Murray, "Explaining Interjurisdictional Variations in Local Sales Tax Yield," *Public Finance Review* 32 (January 2004): 82–104.

22 State of Ohio, Department of Taxation, *Sales and Use Tax*, 141–143.

23 Allegheny Regional Asset District, "Frequently Asked Questions," https://radworkshere.org/pages/FAQ (accessed January 5, 2019).

24 Burge and Rogers, "Local Option Sales Taxes and Consumer Spending Patterns."

25 North Carolina Department of Revenue, "Effective Dates of Local Sales and Use Tax Rates in North Carolina Counties," April 1, 2017, https://files.nc.gov/ncdor/documents/tax-rate-charts/levydates_4-17.pdf.

26 Amber E. Crabbe et al., "Local Transportation Sales Taxes: California's Experiment in Transportation Finance," *Public Budgeting & Finance* 25 (Fall 2005): 91–121.

27 Nebraska Department of Revenue, "Current Local Sales and Use Tax Rates," April 2018, http://www.revenue.nebraska.gov/question/sales.html.

28 B.J. Pritchett, "Arkansas Local Taxes—Understanding the Local Tax Cap," April 25, 2016, https://www.salestaxsupport.com/blogs/state/arkansas/arkansas-local-taxes-understanding-the-local-tax-cap/.

29 Sales Tax Institute, "State Sales Tax Rates," June 1, 2018, https://www.salestaxinstitute.com/resources/rates.

30 Colorado Department of Revenue, "Colorado Sales/Use Tax Rates," January 2018, https://www.colorado.gov/pacific/sites/default/files/DR1002.pdf.

31 U.S. Census Bureau, *2012 Census of Governments,* Table 2.

32 Bowman and Mikesell, *Local Government Tax Authority and Use*, 95.

33 State of Arizona, *2017 Tax Handbook,* 2.

34 Florida Office of Economic and Demographic Research, 2017 *Local Government Financial Information Handbook,* 201-222.

35 City of Chicago, "Tax List," https://www.cityofchicago.org/city/en/depts/fin/supp_info/revenue/tax_list.html (accessed January 6, 2019).

36 National Conference of State Legislatures, "State Lodging Taxes, Specific Statewide Taxes on Lodging - By State," October 1, 2017, http://www.ncsl.org/research/fiscal-policy/state-lodging-taxes.aspx.

37 Joseph Henchman, "Litigation Ongoing against Online Travel Companies for Hotel Occupancy Taxes," Tax Foundation Special Report no. 230, February 2016, https://files.taxfoundation.org/legacy/docs/TaxFoundation_SR230.pdf.

38 Ibid.

39 Divya Mulanjur, "A Quick Guide to Understanding Hotel Occupancy Tax," January 14, 2017, https://www.suiteness.com/blog/hotel-occupancy-tax-guide.

40 Federation of Tax Administrators, "State Motor Fuels Tax Rates," January 1, 2017, https://www.taxadmin.org/assets/docs/Research/Rates/mf.pdf.

41 U.S. Census Bureau, *2012 Census of Governments,* Table 2.

42 Edward Huang et al., *Transportation Revenue Options: Infrastructure, Emissions, and Congestion.* Belfer Center Discussion Paper 2010-13, September 2010.

43 Todd Goldman and Martin Wachs, "A Quiet Revolution in Transportation Finance: The Rise of Local Option Transportation Taxes," *Transportation Quarterly* 57 (Winter 2003): 19–32.

44 U.S. Census Bureau, *2012 Census of Governments,* Table 2.

45 Federation of Tax Administrators, "State Excise Tax Rates on Cigarettes," January 1, 2018, https://www.taxadmin.org/assets/docs/Research/Rates/cigarette.pdf; U.S. Census Bureau, *2012 Census of Governments,* Table 2.

46 Ibid.

47 Kevin Callison and Robert Kaestner, "Do Higher Tobacco Taxes Reduce Adult Smoking? New Evidence of the Effect of Recent Cigarette Tax Increases on Adult Smoking," *Economic Inquiry* 52 (January 2014): 155-172.

48 Jerry G. Thursby and Marie C. Thursby, "Interstate Cigarette Bootlegging: Extent, Revenue Losses, and Effects of Federal Intervention," *National Tax Journal* 53 (March 2000): 59–77.

49 Patrick Fleenor, "How Excise Tax Differentials Affect Cross-Border Sales of Beer in the United States," Tax Foundation Background Paper no. 31 (May 1, 1999), taxfoundation.org/article/how-excise-tax-differentials-affect-cross-border-sales-beer-united-states.

50 Colorado Department of Revenue, "Marijuana Tax Data," June 2018. https://www.colorado.gov/pacific/revenue/colorado-marijuana-tax-data

51 Joseph Henchman and Morgan Scarboro, "Marijuana Legalization and Taxes: Lessons for Other States from Colorado and Washington," Tax Foundation Special Report no. 231, May 2016, https://taxfoundation.org/marijuana-taxes-lessons-colorado-washington/.

52 National Conference of State Legislatures, "Real Estate Transfer Taxes," 2017, http://www.ncsl.org/research/fiscal-policy/real-estate-transfer-taxes.aspx

53 James Alm and William H. Kaempfer, "Who Pays the Ticket Tax?" *Public Finance Review* 30 (January 2002): 27–40.

54 Tonya Moreno, "U.S. Cities that Levy Income Taxes," The Balance, May 31, 2018, https://www.thebalance.com/cities-that-levy-income-taxes-3193246.

55 Office of the Auditor of State of Indiana, Department of Local Government Finance, "Local Option Income Tax Reports," https://www.in.gov/dlgf/2339.htm.

56 U.S. Census Bureau, *2012 Census of Governments,* Table 2.

57 Andrew F. Haughwout et al., "Local Revenue Hills: Evidence from Four U.S. Cities," NBER Working Paper 9686 (Cambridge, Mass.: National Bureau of Economic Research, May 2003).

CHAPTER 5

Service charges and regulatory fees

Be not the first by which the new is tried,
nor the last to lay the old aside.

—Alexander Pope

This chapter provides the following takeaways:

- The difference between service charges and regulatory fees and why it matters.
- The obstacles to using service charges and strategies for overcoming those obstacles.
- An inventory of the wide range of services and regulated activities potentially subject to benefits-based charges or fees.
- The alternative strategies for designing pricing structures and why it is important to use a design that maximizes efficiency in the production of the service.
- Alternative types of development fees and charges and the impact of each on local economies.

While general and excise sales taxes have gained prominence in local government budgets, service and utility charges represent the largest source of local revenue. This shift to charges has occurred in part because of taxpayers' resistance to higher tax burdens, particularly increased property taxes. Service charges and regulatory fees are well suited to the "finance-it-yourself" environment that currently pervades all levels of government.[1]

As discussed in Chapter 1, goods and services produced by government can be divided into three categories: public, private, and merit (or mixed). Public goods and services, such as snow removal from city streets, benefit all citizens, cannot be sold in units, and can be financed only from general tax revenues. At the other extreme are private goods and services, such as water, sewerage, and electric power; unlike private goods produced by the private sector, which are sold in a competitive market, these services are produced and sold by the government because the opportunity for profit is insufficient to attract a private provider (as in the case of public transit) or because the large capital investment naturally limits provision to a monopolist (as in the case of water service). Governments rely on their proprietary powers, granted in state or local law, to charge consumers for these services. If revenue from the sale of a service is sufficient to cover its costs, the government tracks the revenue and **expenses** using a self-supporting enterprise fund.

Between public and private goods lie merit goods, which are private goods endowed with a public purpose. For example, a municipal airport provides individual benefits that can be denied to those unwilling to pay for them, yet it also benefits the whole community by improving business opportunities and thereby helping to create jobs. Thus, a portion of the cost of merit goods should be borne by all taxpayers, with the remaining private portion of benefits financed through service charges to users. Public education, which is probably the best example of a merit good, lends itself to privatization through such measures as the provision of government vouchers to individual users.

Figure 5–1 shows the types of benefits-based levies that governments use. As discussed in Chapter 1, local governments look to different sources of legal authority when adopting these levies. A few benefits-based levies—for example, gasoline and hotel occupancy taxes—derive their legal basis from the taxing powers of local governments. State laws also grant local governments limited regulatory powers for preserving and promoting the health, safety, and welfare of the community by issuing **licenses** and **permits**. A license authorizes an individual or business to engage in an ongoing activity—for example, to operate a motorcycle on local streets. By contrast, a permit authorizes a business or individual to undertake a particular task—for example, to use particular streets at a particular time for an organized parade. Within limits prescribed by law, governments charge a fee for a license or permit as compensation for the cost of regulating the activity.

Development charges, such as impact and building inspection fees, compensate local governments for the cost of regulating new construction and for the impact of the construction on public services. In other cases, a **special assessment** is used to recoup the value of private benefits accruing to property owners. Revenue from the levy usually cannot exceed the increase in property value that results from the improvement, such as widening a street. In some states, regulatory rather than taxing powers provide the legal basis for a special assess-

Figure 5–1 Benefits-based levies commonly used by local governments

Type of benefits-based levy	Legal authority	Example
Benefits-based taxes	Taxing powers	Motor fuels tax for street improvements
User charges	Proprietary powers	Water service charges
License and permit fees	Regulatory powers	Health permit
Development charges	Regulatory powers	Zoning fee
Special taxing districts	Taxing powers	Public improvement district

Advantages of service charges and regulatory fees

Charges reduce wasteful consumption of public services by heightening users' awareness of the cost of providing the service.

Because service charges are based on the quantity consumed by each user, they give local governments a clear indication of the level of service preferred by citizens, thereby reducing the tendency to expand government facilities to meet apparently increased demand.

Service charges are equitable: Those using the service pay in proportion to the benefits they receive from it. Those who do not use the service do not subsidize those who do.

Service charges improve local government productivity by increasing managers' awareness of the cost of services. Charges to users also slow the growth of local budgets by ensuring that decision making is based not on interdepartmental budgetary politics but on the relationship of service levels to demand.

Service charges provide a market-based alternative to regulating through rules and administrative orders. In other words, they can be used to influence private behavior toward socially desirable ends.

ment, as in the case of a sidewalk installation. Public improvement districts (PIDs) provide yet another funding mechanism for local governments. State law may authorize local governments to overlay an area of the city or county with a PID. The PID, acting on the authority of its board of directors, levies a separate tax on property in the district dedicated to providing enhanced services to the district. For example, the City of San Antonio established a PID that overlays the Riverwalk to provide additional landscaping, lighting, sidewalk maintenance, and guest services.[2]

The role of service charges and regulatory fees in local government

Economically, charges and fees score high marks for both equity and efficiency. Undoubtedly, their greatest virtue is to reduce the wasteful use of some government-produced services, thereby reducing the pressure to expand public facilities to meet artificially inflated user demand and constraining the growth of government budgets. When a service is financed with tax revenue, users have no incentive to limit their use, so they create an apparently greater demand, which governments feel obligated to meet. When the same service is *sold* to users, citizens purchase only what they want, and consumption is limited to those who use the service only because they value its benefits, not because it is free. In the terms of economists, prices ration goods and services to those who value them the most, thereby maximizing economic neutrality. The accompanying sidebar summarizes some of the advantages of service charges and regulatory fees.

As an illustration, consider the per capita water consumption in two hypothetical cities—Alpha and Delta. Alpha meters water use and charges users for the full cost of the quantity consumed, but Delta finances all water services through its property tax. Predictably, per capita water consumption in Delta greatly exceeds that in Alpha because users who perceive the water as "free" have no incentive to control their level of use. The greater demand for water leads Delta to increase water production capacity well beyond that of Alpha.

Local government dependence on revenue from service charges

While local governments had increased their dependence on service charges and regulatory fees before California's Proposition 13 was ratified in 1978, the tax revolt accelerated this

Table 5–1 Service and utility charges as a percentage of local government general revenues, FY 2012

Revenue source	Counties	Municipalities[a]
Property taxes	42.7	29.8
All other taxes	16.7	22.3
Service charges	**30.1**	**20.9**
Utility charges	**2.4**	**19.6**
Other nontaxes	8.1	7.4
Total	100.0	100.0
Total general revenue (in millions)[b]	$243,140	$439,100

Source: U.S. Census Bureau, *2012 Census of Governments: State & Local Government Finance*, Local Government Table 2, https://www.census.gov//govs/local/historical_data_2012.html.

a Combines cities and townships.

b Combines general revenue from own sources and utility revenue.

trend. In the past decade, however, the combined effects of a deep recession (2007–2009) and declining state and federal grants-in-aid have forced local governments to return to increased use of local taxes.

A comparison of the role of **user charges** (service plus utility charges) versus property taxes indicates this shift. For municipalities, user charges represented 40.0 percent of general own source and utility revenues in 2012, a decline from almost 42 percent in 2002. Property taxes, on the other hand, increased to 30.0 percent in 2012 from 22.8 percent a decade earlier. For counties, user charges made up 32.5 percent of general own source and utility revenues in 2012, essentially the same as in 2002, whereas property taxes increased from 38.4 percent in 2002 to almost 43.0 percent in 2012.[3]

Generally, smaller municipalities rely more heavily on service charges than do larger ones, probably because the latter have more diversified revenue sources while the former have more limited tax bases.[4] As is apparent from Table 5–1, cities rely much more heavily on utility charges than counties do. For many cities, especially those with large amounts of tax-exempt state or federal property (such as university towns), utilities provide an important mechanism for subsidizing their general funds. Utility operations are often required by local ordinance or charter to provide a return on investment to the city, as well as franchise fees comparable to what a private utility would incur for the exclusive privilege of providing utility services.

Bernd Huber and Marco Runkel use economic theory to explain the growing popularity of user charges, especially for such services as toll roads, higher education tuition, and public health care.[5] They contend that in order for governments to compete effectively for investment capital, which has become increasingly mobile in the global economy, governments must keep their tax rates lower than otherwise would be the case in the absence of intergovernmental competition. Thus, to fill the gap made by foregone tax revenue, local governments increase service charges. Huber and Runkel conclude from their theoretical analysis that the more intense the competition among governments, the greater the reliance on user charges.

Services financed by charges and fees

When local governments review their services to identify candidates for charging fees, they must perform two tasks. First, they must decide which services *can be* sold to users (divisibility). This involves identifying activities that provide private benefits and whose benefits can be denied, with minimum cost, to those not paying for the service (excludability).

The second, more political task involves deciding which services *should be* financed by service charges. In making this decision, managers must consider four issues:

1. Is it more equitable to charge users for the service or to levy a tax? If the service possesses the attributes of a private good, it is more equitable to charge users than taxpayers.
2. Do surrounding cities, towns, or counties levy a charge for the service? Regional precedent makes it much easier politically for a local government to assess a fee for the same service.
3. How do citizens feel about increases in local taxes? Managers should require proponents of a new or expanded service to include the use of service charges in their proposals.
4. What effect will the charge have on the use of the service? Normally, charging for a service reduces demand; that is, demand is price elastic because consumers can choose to reduce their consumption of the service. For services that have widespread benefits to the community, however, such reductions are undesirable. For example, charging full cost for residential use of a landfill may increase illegal dumping along roadways and in vacant lots. When it comes to increasing prices, change in demand varies for different services depending on the availability of substitutes.

   For utility services, price elasticity is low; there are no substitutes short of reducing consumption, and going without the service is usually not an option. But for many other governmental services, consumer demand is more sensitive to price changes. In general, the greater the change in price, the greater the effect on service use. *For this reason, local governments should avoid large and irregular price increases.* Small, annual adjustments in prices have much less adverse effect on demand and thus on revenue yields.

Local government policy makers are often astounded by the lengthy list of activities for which charges and fees are collected. The following sidebar lists some of the more common services for which local governments collect charges, and the sidebar after that does the same for some of the more common regulated activities for which license and permit fees are assessed. For example, utility services, such as water and wastewater treatment, have long been financed by direct charges to users, including wholesale consumers such as other governments. Some governments even generate a profit on these services, which is used to subsidize services paid for from the general fund.

The 1987 amendments to the federal Clean Water Act ushered in a new category of utility charges: storm-water drainage fees. To meet the federal mandate for water quality standards for runoff, many local governments, especially in flood-prone areas, adopted these fees, which are distinct from wastewater treatment fees. Fees may be a flat rate per lot or scaled to lot size. Fee structures that are even more sophisticated consider the permeability of each surface area (lot or property boundary) and the expected amount of runoff it generates.

As resistance has grown to a greater reliance on taxes, local governments have looked to other services for which users can share in the cost. Recreation and leisure, public works, police and public safety, planning, economic development, public health and sanitation, and public transit all have become candidates for at least partial cost recovery through user charges. In recent years, the search for chargeable activities has been enlarged to include advertising in public spaces, such as on government vehicles and buildings. Unlike utility

Services for which local governments commonly charge a fee

Recreation and leisure activities
Athletic fields (P)
Athletic leagues (F)*
Auditorium/civic center rental (F)
Boat harbors (F)
Concession rental (F)
Equipment rental (F)
Greens fees (F)
Law library (F)*
Parks (P)
Public library services (P)
Recreation center rental (F)
Recreation classes (F)*
Swimming pools (P)
Tennis courts (P)
Web-based data services (F)

Utility services
Connection (F)
Drainage (F)
Lateral permits (F)
Pro rata connection (F)
Retail wastewater service (F)
Retail water service (F)
Septic tank dumping (F)
Tap permits (F)
Temporary use of meter or hydrant (F)
Wholesale water and wastewater (F)

Public works
Abandoned-vehicle removal (F)
Barricades (F)
Curb and street cuts (F)
Maps (F)
Right-of-way access (F)
Weed cutting (P)

Police protection
Accident and offense reports (F)
DWI processing (F)
False alarm call (F)
Funeral escorts (F)
Other special-occasion escorts (F)
Police services at special events (F)
Serving warrants (F)
Vehicle impoundment (F)

Planning and economic development
Annexation (F)
Development guide or manual (F)
Fairgrounds rental (P)
Historic landmark designation (P)
Maps (F)
Plat processing (F)
Zoning variance (F)

Sanitation and animal control
Animal holding (F)
Animal impoundment (P)
Carcass retrieval (P)
Euthanasia (F)
Landfill (P)
Large-item solid-waste pickup (F)*
Litter abatement (P)
Rabies vaccination (P)
Solid-waste collection (F)
Street cleaning (P)

Health
Ambulance service (P)
Hospitals and nursing homes (F)*
Inoculations (P)
Mental health services (F)*

Transportation
Airport landing (F)
Bridge tolls (F)
Bus fares (P)
Hangar rentals (F)
Parking garages (F)*
Parking meters (F)*
Special-occasion bus rentals (P)

Miscellaneous
Advertising on public space (F)
Cemeteries (P)
Commodity sales (F)
Document search (F)
Election filing (F)
Farmers' markets (P)
Meeting room rentals (F)
Photocopying records (F)
Public housing (P)
Vending machine space rental (F)
Wi-Fi service (F)

Notes: (F): Price should be set at full cost of providing the service.

(F)*: Full-cost pricing should be required only for certain classes of users; a partial subsidy should be provided for some users, such as the elderly, children, and nonprofit organizations.

(P): Fee for service should be set so as to recover only part of the cost of the service. A partial subsidy is justified for any one or all of the reasons discussed in the chapter.

Activities commonly regulated by local governments

Animal regulation
Dog and cats (license)
Kennels (license)

Amusement and recreation
Bicycles (registration)
Billiard and pool halls (license)
Boats (license)
Camping (permit)
Carnivals and circuses (permit)
Coin-operated machines for entertainment (license)
Dance halls (license)
Fireworks (permit)
Fishing and hunting (license)
Massage parlors (permit)
Movie theaters (license)
Outdoor concerts (permit)
Parades (permit)

Building construction
Alarms (permit)
Billboards (permit)
Building (permit)
Building movers (license and permit)
Concrete contractors (license and permit)
Demolition (license and permit)
Driveway curb cutting (permit)
Electrical contractors (license and permit)
Elevator installation (permit)
Fence contractors (license and permit)
Grading (permit)
Heating contractors (license and permit)
Home repair (license)
Manufactured-housing installation (permit)
Plumbing contractors (license and permit)
Street excavating (permit)

Food service
Alcoholic beverage sales (license)
Food handlers (permit)
Restaurants (health permit)

Businesses and occupations
Bottled water (license)
Christmas tree sales (license)
Collection agency (license)
Distressed goods sales (license)
Dry-cleaning (license)
Electronic repair (license)
Flammable-liquid storage (permit)
Itinerant merchants (license)
Jewelry auction (permit)
Lawn sprinklers (license)
Motor vehicle repair (license)
Motor vehicle towing (license)
Parking lot (license)
Pawnbrokers (license)
Residential garage sales (permit)
Retail cigarette dealers (license)
Rug and carpet cleaners (license)
Sign permits (fee)
Solid- and liquid-waste haulers (license)
Taxi and bus carriers (license)
Ticket brokers (license)
Tree service contractors (license)
Wood vendors (license)

Health care facilities and services
Ambulance drivers (license)
Hospital and convalescent home (license)
Private ambulance vehicles (permit)

Planning, zoning, and development
Barricades (permit)
Certificates of occupancy (fee)
Floodplain development (permit)
Plat approval (fee)
Waterway development (permit)
Zoning variance (fee)

Other
Charitable solicitation (permit)
Concealed weapons (permit)
Loudspeakers (permit)
Trash burning (permit)

Source: This is an updated version of an earlier list in Stanley E. Wilkes Jr., *A Guide to Revenue Administration for Small Cities* (Arlington, Tex.: Institute for Urban Studies, University of Texas at Arlington, 1981). Reprinted with permission.

services, for which revenue is accumulated in separate enterprise funds, revenue from these governmental services is typically comingled with tax revenue in the general fund.

While local governments tend to have wider latitude in the rates they charge for services, state law and court rulings have generally limited fees for licenses and permits to the cost of regulating the activity. Local governments have relied on their authority to promote the health, safety, and general well-being of their communities to license a wide range of private activities, including pet ownership, amusement and recreation, new construction, various professions and trades, food service, and land use. Seldom do the fees for these privileges cover the full cost of regulating the activity, and unless state or federal law stipulates otherwise, the revenues are almost always comingled with general taxes.

Constrained tax revenue has pushed some local governments into imprudent ventures in their quest for nontax revenue. Local governments operate a host of "businesses," from radio stations to casinos, some of which have proven quite profitable. But other ventures have proven financially fatal. Harrisburg, Pennsylvania, invested heavily in a trash-to-energy incinerator that proved unprofitable, leaving the city teetering on bankruptcy.[6]

Local governments often confront unrealistic expectations from citizens to reduce taxes while maintaining or even increasing services. In the case of revenue policy, governments are best served by incremental changes tested on a small scale before being expanded to the jurisdiction as a whole. There are no pots of gold awaiting discovery, and promises to the contrary are certain to lead to disaster.

Local governments have introduced charges for the growing array of services spawned by new technology, such as access to online data and to WiFi, a city- or countywide broadband wireless network that provides high-speed Internet service to citizens at a fraction of the cost of other modes of service. Increasingly, more transactions—from paying taxes, utility charges, and traffic citations to providing input on strategic plans and initiatives—are occurring through online portals. Not only does this technology lower the cost of doing business with city hall, but it also provides cities with a tool for attracting technology-dependent industries. Yu-Che Chen and Kurt Thurmaier conclude that given the mix of private and public benefits from online transactions, local governments should use a combination of service charges and general revenues to finance their e-government services.[7]

Policy issues in the adoption of service charges

Service charges pose policy issues that are quite different from those that local officials encounter with taxes. These issues include

- Keeping charges in line with costs
- Pricing strategies
- Choices in cost recovery
- Provisions for a policy statement on service charges and regulatory fees.

Keeping charges in line with costs

Charges for utilities and other self-supporting services accounted for in a businesslike enterprise fund receive careful scrutiny because governmental accounting standards require that rates be sufficient to recover all costs. Often an outside firm will be retained to undertake a cost-of-services study to identify both the **direct costs** and **indirect costs** of providing a service, arrive at a defensible basis for the charges set, and ensure that the rate structure fairly distributes the cost of the service among users. Charges for general fund services, by contrast, rarely receive the same scrutiny—in part because they are not self-supporting and because the revenue is comingled with tax revenues in the general fund. Because of the infrequent scrutiny, rate adjustments—when they come—are substantial, often to compensate for a substantial revenue shortfall; this has the effect of depressing user demand for the service, at least in the short term.

The following actions are recommended for keeping charges more in line with the cost of service provision.

List services More systematic monitoring of charges for governmental types of services begins by asking each department to compile a list of services, typically a section in a revenue manual that inventories all revenue sources, for which it currently levies a charge or fee. The budget office (or finance office, if no separate budget office exists) should oversee this task. Documentation should reference the statute or ordinance authorizing each charge, along with historical information on the rate and amount of revenue it yielded for previous fiscal years.

Codify charges and fees by function Because legal authorization for charges is scattered throughout the local code, local governments should consider codifying charges and fees by category or function. One approach is to list all charges in one ordinance and all regulatory fees in another, making reference to the underlying ordinances authorizing their use. An alternative is to group charges and fees by function and then adopt an ordinance setting the rates for each functional area.

Review charges and fees annually The next step involves each department reviewing the charges and fees it administers as part of the annual budget preparation process. Departments should complete an online form that identifies the expected revenues from the service at current rates and the cost recovery ratio (revenues divided by cost). Periodically (although not annually), a cost-of-services study of governmental types of services should be undertaken to establish a baseline of the potential revenue available from users of each service, the portion of full cost that should be recovered from consumers, and the indirect costs that should be assessed for internally provided services.

Recommend adjustments where appropriate As part of the detailed revenue analysis submitted to the city or county manager, the budget office should include a list of all governmental services for which a charge or fee is assessed and the proportion of cost recovered by the charge or fee. In consultation with each affected department, it may recommend adjusting the charge or fee to better match the cost recovery target.

Pricing strategies

As a general rule, public managers have less experience in pricing goods sold to their consumers than their counterparts in the business sector. For private sector managers, price decisions involve knowing the prices of competitors and positioning their products or services so as to garner a greater share of the market. Public administrators, on the other hand, have less of an opportunity to learn the demand structure of their market because they have few or no competitors in their service area with which to compare prices and service quality. For example, a university offered a premium reserved parking option in a newly constructed parking garage; the assumption was that patrons would be willing to pay the $1,575 annual charge to park in a reserved space on the first level rather than half that rate for a nonreserved space on higher levels. Two parking spaces were sold in the first year that the option was available.

For public managers, the key to effective pricing of services is to *know your customers.* When formulating their operating budgets, especially for general fund services, managers spend considerable effort trying to assess the preferences of their citizens. When the same level of effort is not expended to know the preferences of customers, a mismatch between price and consumption is inevitable.

Most state laws and court decisions require that prices be reasonable and not arbitrary. In most states, local governments may earn a reasonable return on their investment (a profit), especially for enterprise services such as water, sewerage, and electric power. Deciding on the right price for a service requires that public officials resolve how rates should be structured so as to equitably reflect the cost of serving different types of users.

Where the level of service consumption varies among users and where the cost of serving different user groups varies, charges should approximate the cost of serving each group in order to avoid inequitable and often unintended subsidization of one group of consumers by another. Also, wherever possible, consumption should be measured through metering or other means to ensure a more equitable allocation of the cost of providing that good or service. In addition to the equity gains, metering ensures more efficient use of the service since it is the user who bears the cost of wasteful consumption.

Local governments use one or a combination of several of the following procedures for pricing their services.

Lump-sum pricing In cases where measuring the quantity consumed is not administratively feasible, a **lump-sum price** is usually assessed per person or per object based on the average cost of serving each class of user. Total revenue is the product of the number of persons or objects served and the price per person, per household, or per object. Lump-sum pricing provides no incentive to reduce wasteful consumption, so it should be employed only in cases where it is administratively infeasible to measure the quantity used. Because the lump-sum fee is based on the average cost of providing the service, this strategy assures generating sufficient revenue to meet current year costs, an advantage for services with a large debt service obligation or where it is essential that the service be self-supporting. In Denton, Texas, which uses a monthly lump-sum fee for its residential solid-waste collection (Figure 5–2), even the containerized service is provided using a lump-sum amount; although that fee increases as container capacity increases, it does so at a declining rate because of the lower cost to collect each additional gallon (or cubic yard) of waste. Sometimes, a lump-sum charge is the most cost-effective way of fairly allocating the cost among users even though it has none of the rationing benefits associated with charges scaled to the amount of consumption and below average users of the service are subsidizing above average users.

Single- and block-rate pricing The **single rate**, or two-part tariff, charges users a fixed rate (or facility charge) for the fixed costs of access to the service and a single rate on the volume of service used. A variation on this is a block-rate structure, in which the volume rate changes for each block as consumption changes. A block-rate structure reflects the changes in the per unit cost for overhead, capital, and operations as consumption changes. In some cases, as in the energy charge for wintertime use of electric power by Denton's residential customers, the block price declines as consumption increases. In the summer, however, just the reverse occurs, and higher levels of consumption move consumers into a higher-priced block. Such a pricing strategy approximates the marginal-cost pricing model discussed below. Water rates for summertime consumption in Figure 5–2 illustrate block-rate pricing, and the wastewater rates illustrate a two-part tariff. Universities have begun using a variation of block-rate pricing with differential tuition rates—higher tuition for higher-cost disciplines, such as engineering, medicine, and business. Such pricing strategies reduce inequities among customers by shifting the marginal cost to the marginal user.

Peak-period pricing Peak-period (or congestion) pricing determines prices according to when a service is used. In cases where a service cannot be stored, such as electric power or public transit, peak demand means that capacity must be built to satisfy peak usage. Charging the same rate for such service, regardless of time of use, means that off-peak-period users are subsidizing peak-period users. Public transit provides a good example. Fares should be

Figure 5-2 Rate schedules for Denton, Texas, municipal utilities

CITY OF DENTON

CONSUMER INFORMATION

DENTON MUNICIPAL UTILITIES

ELECTRIC RATES

Residential

Facility Charge	$8.67/bill (single phase)
	$17.33/bill (three phase)
Usage Charge	
Winter (November-April)	6.84¢/KWH (first 600 KWH)
	4.55¢/KWH (all additional KWH)
Summer (May-October)	6.84¢/KWH (all KWH)
Energy Cost Adjustment*	3.41¢/KWH (all KWH)
Transmission Cost Recovery Factor**	0¢/KWH (all KWH)

Residential Renewable Energy

Facility Charge	$8.67/bill (single phase)
	$17.33/bill (three phase)
Usage Charge	
Winter (November-April)	6.84¢/KWH (first 600 KWH)
	4.55¢/KWH (all additional KWH)
Summer (May-October)	6.84¢/KWH (all KWH)
Renewable Cost Adjustment*	3.81¢/KWH (all KWH)
Transmission Cost Recovery Factor**	0¢/KWH (all KWH)

General Service Small

Facility Charge	$16.60/bill (single phase)
	$22.17/bill (three phase)
Usage Charge	
First 2,500 KWH	8.52¢/KWH
All additional KWH	4.46¢/KWH
Energy Cost Adjustment*	3.41¢/KWH (all KWH)
Transmission Cost Recovery Factor**	0¢/KWH (all KWH)

Commercial Renewable Energy

1,000 KWH Blocks	3.81¢/KWH (all KWH)
100% of Actual Energy Consumption	3.81¢/KWH (all KWH)

*The Energy Cost Adjustment and Renewable Cost Adjustment rates are adjusted periodically as the energy market fluctuates. Call for current rates.
**The Transmission Cost Recovery Factor rate is adjusted periodically as Electric Reliability Council of Texas transmission tariffs fluctuate. Call for current rates.

SOLID WASTE RATES

Residential Refuse and Recycling

Trash Cart Size	**One Cart**	**Two Carts**
Large Trash Cart	$29.26/bill	$46.64/bill
Standard Trash Cart	$24.51/bill	N/A

(Each rate includes one standard-size recycling cart.)

Commercial Rates

Side Load Service

Size	**1x** /week	**2x** /week	**3x** /week	**4x** /week	**5x** /week	**6x** /week
3 CY	$104.64	$209.28	$313.92	$439.44	$576.90	$726.84
4 CY	$139.52	$279.04	$418.56	$585.92	$769.20	$969.12

Front Load Service

Size	**1x** /week	**2x** /week	**3x** /week	**4x** /week	**5x** /week	**6x** /week
3 CY	$74.16	$148.32	$222.48	$311.52	$408.75	$515.16
4 CY	$98.88	$197.76	$296.64	$415.36	$545.00	$686.88
6 CY	$148.32	$296.64	$444.96	$623.04	$817.50	$1,030.32
8 CY	$197.76	$395.52	$593.28	$830.72	$1,090.00	$1,373.76

Front Load Compactor	
Front Load Compactor (per CY)	$74.16
Commercial Open Top (Roll-Off)	
Monthly Rental	$167.08
Collection Charge*	$275.00

*Plus landfill fees based on weight.

Landfill Rates

Gate Rate	$44.00 per ton
City Hauled Disposal Rate	$40.00 per ton

WATER RATES

Residential

Facility Charge	
¾" Meter	$16.00/bill
1" Meter	$20.80/bill
1 ½" Meter	$27.20/bill
2" Meter	$34.40/bill
Volume Charge	
Winter (November-April)	$4.15/1,000 gallons (all consumption)
Summer (May-October)	$4.15/1,000 gallons (up to 15,000 gallons/bill)
	$5.90/1,000 gallons (15,001-30,000 gallons/bill)
	$8.15/1,000 gallons (30,001-50,000 gallons/bill)
	$10.90/1,000 gallons (50,000+ gallons/bill)

Irrigation Customers
See rate ordinance for applicable rates.

Commercial/Industrial

Facility Charge	
¾" Meter	$22.60/bill
1" Meter	$32.00/bill
1 ½" Meter	$38.70/bill
2" Meter	$51.50/bill
Volume Charge	$4.45/1,000 gallons
Irrigation Customers	
Winter (November-April)	$4.45/1,000 gallons
Summer (May-October)	$6.15/1,000 gallons

WASTEWATER RATES

Residential

Facility Charge	$11.00/bill
Volume Charge	$3.80/1,000 gallons effluent

(Billing based on 100 percent of average monthly water billed from December-February.)
(18,000 gallon wastewater volume cap.)

Commercial/Industrial

Facility Charge	$26.50/bill
Volume Charge	$4.85/1,000 gallons effluent

(Billing based on 95 percent of monthly water consumption.)

Equipment Services and Eating Establishments

Facility Charge	$26.50/bill
Volume Charge	$6.75/1,000 gallons effluent

(Billing based on 95 percent of monthly water consumption.)

DRAINAGE RATES

Residential

Square Feet in Block	**Monthly Charge per Bill**
0-600	$.50
601-1,000	$1.00
1,001-2,000	$3.35
2,001-3,000	$5.45
3,001-4,000	$7.60
4,001-5,000	$9.75
5,001-6,000	$12.00
6,001+	$15.50

Nonresidential

Square feet of impervious service x $0.00186/bill.

All rates are effective as of Oct. 1, 2018.
A complete copy of utility rates can be obtained at www.cityofdenton.com and at all Denton Public Libraries.

Produced by the Communications Office • www.cityofdenton.com • ADA/EOE/ADEA • TDD (800) 735-2989.

Source: City of Denton Municipal Utilities, October 2018. https://www.cityofdenton.com/CoD/media/City-of-Denton/Government/Water%20Utilities/2018-19-Utility-Rate-Brochure_final2.pdf higher during morning and evening rush hours to reflect the additional capacity in bus and rail service and the additional personnel required to meet demand during these peak periods. Local governments are increasingly using congestion pricing, which adjusts tolls upward automatically whenever traffic increases and downward as congestion eases.[8] Similar capacity costs are incurred for water, sewer, electric power, and natural gas services. Both electric and water utilities for Denton use peak-period pricing in combination with block pricing (Figure 5–2). Similarly, peak-period pricing may be used in combination with single-rate pricing such as with Denton's commercial/industrial irrigation customers. Peak-period prices should vary according to the cycles in use of the service, such as by hour, day, or season.

Table 5-2 provides a summary of the four basic pricing strategies—lump sum, single-rate, block-rate, and peak-period — and their blended strategies when used in combination with peak-period pricing. Block-rate pricing used in combination with peak-period best allocates cost to the marginal user and most effectively reduces subsidies across customers. The blending of lump-sum pricing with peak-period is infrequently encountered in local government. A hypothetical example of this strategy would be a toll road that charges a lump sum of $5 for rush hour regardless of the distance traveled and $2.50 for all other times and distances.

Pricing by classification of users **Classification of users** may be according to type of user (seniors, children, disabled), location of user (resident, nonresident), or location of service (transit zones). Where costs vary by classification of user, prices should be stratified so that low-cost users do not subsidize higher-cost users. Nonresidential rates are usually higher than residential rates because of the greater distance required to deliver services to nonresidents. However, the cost of serving different classes of users is not always the overriding consideration in classifying users; for example, adults generally pay a higher admission charge to recreational services than children do, but this does not reflect actual higher costs in serving adults. In the case of utility services, consumers in Denton are classified generally as residential and commercial (Figure 5–2).

Table 5–2 Pricing strategies

Pricing strategy	Quantity measured (Q)	Price (P)	Peak time (T))
1. Lump sum	Number of persons or objects	Lump sum per object	Not considered
2. Single rate	Consumption per unit	One rate for all Q	Not considered
3. Block rate	Consumption per unit in blocks	Separate rate for each block of Q	Not considered
4. Peak period	Not measured	Separate rate for each time category	Measured in categories
5. Blended:			
#1 (3 and 4)	Consumption per unit in blocks.	Separate rate for each block and time category	Measured
#2 (2 and 4)	Consumption per unit.	Separate rate for each time category.	Measured
#3 (1 and 4)	Number of persons or objects.	Separate rate for each time category.	Measured

Choices in cost recovery

Another policy issue that local governments must resolve is whether to price a service so that it recovers all or only a portion of its cost. The common practice, especially for nonutility services, is to recover only part of the cost through service charges, with the remainder subsidized by general revenues. The sidebar on page 114 listing common services for which charges are collected also identifies those services that should be priced at full (direct and indirect) cost, or at full cost for at least some users, and those services for which partial cost recovery is justified.

The various pricing strategies available to local governments are as follows.

Full-cost and return-on-investment pricing Under most circumstances, enterprise services (e.g., utilities) should be priced at full cost, including both direct and indirect costs associated with service provision. As noted above, in some cases, a reasonable return on investment is legally and administratively justified. Privately owned utilities earn a return on their investment, and it makes sense for government-owned utilities to earn a comparable return. State and local laws vary in the amount of return authorized.

Partial-cost pricing For merit goods and services, a partial subsidy is usually warranted. This poses two issues that local governments must resolve when setting a price: (1) when should a subsidy be provided and (2) how much of a subsidy should be provided? For merit services, partial-cost pricing is justified when any of the following conditions exists:

- Some of the benefits from the service accrue to the whole community. For example, a rabies vaccination program reduces the risk of this disease for all pet owners, not just for those obtaining the inoculation. A portion of the program's costs should be funded from general revenues.
- The local government wants to stimulate demand for the service. For example, a county library provides long-term benefits to a community by enriching its quality of life. Policy makers can encourage library use by fully subsidizing its operations from general taxes or possibly by charging only a token fee for users.
- Enforcement of the charge at full cost would result in widespread evasion. For example, setting a registration fee for dog and cat tags at full cost may give pet owners an incentive to evade purchase of these licenses. This increases enforcement costs and creates an adversarial relationship between owners and the animal control unit. Partial-cost pricing may be justified under such circumstances.
- The service is used primarily by low-income households. For example, rental rates for affordable housing should be set below full cost, with the difference made up by subsidies from federal and state grants.

The second challenge for local governments is deciding how much of a subsidy is justified for services with spillover benefits to the community. Often political considerations enter into this discussion,[9] with the relative political influence of the users weighing heavily in the decision. Politically active groups, such as senior citizens or sports enthusiasts, may effectively lobby to keep a service charge lower than would otherwise be the case.

Competitive pricing A competitive pricing strategy considers the prices charged for comparable services by private or nonprofit providers or by surrounding local governments. For example, a village may set its admission price for a swimming pool to be competitive with the YMCA's charge. In the case of utility services, decision makers give particular consideration to the prices charged by surrounding jurisdictions and private suppliers. In today's deregulated environment, especially for electric power and natural gas, public utilities must keep a close eye on the pricing practices of private providers who have an incentive to "cherry pick" (i.e., lure away the low-cost, high-revenue accounts).

Marginal-cost pricing Marginal-cost pricing sets prices to reflect the cost of producing each additional unit of service. For example, higher prices for summertime electric and water rates, as shown in Figure 5–2, shift the additional cost for this marginal capacity to those who create that need. Economists support this approach because it leads to the most efficient allocation of resources. Since the price reflects the marginal cost, only consumers who value that additional unit will purchase it. However, this strategy poses significant administrative difficulties in determining the marginal cost of each service. It also leads to prices that do not always recover the full cost of producing a service. Some pricing structures may approximate marginal-cost pricing, such as combinations of peak-period, block-rate, and two-part tariff pricing.

Provisions for a policy statement on service charges and fees

Politically and legally, a cost-of-services study or rate analysis provides a defensible basis for the price charged to users. It can buttress a government's contention that its prices were not set arbitrarily, particularly in cases where different rates are charged to different classes of users. In the case of merit goods and services, knowing the full cost also provides the manager with an indication of the value of the subsidy going to the service. Finally, knowing the cost of providing services heightens administrators' awareness of the need to control costs. It aids managers in reviewing cost trends and the effect of those trends on budget allocations.

Costs to include The objective of a cost-of-services study is to identify the cost of providing a service, but governments seldom maintain accounting information on the basis of costs (or expenses). Instead, such information is usually maintained on the basis of expenditures (the value of goods and services purchased during the budget period), which must be converted into costs (the value of the inputs used to produce the particular service during the budget period). Accountants identify two types of costs: direct (those associated with the direct provision of the service, such as wages, benefits, supplies, equipment) and indirect (those associated with supporting operations, such as general management, accounting, purchasing, human resources, payroll, utilities). Direct costs include those expenses that would be eliminated if the service were discontinued. Indirect costs result from the support (or staff) services provided by one department to other government departments.

For utility services, local governments generally set rates so as to recover both direct and indirect costs. For services other than utilities—for example, park and recreation services, animal control, toll roads, public transit, and public health services—local governments almost never recover indirect costs, and even recovery of full direct costs is problematic because most of these services provide community-wide benefits.

One of the thorniest issues in cost analysis is the equitable allocation of indirect costs to each chargeable service. Support services, such as personnel or accounting, constitute indirect costs not only for line services but also for other support services. For example, the finance department provides accounting and payroll services to the water department and also to the personnel department, which is itself a support service for the water department. This complexity suggests the need for a series of simultaneous equations to determine the proper allocation ratio for the indirect costs of all government services. Cost studies usually use two less sophisticated procedures for allocating indirect costs: the direct allocation method and the step method.[10]

Direct allocation method The **direct allocation technique** involves summing the cost of all support services and then allocating these costs to each activity, including services sold for a price, using some allocation criterion such as each activity's share of the total budget or share of total salaries and fringe benefits. However, completely ignores the interdependence of support services and thus allocates more support service costs to line activities (including chargeable services) than is justified.

Step method The **step method** gives some consideration to the benefits that support services derive from each other. Support services are first ranked according to the amount of service each provides to all other support services. Line activities are not ranked. The benefits of each support service are then apportioned to all support services ranked below it. At least some compensation is thereby made for the benefits that support services derive from each other before indirect costs are allocated to line activities. Properly allocating indirect costs will yield more accurate estimates of the true cost of providing services and provide a more accurate basis for pricing those services. However, the success of any allocation ratio ultimately depends on whether department heads are convinced that it is fair.

Administering service charges and regulatory fees

Many of the issues associated with the collection and enforcement of service charges parallel those associated with the property tax, and most of the recommendations for improving the collection of current and delinquent property taxes apply to service charges as well, especially to those for utility services.

Collection

Service charges are collected in one of two ways: at the point of sale (such as a rental charge for the use of recreational equipment or an admission charge to an ice skating rink) or on a periodic basis for the service used (such as a monthly statement for the quantity of water

Strategies for improving collection of charges and fees

Current accounts

Design the utility statements to catch the attention of users and clearly communicate the amount of payment and the due date.

Keep account records current, especially mailing addresses; consider developing a consolidated database of utility and taxpayer accounts.

Provide for web-based payment and automatic bank draft options now commonplace with many private firms. Allow payment by credit or debit card.

Adopt penalties and interest charges that make delinquency unrewarding.

Consider the cost-effectiveness of contracting out collection of current and delinquent accounts.

Delinquent accounts

Establish a legal basis and procedure for collecting delinquent accounts.

1. Establish liability for utility charges.
2. Specify the steps for collecting delinquency charges and increase the intensity of each step in the process.
3. Use discretionary powers such as setoff provisions in contracts and liens on the property of delinquent customers.
4. Require a deposit.

Consider contracting out collection of delinquent payments to a private law firm.

Consider developing an amnesty program to reduce the backlog of delinquent accounts, especially for parking and traffic citations.

consumed). While the first approach eliminates the problem of delinquency, it is usually more costly to administer relative to the amount of revenue collected. Periodic billing of users yields the largest portion of revenue from service charges, especially for utility services. However, managing these accounts receivable creates many of the same problems that a private firm encounters when it extends short-term credit to its customers.

Local governments typically piggyback several utility and related service charges onto one billing system. For example, charges for water, sewer, solid-waste (refuse) collection, and electric power may be listed on one statement. While water usage is usually metered, sewerage charges are usually based on a proxy measure, such as the average volume of water used during the winter months.

Local governments should achieve at least a 95-percent collection rate on current accounts. That is, no more than 5 percent of the current charges for billed services should be delinquent. As with the property tax, achieving this collection rate depends on local economic conditions, including the unemployment level, and on the aggressiveness of the collection effort. The accompanying sidebar summarizes the strategies for effectively administering the collection and enforcement of service charges.

Designing a policy for service charges and fees

Managers may want to propose a broad policy covering all types of charges and fees, with separate sections devoted to particular service areas, such as utility services, parks and recreation, sanitation, and health. The alternative is to adopt separate policy statements for each major service area. A policy statement on charges and fees should address the following issues.

Integration with budget process Because a review of all charges and fees should be integrated into the budget preparation process, the policy statement should assign responsibility for overseeing implementation and review of this task. The responsibility may be assigned to the budget office, or it may be shared with units that have administrative oversight, such as internal auditing or performance management.

Schedule for cost-of-services studies The policy statement should specify the frequency with which a cost-of-services study will be undertaken and the cost-of-living index that will be used in the intervening years to adjust rates.

Levels of subsidy The policy statement should provide guidelines on the types of services that will be priced at less than full cost and the level of subsidy provided. For example, a city may classify its park and recreation services as self-sustaining activities priced at full cost, partially sustaining activities priced at direct cost only, and services for which a token fee is charged.

Collection The policy statement should provide guidelines on the collection of charges and fees. Guidelines are particularly important for utility services, where delinquency is a problem. At a minimum, the policy should specify the amount of deposit required from new customers, the procedures for collecting delinquent charges, and the sanctions to be used against delinquent customers.

Development charges

Local governments that are experiencing rapid population growth are increasingly relying on development charges and fees to finance the capital cost of additional public facilities. Traditionally, the cost of adding facilities to accommodate growing populations has been borne by all users through increased charges and taxes. However, the tax limitation movement and the retrenchment in federal aid have made it much more difficult for local governments to sustain this approach.

Impact fees are collected from developers, often under a local government's regulatory powers, for off-site improvements that are needed to serve the new development.[11] Impact fees were initially used to finance off-site expansion of water and sewer treatment facilities. Their use was extended to cover the cost of expanding arterial roads serving a new development; solid-waste disposal capacity; storm drainage; beach and park acquisition; and police, fire, school, and public transit facilities. While these fees are unpopular with developers, they are understandably popular with current residents, who see them as a more equitable way of providing additional service capacity than imposing taxes and service charges on all residents.

Cities in Colorado have the longest experience with impact fees, although the fees are most widely used by cities and counties in California. Florida holds the distinction of having the most well-developed case law on the use of impact fees, whose legality has been challenged on both statutory and constitutional grounds. State courts have generally held that impact fees do not deny due process or equal protection as long as a rational nexus exists between the need for additional capacity in public facilities and the growth from new development. To provide a clearer legal basis for local authority to assess these fees, states have shifted to granting explicit authority for the fees in statute rather than relying on local governments' more vague regulatory powers.

Economically, impact fees raise contentious issues about their effect on the cost of housing, especially for first-time home buyers. Opponents contend that impact fees increase the cost of housing, are potentially unfair to new residents, and provide a windfall in benefits to current residents. In fact, except under unusual market conditions, impact fees are partially capitalized into lower land values, especially in competitive markets with housing options, rather than being shifted forward to buyers (or renters) as higher prices for housing or commercial space.[12] Burge concludes in his nationwide analysis that the impact fees implemented by local governments are on the whole far below the cost of the infrastructure they are used to fund.[13]

The ordinance that levies the fee should specify the types of improvements financed by the fee, the basis for determining liability, and whether rates should be stratified by the type or the location of property. It should also specify when in the development process the fee will be collected. Most governments collect it at the building permit stage along with other development-related fees. Local governments should develop accounting procedures capable of documenting that fees were used to finance projects directly benefiting those paying the fee.

Connection charges are another type of levy used to recover the cost of off-site improvements. While impact fees provide up-front financing for the expansion of public facilities, connection charges allow the developer to buy into the existing capacity of public facilities.

A third approach is to require developers to **dedicate improvements**—such as new streets, lighting, and drainage—as a condition for local government approval of the new subdivision. Historically, developers have been required to dedicate on-site facilities as a condition of approval. As an alternative to impact fees, local governments may extend that responsibility to include off-site improvements, such as arterial roads or expanded sewer treatment and water facilities needed to serve the new development.

Special taxing districts

Special assessments, another form of benefits-based financing of public facilities, are levies on property owners for the increased property values attributable to a public improvement.

For example, a city-funded street widening project increases the market value for commercial property along the improvement. (More traffic means more business, which increases the locational value of the property.) Some local governments use assessments to partially finance the installation of water and sewer lines and the construction of recreational facilities and off-street parking. Heaviest use of these levies is made by local governments west of the Mississippi River, especially those in Pacific Coast states.

Special assessments differ from other benefits-based levies, including impact fees, in that the maximum assessment is the increase in property value created by the improvement, regardless of the extent to which beneficiaries use the facility.

In the past twenty years, states have introduced variations on special assessments as a way to shift the financing of infrastructure to those benefiting from the improvements. For example, Texas authorizes cities to establish municipal management districts (MMDs) that blend the financing mechanisms of special assessments with the governance structure of tax increment financing districts. MMDs may use a combination of special assessments and impact fees on those properties that benefit from improvements in the district. Additional dedicated property taxes may be levied by the district's governing board.

A special assessment may be applied to each property owner as a pro rata share of the cost of the project. An assessment equal to the increase in each property's value eliminates any windfalls these property owners would otherwise have received at other taxpayers' expense. And by shifting part of the cost of public improvements to property owners who benefit from increased property values, special assessments promote horizontal equity.

Rarely do special assessments recover the full cost of a project. Essentially, they capture the private benefits from an improvement financed in part by general revenues. But in so doing, they promote intrajurisdictional equity and also lower developers' financing costs by giving developers access to tax-exempt debt backed by the assessments.

Public improvement districts (PIDs) and business improvement districts (BIDs), often used in conjunction with a public-private partnership (PPP), are variations of special assessments although much more widely used because of their greater ease to implement. As noted previously, PIDs levy an additional property tax with the revenue dedicated to enhancing the quality of public services in the targeted area. They are more common in larger cities and urban counties. The tax is levied only after a majority of property owners in the district agree to the district's creation. Usually a separate board of directors, appointed by the overlying city or county council, adopts a budget that allocates the tax revenue in the district. The board may have authority to issue debt that is backed by the revenue from the PID property tax. Brooks and Meltzer used simulation models to assess the impact of BIDs on local revenues and tax bases. They concluded that BIDs do not diminish local services to non-BID areas, and that they have modestly increased the tax base of the district.[14]

Authorization and implementation

Unlike impact fees, special assessments are levied under the taxing powers granted to local governments in state law. Every state grants municipalities the authority to levy special assessments, and most extend the same authority to counties and, less frequently, to independent special districts such as utility districts.[15]

Projects financed by special assessments may be initiated by property owners (including developers) or by the local government. At a developer's request, the local government creates a special assessment district to obtain tax-exempt financing for public improvements in the district. Enabling legislation specifies the general procedures that local governments must follow to levy an assessment, the method for allocating the costs of the project, and the terms of payment for property owners affected by the project.

While impact fees are generally collected before the facility is constructed, state laws usually prohibit collection of special assessments until the project is completed, at which point property owners have the option of paying their assessments in installments over a number of years, usually at very favorable interest rates. When financing a project with assessments, a local government typically finances the construction phase with general revenues and then reimburses itself as special assessments are collected. When impact fees are used, beneficiary financing is up front, which places less of a drain on the local government's general revenues.

Allocation of costs

The aspect of special assessments that property owners contest most often is the allocation of construction costs. State law usually specifies the basis for allocating a project's cost among property owners, which is almost always according to the number of feet fronting the improvement (i.e., a front-foot basis). Although by law the maximum assessment can equal the increase in value attributable to a public improvement, local governments rarely levy assessments at this level. Moreover, an appraisal study may reveal that the project's benefits are not uniformly distributed, in which case each property assessment must be adjusted to reflect any differences. Costs may also be allocated on a per acre or per lot basis, especially for water and sewer installations. In some cases, a zone method may be used whereby properties closest to the improvement bear a greater portion of the cost.

Conclusion

Local governments should make greater use of service charges because such charges provide an equitable source of revenue (those using the service pay in proportion to the benefits they receive) and promote efficiency by discouraging wasteful use of government services. Charging for a service reduces the demand for it: the greater the price change, the greater the effect on service use. And charges to users slow the growth of local budgets by ensuring that decisions are based not on interdepartmental budgetary politics but on the relationship of service level to demand. The greatest benefit from service charges comes with regular adjustments in prices that reflect the cost of serving various categories of consumers. Service charges also improve local government productivity by increasing managers' awareness of the cost of services.

A barrier to the increased use of service charges is the political imbalance between the negligible benefits from lower taxes and the noticeable cost to users of the service; consequently, elected lawmakers may find it politically difficult to support the imposition of a visible service charge if there are no significant benefits from a reduction in taxes.

It is recommended that local governments develop a policy statement on service charges and fees. Such a statement should assign responsibility for annually reviewing rates as part of the budget process; specify the frequency with which a cost-of-services study will be undertaken; and provide guidelines on the types of services that will be priced at less than full cost, the level of subsidy provided, and the collection of current and delinquent charges, including the amount of deposit required from new customers.

When the cost of serving different groups of users varies, charges should be stratified to approximate the average cost of serving each group. A lump-sum pricing structure is the simplest to design, but it has the least effect on efficiency because users have no incentive to ration their use of the service. Moreover, it is less equitable because those using less of the service subsidize those using more. Alternative pricing structures that more efficiently and equitably allocate costs include a single rate structure, peak-period pricing, and a combination of strategies that classify users by the cost of serving each category.

For services providing only private benefits, such as utility services, full-cost pricing (with possibly a return on investment) is appropriate. Partial-cost pricing is appropriate for services with some spillover benefits to the community or services for which local governments want to encourage demand.

A sensitive issue in the costing of services is the allocation of the indirect costs of support services, such as those associated with the manager's office or accounting. An equitable basis should be found for allocating these costs to all activities, including those for which charges are not collected.

Development charges and fees, such as impact fees, provide an equitable benefits-based alternative for financing public improvements required by new development. The critical stage in the process of adopting an impact fee is documenting the cost of capital improvements needed to serve new residents.

The principal objection to fees and charges for new development is that they will increase the cost of housing in the community. Although in the long term fees are capitalized into lower prices for undeveloped land, in the short term builders bear the fee's cost on their existing inventory of property. To reduce this burden, local governments should phase in the fee over a two- or three-year period, giving developers and builders an opportunity to adjust their bid prices for raw land to compensate for the fee.

Special taxing districts such as MMDs, PIDs, and BIDs offer a benefits-based strategy for recouping at least part of the costs of public improvements. Successful use requires that affected property owners be involved early in the process. The local government may want to survey owners about their attitudes toward a proposed project and their willingness to pay an assessment for part of its cost. Because special assessments are costly to administer, there should be a sufficient volume of projects capable of being financed in part by assessments to provide some economies of scale in their administration.

Notes

1 Robert J. Kleine and John Shannon, "Characteristics of a Balanced and Moderate State-Local Revenue System," in *Reforming State Tax Systems,* ed. Steven D. Gold (Denver, Colo.: National Conference of State Legislatures, 1986), 33–34.

2 City of San Antonio, *San Antonio Downtown Public Improvement District Draft Service and Assessment Plan for Fiscal Years 2018-2022,* https://www.sanantonio.gov/Portals/0/Files/CCDO/Centro%20PID%20FY2018%20Service%20and%20Assessment%20Plan%20-%20Final%208%2030%2017.pdf?ver=2017-08-30-181538-713.

3 U.S. Bureau of the Census, *State & Local Government Finance, Historical Data: 2002,* Table 2, https://www.census.gov/govs/estimate/historical_data_2002.html, and *2012 Census of Governments: State & Local Government Finance,* Local Government Table 2, https://www.census.gov//govs/local/historical_data_2012.html.

4 Deborah A. Carroll and Terri Johnson, "Examining Small Town Revenues: To What Extent Are They Diversified?" *Public Administration Review* 70 (March/April 2010): 223–235.

5 Bernd Huber and Marco Runkel, "Tax Competition, Excludable Public Goods, and User Charges," *International Tax and Public Finance* 16 (2009): 321–336.

6 Hilary Russ, "Pennsylvania Sues Over Troubled Harrisburg Incinerator Bond Deals," Reuters, May 21, 2018, https://www.reuters.com/article/us-pennsylvania-harrisburg-lawsuit/pennsylvania-sues-over-troubled-harrisburg-incinerator-bond-deals-idUSKCN1IM23N.

7 Yu-Che Chen and Kurt Thurmaier, "Advancing E-Government: Financing Challenges and Opportunities," *Public Administration Review* 68 (May/June 2008): 537–548.

8 Congressional Budget Office, *Using Pricing to Reduce Traffic Congestion,* Publication no. 3133, March 2009, https://www.cbo.gov/sites/default/files/111th-congress-2009-2010/reports/03-11-congestionpricing.pdf.

9 Michael A. Pagano, *Funding and Investing in Infrastructure* (Washington, D.C.: Urban Institute, December 2011).

10 Lumen Learning, "Appendix: Allocation of Service Department Costs," in *Managerial Accounting,* https://courses.lumenlearning.com/tcc-managacct/chapter/allocation-of-service-department-costs/

11 Gregory S. Burge, "The Effects of Development Impact Fees on Local Fiscal Conditions," in *Municipal Revenues and Land Policies,* ed. Gregory K. Ingram and Yu-Hung Hong (Cambridge, Mass: Lincoln Institute of Land Policy, 2010): 182-212.

12 Jennifer S. Evans-Cowley and Larry L. Lawhon, "The Effects of Impact Fees on the Price of Housing and Land: A Literature Review," *Journal of Planning Literature* 17 (February 2003): 351–359; John Yinger, "The Incidence of Development Fees and Special Assessments," *National Tax Journal* 51 (March 1998): 23-41.

13 Gregory S. Burge, "The Effects of Development Impact Fees," 209.

14 Leah Brooks and Rachel Meltzer, "Does a Rising Tide Compensate for the Secession of the Successful? Illustrating the Effects of Business Improvement Districts on Municipal Coffers," in *Municipal Revenues and Land Policies,* ed. Gregory K. Ingram and Yu-Hung Hong (Cambridge, Mass: Lincoln Institute of Land Policy, 2010): 271-302.

15 Thomas P. Snyder and Michael A. Stegman, *Paying for Growth: Using Development Fees to Finance Infrastructure* (Washington, D.C.: Urban Land Institute, 1987), 35.

CHAPTER

6

Tax incentives and tax relief: Using taxes for economic and political purposes

Now the Israelites had been saying, "Do you see how this man keeps coming out? He comes out to defy Israel. The king will give great wealth to the man who kills him. He will also give him his daughter in marriage and will exempt his father's family from taxes in Israel."

—I Samuel 17:25

This chapter provides the following takeaways:

- What businesses look for when considering an expansion or relocation of their operations.
- The tax incentives that provide the best results and how to design an economic development strategy to maximize those benefits.
- The sobering truth on incentives for sports and arts venues and their value as civic symbols.
- Understanding the impact of various types of tax relief measures for citizens and means to mitigate their long-term budget impact.
- Items to consider when preparing a disaster recovery plan.

Local and state governments invest heavily in attracting and retaining business investment. The jobs that investment creates and the value it adds to the tax base provide long-term benefits to local coffers. The incentives for business investment offered by cities and counties create the economic engines that fuel most state economies. Yet the Great Recession of 2007–2009 spawned a wave of municipal bankruptcies and exposed the vulnerability of local and state budgets to economic cycles. The slow recovery following the Great Recession has not abated taxpayers' demand for relief and businesses from shopping for the best package of incentives to relocate their operations.

Not only do taxes provide the resources needed to finance local government operations, they also have become tools in two politically powerful but potentially antithetical trends: stimulating new investment by businesses and providing tax relief for citizens. The former finds expression in the array of economic development incentives offered by local and state governments. The latter is seen in such measures as tax limitations, beginning with Proposition 13 in California, and targeted relief to select groups of citizens, particularly senior citizens.

This chapter examines the role of local taxing decisions in economic development and tax relief, specifically as it relates to these issues:

- What criteria do businesses use when making locational decisions?
- Do locally financed tax incentives, such as tax abatements and tax increment financing, attract new business investment?
- How effective are targeted incentives—for example, for sports stadiums and arts venues?
- How has the tax limitation movement affected local government budgets? Do limitations on taxing powers stimulate an increase in household income and new job creation?

Taxes and economic development: Finding the balance

This chapter begins where it ends: No amount of creative financing to attract business investment will compensate for poor budgeting practices. The most cost-effective economic development strategy that local governments can pursue is to maintain sound budget practices, competitive tax and utility rates, and professional leadership.

Pursuing an aggressive economic growth policy makes good political sense. A successful economic development initiative communicates to industries making locational decisions that the business environment is a favorable one. If one industry is attracted to a community, related industries are likely to follow. Economic development initiatives also express to voters that public officials are concerned about job opportunities and are making efforts to expand them.

However, a more fundamental objective underlies the effort to attract business investment: to improve the local government's revenue condition by expanding its tax base. Investment in plant facilities and equipment expands the property tax base and creates new employment opportunities. New jobs bring more workers—or at least help to retain the existing workforce—and that further expands the local tax base. If the municipality or county has access to an income tax or a sales tax, it will reap even greater budget returns from economic development as a result of increased income and consumption.

Defining a favorable business environment raises two fundamental questions: (1) how do local taxes affect business investment and (2) under what circumstances should local governments offer tax incentives? Both issues have been the focus of considerable research, and studies can be found to support almost any position on these questions; the issues are complex, and isolating the effect of local taxes or tax incentives on business locational patterns requires highly sophisticated techniques and theories. Anecdotal analyses that compare the number of jobs or the size of the business tax base before and after completion of a major business investment but that do not simultaneously control for other factors should be disregarded.

Factors affecting business locational decisions

Although business leaders often contend that different tax policies at the state or regional level have a significant bearing on their investment decisions, the research generally shows that "this effect is fairly small and easily outweighed by differences in other factors."[1] However, once a firm has narrowed its locational choice to a particular region, that region's tax

Summary of research on local taxes and business location

- In a firm's initial search for possible sites, taxes have virtually no bearing on locational decision. As the number of possible sites is narrowed, however, differences in the effective tax rates of local governments increase in importance.
- Nontax factors such as labor supply and cost, energy cost, transportation networks, space availability, agglomeration economies, and educational level of the workforce are more central to a firm's final locational choice than tax-related factors.
- The effect of local taxes on business investment decisions varies with the type of business. Firms in manufacturing and wholesale trades are more sensitive to effective property tax rates (property tax liability as a percentage of the property's market value) than are firms in other types of industries. Tax incentives to attract new manufacturers *do* increase local economic activity, especially where agglomeration economies exist.[1]
- Inordinately high local tax burdens may affect business investment indirectly by promoting the emigration of labor. As workers leave, so too will manufacturing firms, followed by retail and service industries, in order to be closer to the labor supply and consumers.
- In the long term, above-average property tax burdens prompt businesses and households to relocate to lower-tax areas, thereby causing property values to decline. Thus, to maintain a competitive level of public services, governments with declining property values must levy even higher tax rates, precipitating further decline in the tax base.

1 Michael Greenstone, Richard Hornbeck, and Enrico Moretti, "Identifying Agglomeration Spillovers: Evidence from Winners and Losers of Large Plant Openings," *Journal of Political Economy* 118, no. 3 (2010): 536–598.

burden—and particularly its property tax burden—becomes more important, even if not paramount. Firms that are otherwise indifferent to two or more possible sites may consider the effective local tax burden of the finalists in their evaluation. Thus, at the margin, a local government's tax burden *does* affect business investment decisions.

However, no firm rule can be offered because a lower tax burden does not necessarily lower the cost of doing business in a jurisdiction. If lower taxes mean fewer public services, particularly those used by businesses, the operating costs may be much higher for businesses that have to absorb the cost of providing those services. Moreover, state and local taxes usually represent just a small component of the cost of doing business, and those expenses are deductible for federal income tax purposes, which further lowers businesses' marginal costs.

The inefficiencies of local tax incentives

From a political perspective, providing tax breaks to businesses is a win-win proposition. Businesses reduce their operating costs, and the local community expands employment opportunities for its citizens, augments its tax base, and promotes its reputation for having a favorable business climate.

From an economic perspective, however, local government use of tax abatements, tax credits, and tax increment financing (TIF) is inefficient for two reasons: (1) it represents government interference in the marketplace, and (2) it creates a mismatch between the benefits from new job opportunities that inevitably spill over into surrounding or overlapping governments and the cost that is paid for by taxpayers only in the jurisdiction providing the tax incentives.

Market interference A locally financed tax abatement lowers the cost of production for qualifying firms, which makes the jurisdiction more cost competitive with another city or county. However, even in the absence of a government-provided incentive, a business will choose the location for new investment that minimizes its production costs. Energy-intensive firms search for locations with lower energy costs; labor-intensive firms seek out locations with low labor costs; and technology-dependent firms locate in areas with an ample supply of technologists. The point is that not all locations are equally desirable alternatives for firms seeking to relocate. Economic incentives interfere in the decision-making process by enhancing a community's locational advantages beyond what they would have been without such incentives, and in so doing, these incentives may lure business investment to less than optimal locations. In other words, tax incentives reduce the neutrality of local revenue policies.

Spillover benefits People and money move unhindered across state and local borders. If a city uses a tax-incentive package to attract a new business, the cost of those incentives is borne by local taxpayers while the benefits may accrue to a much broader area. For example, job creation financed by a city benefits job seekers from surrounding areas, too. No economic development initiative has ever successfully included a residency requirement for job beneficiaries.

Revenue windfalls that can accrue to overlapping governments are another type of spillover benefit. For example, locally financed tax relief enhances a firm's profitability, resulting in increased income tax revenue for state and federal governments. State sales tax revenue also increases as businesses and households increase their consumption.

Why local governments use tax incentives

Given the inherent inefficiencies of locally financed incentives for economic growth, why do so many jurisdictions use these incentives? Local government managers must formulate decisions and make policy recommendations in the context of *public perceptions* that business "pays its way" and that a tax incentive will more than "pay for itself" in the long term as new jobs and additional business investment follow.

Research supports these perceptions. In a study of Midwestern states, William Oakland and William Testa found that, on average, businesses pay 2.4 times in taxes what they receive back in tax-supported services. The minimum ratio in their sample was 1.9, meaning that in the worst case, businesses pay almost $2 in taxes for every $1 in tax-supported benefits they receive.[2] Tax incentives provide local governments with a mechanism for better aligning the tax burden that businesses incur with the public benefits they receive.

A second reason for the popularity of tax incentives is the need to signal a hospitable business environment. Tax incentives provide compelling evidence of a local government's commitment to keeping existing jobs and attracting new ones.

A related reason is that businesses may pressure local leaders to offer incentives, playing one local government against another. Municipalities in economic decline are especially vulnerable to such pressure: they can afford neither the tax incentives nor the political consequences of refusing to offer them. A related issue concerns whether incentives result in no net change in overall business investment as capital flows from areas with less competitive incentives to areas with greater incentives. Research indicates that in the case of enterprise zones the increase in new business investment was offset by the loss from disinvestment by existing businesses, and this loss was most evident in states with larger areas devoted to enterprise zones.[3] At the local level, an aggressive economic development strategy does generally produce benefits for the host city or county but those benefits may come with a commensurate decline in business investment within the jurisdiction or the region.

Thus, the issue for local leaders has become not *whether* to influence the locational decisions of businesses but rather *how* to create a favorable business environment. And in this respect, interlocal competition for business investment and the mobility of business capital have made tax incentives a standard tool in the local economic development toolbox.

Tax relief for business investment

The fundamental purpose of tax incentives is to encourage a firm to reduce its cost of doing business by relocating to the host city or state. Incentives for business investment fall into three general categories: (1) tax incentives, such as TIF, tax abatements, tax exemptions, and tax credits; (2) nontax incentives, such as subsidized loans and industrial development bonds (IDBs); and (3) direct services such as land acquisition, site preparation, preemployment training, and publicly provided infrastructure.[4] The following discussion considers only the four types of tax incentives.

Initially, local and state governments used specifically designated federal aid to target their economic development initiatives and stimulate reinvestment in blighted areas. With the decline in that aid, those governments have increasingly broadened their use of incentives to include nonblighted areas and have sought other revenues, such as the sales tax and development and utility charges, to support economic development. Meanwhile, states have reduced their own economic development expenditures by giving local governments the financial responsibility to provide incentives on their own and the discretion to determine the type and amount of incentives they will offer. This has allowed states to avoid mandating that local governments provide such aid while knowing that interlocal competition will compel them to make concessions available. In most cases, it is a city- or county-designed package of incentives that provides the primary lure for businesses seeking an inducement.

Types of tax incentives offered by local governments

Next to IDBs, tax incentives are the most frequently used method for promoting economic growth. They are relatively easy to implement, and unlike IDBs and public financing for infrastructure, they immediately improve a business's income statement by reducing its operating costs. Of course, if all competing firms in an industry receive the same tax incentives, compe-

A typology of tax incentives

One way to classify tax incentives is by the component in the basic tax equation (tax base x tax rate = tax liability) that is initially targeted by the incentive. Ultimately, all incentives are intended to influence tax liability, but they differ in which component is targeted. The following typology profiles tax incentives by whether they initially alter the tax base, tax rate, or tax liability. For example, a tax exemption excludes a portion or all of the value of a category of property, sales, or income from the *tax base*. A split tax roll, by contrast, creates a multitiered rate structure that levies a lower *tax rate* on preferred types of property, sales, or income—for example, the two-tiered property tax rate used by Michigan for public education (discussed in Chapter 3). A tax credit, on the other hand, is a dollar-for-dollar reduction in *tax liability*.

Tax base	Tax rate	Tax liability
Tax abatement	Split tax roll	Tax credit
Tax exemption	Tax rate freeze	Tax rebate
Tax increment financing		
Tax base sharing		

tition will lower prices for the firms' products rather than increase the firms' profits.

Tax incentives enjoy widespread public approval when presented as aids to job creation. As mentioned earlier, most people assume that incentives more than pay for themselves. Whether this is true, however, must be determined on a case-by-case basis and only after careful analysis of the economic impact of the firm's investment. The accompanying sidebar summarizes the range of tax incentives used by state and local governments, and the sections that follow focus on the three most popular locally provided incentives: abatements, exemptions, and TIF.

Tax abatements Tax abatements, the most popular incentive and the least costly to administer, temporarily reduce the property (or sales) tax burden of a business. They work in several different ways, depending on state law. In the case of a property tax abatement, one common method is to exempt all or a portion of the taxable value of the new investment in a building and equipment for a specified number of years (usually ten to fifteen), after which the property is assessed and taxed at the prevailing rate. An alternative involves freezing the tax liability at its predevelopment level for the abatement period; in exchange, developers must make contractually agreed-upon improvements in the designated area, which may include hiring from the local labor pool. Yet a third approach is to abate all tax liability but require payments in lieu of taxes (PILOTs) on the predevelopment value of the tax base. PILOTs, which would constitute a provision of the abatement agreement, are subject to negotiation.

Tax abatements were originally used for property taxes. More recently, local governments have abated sales taxes, or at least a portion of them, for new retail developments such as "big-box" retailers. In this case, the abatement typically takes the form of a tax credit. The retailer retains a portion of the sales taxes collected rather than remitting the full amount to the local or state government.

According to compilation from state and federal reports, thirty-seven states now sanction the use of tax abatements by local governments.[5] These states may also provide for the partial abatement of state taxes. Although states and their local governments usually pursue their economic development initiatives independently of each other, states that permit local tax abatements typically require that local governments adopt policies to guide their use of abatements. These policies specify the qualifications for an abatement, the approval process, and the terms of the abatement agreement.

Qualifying businesses Most states allow a broad range of industries to participate, especially if the abatements are targeted to blighted areas. Some states or local policies may restrict abatements to predetermined reinvestment zones where business investment is targeted to stimulate economic growth. Iowa and Illinois restrict their abatements to new firms moving into a local jurisdiction from another state or country or to an existing firm expanding its production capacity by adding to an existing facility.

In stipulating the qualifications for a partial or full abatement of property or sales taxes, the local policy may specify a minimum investment that must be made in new construction or renovation, which may include new equipment; the number of new jobs to be created by the proposed investment; and the economic life of the proposed project (i.e., the number of years the facility is expected to be operational). Some policies may impose even more specific criteria, especially where a municipality or county has already well-established agglomeration economies. Even if a business qualifies for an abatement, however, local governments typically have the discretion to grant such benefits on a case-by-case basis.

Approval process States typically give their municipalities or counties responsibility for approving abatements. But other overlapping local governments, such as schools and special districts, also levy property or sales taxes. Thus, for its benefits to be maximized, the abatement should be extended to these other jurisdictions—an issue that has become the focus of considerable disagreement and litigation. Those on one side of the issue say that all local jurisdictions, including school districts, should participate in encouraging redevelopment of an area because all will enjoy the future revenue benefits from the increased property value. Those on the other side contend that maintaining or improving the urban environment is the responsibility of a municipality, not a school district. Not surprisingly, overlapping jurisdictions resist the loss of tax revenue, and states often give them the choice to participate in an abatement.

Louisiana is the only state in which the state commerce department may exempt new or expanding firms from *local* property taxes without the approval of the local governments affected by the decision. At the other extreme, Maryland compensates local governments for up to half the lost revenue from property tax credits approved for firms locating in enterprise zones, to the extent that funds are appropriated by the state legislature.

Terms of abatement agreements Once an abatement is approved, local governments usually enter into contractual agreements that specify the improvements or restorations that both government and business are to make as a condition for abatement. These agreements, which are typically made with the developer of the property, may specify the amount of exemption and the method of calculating it; the improvements to be made and the time line for completion; any documentation that the property owner must provide periodically to demonstrate compliance with the agreement; the number and types of new jobs, if any, that must be added by the project; the provisions for access and inspection by city personnel; the minimum wage on projects receiving an incentive; and a **clawback clause** that specifies the terms for recovering lost property tax revenue should the owner fail to honor the contract's terms.

Reporting abatements In 2015, the Governmental Accounting Standards Board issued Statement No. 77 requiring state and local governments to include in their annual financial reports the total reduction in tax revenues caused by tax abatements, the mechanism used to reduce tax liability (e.g., reduction in assessed value), and the provisions, if any, for recapturing lost revenue.[6]

Tax exemptions Tax exemptions permanently exclude from the tax base particular types of transactions or property. For example, building materials used in construction may be exempted from a local-option sales tax. A common form of property tax exemption—a freeport exemption—extends to inventory items, both raw materials and finished goods, that move across state borders for fabrication or sale. By targeting exemptions to businesses with inventories, local governments can stimulate significant agglomeration economies. For example, a community that serves as a transportation hub—either by highway, railroad, or airline—may use its competitive advantage to become a center for warehousing. Most states now extend some sort of partial exemption for goods in transit, but the parameters vary.

In Texas, for example, the freeport exemption is a local option for cities, counties, and school districts. One, two, or all three overlapping local governments may extend an exemption, which is available on all inventories brought into the state for "fabrication, assembling, manufacture, storage or processing" and then exported outside the state within 175 days. If the local governing body adopts the exemption by ordinance, Texas law provides that the exemption can never be revoked.

Of the four types of tax incentives, exemptions are the most powerful at stimulating growth. At the same time, they are the least amenable for targeting economic development efforts because they almost always exist as a blanket provision (covering all inventory or all sales of a particular type) in state law. Moreover, they deprive a local government of the discretion to target its tax incentives to industries that will provide the greatest benefits to its economic development goals. Businesses, however, generally prefer tax exemptions because those that meet the provisions of state law qualify for the exemption, and the exemption, once approved, is virtually impossible to repeal.

Tax increment financing TIF is authorized in forty-eight states; only Arizona does not authorize TIF and California has terminated its use.[7] Although California was the first to adopt TIF in 1952, the state disbanded all 400-plus redevelopment agencies in 2012 after a report prepared by the Legislative Analyst's Office concluded that they had not been effective at attracting business development to California.[8]

Purpose and design Unlike tax abatements, which are typically awarded to businesses on a case-by-case basis, TIF targets local tax incentives to an area that has lagged in development; this area is thus designated a TIF district. The design of TIF is basically the same across all states: the increased property tax revenue resulting from redevelopment in the TIF district is dedicated to financing the development-related costs in that district. Property in the TIF district is taxed at the same rate as all other property in the host city or county. However, its property tax revenue is divided into two categories: (1) taxes on the predevelopment value of the tax base are kept by each overlapping taxing jurisdiction and (2) taxes generated from the increased property value resulting from new development in the district are retained in a tax increment fund, usually administered by an appointed board.[9] TIFs grant preferential treatment only in that tax revenues *produced by* the district are dedicated to financing public improvements in the district thereby making the TIF a bounded benefits-based levy.

Typically, tax-exempt TIF bonds are sold up front to provide financing for the purchase and preparation of the land, including preparation for industrial, commercial, or residential development, and for the installation of public infrastructure, such as streets, lights, water and sewer lines, curbs, gutters, and landscaping. Once prepared, the land is sold to developers at a price that is often below the local government's cost of preparing the site, a technique known as a **land write-down**. The predevelopment costs, including write-downs, are recouped through the tax increment fund over the life of the project, and the money in the fund is usually used to repay TIF bonds.

The underlying assumptions of the TIF approach to economic development are that locally financed improvements will draw private investment into the TIF district, and that without those improvements, private investment would not occur. Whereas a tax abatement draws business investment by lowering the property (or sales) tax burden, TIF lures such investment by providing a ready-made site for construction, usually provided by the local government at a subsidized price, with publicly funded amenities. The upfront financing for site preparation is repaid by developers, whose property taxes on the incremental increase in property values are earmarked to repay the bonds as they mature over several years. The strongest appeal of a TIF district is the greater returns to businesses investing in the district that come from the agglomeration economies. For example, Dallas has designed TIF districts that cater to professional sports, the visual and performing arts, public transit corridor, and wholesale business.

Responsibility for costs Although TIF is more complex and costly to administer than tax abatements, private firms generally prefer it. With TIF, the local government shares the financial risk of the TIF district's failure with developers who invest in the district. But should the increment in property tax revenues be insufficient to meet the annual debt service costs, the city is responsible for repayment of the outstanding debt—in which case the city must find some other source of funds to prevent a bond default. Local governments also use TIF to

Figure 6–1 Stages in the TIF Life Cycle

Proposing a TIF district

State law typically restricts TIF to blighted areas, although laws are usually lax in definition of blight.

- All states require notifying overlapping local jurisdictions;
- Hold a public hearing where affected individuals and governments may weigh in on the proposal.

↓

Preparing a redevelopment plan

Host government appoints a board of directors; responsible for preparing project and financial plans for the district.

- Redevelopment plan guides the implementation of projects and identifies commitments made by public, nonprofit, and private sector participants.
- Financial plan should include realistic estimates of the proposed public expenditures; cost of site preparation, including land acquisition, relocation, and demolition; and the cost of project administration.
- Plan should identify the type of business investment targeted for the district (arts, sports, historical preservation, retail) to build an agglomeration economy.

↓

Creating a TIF district

Formally establish the TIF district by ordinance.

- Authorize creation of a fund to track associated revenues and expenditures.
- Determine predevelopment value of its tax base; all affected local and state agencies are notified of that value.
- Council may authorize issuance of TIF bonds to initiate land preparation and construction.
- Establish a reserve fund, possibly using money accumulated from other successful TIF district projects, to cover such exigencies.

↓

Implementing a TIF district

Obtain funding for land acquisition and site preparation from (1) TIF-backed bonds, (2) current revenues from host governments, or (3) upfront funding of capital improvements by private sector who are then reimbursed from future TIF revenues.

- Prepare annual audited report of financial activities of the TIF district.
- Report documents sources of revenue, amount and purpose of expenditures, amount of principal and interest due on TIF debt, and current appraised value of property.

↓

Terminating a TIF district

State law typically restricts TIF to blighted areas, although laws are usually lax in definition of blight.

- Illinois limits the life to twenty-three years or until all project costs are paid.
- Once terminated the property value reverts to the overlapping taxing jurisdictions who can now collect the full levy from the taxable value.
- On termination, all obligations liquidated and the TIF board is disbanded.

stimulate agglomeration economies in and adjacent to the redevelopment district, a strategy essential to building a sustainable local economy.[10]

State laws vary on whether overlapping local jurisdictions, such as counties and school districts, that levy property taxes on the TIF district must share in the cost of redevelopment by forgoing the tax increment captured by the district. Without TIF, cities bear the full cost of redevelopment while overlapping jurisdictions reap revenue windfalls from increased property values. Opposition to TIF comes primarily from those overlapping jurisdictions that are required to share in the costs.

Effectiveness in stimulating economic growth TIF relies on public–private partnerships to add new construction and employment in the district that would not occur in the absence of the partnership.[11] The benefits that accrue to each partner in the TIF district are dependent on the success of the other partners. One consequence of TIF and of the new order of governance is their appeal to creating public goods with bounded benefits. The first issue raised by TIFs concerns their effectiveness at increasing taxable property values in the TIF district as well as throughout the city or county. In a study of eighteen TIF districts in the City of Dallas, Robert Bland and Michael Overton found that investment in infrastructure and other public amenities by the city leveraged private investment such that the outcome was greater than otherwise would have been the case.[12]

The second issue concerns the factors that help achieve success in using TIF. Using property sales from the Milwaukee area, Deborah Carroll found that a property's location within a TIF district is positively related to its assessed property value.[13] She also found that older TIF districts have higher property values compared with newer ones. Bland and Overton found in their study of Dallas's TIF districts that, as the city gained experience in establishing additional TIF districts and in administering existing ones, property values increased substantially.[14] Two important implications come from this finding: first, early attempts at using TIF are likely to be less successful than later initiatives, and second, local managers gain operational knowledge in building a successful TIF district as it ages.

Tax credits The fourth approach to tax incentives—tax credits—provides a dollar-for-dollar reduction in tax liability. From a business perspective, the appeal is the direct effect that a credit has on a company's bottom line. From a local government perspective, the appeal is that the business shares in the success of the development initiative. A common approach for sales tax abatements, for example, is to give a retailer a tax credit on sales tax receipts in exchange for the business investment. The retailer shares in the success of the venture by sharing a percentage of the sales tax revenue generated by the retail business. Property tax abatements may also be provided on a tax credit basis.[15] The company receives a remittance for a predetermined percentage of the property taxes paid over the life of the agreement.

The downside of credits is that the city or county must make a cash payment to the business, and that payment often must be accounted for in the operating budget. That visibility raises the political stakes for the city or county, especially from competitors who do not receive the largesse.

Assessment of locally financed tax incentives

Tax incentives can be used to negotiate benefits for the local economy. As has been noted, tax incentive agreements commonly stipulate the number of new jobs that a firm must create and even the percentage of new hires who must reside within the city or county. Enforcing these agreements, however, has proven challenging for city administrators. For example, after conducting a compliance audit of incentive agreements, the City of Fort Worth found that several firms had not met their employment requirements. In such situations the city must decide whether to void the agreement and suffer even further reductions in its tax base, modify the agreement to reflect more realistic employment targets, or disregard the terms of the agreement.

But agreements notwithstanding, public finance experts disagree about the cost-effectiveness of tax incentives. It is indisputable that tax concessions improve the competitive position of a local government, but are their costs, measured in foregone revenue, worth the benefits from the business investment? Are tax incentives essential to attracting new business investment or do they merely encourage businesses to relocate within the region? The general conclusions about tax incentives can be summarized as follows:

- Tax incentives are economically most easily justified in marginal cases, where a firm is otherwise indifferent to the choice between two or more possible locations. Yet even in these instances, competing local governments tend to offer nearly comparable incentives that effectively cancel each other out.
- Tax incentives are politically most appropriate for state and local governments with relatively high and persistent rates of unemployment. Unfortunately, these governments are the least able to bear the cost of tax incentives, particularly when competing with more prosperous jurisdictions.[16]
- Tax incentives are also most appropriate near state or local boundaries, which is where governments often encounter the most intense competition for business investment (i.e., border-city/state effects), and especially in retail centers such as shopping malls. This is also why a number of states have curious exceptions to their tax policies, such as no state income tax for residents of Texarkana, Arkansas, which shares a border with Texarkana, Texas, where there is no state income tax.
- To the extent that local taxes on businesses exceed the benefits in public services that those businesses receive, tax incentives provide local governments with a mechanism for more equitably aligning the tax burden on business, particularly for mobile sectors. Thus, tax incentives make the most sense, politically and economically, for high-tech industries and services and the least sense for retail and residential development.[17]
- Once a city or region establishes agglomeration economies, the necessity for tax incentives declines. However, anecdotal evidence suggests that it is difficult to turn off the incentive spigot once it has been opened.[18] And if a local economy is heavily dependent on one industry or service—for example, the entertainment industry in Nashville, auto manufacturing in Detroit, oil refining in Houston—city and county budgets become more vulnerable to the cycles in that industry.
- Local governments with taxing powers limited to the property tax are less able to recover the cost of a tax incentive through increased revenues than those with access to an income tax or a sales tax.
- Local governments in economically linked metropolitan areas retain fewer benefits from tax incentives within their jurisdiction. For example, a tax abatement offered by a central city will produce spillover benefits in surrounding suburban communities that supply some of the labor force. The smaller the geographic size of a city or county, the more the benefits of tax incentives are exported to surrounding communities. For this reason, central cities tend to use TIF more aggressively because they can better create bounded benefits from the city's investment. In order to distribute the benefits of commercial and industrial development more equitably, a few metropolitan regions, such as Minneapolis/St. Paul, Minnesota, have adopted tax base–sharing plans, in which increases in the property tax base from new business development are shared with all local governments.
- Political expediency requires that local governments offer some type of tax incentive if for

no other reason than to send a message that they have a "favorable business environment." Public managers must consider what it costs in tax incentives to lure new business investment without alienating existing businesses. Research evidence also shows that, in the case of TIFs, success increases with each successive district that is established and the longer a district exists. Local managers acquire both institutional and operational knowledge from the public-private collaborations that characterize TIF.

Tax incentives for professional sports and the arts

Professional sports stadiums and performing and visual arts centers that demand tax-supported assistance present special challenges to local governments. Even the spreading use of subsidies for outdoor displays—Cincinnati's pigs, Dallas's cantilever bridge—raises questions about the extent of public support for such community symbols. Just how long is the "arm of economic development"?

Such symbols have their origins in antiquity. The Athenians built the Parthenon and the Romans the Coliseum, both monuments to their cultural accomplishments. But the past four decades have witnessed a significant increase in public funding in the United States for such initiatives under the guise of economic development. Of the thirty Major League Baseball teams, twenty-four play in stadiums built since 1989;[19] fifteen stadiums alone have been constructed since 2000, many partially or fully funded by the host city.

In the case of the National Football League (NFL), twenty-three stadiums were constructed for teams since 1992, many with substantial tax subsidies, mostly sales and hotel/motel tax revenue.[20] Both Los Angeles and Las Vegas are constructing new stadiums, each costing in excess of $2 billion and both expected to open in 2020. Only two of the NFL's thirty-two teams—the Green Bay Packers and the Chicago Bears—play in stadiums constructed before 1960, although both stadiums—Green Bay's Lambeau Field, built in 1957, and Chicago's Soldier Field, built in 1924—have been extensively renovated.

Performing and visual arts centers also receive dedicated tax revenue to subsidize their operations or capital improvements. Americans for the Arts, a national advocacy organization, estimates that in 2015 the 4,500 local arts agencies in the United States received approximately $738 million (54 percent) of their funding from a city or county government.[21] The most common form of local tax support is a hotel/motel tax, although occasionally local governments may dedicate a portion of the property tax or sales tax for local arts and historical preservation. For example, the City of Denton, Texas, dedicates 3 percent of its 7-percent hotel/motel tax to the annual operating costs of the arts. This support is over and above the locally funded facilities that are owned by cities but leased to sports franchises or arts organizations, such as AT&T Stadium, which the City of Arlington, Texas, owns and leases to the Dallas Cowboys for $2 million per year through 2038.

But again the question is whether these investments provide economic returns greater than their cost in public subsidies. And the resounding answer from numerous studies—particularly those analyzing the economic benefits of professional sports teams to household income and job creation—is no.[22] So if they are not justified economically, what justifies such massive public investment in these facilities?

Assessing the case for government financing

The case that is made for public financing of stadiums and arts venues is that these facilities either (1) provide public (collective) benefits or (2) contribute to the economic growth (job creation, increases in property values, growth in personal income) of the community. For true public goods, or even merit goods with substantial collective benefits, tax support is justified up to the value of the collective benefits. But professional stadiums and arts complexes, however meritorious, do not meet the criteria of nondivisibilty and nonexcludability. Admission tickets are required to their events, and nonsubscribers are excluded from enjoying any direct benefits. Thus, they do not qualify as pure public goods.

A more convincing case might be that because of the intangible public benefits they provide—a professional sports team or symphony orchestra, like a library or a museum, enriches the life and character of a community and contributes to civic pride—these facilities qualify as merit goods and so a partial subsidy is justified. In an analysis of attitudinal data for residents in the Indianapolis area, one study found that "attendance is an important element in determining pride."[23] That is, those who attend sporting and cultural events derive more pride from the event than those who do not attend. A nationwide survey of the public's perception of megasport events found that a majority did not think these events produce benefits in excess of their costs.[24] And a study of Portland, Oregon, found modest collective benefits from hosting a major league baseball team, although the value of those benefits was much smaller than the huge public subsidies that stadiums typically receive.[25]

In terms of the second justification for public subsidies—the impact of sports stadiums and arts venues on economic development—the research is conclusive: not only do the benefits to economic growth fall short of the cost of the subsidy, but these venues may even have an adverse effect on economic growth.[26] Whether measured by job creation, changes in consumer spending, or revitalization of a blighted area, independent analyses consistently show that public investment in stadiums, in particular, has no effect on economic growth.[27]

Part of the reason is that household spending for entertainment is limited. If people buy more tickets for professional sports, they simply reduce spending for other entertainment purposes, and the result is no net economic gain for the region. Only 5 to 20 percent of the fans at professional athletic events are from outside the area.[28] While some visual or performing arts events may have a strong regional draw, it is unlikely that, on average, the percentage of out-of-area patrons is any greater. Thus, apart from rare events such as the World Series and the Super Bowl, athletic and arts events are not effective mechanisms for exporting the burden for financing stadiums and performance halls.

Finally, the benefits of professional athletics and the arts to economic development are constrained by the absence of significant **multiplier effects**. While the relocation of a manufacturing or technology firm may yield as much as a $2 impact on the local economy for every $1 in new investment, professional sports teams have a much lower multiplier effect.[29] This is explained by their limited season, use of lower-skilled labor for services, and narrow opportunities for agglomeration economies.

Civic symbolism

Why do local government leaders acquiesce to the demands of professional sports team owners for new and increasingly more costly stadiums? Why do cities feel compelled to build and operate concert and opera halls, theaters, and art museums? In fact, cities and civic leaders, from pharaohs to presidents, have always erected monuments as a visible legacy of their leadership. What greater testimonial can there be to your tenure as a leader than to have your name on a brass plaque discreetly but visibly displayed near the main entrance of a new facility?

Seen in this historical context, sports stadiums and arts centers serve much the same function—particularly in Western culture, where benefits to the whole are valued over the immortalization of individual leaders. Beyond the civic pride, quality of life, and "bragging rights" that these venues bring to a community, they serve as permanent reminders of the community's past accomplishments and as proclamations of anticipated achievements. Just as the arch defines St. Louis and the Eiffel Tower Paris, so too does Bass Hall symbolically herald

Fort Worth's cultural achievements and Madison Square Garden New York City's athletic and artistic triumphs.

Regardless of what team owners and arts proponents may say, the value of stadiums and arts venues is symbolic, not economic. They are more than public art. These structures have tangible—albeit political—value, particularly for those leaders responsible for their development and construction. But Americans' preoccupation with economic growth and general lack of historical perspective complicate the local leader's task of rationalizing the construction of new facilities. When such initiatives are presented as civic symbolism, arguments faulting their lack of value as engines for economic growth fall by the wayside. But promoting them as symbolic tributes to a community's accomplishments poses political hurdles that the more pragmatic would prefer to avoid. Not surprisingly, when put to a vote, such initiatives result in highly contentious elections with each side making dubious claims about expected benefits and costs.

But public values change and monuments may lose their civic significance and even become embarrassments. They may cause division within a community when they herald persons or events that, on more reflective discussion, denigrate the dignity of others. In recent years, the extensive number of monuments memorializing the Confederacy or the subjugation of Native Americans have opened up conversations about what is appropriate to immortalize in a monument and what is not. Some maintain that these monuments recognize legitimate historical persons or events and to remove them is to deny their historicity. Others maintain that these monuments glorify persons or events that effectively denigrate the dignity and rights of oppressed persons. As these conversations progress, community leaders must recognize the role of such civic symbols as statements of our respect for each other. Monuments lose their symbolic value when they no longer extol that dignity.

Guidelines for using tax incentives

Every local government has a unique set of attributes that make it a more attractive location for some types of industries than for others. When considering the use of tax incentives to enhance a community's attractiveness for new business development, local government leaders would do well to keep the following guidelines in mind:

- Before launching an economic development program, local leaders should develop a **strategic plan** that identifies (1) the community's economic strengths, weaknesses, opportunities, and threats; (2) their economic development goals, measurable objectives, and strategies for achieving those objectives; and (3) measurable benchmarks for assessing the progress toward achieving their goals. Local leaders should commit to annually reviewing the strategic plan and revising its elements where warranted. Several studies have found evidence that having a strategic plan for promoting economic development was of greatest benefit to existing businesses.[30]
- A local government offering tax incentives should have access to at least one broad-based nonproperty tax, such as a general sales tax or an income tax, in order to capture more revenue benefits from economic growth.
- The larger the jurisdiction, the better the match between those taxpayers bearing the cost of the incentives and those benefiting from the increased economic activity; by implication, counties are better suited for providing tax incentives than are cities, towns, or villages.
- Economically declining jurisdictions are the most vulnerable to "giving away too much" when negotiating with a business that is contemplating the relocation or expansion of an existing facility.

- Incentives may be appropriate as a strategic measure to diversify the local tax base and thereby reduce a local government's budget to the vulnerabilities of the business cycle. The greatest benefit of tax incentives comes when they are used sparingly and strategically to build agglomeration economies. For urban areas already benefiting from agglomeration economies, it is not necessary to use tax incentives to attract other firms in the same industry.
- TIF is preferred to tax abatements and tax exemptions as a more equitable approach to attracting business investment. Numerous studies have shown that tax incentives do not add to the overall taxable value of property in a city. However, they do increase the value of property within the TIF district.
- In the long term, locally financed tax incentives may prove counterproductive because they shift the cost of services to other taxpayers, who then have an incentive to move to a lower-tax jurisdiction.

For cities and counties with vibrant economies and moderately growing populations, the best approach to promoting economic growth is to maintain property tax rates at competitive levels. Tax incentives are no substitute for prudent budget policies that promote responsible financial management practices. As a case in point, three major employers in the city of Hartford, Connecticut, committed to give the city $50 million if city leaders developed "a stable and sustainable fiscal climate" in the city.[31] Business leaders value local governments that invest in good management practices and professional public administration.

Tax relief for citizens

While local governments have pursued tax relief for business through targeted tax incentives, citizens have grown increasingly resistant to paying more taxes, particularly property taxes. The groundswell of resistance began in 1978 when Californians ratified Proposition 13, rolling back property tax rates to a combined maximum of 1 percent for all overlapping local governments and limiting annual increases in taxable (assessed) values to 2 percent or to the purchase price whenever the property is sold. Tax and expenditure limitations (TELs) at the state and local levels have drawn on the California experience. Although states have always imposed limitations on the taxing capabilities of local governments, the following discussion focuses on recent efforts to limit the local tax base, tax rates, and tax levies. While efforts to limit growth in local expenditures have also been undertaken, these have proven less attractive politically as strategies for constraining local budgets.

Tax relief for citizens has the potential to undo the gains made through tax incentives designed to attract business investment. The local manager walks a tightrope, addressing the political need to provide such relief while not unduly shifting the burden to more mobile businesses. Much of the relief has targeted taxes paid by individuals and households, as summarized in the accompanying sidebar. While each state has pursued its own approach to providing relief, their various approaches can be grouped into broad-based measures and more targeted measures.

Broad tax relief measures

Four states—Colorado (1992), Missouri (1996), Nevada (1996), and Oklahoma (1992)—responded to citizens' pleas for tax relief by adopting a requirement that increases in tax rates could not be made without voter approval. Colorado's Taxpayer Bill of Rights (TABOR) not only requires voter approval for any increases in local tax rates but also restricts revenue growth in local governments to inflation plus population growth—unless voters approve otherwise. Missouri's Hancock Amendment, one of the more sweeping local revenue limitations in the

A typology of tax relief measures for citizens

As with tax incentives, tax relief measures initially target one of the factors in the basic tax equation (tax base × tax rate = tax liability). Ultimately, all tax relief measures alter tax liability, but they differ in what component is targeted. The following typology profiles tax relief initiatives by whether they initially alter the tax base, tax rate, or tax liability.

Tax base	Tax rate	Tax liability
Cap on increases in taxable value	Split tax roll	Tax credit (circuitbreaker)
Acquisition appraisals (Prop 13)	Tax rate freeze	Tax levy freeze
Tax exemption	Truth-in-taxation	Tax liability freeze
Homestead exemption	Voter approval	Tax rebate
Fractional assessments		Tax amnesty
Sales tax holiday		

nation, requires voter approval not only of taxes but also of fees. Nineteen states limit annual increases in the taxable value of property, but the limit usually applies only to single-family residential property.[32]

A number of states cap tax rates, particularly for the property tax. Thirty-five states limit property tax rates—some to a fixed percentage (as in California) and some with limits that can be overridden by a majority or supermajority of the council or of voters—and some states limit the percentage increase in the property tax rate.[33] Although many states have constitutional limits on the maximum rates that particular types of local governments can impose, such as $1.50 for cities in Texas not operating with a home rule charter and $2.50 for those with a home rule charter, Proposition 13 unleashed citizen efforts to limit the combined tax rates of overlapping local governments. Massachusetts limits the overlapping tax levy to 2.5 percent of the tax base, and yields in the property tax cannot increase by more than 2.5 percent annually unless approved by at least two-thirds of the voters. Idaho and Arizona both impose a combined cap of 1 percent of the tax base. By contrast, a tax liability freeze (discussed in the accompanying sidebar, "Freezing tax liability of older homeowners") limits changes in an individual property owner's tax liability.

Thirteen states use some variation of truth-in-taxation to hold local councils and commissioners more accountable for increases in the local property tax burden.[34] Two states, Kentucky and Texas, give voters the power to overrule their local governments should their lawmakers approve an extraordinary increase in the tax revenue. The advantage of truth-in-taxation—particularly in states such as Florida and Utah, where a mailed notice is sent to each property owner before a final tax rate is approved—is that it elevates the visibility of the tax rate–setting process while preserving local autonomy from state fiat.

A comparative analysis of the effectiveness of TELs in Kansas made the interesting discovery that truth-in-taxation is more effective at limiting increases in per capita property taxes than the presumably more rigid tax levy limitation.[35] The researchers conclude that "these results would seem to support the notion that local officials in Kansas demonstrated a clear measure of self-imposed fiscal restraint when given greater local choice and flexibility in budgetary priorities" that comes with truth-in-taxation.[36]

Freezing the tax liability of older homeowners[1]

An emerging trend is ballot measures to permanently freeze city and county property taxes for homeowners who are at least 65 or who are disabled. Who could be opposed to such an idea? Tax relief has great appeal across demographic and political lines.

However, a freeze on seniors' tax liability negatively impacts property owners who are not eligible for the freeze (existing businesses and young families, for instance), adversely affects attracting new job-creating businesses, and compromises the future prosperity of a community.

Why is the senior tax freeze bad for noneligible property owners? A freeze does not decrease the total tax collections; it simply shifts the tax burden onto other property owners (those who are less than 65 and businesses). While senior citizens continue to enjoy all the benefits of locally produced services, the freeze shifts to these other property owners a greater share of the cost of local services.

A basic principle of fiscal conservatism is that each generation should take responsibility for the cost in public services it creates. A senior tax freeze shifts even more of that burden to a shrinking pool of property owners.

Some may argue that senior citizens are unfairly taxed and that equity concerns justify this additional tax relief. If fairness is the driving force behind property tax relief, such relief should benefit all property owners rather than a select demographic group. It is likely that not only does a senior tax freeze shift the property tax burden to other property owners but also incentivizes seniors to pressure their local councils for more services since the cost is borne by others. In other words, a freeze creates incentives for local governments to spend more than they otherwise would.

Why is the senior tax freeze bad for job creation? Given that the freeze shifts more of the cost of services to other property owners, it increases their cost of doing business in a community. A local government must now up the ante even more to attract job-creating businesses.

A freeze increases the cost of homeownership for those under 65 by increasing their tax burden. That discourages new housing construction, especially for young, first-time home-buyers. Younger households are drawn to neighboring cities without a freeze.

At the same time, the freeze lowers the cost of homeownership for those 65 and older and makes neighborhoods serving them more attractive. The freeze artificially alters the housing market and tips the balance to favor homeownership by seniors.

Some have advanced the bogus argument that the freeze will benefit lower-income homeowners. Do not be deceived. The big winners in the tax freeze are owners of higher-valued homes. These homes have the greatest appreciation in value, and their owners stand to benefit handsomely from the freeze over the long term. In short, the freeze widens the gap between wealthy and poor homeowners at the expense of all other property owners.

A freeze is bad for a community because it narrows the funding options available to elected leaders. In short, a senior tax freeze increases the tax burden on other property owners, tips the housing market to favor senior homeownership, and alters the budget choices for local leaders.

1 Portions of this sidebar were taken from Robert L. Bland, Guest Editorial: "Should seniors get tax break?" *Denton Record-Chronicle*, April 23, 2017. Courtesy of *Denton-Record Chronicle* and www.dentonrc.com.

Targeted tax relief measures

In recent years, a number of states have also pursued tax relief measures targeted to specific classes of citizens, particularly senior citizens. For example, Pennsylvania's Act 77 freezes property assessments of senior citizens in counties levying a sales tax. As part of a sweeping tax reform initiative, Michigan adopted a two-tiered rate structure for school property taxes that was designed to reduce the burden on homeowners. In lieu of locally set school taxes, the state now imposes a 6-mill tax on all primary residences and a 24-mill tax on secondary homes and businesses that fund schools. Still other states, such as Texas, freeze the school taxes of senior citizens at the amount they pay in the year that either spouse turns 65. In 2003, Texas voters amended the state constitution to give cities and counties the option to extend the senior tax freeze to their property tax levies. City and county officials have been reluctant to adopt the freeze because of the long-term adverse impact it has on local budgets.

The impact of tax and expenditure limitations

Proponents of TELs contend that reductions in state and local taxes will increase economic growth. Specifically, they contend that increases in per capita income will mean more consumption and investment so that more resources will shift to the private sector, and since the private sector is assumed to be more productive than the public or nonprofit sectors (an assumption that has little support from research), the increased consumption and investment will lead to greater growth in job creation and per capita income. This is a testable proposition: Do tax limitations lead to increased economic growth at the state and local levels?

A related question concerns the effect of TELs on state and local budgets. Do they lead to reduced spending by state and local governments? Do they affect states' capacity to counter the adverse effects of recessions? These are also testable research questions that, not surprisingly, have captured the interest of public administration researchers.

Turning to the first question, if the theory underlying the tax limitation movement is accurate—that lower taxes lead to greater economic growth—then those states with the most restrictive TELs should experience the greatest economic growth. Therese McGuire and Kim Rueben specifically tested this hypothesis using data from Colorado after the state adopted its highly restrictive TABOR in 1992. While they found "some limited evidence for short-term increases to growth (in employment but not household income), these were not sustained in the long term."[37] In fact, five years after TABOR's adoption, job growth in Colorado lagged significantly behind that in other states with comparable economies. In another study, researchers used data from 1985 to 2005 to study the effect of TELs in the forty-eight contiguous states and found that these limitations had no effect on per capita personal income or level of employment.[38] In other words, there was no evidence that TELs affect job growth or household income at the state level. And in yet another study, the more restrictive TELs were found to slow economic growth at the state level and actually lead to a decline in economic growth at the local level.[39]

As for the second question—the effect of TELs on state and local budgets—the evidence is also substantial. Limits on the use of the property tax cause local governments to shift to other resources, especially service charges and user fees. To the extent that some of those revenue sources are more volatile, they put state and local budgets on a roller coaster, experiencing greater and greater swings in revenue yields across the business cycle.[40] TELs also lead local governments, especially school districts, to depend more heavily on state aid, which increases their vulnerability to budget reductions in recessions.

Accumulated evidence from several tax limitation initiatives suggests that their full impact is often delayed by several years—in the case of Proposition 13, even decades—but that their effects become cumulative and most apparent in recessions. It was during the recession of 2001 that Californians began to experience the cumulative effects and drag on economic growth from Proposition 13, effects that built up to a crisis level during the Great Recession of 2007–2009. A study of the property tax cap in Illinois found that in the first few years following its adoption, it slowed the growth in property tax revenues for municipalities and school districts, an effect that was even more pronounced ten years later.[41]

Finally, tax limitations, while providing relief to some fortunate taxpayers, shift the burden to other, often less equitable and economically efficient revenue sources—in particular, more narrow-based excise taxes. Most disconcerting is their long-term impact on state and local governments' capacity to pursue countercyclical measures. Casual observation suggests that recessions are steeper and more protracted in states with limited tax and spending options. TELs make it more difficult for state and local governments to take preemptive action to restore economic stability and strengthen employment opportunities.

Do tax limitations work?

There are two general answers to this question: First, it depends on the type of tax limitation, and second, tax limitations almost never work as proponents intend and often have unintended and counterproductive consequences. Although no comparative analysis of tax limitation measures has been undertaken, casual observation suggests that the measures that limit increases in the tax burden most effectively are those that require voter approval to change tax (or fee) rates, followed by those that require extraordinary majorities of legislative bodies to change the rate or base.

Formal analyses of tax limitations suggest, however, that these measures have consequences that are often unanticipated and even antithetical to the proponents' original intentions. For example, several studies of California's Proposition 13 have found that the amendment has resulted in

- Greater concentration of decision making at the state level
- A significant reduction in the fiscal and political autonomy of local governments, particularly school districts and counties, thereby impeding the home rule capabilities of local governments and their capacity to shape their local economies
- Less accountability for local governments as they shift dependence to more indirect (hidden) taxes and to property exactions such as impact fees
- Marked increases in horizontal inequities between new buyers of property, whose property is assessed at its purchase price, and long-term residents, whose increases in property assessments are limited to 2 percent per annum (resulting in tax burdens for comparable properties that are as much as five times greater for the recent buyer)
- A significant shift in the property tax burden to homeowners and away from business owners because of the more frequent turnover of residential property
- Chronic housing shortages, especially for multifamily units, because of the punitive tax burden for new housing and thus the lower profit margins for newer developments compared with existing developments
- Competitive advantages for established retail and service industries over newer commercial businesses for the same reasons cited immediately above. As a result, retail markets in California are less competitive, which means higher prices for consumers.[1]

1 Gregory D. Saxton, Christopher W. Hoene, and Steven P. Erie, "Fiscal Constraints and the Loss of Home Rule: The Long-Term Impacts of California's Post–Proposition 13 Fiscal Regime," *American Review of Public Administration* 32 (December 2002): 423–454; Carol Douglas, "Proposition 13—25 Years Later," *State Tax Notes* 30 (October 20, 2003): 222–226; Lenny Goldberg and David Kersten, "Huge Disparities Found in California Commercial Property Taxes," *State Tax Notes* 31 (May 10, 2004): 437–457; Randall G. Holcombe, "Tax and Expenditure Limitations: Issues for Florida," *Policy Report* no. 932 (April 2001); Terri A. Sexton, Steve M. Sheffrin, and Arthur O'Sullivan, "Proposition 13: Unintended Effects and Feasible Reforms," *National Tax Journal* 52 (March 1999): 99–111.

Sustainable and resilient community development

There has been a growing sense of collective anxiety about the world's diminishing supply of nonrenewable energy and inability to support, for the long term, the growing affluence of developed and developing nations. **Sustainable economic development**—providing incentives at the community level to promote ecofriendly growth by shifting production to renewable resources—has gained adherents in some cities, especially in North America.[42] At its most basic level, sustainability is a resource allocation issue: "meeting the needs of the present without compromising the ability of future generations to meet their own needs."[43] Some local governments have modified their economic development policies to attract ecofriendly industries and provide incentives for existing industries to convert to more resource-efficient technology.

Sustainable economic development uses many of the conventional tools described in this chapter but targets them for sustainable purposes. For example, sustainable tax incentives would target new development that promotes in-filling (using vacant land within a city's core area), the production of locally grown food, the creation of cooperative ventures, or the financing of a microenterprise loan program. Alternatively, incentives may be used for research and development of new ecofriendly technology. Whatever approaches are taken, citizens will increasingly look to their local government to encourage innovation and experimentation through tax incentives.

Managers have recognized that in communities prone to disasters, including the impact of rising sea levels caused by global warming, the goals of sustainability are closely aligned with those of **disaster resiliency.**[44] Resiliency means the ability to anticipate, withstand, and recover from the consequences of a disaster so as to reduce its cost and the disruption to normal activity that it may cause.[45] Environmental disasters have an immediate adverse impact on own-source revenues and concurrently on require increased expenditures as the community seeks to restore economic and social normalcy.

Sustainable economic development and disaster resiliency share a common goal of adapting communities and their economies to their natural environment. In both cases, local revenue issues should be part of the planning and decision-making processes. Although each community's vulnerability to natural and technological disasters is unique, including policies that promote budget resilience in a comprehensive emergency plan will mitigate the long-term economic effects of those events and its timely return to normal.[46]

Even after their communities have been destroyed by natural or man-made forces, people have a curious habit of returning to rebuild their homes—what might be called the anthill phenomenon. Economic growth has its limits. Cities build out and have no further available space for expansion. Should they try to recreate themselves as they age? Venice, Italy, was once a glorious center of culture and trade. But no amount of investment can stop the inevitable demise of this once glorious jewel of Europe as it slowly sinks into the Adriatic Sea.

While federal and, to a lesser extent, state aid help to offset the cost of responding to and recovering from a disaster, much of that cost goes uncompensated. And increasingly the cost of recovery is being shifted away from the Federal Emergency Management Agency (FEMA) to the states and ultimately local governments. A series of major disasters impose long-term costs on local governments that must be absorbed locally through delayed growth and ultimately higher state and local tax burdens. Thus, when assessing a community's disaster resiliency, the following questions should be considered:

- Is our insurance coverage sufficient for large-scale losses of city or county property?
- What impact would the most likely types of disasters or emergencies have on the property tax base? Sales tax base? Water and wastewater service charges? Other major revenue sources?

- What level of **budget reserves** is appropriate given our community's vulnerability to particular types of disasters or emergencies?
- What protection should be available to cover debt service costs in the event of a disaster?
- What is the cost and what procedures should be followed to restore collections and enforcement of revenues in the event of a disaster?
- Do mutual aid agreements include assistance with revenue administration in the event of a disaster?
- What agreements should be in place with local nonprofits whose mission is to assist households and businesses in times of disaster?
- Under what conditions can the local government incur **short-term debt** to cover the operating costs associated with an emergency or disaster?
- What loans or grants are available from the state or federal government to ensure continuity in operations for the local government?

Conclusion

Local government tax policy pursues two strategies: (1) providing tax incentives to businesses to advance economic prosperity and (2) providing tax relief to residents to curry political favor. Both place heavy demands on local budgets in forgone revenues.

When making locational decisions, businesses are most influenced by business opportunities—the cost of land and labor, the availability of transportation networks, and the presence of agglomeration economies—especially in manufacturing and warehousing. Once they have narrowed their locational choices, especially to a regional or metropolitan area, taxes become an increasingly important factor. At the margin, a local government's tax burden does affect business investment decisions.

And it is at the margin, where a firm is otherwise indifferent to the choice between two or more possible locations, that locally financed tax incentives, such as tax abatements and TIF, are economically most justified. Among local governments, TIF is the most widely used tax incentive; while it is more complex to administer, it creates the least inequities with existing businesses. But studies on the effectiveness of tax incentives, especially TIF, show that while they may increase property values within the redevelopment district, citywide property values do not show any change that can be attributed to TIF.

Similarly, although public subsidies for professional sports and artistic venues have assumed overbearing influence in some large-city budgets, studies consistently find that these venues also add nothing to the local economy (no net increase in jobs or household income). In this case, however, the subsidies are justified because these venues provide intangible benefits: civic pride, symbolic tributes to a community's artistic and athletic accomplishments, and, not unimportantly, tributes to the elected leaders who pushed them through.

While much attention has been focused on strategically using tax incentives to promote economic growth at the state and local levels, taxpayers have intensified their demands for tax relief. Much of the relief has targeted taxes paid by individuals, particularly owners of single-family residences. But because tax relief to citizens shifts more of the local burden onto businesses, it has the potential to undo any gains made through tax incentives designed to attract business investment. Thus, the local manager must find an acceptable balance between the political need to grant tax relief to households and the economic need to attract, encourage, and retain successful business ventures.

Although advocates of TELs contend that reductions in state and local taxes will increase economic growth, a number of studies have found that TELs, in fact, lower economic activity especially at the local level and that their adverse effects accumulate over time. Limits on the property tax in particular cause local governments to shift to other resources and lead to greater dependence on state aid, increasing their vulnerability to budget reductions in recessions.

For cities and counties with vibrant economies and a stable to moderately growing population, the best approach to promoting an economic development strategy is to maintain their property tax and utility rates at competitive levels. Tax incentives are no substitute for prudent budget policies that promote responsible financial management practices.

Notes

1 Daphne A. Kenyon, Adam M. Langley, and Bethany P. Paquin, *Rethinking Property Tax Incentives for Business* (Cambridge, Mass.: Lincoln Institute of Land Policy, 2012), 29, lincolninst.edu/pubs/dl/2024_1423_Rethinking%20Property%20Tax%20Incentives%20for%20Business.pdf/.

2 William H. Oakland and William A. Testa, "The Benefit Principle as a Preferred Approach to Taxing Business in the Midwest," *Economic Development Quarterly* 14 (May 2000): 154–164.

3 Daniele Bondonio and Robert T. Greenbaum, "Do Local Tax Incentives Affect Economic Growth?" *Regional Science & Urban Economics* 37 (2007): 121-136.

4 Ronald C. Fisher, *State & Local Public Finance,* 4th ed. (New York: Routledge, 2016), 619-621.

5 Kenyon, Langley and Paquin, *Rethinking Property Tax Incentives,* 5.

6 Governmental Accounting Standards Board, *Statement No. 77 Tax Abatement Disclosures,* Governmental Accounting Standards Series No. 353, August 2015.

7 Kenyon, Langley and Paquin, *Rethinking Property Tax Incentives,* 5.

8 Ibid., 37.

9 Robert L. Bland and Michael Overton, "Assessing the Contributions of Collaborators in Public–Private Partnerships: Evidence From Tax Increment Financing," *American Review of Public Administration* 46 (July 2016): 418-435.

10 Gerald A. Carlino, "Three Keys to the City: Resources, Agglomeration Economies, and Sorting," *Business Review* (2011): 1–13, philadelphiafed.org/research-and-data/publications/business-review/2011/q3/brq311_three-keys-to-the-city.pdf.

11 Bland and Overton, "Assessing the Contributions of Collaborators in Public–Private Partnerships," 419.

12 Ibid., 431.

13 Deborah Carroll, "Tax Increment Financing and Property Value: An Examination of Business Property Using Panel Data," *Urban Affairs Review,* 43 (March 2008): 520-552.

14 Bland and Overton, "Assessing the Contributions of Collaborators in Public–Private Partnerships," 430.

15 Robert W. Wassmer, "Property Tax Abatement as a Means of Promoting State and Local Economic Activity," in *Erosion of the Property Tax Base,* ed. Nancy Y. Augustine et al. (Cambridge, Mass.: Lincoln Institute of Land Policy, 2009): 237.

16 Kenyon, Langley, and Paquin, *Rethinking Property Tax Incentives,* 12.

17 Ibid., 8.

18 Gary Sands and Laura A. Reese, *Money for Nothing: Industrial Tax Abatements and Economic Development* (Lanham, Md.: Lexington Books, 2012).

19 "List of current Major League Baseball stadiums," Wikipedia, https://en.wikipedia.org/wiki/List_of_current_Major_League_Baseball_stadiums (accessed January 21, 2019).

20 "List of current National Football League stadiums," Wikipedia, https://en.wikipedia.org/wiki/List_of_current_National_Football_League_stadiums (accessed January 21, 2019).

21 Americans for the Arts, *Local Arts Agencies in America: 2016,* https://www.americansforthearts.org/sites/default/files/25%20Highlights%20from%20the%202015%20LAA%20Census_0.pdf.

22 Geoffrey Propheter, "Are Basketball Arenas Catalysts of Economic Development?" *Journal of Urban Affairs* 34 (2012): 441–459; Andrew Zimbalist, *May the Best Team Win: Baseball Economics and Public Policy* (Washington, D.C.: Brookings Institution Press, 2003); David Swindell and Mark S. Rosentraub, "Who Benefits from the Presence of Professional Sports Teams? The Implications for Public Funding of Stadiums and Arenas," *Public Administration Review* 58 (January/February 1998): 11–20.

23 Swindell and Rosentraub, "Who Benefits from the Presence of Professional Sports Teams?" 16.

24 Peter A. Groothuis and Kurt W. Rotthoff, "The Economic Impact and Civic Pride Effects of Sports Teams and Mega-Events: Do the Public and the Professionals Agree?" *Economic Affairs* 36 (February 2016): 21-32.

25 Charles A. Santo, "Beyond the Economic Catalyst Debate: Can Public Consumption Benefits Justify a Municipal Stadium Investment?" *Journal of Urban Affairs* 29 (2007): 455–479.

26 Zimbalist, *May the Best Team Win,* 125.

27 See, e.g., Gerald A. Carlino and N. Edward Coulson, "Should Cities Be Ready for Some Football? Assessing the Social Benefits of Hosting an NFL Team," *Business Review* (2004): 7–17; Santo, "Beyond the Economic Catalyst Debate"; Zimbalist, *May the Best Team Win.*

28 Zimbalist, *May the Best Team Win,* 126.

29 Carlino and Coulson, "Should Cities Be Ready for Some Football?"

30 Bondonio and Greenbaum, "Do Local Tax Incentives Affect Economic Growth?" 135.

31 Joe Cooper, "Hartford Insurers Gift $10 million to City," HartfordBusiness.com, June 29, 2018.

32 Alan S. Dornfest et al., "State and Provincial Property Tax Policies and Administrative Practices: Compilation and Report," *Journal of Property Tax Assessment & Administration* 7 (July 2014): Table 6, p. 30.

33 Jared Walczak, "Property Tax Limitation Regimes: A Primer," Tax Foundation Fiscal Fact No. 585, April 2018.

34 Robert L. Bland and Phanit Laosirirat, "Tax Limitations to Reduce Municipal Property Taxes: Truth in Taxation in Texas," *Journal of Urban Affairs* 19 (Spring 1997): 47.

35 Job D. Springer et al., "An Evaluation of Alternative Tax and Expenditure Policies on Kansas Local Governments," *Public Budgeting & Finance* 29 (Summer 2009): 48–70.

36 Ibid., 68.

37 Therese J. McGuire and Kim S. Rueben, "The Colorado Revenue Limit: The Economic Effects of TABOR," Economic Policy Institute Briefing Paper (March 21, 2006): 2, urban.org/uploadedpdf/1000940_TABOR.pdf.

38 Suho Bae, Seong-gin Moon, and Changhoon Jung, "Economic Effects of State-Level Tax and Expenditure Limitations," *Public Administration Review* 72 (September/October 2012): 649–658.

39 Steven Deller, Judith I. Stallmann, and Lindsay Amiel, "The Impact of State and Local Tax and Expenditure Limitations on State Economic Growth," *Growth and Change* 43 (March 2012): 56–84.

40 Mathew D. McCubbins and Ellen Moule, "Making Mountains of Debt out of Molehills: The Pro-Cyclical Implications of Tax and Expenditure Limitations," *National Tax Journal* 63 (September 2010): 603–622; Travis St. Clair, "The Effect of Tax and Expenditure Limitations on Revenue Volatility: Evidence from Colorado," *Public Budgeting & Finance* 32 (Fall 2012): 61–78.

41 Richard F. Dye, Therese J. McGuire, and Daniel P. McMillen, "Are Property Tax Limitations More Binding over Time?" *National Tax Journal* 58 (June 2005): 215–225.

42 Susan M. Opp and Jeffery L. Osgood Jr., *Local Economic Development and the Environment* (Boca Raton, Fla.: Taylor & Francis Group, 2013).

43 World Commission on Environment and Development, *Our Common Future* (New York: United Nations, April 1987).

44 Steven D. Stehr, "The Political Economy of Disaster Assistance," *Urban Affairs Review* 41 (March 2006): 492–500.

45 Philip Berke and Gavin Smith, "Hazard Mitigation, Planning, and Disaster Resiliency: Challenges and Strategic Choices for the 21st Century," in *Sustainable Development and Disaster Resiliency* (Amsterdam, The Netherlands: IOS Press, 2009).

46 Shayne Kavanagh, *Building a Financially Resilient Government through Long-Term Financial Planning* (Chicago: Government Finance Officers Association, circa 2011).

PART II:

PREPARING AND APPROVING THE LOCAL BUDGET

CHAPTER 7

Budget choices: Principles to guide the manager

One cannot speak of "better budgeting" without considering who benefits and who loses or demonstrating that no one loses.

–Aaron Wildavsky

This chapter provides the following takeaways:

- The reasons why budgeting processes in the private sector cannot (and should not) be replicated in the public arena.
- The rich heritage of budget innovations in American local government and their cumulative impact on budget processes.
- How smaller cities and counties adapt their budgets to their institutional constraints.
- The budget analyst as a commodity broker; the budget process as a local government's commodity exchange.
- Why the quest for truth-in-budgeting requires consideration of organizational placement of the budget office and the search for understanding the linkage among inputs, outputs, and outcomes.

No other aspect of public administration has undergone as much reform or been the focus of as much attention from political leaders—from city and county managers to presidents—as the budget. As was noted at the beginning of Chapter 1, the budget document is foremost a tool for maintaining financial accountability, and its preparation has evolved into a forum for establishing strategic goals and performance expectations.

The quality of budget decisions made and policies formulated, however, depends fundamentally on the quality of information fed into the budgeting process, and that process tends to produce far more information than is used in decision making. Thus, as the chief budget officer for the organization, the chief executive must identify the central issues to be resolved in the budget process and the essential information needed to resolve them. As Edward Lehan, former finance director for the city of Rochester, New York, observed: "Formats are important. People tend to think about what is put in front of them. Budget classifications tend to define reality for budget makers and reviewers, channeling their attention and thought."[1]

A thoughtfully designed and strategically oriented budget process results in more complete and accurate documentation. Not insignificantly, it also reduces resentment toward budget preparation among those department heads who bear the burden of compiling and presenting

Public sector budgeting versus private sector budgeting

As with most administrative practices, budgeting fulfills fundamentally different purposes in the public sector than it does in the private sector. In the private sector, it fulfills a limited internal management function: providing targets for a firm's sales volume. Often businesses create responsibility centers and charge them with preparing a budget based on both the cost of production and the expected revenue from sales. These center budgets are then compiled into a single document, which becomes a statement of the firm's sales and profit targets by each month or quarter for the year.

Governmental budgeting, by contrast, is more than a process of costing out public services and then setting a tax rate. It involves building consensus among residents on what services government should provide and at what level of effort; finding compromises among powerful interest groups over their relative share of taxation; and reconciling the public will with what leaders in the budget process perceive as the long-term public interest. Governmental budgeting also differs from private sector budgeting because of the nature of services provided (public and merit) and the need to provide them equitably.

Even accounting practices reflect differences in the way the two sectors track and report their financial affairs. Whereas businesses track their financial transactions by treating the organization as a single, unified entity, virtually all governments in the United States use fund accounting, which breaks transactions into separate funds, each with its own revenues, expenditures, and financial statements. Unlike businesses, which have a single bottom line for the whole company, governments must contend with multiple bottom lines, one for each fund.

Mandates from state and federal governments—requirements that specify which services local governments must provide and at what level—have compounded budgeting at the local level. Mandates typically contain regulations with which local governments must comply, often at great expense, thereby skewing local spending priorities. Some mandates reflect the effectiveness of lobbying groups that find it more efficient to deal with a state government, which sets state policy at odds with local control.

Ultimately, however, comparing public and private sector budgeting is pointless because the two sectors produce fundamentally different types of goods and have fundamentally different criteria for measuring performance. Government produces goods for which there is no profit incentive and/or that address political or social concerns for fairness. This greatly complicates the public manager's task of managing and budgeting. Moreover, unlike the private sector manager, the public manager cannot make budget decisions solely to maximize the organization's profit; while efficiency is important, it is not the only consideration. And further complicating the public manager's task is the fact that decision making in government is much more open to outside influence than it is in the private sector. This means that the public budgeting process will be more riddled with conflict, requiring public managers to possess superb negotiating skills if they are to be effective decision makers.

information. The views debated throughout the budget process and the interpretation of the data generated from that process shape the allocation of resources. Managers know that this process is the one common thread that links the parts of the organization together and steers them toward common goals. The budget is the rudder for any public organization.

A common misperception is that governmental budgeting is like budgeting in the private sector and so most of the innovations developed in the business sector can be easily transferred to the public arena with the same laudable results. All that is needed to improve government productivity is to import the financial management innovations developed in the private sector. As the accompanying sidebar makes clear, however, this is a false equivalency.

A century of budget innovations

Budgeting in the last century was characterized by a series of innovations that parallel many of the innovations in management practices. Modern budgeting began in New York City in 1906, when the city's Bureau of Municipal Research called for all city agencies to use a budget. Since then, what began as an accounting function has also become a tool for implementing strategic plans, measuring performance, and evaluating progress toward achieving goals. Particularly at the local level, the tendency has been to retain those elements of a budget innovation that work well and to discard those that are less suitable. The result is that local budgeting practices are often layered with elements of various innovations that, much like an archaeological dig, reveal successive stages in budget development.

Budget reforms fall into one of two general categories: (1) innovations designed to improve budget data—that is, the content and presentation of budget information (budget focus), and (2) innovations designed to improve the budget process (budget locus) (Figure 7–1).[2] In practice, these categories overlap.

In his classic 1966 article, "The Road to PPB: The Stages of Budget Reform," Allen Schick traced the evolution of the budgeting function from (1) imposing control to (2) improving the management of operations to (3) improving the prioritization of programs.[3] With the transformation in budget focus came an increased reliance on more and different kinds of data, particularly data that help top management and lawmakers better connect the impact of their spending decisions to conditions in their community; this has led in turn to changes in the organizational location of the budget function to accommodate new informational needs. Thus, the budget has evolved from being a tool for accounting and financial management to

Figure 7–1 The evolving locus and focus of budgeting

Budget locus	Accounting	Finance	Independent budget office	Chief executive's office
Budget focus	• Line-item budgeting • Zero-base budgeting • Target-base budgeting	• Performance budgeting • Management by objectives	• Program budgeting	• Entrepreneurial budgeting • Balanced scorecard • Budgeting for outcomes • Responsibility-centered management

Figure 7–2 FY 2019 Proposed operating budget, City of Syracuse, New York

DPW Street Cleaning
01.81700

	FY17 Actual	FY18 Adopted	FY18 Projected	FY19 Proposed
Personal Services				
510100 Salaries	48,024	59,960	61,336	61,336
510200 Wages- F/T Weekly	690,487	784,580	866,470	802,822
510300 Temporary Services-P/T	4,823	25,215	25,215	0
510400 Overtime Wages	57,129	55,000	55,000	55,000
511000 Uniform Allowance	7,300	11,100	9,350	11,100
Total Personal Services	**807,764**	**935,855**	**1,017,371**	**930,258**
Contractual & Other Expenses				
540500 Operating Supplies & Expenses	134,659	244,200	262,900	230,100
540700 Equipment Repair, Supplies & Services	0	1,500	1,000	0
540800 Uniforms	4,020	8,500	7,000	7,000
541600 Travel, Training & Development	0	400	250	250
543000 Payments to Other Governments	0	1,500	1,500	1,500
Total Contractual & Other Expenses	**138,678**	**256,100**	**272,650**	**238,850**
TOTAL:	**946,442**	**1,191,955**	**1,290,021**	**1,169,108**

Source: City of Syracuse, July 2018-June 2019 Mayor's Recommended Budget Estimate, April 8, 2018. http://www.syracuse.ny.us/uploadedFiles/Departments/Budget/Content/Proposed%20Budget%202018-2019%20(updated%2006042018).pdf

being a tool for strategically and logistically positioning a community to capitalize on historical strengths and emerging opportunities.

Line-item budgeting

The line-item (or **object-of-expenditure**) budget, the format most often associated with budgeting, originated in the late nineteenth century in response to the excesses of the political machines that controlled many state and local governments. This format shifted power away from political bosses to legislative bodies, which were more accountable to voters. It is still the most widely used budget format.

The line-item budget collects and reports information on inputs (resources) used in the production of government goods and services (Figure 7–2). It lists the goods or services to be purchased—labor, supplies, utilities, capital items, and miscellaneous. Its focus is the objects of expenditure allowed for each department or agency; once the council appropriates the funds (i.e., approves the proposed budget), department heads can acquire the objects authorized in the line-item budget. Line-item budgets typically compare spending levels for the prior year (actual), the current year (both adopted and projected) and the budget year (proposed). The locus of budgeting is the accounting office, where the detailed line-item information is collected and made readily available.

It is clear why a line-item budget format is associated with a control-oriented budget process: the line items correspond to the accounts in the accounting system and make it easy for budget overseers to compare budgeted amounts with actual levels of spending. The more detailed the objects of expenditure, the greater the governing body's control over administrative agencies.

Zero-base budgeting In response to pressure to limit government spending, **zero-base budgeting (ZBB)** emerged in the 1970s as an adaptation of the line-item budget. Initially developed in the private sector by Texas Instruments, ZBB quickly spread to local and state governments. Much of its popularity was due to the fact that it relies on existing accounting information and is simple to understand and implement. Although many local governments had moved budgeting out of the accounting department by the 1970s, ZBB reasserted the value of accounting information to budget deliberations.

ZBB focuses on budget inputs (i.e., the resources used by local governments to produce goods and services), organizing them into **decision packages** that reflect various levels of effort and cost. In theory, each department (or decision unit, which is the lowest level in the organization at which budgetary decisions are made) prepares at least three packages: a base-level package, which meets only the most basic service needs (hence, the term *zero base*); a current services package, which ensures delivery of services at the current level; and an enhanced package, which allows the decision unit to extend its services to currently unmet needs. Decision units can prepare more than one enhanced package, each representing a different level of expanded effort. Packages from all the decision units are then ranked according to the perceived need for the package; rankings are based on the subjective judgment of decision makers, who annually evaluate each program's purpose and priority, weighing the program against all other spending possibilities.

As a consequence of this evaluation, decision makers may decide not to renew funding for an existing program, choosing instead to fund an enhanced spending package for another decision unit or even to provide base-level funding for an entirely new initiative. In fact, however, such reallocation rarely occurs.[4] Chief executives quickly found that department heads were unwilling to provide them with estimates of the base package because, as the department heads argued, the estimates were already at the minimum level and any further reductions would make it difficult to continue providing service. Thus, the base-level (or minimum) package has all but disappeared from the scene. But vestiges of ZBB still persist in many local governments, particularly in the use of enhancement packages, which receive separate and more thorough scrutiny from top administrators and lawmakers.

Target-base budgeting **Target-base budgeting (TBB)**, which entered the picture in the 1980s, reversed the trend toward increasingly complex budget innovations. It was intended to simplify budget preparation, mitigate interdepartmental conflict, and reduce gamesmanship in the preparation of budget requests. Under the simplest form of TBB, the budget office gives each department a maximum dollar figure for its budget request,[5] basing its targets for each department on revenue estimates for the forthcoming fiscal year and on any changes in policy makers' priorities (e.g., more for public safety, less for park maintenance).

The more complex part of TBB involves estimating each department's **current services budget**, which is defined according to rules that are sometimes rather elaborate. Generally, the current services budget is the department's appropriation for the current year unless it happens to contain funding for one-time purchases or for a position that was filled well into the fiscal year. Once the current services budget is established, the target is typically set at some percentage of that level—for example, 95 percent if the program has a lower priority in the current year or 105 percent if it has a higher priority. Although TBB includes some elements of ZBB, it greatly reduces the level of conflict and the role of subjective judgment found in ZBB: departments know from the outset what their likely level of funding will be for the forthcoming year.

Performance budgeting

While line-item budgets are effective at controlling expenditures, they provide no information on outputs (how much work gets accomplished) or level of efficiency (how much input is required to produce each unit of output). Local governments had already begun experimenting with **performance budgeting** when the approach gained popularity in the 1950s after the second Hoover Commission issued a report that recommended collecting and reporting output measures in the federal budget as a tool for controlling costs.[6] They began to use performance measures to monitor the use of funds and to identify ways to improve productivity and the management of public programs.

In the 1990s, performance budgeting experienced a resurgence in interest as a result of the national performance review undertaken by the Clinton administration. In both its original and more recent incarnation, performance budgeting is designed to improve program efficiency, to evaluate the outcomes of program operations, and to provide decision makers and the public with better information on what they are getting for their tax dollars. Budgets not only report information at the line-item level but also indicate what is to be accomplished with those funds.

Budgeting has thus become a financial management tool (Figure 7–1), and local governments increasingly locate the budget function where they can ensure that the necessary information on performance and outcomes (actual results achieved) is being provided in a form appropriate to the organization's needs. The trend has been to move budgeting out of the accounting area and align it with other finance functions that share a broader management focus.

Management by objectives (MBO), an innovation of the legendary management scholar Peter Drucker, had a short-lived courtship with budgeting in the 1960s and early 1970s. MBO is a top-down process: each level in the organization develops performance objectives for the forthcoming year. Employees negotiate a performance agreement with their supervisors, which becomes the basis for evaluating the employee's year-end job performance. The intent is for every employee to have a clear understanding of both the organization's priorities for the fiscal year and its expectations for their individual contributions to meeting those priorities. MBO is more of a personnel management tool than a budgeting tool, but the budget process provided a suitable forum for negotiating the performance agreements.

Program budgeting

Performance budgets focus attention on outputs, but they do not address more fundamental policy questions, such as whether a program is necessary at all or how best to allocate limited resources among competing purposes. The quest to add a policy focus to budgeting gained momentum in the 1960s with the introduction of planning, programming, budgeting systems (PPBS), or **program budgeting** for short.

Program budgeting organizes government activities into programs—activities or services with a common goal—and identifies alternatives for achieving each goal, determines the costs and benefits of each alternative, and selects the alternative that maximizes net benefits. In short, it seeks to interject policy analysis into fundamental budgetary decision making—that is, to determine how much to allocate to activity A as opposed to activity B.[7]

To accommodate this new analytical focus, the budgeting function grew independent of accounting and even of finance, and the stand-alone budget office emerged, reporting directly to the city or county manager or to an assistant manager of administrative services. The newfound autonomy of the budgeting function opened up opportunities for more independent and comprehensive analysis to guide budget deliberations. The merger of budgeting with management was now complete organizationally (locus) and functionally (focus).

While a few local governments continue to build their budgets using the program format, most have abandoned that format, at least as it was originally designed. Like other budget reforms, program budgeting has morphed into other approaches, one of which is **total quality management (TQM)**.

Entrepreneurial budgeting

As strategic planning gained widespread acceptance among local governments as an effective tool for harnessing and channeling the energy of their organizations as well as for containing their growing costs, managers began to cast about for ways to use the process to prioritize programs and reallocate funds to those priorities. Attention quickly turned to the budget process as the vehicle for merging strategic planning with the indicators of demand provided by a competitive market.

The cutting edge in budget innovation over the past decade has been the attempt to transform local governments into entrepreneurial enterprises (Figure 7–1); this effort has introduced competition into the process for setting spending priorities—an area where a competitive market does not exist. At the same time, governments have added a community value perspective to budgeting: how do spending proposals achieve the strategic priorities of the city or county to the satisfaction of customers? (Note the transition of residents from "citizens" to "customers of government services.") Given the new information and management needs, some budget personnel are now finding their duties mingled with those of the chief executive's office.

Three different approaches to entrepreneurial budgeting have gained attention in the past few years: the **balanced scorecard**, budgeting for outcomes, and **responsibility-centered management**. Although the three methods are very different, they each introduce a form of competition into budgeting and management.

Balanced scorecard Robert Kaplan and David Norton, two Harvard management experts, developed the balanced scorecard as a tool for translating an organization's mission into a series of action plans that link together financing, customer satisfaction, internal operations, and the learning and growth of employees.[8]

In a fully operational balanced scorecard approach, a local government begins by developing a mission statement that clearly articulates the organization's purpose and values. Then it carefully assesses the expectations and needs of its customers (citizens and businesses, presumably) and develops a strategic plan (goals, objectives, and strategies), while the administrator prepares a budget that allocates funds to the strategic priorities. In accordance with its mission and strategic plan, the local government leadership develops ten to fifteen key measures of success that the organization will pursue, and each department develops performance measures that show how it will contribute to the expected outcomes.

Since the balanced scorecard was designed for private business, customer satisfaction is a key indicator of success. To fully develop the scorecard concept, a local government must know how a change in performance—for example, the fire service reducing its average response time to top-priority fire alarms by ten seconds—will affect citizen satisfaction. The organization is expected to learn from its experiences and improve its internal processes in order to achieve its key measures of success. One local government that has implemented the balanced scorecard is Charlotte, North Carolina, which it has used to make strategic and budget decisions since 1994.

Budgeting for outcomes Budgeting for outcomes, also called priority-based budgeting,[9] is a relatively recent adaptation of several previous budget reforms. The goal is to provide better information that helps council members make better decisions, provide better procedures to increase the accountability of local governments to their citizens, and thereby increase the efficiency and effectiveness of government. Budgeting for outcomes relies on competition among city departments as well as with businesses and nonprofits outside government to bid on the provision of city services.

Budgeting for outcomes begins with the council determining "the price of government." Fort Collins, Colorado, for example, sets the maximum amount of revenue that it will collect from all local sources as a percent of personal income. The city collects about 5.6 percent of residents' personal income in taxes and service charges to support city operations, a percentage the city has held relatively constant over time.[10] Revenue projections for the biennium are prepared, and that revenue target becomes the spending limit for the budget period.

The next step involves articulating the community-wide outcomes, or priorities, taken from its strategic plan that it wants to focus on in the forthcoming biennium. For the biennium, Fort Collins has seven such outcomes to which all budget requests are anchored. They commit the city to:

- Provide a high-quality built environment and support quality, diverse neighborhoods
- Provide diverse cultural and recreational amenities
- Promote a healthy, sustainable economy reflecting community values
- Promote, protect, and enhance a healthy and sustainable environment
- Provide a safe place to live, work, learn, and play
- Provide safe and reliable multimodal travel to, from, and throughout the city
- Exemplify an efficient, innovative, transparent, effective, and collaborative city government.[11]

The projected revenue is then allocated to the seven outcomes based on the council's priorities.

At this point in the process, city departments, interdepartmental work teams, and, where relevant, teams formed through external partnerships prepare bids or requests for results (RFRs) to meet the council's priorities and deliver the targeted results. Most spending requests in a city's budget have to be part of a bid offer, and each offer has to include quantifiable measures of the results to be delivered. Much like the decision packages in ZBB, RFRs form the city's budget building blocks. Department and program managers are recast as "sellers" in this budget construct.

Bidders compete with each other on the basis of their RFRs. They may also form partnerships with other units, inside or outside government, to prepare an RFR for a particular service need. If a bidder does not cost out its RFR accurately, it may not meet its performance requirements. The RFRs are then ranked by the city's leadership team and manager, and the manager uses them to prepare a budget for submission to the council based on the revenue target established at the outset. Those proposals above the revenue target cutoff line receive funding; those below the line do not, a process analogous to ZBB's ranking of decision packages.

Budgeting in the twenty-first century represents a rich blend of all these innovations. Especially at the local level, where budget format and process are substantially shaped by the chief executive's management philosophy, the budget is likely to contain some combination of line items, performance measures, and even enhancement packages for new spending initiatives, and departments are likely to be given target funding levels at the outset of budget preparation.

Responsibility-centered management Responsibility-centered management (RCM) represents the most clear-cut application of private-sector budgeting methods to the public sector. Corporations with multiple lines of businesses typically classify organizational units, usually departments, as responsibility centers. Businesses further distinguish these centers as either cost centers or profit centers. A manager of a profit center has responsibility for both the revenues generated by the center and the costs incurred to produce those revenues. In the case of a cost center, such as the finance department or IT department, the manager is held responsible for only the costs incurred by the unit.

Budgeting in small cities and counties

While larger cities and counties have received much of the focus for budget innovations, local government in America is heavily tilted toward smaller, less populated, cities, towns, and counties. Over two-thirds of the American population live in an incorporated city.[1] Over 84 percent of the cities and towns in the United States have populations of 10,000 or less. Many of these communities are in or near large metropolitan areas. For example, Allegheny County, Pennsylvania, has 87 incorporated cities, towns, and boroughs; Los Angeles County has 88 incorporated cities; the 13 counties in the Dallas/Fort Worth metropolitan statistical area (MSA) are home to 186 incorporated cities, 143 of which have a population under 10,000.

The numerous rural cities and town located outside a metropolitan area constitute a distinct subset. These communities, many dependent on agriculture or mining industries, often face the opposite issues from their metropolitan counterparts: an aging and declining population, stagnant or declining tax base, and increasingly grim prospects for future prosperity.

How does budgeting differ in these smaller governments? Although staff sizes are proportionately smaller than those of their larger counterparts, the chief executive, often a city secretary or city clerk, confronts the same challenges of matching limited revenues to an expanding demand for services. Smaller communities within an MSA benefit from the large and mobile pool of talent in the area. While they may lack the more specialized promotional opportunities available in larger cities and counties, they do offer a wider range of opportunities for gaining professional experience and administrative responsibility. As such they are strong draws for newly minted MPA graduates.

The greatest disadvantage arises from their more limited technical capabilities. Smaller governments lack the funding or need to acquire more advanced enterprise systems and the expertise to support that technology, particularly as it applies to budget preparation and financial reporting. But the deficit in technology offers an opportunity for budget analysts to develop their Excel competency and creativity in customizing data collection and analysis to their budget process.

For smaller governments outside metropolitan areas, access to a pool of talent is quite limited. Often, the chief administrator is also the chief finance officer. The professional staff typically is comprised of lifelong residents of the area who are, themselves, long-term employees of the town or city. Turnover at city hall is low because of the lack of job opportunities. Budget preparation is a straightforward line-item process with little justification or need for more innovative methods. Revenue forecasts rely on a relatively stable tax base, although one more vulnerable to business cycles that affect the dominant industry in the community.

City hall, a post office, and the local school provide the civic symbols for these rural communities. The unheralded anchor in the community is the city secretary who ensures that elections are conducted according to state law; that reports are filed on time; that council meetings are posted as required and conducted according to law; and that city government operates responsibly and responsively. Council discussions on the budget involve the same concerns and constraints as their larger counterparts, but without the flexibility or staff capacity to test options. Professional development in these communities requires a broader range of skills and interpersonal competency that characterizes the professional associations that support the city secretary profession.

1 Darryl T. Cohen, *Population Trends in Incorporated Places: 2000 to 2013*, U.S. Census Bureau Crrent Population Reports, March 2015, https://www.census.gov/content/dam/Census/library/publications/2015/demo/p25-1142.pdf.

RCM, also known as responsibility-centered budgeting and revenue-centered budgeting, has been adapted to the public sector, most notably by several major universities in the United States. The academic divisions within universities incur costs but also generate revenues through the tuition and fees paid by students, making them candidates for RCM.[12] These profit centers compete for students, now called customers, by offering marketable degrees, using titillating titles for courses, and recruiting professors who deliver spellbinding lectures either in face-to-face or online classes. Managers of these centers, previously called deans and department chairs, must manage their "center's" costs by configuring their instructional staff to maximize profits. Profit centers pay a "tax" that is reallocated to support the university's cost centers, such as central administration, that provide indirect benefits to the university's educational mission but generate little or no revenue.

For departments that generate little or no revenue, which is the case for most multipurpose cities and counties, RCM lacks applicability. A multiservice utility district with revenue-producing departments may find RCM a useful budgeting tool. But managers should be aware of the perverse incentives RCM creates among departments by further promoting organizational units to become self-serving silos.

Discovering budget linkages

Budgeting involves converting data and information on community needs and wishes into an action plan with resources. Economically, the budget process converts the factors of production—labor and capital (money, fixed assets, technology)—into goods and services. The process of preparing a budget is about discovering the linkages between budget inputs and outcomes. For example:

- Does an increase in police officers reduce crime and make our city safer?
- How will a reduction in park or recreational services affect the livability of our community?
- Does an increase in the number of code enforcement officers improve property values?
- Will a mosquito spraying program reduce the incidence of West Nile virus?

Divining the link between budget inputs and the impact on the community is the key budget problem that leaders at all levels of government must wrestle with as they sort out various spending requests.

Inputs, outputs, and outcomes

The "probable linkages" in a particular city, town, or county are determined by the community's unique mix of economic, social, political, cultural, and historical events. For example, changes in spending for law enforcement have an impact on outcomes (response times, crime rates, recovery of stolen property rates), but that impact will be unique for every city or county. Through the budget process, community leaders learn what works effectively in their communities and what does not.

The budget process is not only about understanding the linkage between inputs and outcomes, but also about reducing unintended effects. Every budget decision has unintended consequences, and budget deliberations help community leaders ferret out a better, albeit still imperfect, understanding of both the intended and unintended consequences of their choices. It is through this learning process and the conflict inherent in budget deliberations that budget data are converted into budget decisions.

The true cause-and-effect links between spending and outcomes—budget "truth"—are never known with certainty. As leaders, public administrators and elected officials make informed decisions about what will work. But they don't really know; nor does anyone else. It is, as characterized by Charles Lindblom more than fifty years ago, management by "muddling through."[13] Good leaders continuously search for more data and better interpretations of those data. They intuitively know that the better the information, the better the decisions that will follow.

Seeking truth-in-budgeting

In the 1960s, the U.S. Advisory Commission on Intergovernmental Relations promoted a reform dubbed "truth-in-taxation," which was designed to make the property tax more transparent and accountable to taxpayers. Although imperfect, the idea behind truth-in-taxation was laudable, and the policy is used today in varying forms by several states. It may now be time for governments to embrace **truth-in-budgeting:** an organizational culture that ensures that the budget office is a dependable and credible source of analyses.

What measures can managers take to pursue an organizational culture that promotes truth-in-budgeting? First, the budget office must be protected from political influence. While it is naïve to expect complete insulation, there must be a clear boundary around the budget office to ensure that its analyses are completed independent of any political agenda. Managers will likely be uneasy about giving the budget office too much independence because of its central role in managing operations. One possibility is to create a quasi-independent research unit made up of analysts drawn from inside and outside the organization.

Second, progress has been made in evaluating and rating budget information and documentation. A next step may be to evaluate the quality of work performed by budget offices, particularly their analyses of policy and administrative issues. Just as criteria have been developed to evaluate budget documentation, criteria would be needed to guide external evaluators of budget analyses.

The key to good budgeting is recruiting good people and providing them with the technology to support their work. Qualified analysts bring an array of analytical and intuitive skills to their tasks, and they must have access to the data and the methodologies to accomplish their tasks.

Finally, every local economy is unique, and the mix of revenues and expenditures responds differently to economic cycles. With experience, the budget office accrues institutional expertise in understanding the interaction among the economic factors that influence its budget and, with experience, is better able to predict how its budget will respond to economic cycles. That experience must be nurtured and rewarded if the organization is to achieve a reputation for accurate and thorough analyses.

The role of the budget analyst

In this context, the budget process is the public sector's commodity exchange, and budget analysts are its commodity brokers. But their brokerage skills entail providing an independent assessment of the linkage between proposed appropriations and anticipated results. Governments (and in many cases nonprofit boards) use the budget process to sort out their collective values, determine the quantity of services to produce, and set prices for those services. Rather than being traded in a few centralized commodity exchanges in the financial centers of America, public-produced commodities are valued, priced, and authorized in thousands of decentralized exchanges in cities, counties, special districts, and states across the nation. The cumulative impact of these annual or biennial budget processes determines the mix of services produced by government.

In their role as brokers, budget analysts and those responsible for overall budget preparation collect data, interpret it, and compile it into the budget document that becomes the focus of legislative deliberations. Unfortunately, the budget analyst works in a world of incomplete information. First, as noted above, the organizational locus of the budget office shapes the focus of subsequent deliberations. A budget prepared by an accounting office will have a much different focus than one prepared by the strategic management division in the city manager's office. Each locus has its preferences for the type of data collected, analyzed, and reported.

Second, while department heads grapple with converting budget inputs—labor and capital—into outputs, it is the budget office and ultimately the chief executive who must reconcile inputs and outputs with outcomes. The budget analyst must formulate answers using limited data and an imperfect knowledge of the causal linkages among inputs and outputs and the more critical inputs and outcomes. These are the relationships that command the attention of legislators, the media, and community activists. Will a household hazardous-waste collection program reduce illicit dumping and encourage conservation? More fundamentally, will such a program significantly help protect the environment? Is the cost of such a program worth the benefits? And what will be the unintended consequences? Managers who are successful at helping their community discover its budget linkages will be more successful in their professional careers.

Third, the analyst works in a world where discovering comparable standards of performance has been difficult. Budgets report a manager's best guess as to the optimal mix of labor and capital at a particular time. Because each community has a unique production function—the combination of inputs that gives rise to outputs—comparing performance across jurisdictions becomes problematic. The spatial location of fire stations, building density, and age of vehicles can readily explain why a fire department has a slower (or faster) response time than its neighbor across the river. Budget innovations are important if for no other reason than trying to acquire better data and subjecting it to more exhaustive analysis.

Budgeting is, in essence, social science inquiry.

Lessons for budgeting

Several implications for budget theory and practice emanate from this discussion:

- The quality of the data and information coming into the budget dialogue is critical to the successful discovery of a community's budget linkages. The manager performs a pivotal role in authenticating information and providing budget participants with credible sources.
- The fewer the resources available to a community, the less room the community has for error in discovering budget linkages.
- Comparisons of performance across cities and counties are fraught with problems. The uniqueness of every community makes it improbable that the link between inputs and outputs or between inputs and outcomes will be the same for any two communities. The most defensible comparison is historical trends within a city or county.
- The search for the linkage among inputs, outputs, and outcomes is iterative and unending. As communities age, the relationships among the three factors also change. Budgets reflect a community leadership's best guess as to what those relationships are at a particular point in time.
- While businesses can measure with some degree of accuracy their production function (the relationship between labor and capital and their profitability), the complex interaction among public services suggests that local governments face a greater challenge when measuring their performance.

Budget lessons from recessions

Financial crises, such as the Great Recession of 2007–2009, drive home the lesson that recessions have widely varying effects on state and local budgets. The collateral damage of a recession, like that of an earthquake, reverberates long after the initial shock wave. And aftershocks continue for many months, even years, thereafter, striking unsuspecting communities and states. Our lack of knowledge on budget causality makes it nearly impossible to gauge with precision the impact of a recession on any one government's budget. But local governments do control their budget processes, and they can adopt recession-resistant policies and processes that mitigate the financial impact of recessions.

Recessions expose the disconnect between the political forces calling for more and better government services and the political will to finance those services over the long term. Budget analysts provide the key to reconciling these two opposing forces by bringing truth to budgeting estimates. What are the long-term costs of the proposed new program or service? Will the long-term revenue base provide sufficient resources to meet this new commitment? Do the benefits of the new service outweigh the costs? Truth-in-budgeting means providing public officials and citizens with the full budgetary impact of a proposal and the revenue requirements needed to support it over the long term. It means accurately assessing the impact of the proposal on the current operating and capital budgets and knowing up front what revenues will be needed to support the initiative in prosperous as well as less prosperous times.

Because recessions make state and federal aid highly vulnerable to reduction or elimination, they expose the peril of depending on that aid to balance local budgets. Those local governments most dependent on state and federal aid are also the most vulnerable to its elimination. State revenue structures are not capable of financing both state and local operations.

Recessions reveal that delaying difficult budget decisions only narrows the options available in subsequent years and elevates the magnitude of the adjustments needed to bring about budgetary balance. In the absence of credible analyses and a commitment to truth-in-budgeting, it becomes politically expedient to defer making difficult spending and taxing decisions and leave them to the next administration. Recessions shorten the time line and elevate the urgency to resolve political impasses involving past budget decisions on issues such as federal and state entitlements, unfunded pension liabilities, or programs that have fulfilled their mission.

Democracies depend on making quality information available to citizens. The key to better financial decision making is better analyses up front of the short- and long-term budgetary effects of new or expanded initiatives. It means investing in analysts who can provide rigorous analyses of the budgetary effects of proposals and promoting an organizational culture that advocates for truth-in-budgeting. It means pursuing budget policies and procedures that make local budgets more recession resistant.

The budget office

For the most part, budget offices provide accurate, timely, and comprehensive budget analyses. Where those analyses fail to accurately or fully anticipate the costs, benefits, or collateral effects of a proposal, it is usually because of poor or incomplete data, insufficient time, a lack of expertise, or a lack of knowledge about the causal linkages among the inputs, expected outputs, and the desired outcomes. In those relatively rare instances where the failure is the result of human error, the cause is often traceable to understaffing or to insufficient training and investment in technical support for analysts. And, of course, political spinning may alter budget estimates or

Figure 7–3 Impact of budget location on core values and focus

	Organizational location				
	Accounting department	**Finance department**	**Administrative services department**	**Budgeting department**	**Chief executive's office**
Supervisor	Comptroller	Finance director	Director of administration or assistant city manager	City manager or deputy city manager	City manager
Core values	Controlled spending	Financial accountability	Productivity improvement	Program evaluation and responsiveness	Policy development
Focus	Revenue forecast Budget preparation Budget compliance	Long-range forecasting Interim budget reports and projections Financial impact analysis	Cost of services Performance measures Performance monitoring and reporting Policy research Improved organization	Citizen satisfaction Community needs Program goals and effectiveness	Strategic planning Policy analysis

at least foster a tendency to cherry-pick those estimates that most closely align with an advocate's political agenda, creating the potential for good analyses to be misrepresented.

Budget accuracy also suffers because of the unpredictability of economic cycles. Accurately forecasting the turning points of a recession, not to mention the recession's depth or length, is nearly impossible. Forecasting the yields for the more elastic revenue sources—income and consumption taxes—is particularly problematic for analysts. And each local and state economy reacts differently to economic cycles.

Organizing the budget office

When budgeting first became an accepted financial management tool of government in the late nineteenth century, it typically entailed a clerk in the accounting department who was responsible for preparing a list of expenditures by department; this list was presented directly to the legislature for review and approval. Budget preparation involved tabulating requests and required only a few weeks of attention. As has been described, however, the role of budgeting has since expanded, and responsibility for it has shifted from a subunit in accounting and finance to, in some cases, an independent executive-level agency with a budget director reporting to the chief executive. At the same time, the focus of the budget process has expanded as well—from controlling spending (e.g., by means of a line-item budget) to implementing the strategic plan.

Location, values, and functions The most fundamental issue for the manager is the organizational placement of the budget function. As noted above, locus shapes focus, and the budget office's locus has undergone considerable transformation over the past century. Figure 7–3 shows the different organizational placements commonly used by local governments today; each has its merits and advocates.

A budget office located in an accounting or finance department focuses on financial controls, reporting, and line-item expenditures; its core values are controlled spending and financial accountability for the use of funds. In smaller local governments, budgeting responsibility may be assigned to an accountant who, for most of the year, records and reconciles transactions, and for the rest of the time prepares the budget, including a revenue forecast.

An alternative model, more often found in midsized cities and counties, places the budget office in an administrative services department that brings together a number of other support services, such as purchasing, risk management, tax administration, finance, and information technology. In this organizational scenario, the budget office is a unit on par with finance, internal auditing, and other finance-related activities. The core value is now productivity improvement: budgeting is seen as an opportunity to improve management performance by optimizing outputs relative to inputs.

A variation on the administrative services model is the independent budget department, whose head reports to the city or county manager or assistant manager. As an independent unit, the budget office has the most latitude to shape its agenda and can add responsiveness to community priorities as a core value along with productivity improvement. Its budget analysts assume a wider range of duties: measuring and monitoring program performance, assessing citizen preferences and satisfaction with public services, determining community needs and their relative priority, and finding ways to better link program and agency goals to addressing those needs.

Some governments opt to locate the budget office in the chief executive's office. (A quick way to assess a chief executive's priorities is to examine an organizational chart to see what activities report directly to the city or county manager.) In this setup, it is quite common to find the budget office's focus on big-picture issues of strategic planning, mission, and vision. Budget analysts may be more directly involved in policy analysis, particularly in those areas that hold political importance for the governing board. Not surprisingly, the budget function in this environment will have a more political focus than it would in a unit located further down in the organization.

In a few rare cases, primary responsibility for budget preparation lies with an elected council or board rather than with the manager; in such cases, a comptroller may assist in preparing the proposed budget. A few governments, most notably at the state level, rely on a legislature-initiated rather than an executive-initiated budget proposal and have a separate legislative budget office with its own analysts.[14] Where dual budget offices exist—one that assists the executive and the other, the legislature—they usually work closely with each other, at least through the budget preparation phase. However, the norm in the United States is for a single budget office that is located in the executive branch.

The focus of the budget office depends not only on the location of the office but also, to some extent, on the size of its staff. Where the budget office consists of just one person, it usually does not carry out any functions other than budgeting—not even finance functions, such as accounting, treasury, purchasing, or internal auditing. If it employs several analysts, it may include some program and performance evaluation functions. In larger governments, the budget office typically employs a larger staff, many of whom hold graduate degrees in public administration. Each staff member may specialize in a particular area of the budgeting process—for example, long-term financial forecasting, revenue estimation, grants administration, or capital planning and budgeting.

Larger governments also have budget analysts to help provide objective assessments of departmental performance and capabilities; these analysts advise departments on policy issues, review their requests for the forthcoming budget period, and help them tighten their spending requests. A particular budget analyst may be responsible for several departments. In larger governments, the departments will also have their own budget specialists, who represent the department head on budget matters and who interact closely with their assigned analyst in the budget office.

Principal duties Regardless of its location or size, the budget office has traditionally collected spending requests from departments and, with the advice of the chief executive, trimmed those requests to meet expected revenue levels. Even though the focus of the budget office has expanded over the years, its main duties remain constant: estimating revenues, preparing a budget calendar, reviewing and compiling budget requests into a proposal, ensuring that total requests do not exceed estimated revenues, monitoring compliance with the budget during implementation, and periodically preparing a status report comparing actual revenues and expenditures with what was budgeted.

In carrying out these duties, the budget office typically assumes a number of roles: it educates participants about the budget process, adjudicates among participants both within and outside government, manages data processing, promotes accuracy and integrity in budget requests, provides information to budget participants, and reports on how well the approved budget plan is being followed.

When the primary function of the budget office is monitoring departmental budget requests, conflict between it and the various departments is inevitable: departments advocate for more resources, but as guardian of the treasury, the budget office scans budget requests for waste and excess. In the past, the budget office's denial of requests prompted department heads to devise strategies—padding the budget, making partial-year requests, seeking a state mandate or regulatory requirement—in order to outmaneuver the budget office and ensure that their departments get the resources needed to meet the expectations of the community, its elected representatives, and the chief executive. This budget gamesmanship created an adversarial relationship between budget analysts and department heads.

To reduce this conflict, administrators introduced TBB and variations of ZBB to let department heads know up front the boundaries of their budget requests. At the beginning of the budget cycle, the budget office gives each department a target that its proposed budget cannot exceed. In times of stagnant or declining revenues, budget guidelines may require that department heads prepare a budget request that is less than the current spending level, for example 95 percent of current authorized expenditures. In other times, new initiatives that exceed the target may be proposed as separate requests for the budget office to consider on a case-by-case basis. TBB enables the budget office to limit total budget requests to expected revenue levels while giving department heads an opportunity to make a case for extraordinary needs.

The budget office of the twenty-first century seeks a collaborative relationship with departments that promotes and models good management throughout the organization. A clearer division of labor has lessened antagonism, and the budget office provides technical expertise to departments on such matters as strategic planning, developing performance measures, analyzing policy choices, and even identifying entrepreneurial options for raising needed revenue.

The budget cycle

The system of checks and balances between the executive and legislative branches of government that has emerged in most western democracies is evident in the four phases of the budget process (Figure 7–4). The seesaw relationship begins with the executive proposing expenditures and the legislative branch then empowering the executive to enter into financial commitments; it culminates with the council verifying the executive's compliance with its

Figure 7–4 Phases of the budget cycle

Phase	Product	Key participants	Time frame
Preparation	Executive's proposed budget	Budget director; chief executive, department heads	3 to 6 months before fiscal year begins
Legislative adoption	Appropriation act	Council; governing board	2 to 3 months before fiscal year begins
Executive implementation	Encumbrance and disbursement of funds	Department heads; budget office	The fiscal year (12 months)
Accounting and auditing	Comprehensive annual financial report	Accounting office; comptroller	Fiscal year plus 3 to 6 months after year ends to complete audit

wishes. The four-phased cycle—characterized by the acronym PLEA—is nearly universal among state and local governments regardless of size or the organizational location of the budget function:

1. *Preparation phase.* A proposed spending and operational plan for the forthcoming budget period is drafted, usually under the guidance of the manager or elected chief executive.
2. *Legislative approval phase.* The council or governing board approves the spending plan through an appropriation act.
3. *Executive implementation phase.* The executive branch implements the approved spending plan by approving contracts, purchase orders, and other agreements that legally commit the government to the disbursement of funds once goods and services are delivered.
4. *Accounting and reporting phase.* All transactions, both expenditures and revenues, are tracked, tallied continually, and summarized into financial reports. At the end of the fiscal year, a **comprehensive annual financial report** (**CAFR**) of all city activities is prepared and audited for accuracy.

The next three chapters discuss the elements of these four phases in detail. Preparation and legislative approval, which occur in tandem, are the topic of discussion in Chapter 8; Chapter 9 then turns to the third phase of the budget cycle, executive implementation; and Chapter 10 examines the final phase, accounting and financial reporting.

Conclusion

Elected leaders, often those newly elected to public office, incur considerable frustration as they try to remake governmental budgeting to look more like the processes and methods used by businesses. In a representative democracy, governmental budgeting performs the essential social functions of building consensus among residents on what services government should provide and at what level of effort; formulating compromises among powerful interest groups; and reconciling the public will with what leaders in the budget process perceive as the long-term public interest.

Since 1906, when New York City's Bureau of Municipal Research required all city agencies to use a budget, innovations have changed both the focus and locus of budgeting. Line-item budgeting remains the focus of municipal budgeting, and the accounting unit remains the primary locus of budget decisions. However, as the focus of the budget has expanded to include performance measures, policy analysis, and even entrepreneurial approaches, the budget has increasingly become the responsibility of an independent department that reports directly to the manager, or of a unit in the manager's office that brings together strategic planning and performance monitoring.

Budget analysts are local government's commodity brokers and the budget process its commodity exchange. As with any market, participants depend on accurate information. A key responsibility of the manager is promoting truth-in-budgeting. Organizational placement of the budget office shapes the focus on the type of data analyzed, its relevance to the decisions being made, and its ability to aid decision makers in making causal linkages among inputs, outputs, and most importantly, outcomes. The budget office and ultimately the chief executive must reconcile and justify inputs and outputs with outcomes. Over time a budget office accrues institutional expertise on the interaction among the economic factors that influence its budget. That experience provides invaluable benefits to better predict how its budget will respond to economic cycles.

One of the most important decisions that a manager can make is the placement of the budget function within the organization. That decision shapes the core values that will guide the unit as well as the way in which the unit defines and carries out its duties. The budget function has become the locus of arbitration between the government and those it serves.

The budget cycle consists of four distinct phases that involve an interplay of checks and balances between the executive and legislative branches: preparation, legislative approval, executive implementation, and accounting and reporting. The following three chapters examine these phases in greater detail.

Notes

1 Edward Anthony Lehan, *Simplified Governmental Budgeting* (Chicago: Government Finance Officers Association, 1981), 2.

2 The use of locus and focus in local government budgeting is adapted from Nicholas Henry, who used the dichotomy to trace the development of the study of public administration through five successive paradigms; see Nicholas Henry, *Public Administration and Public Affairs*, 13th ed. (New York: Taylor & Francis, 2018), 35.

3 Allen Schick, "The Road to PPB: The Stages of Budget Reform," *Public Administration Review* 26 (December 1966): 245-256.

4 Thomas P. Lauth, "Zero-Base Budgeting in Georgia State Government: Myth and Reality," *Public Administration Review* 38 (September-October 1978): 420–430.

5 Irene S. Rubin, "Budgeting for Our Times: Target Base Budgeting," *Public Budgeting & Finance* 11 (Fall 1991): 5–14.

6 Wouter Van Dooren, Geert Bouckaert, and John Halligan, Chapter 3, "The History of Performance Management" in *Performance Management in the Public Sector*, 2nd edition. (Routledge: New York, 2015): 42-61.

7 Verne B. Lewis, "Toward a Theory of Budgeting," *Public Administration Review* 12 (Winter 1952): 42–54.

8 Robert S. Kaplan and David Norton, *The Strategy-Focused Organization* (Cambridge, Mass.: Harvard Business School Press, 2001).

9 Shayne C. Kavanagh, Jon Johnson, and Chris Fabian, *Anatomy of a Priority-Driven Budget Process* (Chicago: Government Finance Officers Association, March 2011).

10 City of Fort Collins, 2017-18 Biennial Budget, January 2017, 24. https://www.fcgov.com/citymanager/pdf/budget-2017-2018.pdf.

11 City of Fort Collins, Colorado, "Budgeting for Outcomes," https://www.fcgov.com/bfo/.

12 Amanda Rutherford and Thomas Rabovsky, "Does the Motivation for Market-Based Reform Matter? The Case of Responsibility-Centered Management," *Public Administration Review* 78 (July/August 2018): 626-639.

13 Charles E. Lindblom, "The Science of 'Muddling Through,'" *Public Administration Review* 19 (Spring 1959): 79–88.

14 Ronald Snell, *The Power of the Purse: Legislatures That Write State Budgets Independently of the Governor* (Denver, Colo.: National Conference of State Legislatures, March 2008), http://www.ncsl.org/research/fiscal-policy/the-power-of-the-purse-legislatures-that-write-st.aspx.

CHAPTER 8

The budget cycle: Preparation and legislative approval

There is always something to upset the most careful of human calculations.

—Ihara Saikaku, Japanese poet

This chapter provides the following takeaways:

- Why it is essential to prepare a long-range forecast of the impact of past commitments on future expenditures and fund balances.
- Tips for creating a smooth process for preparing an executive budget.
- How to clarify what is meant by a balanced budget, and what to do if it is not.
- Understanding the conflicts inherent in budget preparation and in legislative approval.
- Then how to manage those conflicts through budget policies that reflect best practices.

The top priority in the preparation and legislative approval phases of the budget cycle is to create a process that produces information and, ultimately, decisions that reflect the priorities of elected representatives while also advancing the long-term interests of the community. Close behind this priority is the need to ensure that budget deliberations proceed constructively, efficiently, and prudently. As noted in the previous chapter, part of the challenge is ensuring that the budget staff has adequate information with which to evaluate options objectively and provide a credible assessment of the link between budgetary inputs and the most likely outputs and outcomes. The key to good budgeting is making certain that the process provides a forum for vetting responsible ideas and building consensus on the best course of action.

This chapter covers in depth the first two phases of the budget cycle: budget preparation and legislative approval. Because conflict is endemic to budget deliberations, particularly during these first two phases, this chapter examines the sources of conflict and the importance of well-crafted budget policies in helping managers deal with conflict.

Preparation phase

Budget preparation begins well before the start of the new fiscal year. For example, if the fiscal year begins on October 1, larger governments begin preparing the proposed budget as early as the preceding January; smaller ones, in early summer. State law or local charter may specify the time frame, but the timing for launching budget preparation is more commonly dictated by historical precedent.

The preparation of a budget requires these critical tasks, most of which originate with the budget office:

- Update long-term forecast for revenues and expenditures.
- Publish a calendar identifying deadlines for tasks and the individuals responsible for meeting those deadlines.
- Prepare and update current-year revenue projections.
- Develop budget instructions and targets if applicable.
- Design and revise a budget manual with instructions and forms.
- Update web-based templates and macros for departments to use when submitting budget requests online.
- Review departmental requests for accuracy and consistency with guidelines.
- Conduct budget hearings first with analysts and then with the executive team.
- Prepare the final executive budget request and make it available on the website.

Long-term financial forecast

Before the actual preparation of a budget begins, the budget director in concert with the manager's office should review and update the long-term financial forecast for the local government. Maintaining this forecast is an ambitious, but critically important, endeavor. A widely common practice among local governments is the preparation of a multiyear capital improvement plan (CIP) that projects by year the major capital outlays for the next five to eight years. A less common practice among local government is the preparation of a comparable plan for the operating budget.

An essential precursor to a multiyear financial plan is the preparation of a strategic plan that identifies a local government's vision, mission, strategic priorities, goals, and objectives. Such a plan charts a course of action for at least five years into the future with regular updates to council on the progress toward meeting the plan's goals. Like the CIP, it should be used as a rolling plan with periodic updates to the intervening years and the addition of plans for the outlying years.

The strategic plan provides particularly helpful direction on new initiatives or changes in spending priorities that affect expenditures in the next five to eight years. A long-term financial plan can then serve as the backdrop to the strategic plan by providing local leaders with a realistic assessment of the forthcoming annual revenues, expenditures, and their cumulative impact on the fund balance.

Long-term financial plans also aid local leaders in understanding the impact of long-term commitments on the annual expenditures in the operating budget. Commitments such as pensions, multiyear union contracts, other post-employment benefits, debt service, and other multiyear contracts at some point become short-term obligations in the operating budget. A long-term financial plan with graphical trend lines provides a visual summary of the impact of these long-term commitments on the annual operating budget.

Successful long-term plans, those that effectively anticipate the future trends in revenues and expenditures, depend on several key factors. First, they require qualified experts who have the analytical skills to develop and refine forecasting models and the communications skills to convey the implications of their findings. The challenge in forecasting is anticipating turning points in the local economy. To the extent the local economy tracks with national trends, one reasonably dependable bellwether to recessions has been the emergence of an inverted **yield curve** for U.S. Treasuries. Such an abnormal curve occurs when short-term interest rates exceed longer-term rates. Investors seek to lock in long-term interest rates in anticipation of a drop in those rates as the economy slows.

Second, the assumptions underlying the forecast models are identified and tested. They include assumptions on changes in the local economy and their impact on tax bases, yields, and rates; economic assumptions on inflation, interest rates, and unemployment; and assumptions on the political environment including tax limitations, loss of major employers or taxpayers, and changes in the demographics of the community and the preferences that underlie those demographics. A good forecast must show the sensitivity of the projections to changes in these assumptions.

Finally, effective use of a long-term financial forecast requires council involvement. For example, Tempe, Arizona, semi-annually presents an updated five-year forecast to council, once at the beginning of budget preparation and then again midyear.[1] The City of Dallas incorporates its five-year forecast of revenues, expenditures, and fund balance into the city manager's proposed budget, an increasingly common practice by local governments. Typically, these forecasts show expenditures exceeding revenues in the outlying years as the full impact of spending commitments takes effect (Figure 8-1).

Some may question the benefit of a long-term financial forecast given the additional cost. One of the basic purposes of planning is to reduce uncertainty. In the case of financial planning, a five-year forecast reduces unanticipated consequences of the long-term impact of com-

Figure 8–1 Five-year budget forecast for General Fund, Tempe, Arizona

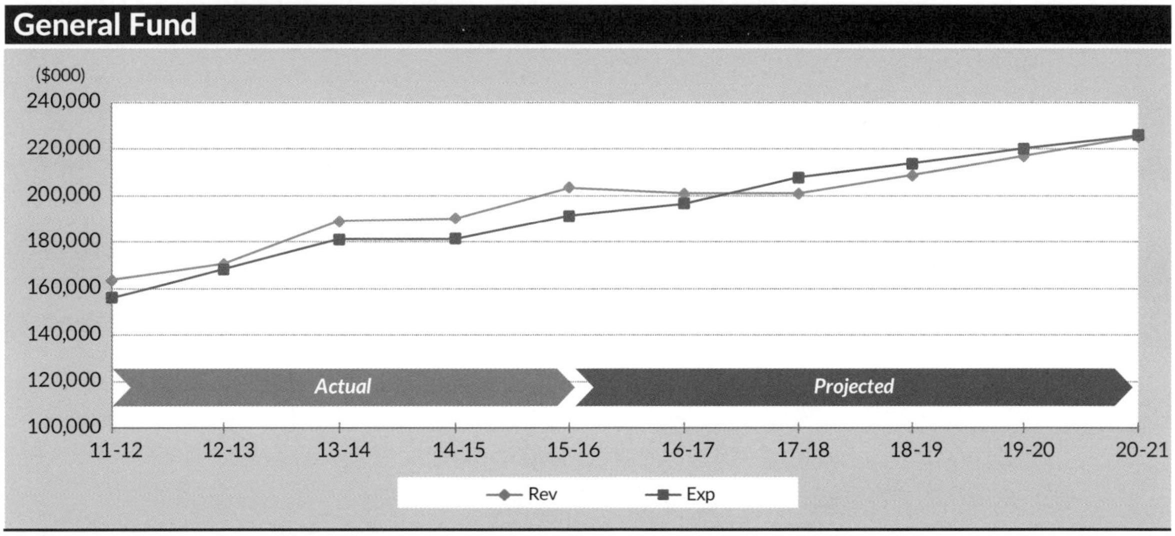

Source: Memorandum from City Manager's Office to City Council, City of Tempe, Arizona, February 16, 2016, p.4. https://www.tempe.gov/home/showdocument?id=48490

mitments made today on future budgets, and it gives administrators the flexibility to make a more timely response to external shocks to local budgets. Ultimately, a long-term forecast promotes financial sustainability in an era fraught with increasing uncertainty.

Budget calendar

Although budget preparation is never popular with department heads because it takes them away from running their departments, the budget calendar provides a roadmap to the preparation and adoption of the budget for the next fiscal year. The calendar establishes deadlines for key activities in the process and names those responsible for completing the tasks.

In midsized and larger local governments, departments commonly make their initial requests for funding, especially requests that exceed their target base, to the lead budget analyst in an informal meeting. The budget calendar specifies the date and time for making these requests; due dates are typically staggered to create a more uniform workload for budget personnel during this peak period, and to give departments with more complex budgets a longer time to compile their requests. The budget office may respond with a set of questions that require further research and analysis by the department.

The next step may be more formal hearings before the city or county manager and a team of senior executives. Usually the budget director will join these hearings, and the department will be expected to address the questions that were raised in the earlier meeting. The formal hearings provide a forum for resolving any lingering conflicts between the recommendations of the budget office and a department's spending requests. They are included in the budget calendar to give participants sufficient notice to clear their schedules and prepare for them.

Revenue projections for current year

Without exception, accurately forecasting the current year's revenues is the most important task in budget preparation. Because, as discussed in the accompanying sidebar, most state and local governments have some type of balanced budget requirement, available revenues determine the level of spending for the fiscal year or biennium.

The beginning point in budget deliberations is the available revenues for the forthcoming year. The long-term forecast provides the context for estimating the current year's revenues. If revenues have dropped, the governing board, with the manager's advice, must immediately look for ways to reduce spending levels. If revenues have risen, the board typically looks for ways to approve tax cuts while also accommodating modest spending increases. State and local governments sometimes have no choice but to seek new revenues, such as a tax or fee increase, or to try to shift the cost of services to another government or to consumers—for example, through higher tuition for a state or local university. Tax revenues can be increased by broadening the tax base or increasing tax rates. Occasionally governments will reduce or remove a tax break—perhaps by reducing a homestead exemption on the property tax or by eliminating a locally authorized tax exemption.

Well before the budget preparation is officially under way, the budget office begins compiling estimates of yields from the major sources of revenue (property and sales taxes for most cities and counties). These estimates are regularly updated throughout the budget preparation and legislative approval phases and into executive implementation. The budget office also solicits estimates of expected yields from departments that collect revenue—for example, investment income (from the treasurer), park and recreation fees, library fines, airport fees, municipal court fines, utility charges (water, wastewater, storm drainage, electric, and in some cities natural gas).

For some revenue, a range of forecasts may be appropriate. The amount of rainfall anticipated in the coming year, for example, affects the forecast for water use. Thus, the water

Defining budget balance

The issue of a balanced budget—one in which current revenues cover current expenditures—has been at the fore of public debate for several decades as a result of the continuing deficits incurred by the federal government. Those annual budget deficits must be funded somehow, and the federal government chooses to fund them with debt—that is, by borrowing through the issuance of Treasury bills, notes, and bonds. (The Bureau of the Public Debt's website, publicdebt.treas.gov, contains details on the amount of debt and who owns it.) Local governments, however, are usually required to adopt a balanced budget. There have been numerous calls for an amendment to the U.S. Constitution requiring the same discipline from the president and Congress.

There are several points in the life of a budget where it can be balanced (see figure below). But a balanced budget is elusive.[1] For example, the manager may be required to propose a balanced budget, but the council may have the latitude to approve an unbalanced one. Or state or local law may require that both the proposed and approved budgets balance but allow deficits at year-end to be carried over to the next year. (Councils typically amend the budget during the fiscal year and approve **supplemental appropriations,** but a local government may still conclude the fiscal year with a deficit.) The most stringent balanced budget condition specifies that the budget must be in balance when it is proposed, when it is adopted, and at year-end.

Because there are no uniform and enforceable standards for budgets as there are for financial reports, budgets are much more amenable to manipulation.[2] Local governments facing a budget crisis may resort to financial sleight of hand to temporarily achieve budgetary balance: they may approve overly optimistic revenue forecasts, shift the last payday of the fiscal year to the next fiscal year (thus saving one pay period in the current budget), accelerate the due date on taxes, defer payments for pensions or other obligations, book the sale of assets as revenue before the sale actually occurs, defer maintenance expenditures, or borrow against a future revenue source. These actions may temporarily balance the budget. However, budget shenanigans have consequences. Unless the local government changes its budget practices, the imbalance will return with a vengeance, leaving local leaders with fewer options and increasingly more costly remedies.

Preparation phase	Legislative phase	Executive implementation	Accounting and financial reporting
1. Chief executive must submit a balanced budget	2. Budget approved by council must be balanced 3. Budget signed by elected chief executive, after any vetoes, must be balanced	4. Budget amendments and supplemental appropriations must include offsetting revenue sources.	5. Must end fiscal year with a balanced budget.

1 National Conference of State Legislatures Fiscal Brief, *State Balanced Budget Provisions*, October 2010.

2 Yilin Hou and Daniel L. Smith, "A Framework for Understanding State Balanced Budget Requirement Systems: Reexamining Distinctive Features and an Operational Definition," *Public Budgeting & Finance* 26 (Fall 2006): 22-45.

department may prepare three scenarios for revenue yields: one for above-average rainfall, another for below-average rainfall, and a third for an average year. This gives budget planners a better idea of the sensitivity of revenue yields to changes in external conditions.

Revenue forecasting involves a variety of measures, which are described in the accompanying sidebar. Some measures, such as econometric modeling, involve sophisticated statistical methodologies; others, such as informed judgment, are more intuitive. Typically the budget office will use two or more techniques in combination to estimate the major revenue sources. Sales (and income) taxes pose the greatest challenge to revenue forecasters because of the difficulty of predicting changes in the local economy, especially downturns.

While the budget office has administrative responsibility for preparing and updating revenue projections, these projections can become politicized, especially if revenues are falling. Should that be the case, the safest approach for the budget office is to keep revenue projections conservative—that is, somewhat below what it actually anticipates receiving. On the other hand, sometimes the city or county administrator and council prefer more optimistic revenue forecasts—projections that assume more favorable economic conditions—because an optimistic revenue forecast makes it easier for them to balance the budget.

The chief executive plays a key role in bringing integrity to revenue forecasts and discouraging the manipulation of revenue forecasts, which can become counterproductive. In the long term, the manager's most prudent course is to insist on accuracy in all revenue forecasts and to stand firm against their manipulation, whether it is done to protect the budget office or to promote the council's agenda. In revenue forecasting, your sins find you out, and they do have a cost.

Budget preparation instructions

To help departments develop their budget requests, the budget office, in consultation with the top management team, develops detailed guidelines for preparing requests. These guidelines present general information on the budget environment: the expected changes in demand for services, trends in the major revenue sources, unemployment trends, major projects affecting the operating (or capital) budget, and any shift in emphasis on community-wide goals. They also include instructions on preparing a **base budget** request, supplemental (or enhancement) requests, revenue estimates for departments with revenue-generating activities, and performance indicators and other program measures, as well as instructions on entering budget data into an online database. In addition, they provide contact information for specific types of questions.

Along with the budget guidelines, departments receive their target allocation for the budget period and a re-estimate of their current year's level of expenditures and revenues. This midyear re-estimate reflects changes in the local economy that may alter the budget conditions not only for the current year but also for the forthcoming one.

The budget calendar and budget guidelines, as well as forms to be used, are compiled into a document called the **budget manual**. For department heads and their staff, the manual provides information needed to prepare and justify budget requests. Budget manuals vary widely in their content and level of detail. Smaller local governments rely on minimal documentation—the basic forms and instructions needed for submitting requests and a narrative from departments explaining any deviations from their historical budget base. Larger governments require more detailed documentation.

Budget offices tend to ask for more information than they need because, in the uncertain environment in which budget decisions are made, data and information are key to the quality of decisions. But at some point, additional information has diminishing value to decision making, and its cost is borne by the departments, which have a limited amount of staff time to devote to budget preparation. An open dialogue among the budget office, department heads,

Revenue forecasting techniques

Because local government expenditures are revenue driven—that is, the total amount of available revenue frames budget deliberations throughout the preparation and legislation phases—estimating the amount of revenue available for the budget year is one of the first steps in budget preparation. Typically, a revenue forecast is prepared for each major revenue source, such as the property tax, sales tax, and each utility service. For smaller revenue sources, such as license or recreation fees, a forecast is prepared for the combined totals, often based on historical trends.

Because local governments collect revenue from dozens, even hundreds, of sources, they often prepare a **revenue manual** that provides details on each source: its legal basis in state or local law, annual yields and rate history, principal payers, and the entity in local government responsible for collection and enforcement.

The methods used to project revenues can be classified into four generic types: informed (or professional) judgment; deterministic, or formula-based, projections; time series analysis; and econometric, or causal, modeling. Most budget offices use several methodologies in combination, depending on the type of revenue source.

Informed (professional) judgment is essential to preparing defensible estimates regardless of what other methodology is used. Even the most elaborate statistical projections require the discerning eye of an experienced budget director. Budget directors and local government managers who may have been caught short in the past learn to watch for changes in the local economy, in state and federal laws, or court decisions that could affect revenue yields. In addition, a panel of local experts and business leaders can be recruited to assess the business environment for the forthcoming budget period. The budget office may reconvene the panel periodically during the year to update projections for the current and future fiscal years.

Deterministic (formula-based) revenue projection relies on a simple mathematical formula to provide an estimate of expected revenue. The property tax, which is usually the most important source of general revenue for local governments, is calculated on a formula basis (total assessed value x tax rate = tax yield). The assessed value represents the taxable value of all property—both real and personal—in the taxing jurisdiction. Typically, the property tax rate is set concurrent with the council's adoption of the budget at a level that will generate sufficient tax revenue (yield) to balance the operating budget. Sometimes collection rates fall or estimates of assessed valuation are off because of delinquencies or bankruptcies, in which case the forecast must be adjusted.

Utility charges are also forecast using the deterministic method (volume of consumption x rates = revenue yield), although forecasting the volume of consumption, such as the demand for water or electric power, requires more sophisticated forecasting methods.

Time series (trend) analysis involves looking for trends from prior years' data. It provides a useful estimate for revenue sources that are less elastic with respect to economic growth—that is, those for which yield does not change much whether the economy is growing or shrinking. For example, license fees and certain excise taxes, such as those on cigarettes and alcoholic beverages, are relatively stable; thus, because they may depend roughly on population size, a simple trend analysis provides reliable estimates.

For revenue sources that produce more volatile yields but that grow at a reasonably constant rate, a common approach is to average several recent years (or months) together to project the next year's yield, a method called moving or rolling average. By taking the average of recent years, the budget forecaster smooths out the peaks and troughs and thereby reduces the chance of over- or underestimating revenue yields. This technique is especially useful to monitor current trends in revenue yield, such as for monthly sales tax collections, and can provide a valuable harbinger of changes in the local economy.

Econometric (causal) modeling is a more sophisticated statistical forecasting method that can help anticipate turning points in the local or state economy, something that time series methods cannot do. Econometric models assume that the yield from a particular revenue source is affected by a number of underlying determinants, such as per capita income, inflation, and population change. Econometric modeling does not work perfectly, but a statistical model can be helpful in showing how the local economy and the tax revenues that come from that economy respond in comparison to a state or regional economy.

The larger and more complicated the economy of a state or local government and the more complicated its revenue sources, the more useful econometric models become. The comptroller for the state of Texas, who is constitutionally charged with preparing revenue estimates for the state's biennial budget, has developed a highly sophisticated series of simultaneous equations whereby one model's prediction becomes a predictor for another. The comptroller's forecasts have proven remarkably accurate, strengthening their credibility and influence in the budget preparation process.

In practice, budget forecasters use a variety of techniques concurrently.[1] They combine their expertise and professional judgment with simple or more complex trend analysis. Striving for accuracy, they have a strong incentive to keep their forecasts conservative. It is far better politically to bring good news midyear of additional revenues coming into the treasury than to report that revenues were overestimated and that emergency budget actions are needed to reduce spending.

1 Shayne C. Kavanagh and Daniel W. Williams, *Informed Decision-Making Through Forecasting: A Practitioner's Guide to Government Revenue Analysis* (Chicago: Government Finance Officers Association, 2016).

and the chief executive office reduces the risk that the budget office will ask for obsolete or redundant information.

The flip side of the coin is the tendency for budget offices to shower departments with endless reams of data, making it difficult for those responsible for preparing budgets to know what is essential to the process. Again, the information distributed to departments must be clearly linked to the documentation that departments must submit.

A new department head unfamiliar with the jurisdiction's budget procedures must invest considerable time learning the mechanics of budget preparation. While some elements of the process are fairly common across governments, enough variation exists, especially in data entry and processing, to require significant time and energy from someone learning a new system. Similarly, when a new city or county administrator introduces major changes in the process and documentation, department leaders must spend time learning the new material. Ultimately, the department head skilled in data analysis and written communications will have a competitive edge.

Department budget requests

Once the budget manual is prepared, the budget office typically begins the preparation process with a kickoff event, a somewhat celebratory occasion that brings together department heads, budget analysts, and top management. Participants are briefed on the budget calendar, guidelines, and budget manual; they may also be briefed on targets, either for each spending category in the department's budget or for the department's budget request overall. In larger governments, budget analysts are introduced and their departmental assignments announced if different from past years; the number of departments that an analyst serves will vary, depending on the size and complexity of the departmental budget.

The kickoff event may be followed by a training session that lasts anywhere from part of a day to two or three days, depending on the extent of changes in the budget process. For example, if a new information management system is being introduced, the training may extend for several days as users become familiar with its features. With new executive leadership often comes new approaches to budget deliberations; these may have catchy titles, such as the "balanced scorecard" approach or "responsibility-centered management" or "budgeting for outcomes." Wholesale changes in the documentation required from departments and the criteria used to evaluate departmental proposals will require extensive retooling of the administrative staff, whose task will be to collect and analyze the data and prepare the documentation needed for budget deliberations.

As departments begin to prepare their requests, a number of concerns will surface, some of which may require consultation with the departments' assigned budget analysts. For example, given the trend toward a more expansive role for budgeting, budget analysts and department administrators must collect and analyze a wider array of data, including performance measures, citizen attitudes, consumer satisfaction levels, and outcome measures. If the government uses a unified budget, departments must prepare capital spending requests alongside operating requests. Further complicating the process are spending requests that are funded from federal or state grants and that typically require separate documentation, justification, and hearings. Departments inevitably have questions about collecting and reporting all these types of information.

Departmental budget requests must also include information on salary savings—that is, the savings in unpaid salaries that result whenever positions remain unfilled for part of a year because of personnel changes. Some governments estimate salary savings for each department using historical data and exclude that portion of the salary expenditures from their budget base for the forthcoming year. Others record salary savings only as they occur during the fiscal year and allocate them to a separate account that can be used to fund supplemental requests or to supplement salary offers where the budgeted salary is below market rates. And still other governments allow departments to keep salary savings, placing limits on how they may be used—for example, to fund a temporary position for an MPA intern.

Another issue involves the use of unused budget authority. In most cases, budget authority lapses at the end of the fiscal year, creating an incentive for year-end spending. City councils consider money carried over as evidence of budget padding and generally reduce the department's budget for the next year, especially if funding is tight.

As department heads agonize over their budget proposals, they will carefully scrutinize the numbers and justification, looking for ways to link each spending initiative to a strategic goal or priority articulated by the council. In some cases, union agreements require the addition of personnel or equipment. In most cases, however, department heads must defend each new spending initiative as well as their current levels of spending. Generally, departments must also supply performance measures as part of the justification for spending requests.

Local governments vary widely in the form and content of information they request from their departments and other subunits. The basic budget format—line-item, zero-based, performance budgeting, program budgeting, balanced scorecard, or budgeting for outcomes—dictates the type of information requested and the content of the manager's final proposed budget. The performance-based format used by the Office of Management and Budget for the Navajo Nation is indicative of the documentation submitted during the preparation phase:

- Program budget summary
- Program performance criteria
- Listing of positions and assignments by business unit
- Detailed budget and justification
- Summary of changes to budgeted positions
- External contract and grant funding information.[2]

The zero-based budgeting format used by Escambia County, Florida, uses forms that collect different data, although the same basic information as the Navajo Nation is obtained—cost of personnel services, cost of other nonpersonnel operating services, and capital outlay.[3] Escambia County adds a separate form for program enhancements, a feature of zero-based budgeting.

The availability of Excel-based platforms makes electronic departmental submission of data commonplace. These platforms also facilitate updating or modifying budget requests. As the budget progresses through the winnowing forks of the legislative approval process, department heads may be called upon to provide additional data or an explanation of requests. However, most of the data collection and reporting is now complete.

Assembling the executive budget

To smooth the workload for budget analysts, midsize and larger governments stagger the due dates for departmental budget submissions. Usually smaller departments' requests are due first, followed by larger departments' requests. As requests filter in, budget analysts verify that all the required information has been submitted, that the estimated costs conform to the guidelines specified in the budget manual, and that measures of performance and other indicators of accomplishments are appropriate to the departments' missions and goals. The budget office may verify that mandated costs are included in a department's request and that the full cost of projects or new staff is also included.

The budget analyst's initial review usually results in a follow-up with the department for clarification, correction, or further documentation, especially on requests for new initiatives. Often the department is asked to describe the consequences of not funding the proposed initiative. There may also be questions about performance and outcome measures. The budget office will typically push for measures that better reflect the department's mission and that provide top management and council members with a better understanding of how the department's programs address the priorities of the council.

As it refines its revenue forecast for the forthcoming budget year, the budget office merges the forecasts prepared by revenue-producing departments. These forecasts have been organized by fund and type of revenue source, grouped into larger categories such as property tax, sales tax, other local taxes, general service charges, license and permit fees, fines and forfeitures, investment income, revenue from other governments, and other revenue.

The budget office also begins compiling expenditure data for continuing activities and preparing a prioritized list of proposed new initiatives or of possible areas targeted for reallocation of existing funds. Its staff pays particular attention to the priorities developed by the council, whether that was done through a strategic planning process, citizen focus groups, or some other method. The goal is to fit department-centered information into a framework that responds to the priorities of the legislative oversight body and the citizens it serves.

The budget analyst typically makes field visits throughout the year to observe the department's activities and the quality of its performance. If an analyst is assigned to a particular department year after year, he or she becomes familiar with that department's budget and

Strategies for balancing an operating budget

The manager's top priority in assembling the executive budget is ensuring its compliance with state and local laws and policies. Ultimately, all budgets are balanced, but the types of resources used to achieve that balance vary. Four options exist:

1. Balanced budget: Current Revenues (CR) = Current Operating Expenditures (COE)
2. Deficit budget
   a. Deficit covered by fund balance: CR + Fund Balance = COE
   b. Deficit covered by debt: CR + Debt = COE
3. Surplus budget: CR > COE

Deficit budgets, and specifically those caused by insufficient own-source revenues, pose the greatest challenge. However, even deficits precipitated by the loss of non-local revenues, such as state or federal grants, can precipitate a deficit budget.

As noted in Figure 2–4, deficit budgets result from one of four types of fiscal crises depending on the severity (low to high) and duration (short-term to long-term) of the crisis. Chapter 2 described the revenue strategies to mitigate the effects of a fiscal crisis. In the case of a crunch (short duration and low severity) or squeeze (longer duration but low severity), a manager should seek revenue solutions that build budget capacity for the long term. These less severe crises often originate from external events such as a recession, reduction or loss of federal or state aid, or a costly court settlement. In these cases, the manager should use own-source revenues in combination with the expenditure reductions described in Figure 9–4 to resolve the deficit. Aggressive action is needed to avoid a deficit lapsing into a more severe fiscal crisis.

Once a deficit lapses into the high severity row, however, and becomes either a crisis or crush, it becomes a structural deficit. These deficits typically originate from structural weaknesses in the local economy, such as loss of tax base, population, and employment opportunities, or an overextended budget. Structural deficits require a significant reduction in long-term commitments (debt, wage agreements, pensions) and a long-term approach to rebuilding the local economy. In the intervening years while the local economy goes through a rebuilding process, local services will be sharply curtailed and the remaining taxpayers may see higher tax burdens with fewer services.

history of requests and thus becomes a critical adviser to the executive on the merits of that department's requests.

Executive budget hearings

The final step in assembling the executive budget is a series of executive-level hearings involving each department head, the budget office, and a team of top managers. Department heads meet one-on-one with the budget director, with the manager, or more commonly with a budget committee comprising representatives from the chief executive's leadership team (city manager, assistant city manager(s), budget director, human resource director, and finance director). These hearings are not open to the public, and there is no public record of the proceedings. Given the stakes involved, departments expend considerable effort developing PowerPoint presentations, honing their speaking points, and justifying their spending priorities. Some department heads role-play the presentation with their staffs, trying to anticipate questions that the budget committee may ask.

Executive budget hearings typically proceed over several days, depending on the size of the organization. Each department has a fixed amount of time to make its presentation, describe new initiatives, justify any extraordinary changes in spending requests, explain new funding options, and answer questions. Larger departments may be allocated more time given the complexity of their operations. The finance director may also be allotted extra time to explain debt service payments or new state or federal legislation that is expected to affect spending choices.

During the question-and-answer period, the committee typically focuses on the more controversial proposals, especially those that involve increased spending. It may again ask about the consequences of not funding a particular item. Department heads with a reputation for fiscal prudence and an innovative management style have an advantage at this point because they tend to be given the benefit of the doubt when it comes to funding a new initiative or reallocating existing spending. Departments that have developed defensible measures of the impact of their programs on community priorities also have an advantage, as do departments that can document an increase in efficiency, have enhanced responsiveness to citizens, or have otherwise improved the delivery of public services. And, finally, those departments that are known to have strong support among community groups will also have a competitive advantage even at this stage of the budget process.

Once the executive budget hearings are completed, the executive budget committee makes its recommendations to the city or county manager. Some committees use elaborate rating schemes to rank new spending proposals. Others use a simple voting process to identify new initiatives to be included in the budget request, initiatives recommended for possible inclusion should sufficient funds become available, and initiatives not recommended for funding in the current year.

The budget office then prepares a draft of the recommended executive budget and distributes it to each department head. At this point, if the department feels that its proposal was not fully understood or if additional information has become available that would have a bearing on the recommendation, the department head may be allowed to appeal to the chief executive to restore a deleted item or increase its priority. The department head should carefully weigh the wisdom of making such an appeal: failure to succeed may lower the department's standing among its peers, while success may lay the department open to accusations of making an "end run"—circumventing the normal chain of command to gain support for its agenda. The opportunity for appeal is usually reserved for truly extraordinary matters. If the budget office and budget committee have effectively screened the requests coming from departments, only the most controversial items will be passed on to the manager for resolution.

The budget document

The culmination of the preparation phase is the executive budget, which represents the chief executive's proposed spending plan for the forthcoming year. The initial version may be posted on the web or circulated internally for departments to review. Depending on the council's preferences, the final version may also be posted on the web for council review, or it may be printed and distributed for council members to mark up and make personal notes as they prepare for the next phase: legislative approval.

After reviewing and revising the executive's proposal, the legislature adopts the budget into law by passing an appropriation, a legally binding act that sets the spending limits for each government department and agency, including those in the legislative and judicial branches, for the forthcoming fiscal year.

Administrators responsible for budget implementation then enter into contracts and issue **purchase orders** that create **encumbrances** to each department's appropriation. The accounting department is responsible for recording encumbrances and approving the subsequent **disbursement** of funds once the contracted service is completed. As a fiscal year unfolds, unexpected events—for example, a recession or the loss of a major taxpayer—often require alteration of the approved spending plan; this is sometimes done through a formal amendment by the council, a supplemental appropriation, or a revision of revenue projections. And in today's world, the increased frequency of disasters and the ever-present threat of mass attacks complicate budget planning and compel even greater flexibility and creativity from public servants at the forefront of preserving social order.

On completion of the fiscal year, the chief accountant prepares a comprehensive annual financial report (CAFR) that, among other things, compares the appropriation for each department, as amended, with the actual amount of expenditures. An **independent auditor** reviews the CAFR and reports to the council on its accuracy and on the local government's compliance with federal, state, and local laws.

Figure 8–2 Total budget overview, Dallas, Texas

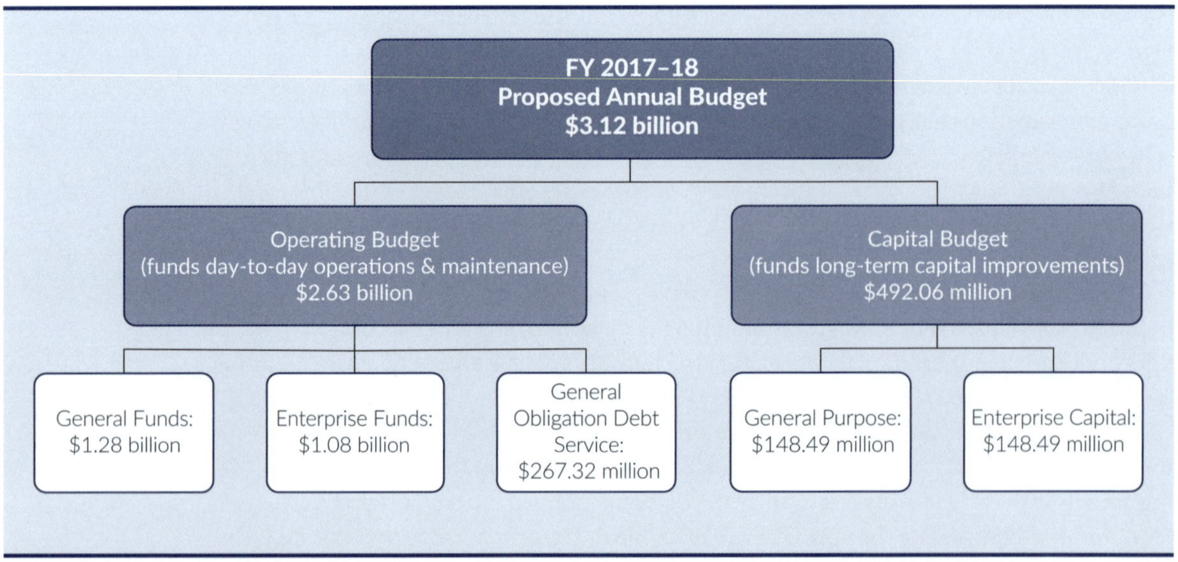

Source: City of Dallas, Texas, *City Manager's Proposed Budget as Recommended to the Mayor and Members of the Dallas City Council, Fiscal Year 2017-18*, 7, https://dallascityhall.com/departments/budget/financialtransparency/DCH%20Documents/Town-Hall-Meetings-Presentation.pdf.

For most local governments, the budget consists of two documents: the operating budget and the **capital budget**. An operating budget reports the spending plan for a government's ongoing services, such as police and fire protection, parks and recreation, water, and sewer service. It typically organizes information by departments and provides details on such line items as personnel, supplies, contract services, travel, utilities, and smaller capital items (e.g., office equipment). Money for the operating budget comes from current revenues, such as property, sales, and income taxes; service charges; fees and fines; and grants.

The capital budget (the preparation of which is discussed in Chapter 11) represents a spending plan for the acquisition of fixed assets, such as highway and building construction, water and sewer line installation, and park development. This budget is usually part of a more comprehensive **capital improvement plan (CIP)** that projects major construction and acquisition needs for a five- to eight-year period. Funding for the capital budget usually comes from the sale of bonds or other long-term obligations, supplemented by funds from grants and current revenues. Information contained in the capital budget is usually organized by projects.

These budgets may be prepared as part of two distinct processes during the fiscal year, each resulting in a separate appropriation, or they may be prepared concurrently, as is done in Dallas, Texas (see Figure 8–2).

Legislative approval

Home rule charters generally stipulate a date by which the city or county manager must submit a proposed budget. For example, the charter for the City of Fort Worth, Texas, requires that on or before August 15 of each year, "the city manager must submit to the city council a recommended balanced budget that provides a complete financial plan for all city funds and activities for the ensuing year."[4] General law local governments and those that operate without a home rule charter follow the time line spelled out in state law. Some states specify detailed timetables; others have relatively few requirements other than that the local government annually adopt and publicize a comprehensive spending plan before the fiscal year begins.

In state governments and in larger local governments, the budget document submitted to the legislature provides a summary compiled from the budget database. This document typically includes

- An organizational chart for the city, county, or state
- A message from the city or county manager or governor summarizing the major policy issues
- Background information, such as budget procedures, a summary of citizen surveys or other public perceptions, financial management policies, strategic goals, a summary of the long-range financial forecast, and a statement of the economic outlook for the city, county, or state
- A section summarizing the key issues considered in the current budget proposal and the chief executive's recommendations
- A series of tables summarizing revenues by source, expenditures by fund and department, **full-time equivalent (FTE)** positions by fund and department, and proposed changes in FTE positions
- More detailed information by department on spending requests (sometimes aggregated into broad categories such as personal services, supplies, contractual services, and capital items to be funded through the operating budget); departmental goals, objectives, and performance measures; and FTE positions by rank
- A separate section on debt service obligations for the budget year
- Additional sections on enterprise activities, such as water and wastewater management, the municipal golf course, the airport, and other fee-for-service ventures

- Detailed spending proposals for internal service activities, such as data processing, the motor vehicles pool, and office supplies
- A separate section on expenditures for trust funds, such as employee pensions, insurance, workers' compensation, and pending litigation
- A separate section or volume containing detailed information on the proposed capital spending plan for the year (if the capital budget is prepared concurrent with the operating budget).

Council members often have particular areas of interest and will devote more time to those areas, scrutinizing the information and making certain that they understand the implications of proposed changes. Rarely will a council "rubber stamp" the manager's proposed budget. The manager and budget office will be called on during the legislative approval phase to explain requests, clarify justifications, and prepare at the council's request documentation on alternative spending scenarios.

Legislative deliberations

Up to this point, deliberations on the budget have been largely outside the purview of public scrutiny. Council involvement in the early stages of budget preparation also varies, depending on the manager's leadership philosophy and on precedent in that city or county. For example, before the budget kickoff meeting, some managers poll their councils to determine their spending priorities for the coming budget year. Others hold a leadership retreat for the council and city staff before departmental budgets are prepared so that they can review economic conditions, strategic priorities, and the results of the most recent citizen survey. Council and staff might use this retreat to update the government's strategic plan, developing new priorities that will guide departments as they prepare their budget requests and the executive budget team as it chooses the new initiatives to include in the proposed executive budget.

The process has now come full circle as the council reenters the dialogue to assess how well the executive branch has responded to its priorities. If there has been little legislative involvement up to this point, the proposed executive budget may contain surprises for members of the council—never a good idea. Thus, the astute manager will have prepared the council for new initiatives or other spending and revenue issues well before the budget is released, thereby avoiding the need to educate council members on the details in the spending plan in order to "sell" the budget. Although council members should be prepared in advance for requests for new revenue sources or proposed increases in taxes or fees, open and frank discussions of the proposed changes and increases should be expected and encouraged.

Some councils prefer to work through committees. The executive budget may go to a budget and finance committee that first reviews the spending plan and the accompanying proposed revenue requirements. Other councils work as a committee of the whole, and all members of the legislative body participate in all aspects of the adoption process.

Local governments have experimented with citizen budget advisory committees with varying degrees of success. Such committees, composed of council- or board-appointed representatives, provide legislators with a citizen's perspective on the proposed spending plan. However, if the citizen committee is no more representative of the community than the council itself or the department heads who submitted the original requests, it may unnecessarily complicate budget deliberations and ultimately add little value to the final product. Citizen committees tend to work best and add the most value when there is continuity of membership from year to year so that they gain some understanding of the economic issues, budget processes and procedures, and performance measures. Ensuring that the committee composition is diverse and represents a true cross section of the community also can make the process more valuable to councils.

Shortly after delivery of the executive budget, the council begins holding a series of budget work sessions, in which members of the budget office and the manager's office walk the council through the proposed budget page by page. These sessions are open to the public, and state or local law may require public notification, including posting or publishing a summary of the proposed budget. Public notice of tax or fee changes may also be required, which the city secretary or county clerk posts in the appropriate venue (local newspaper, city website, city hall bulletin board) and for the appropriate time period (e.g., at least fourteen days in advance of the council's expected action). A continuing challenge for local governments at this stage is to generate broad citizen interest and participation in the budget process.

As the legislative body works through the budget, the requirement for a balanced budget means that most of the discussion will usually center around activities and services funded from taxes. For local governments, adjusting the property tax rate provides the means to bring revenues into balance with planned expenditures. For the vast majority of local governments in the United States that levy a property tax, adoption of the budget is accompanied by adoption of a property tax ordinance that sets the tax rate at a level sufficient to fund operations (not necessarily capital) for the forthcoming year or biennium. Sometimes growth in the tax base (assessed value) is more than sufficient to cover increases in expenditures. As it works through the spending options, the council keeps an eye on the impact of proposals on the property tax rate and often consults with the budget office on the effect of proposed initiatives on that rate.

Councils usually devote much less attention to the budgets for utilities and other government-sponsored enterprises and for internal services (the proprietary group of activities) unless those budgets include a significant fee increase. Unlike the tax-supported operations in the general fund, proprietary fund activities, including internal services, are usually self-supporting; their level of activity is determined by market forces, not the political process. Proprietary activities fund their expenditures with user charges, so outlays fluctuate with consumption. The ordinance approving their budgets typically limits expenditures to the purpose of the enterprise activity and sets a maximum appropriation for the fiscal year. Figure 8–3 shows a sample budget ordinance from DeKalb, Illinois. A separate ordinance (2017-049) was devoted to approval of the property tax rate.

Councils must also approve the budget for debt service—the annual payment of principal and interest on borrowed funds. Sometimes debt service is funded through a transfer from the general fund to the debt service fund. In other cases, a separate dedicated tax levy—usually a portion of the property tax—is collected and deposited directly into the appropriate debt service fund. Again, there is little discussion by council on this appropriation since it represents a legally binding commitment that no government that wants to retain its credit rating will renege on.

The debt service funds account for only the general obligation (GO) debt, which is used to finance capital improvements that support the general operations of government. Most of this debt service is funded through general revenues, such as the property and sales taxes. Estimating the amount of annual debt service is a fairly straightforward task for the budget office in that few policy issues are involved.

The appropriation bill

Since adoption of the budget and accompanying taxes or fees constitutes a legal action, specific procedures apply. In the case of the appropriation—the act adopting a budget and granting authority to the executive branch to enter into agreements that will result in the future disbursement of funds—a council may be required to have a first and second reading of the proposed ordinance. The first reading puts the proposed bill on the table for council action; the second, and final, reading enacts the budget. If there is opposition to the spending

Figure 8–3 Budget ordinance, DeKalb, Illinois

ORDINANCE 2017-051 PASSED: DECEMBER 11, 2017

ADOPTING THE ANNUAL BUDGET OF THE CITY OF DEKALB, ILLINOIS, FOR THE FISCAL YEAR BEGINNING JANUARY 1, 2018, AND ENDING DECEMBER 31, 2018, IN THE AMOUNT OF $93,720,356.

WHEREAS, the City has previously adopted Sections 8-2-9.1 through 8-2-9.10 of the Illinois Municipal Code, 65 ILCS 5/8-2-9.1 through 8-2-9.10 ("State Budget Law') by a two-thirds majority vote of the City Council then holding office, in accordance with Section 8-2-9.1 of the State Budget Law; and

WHEREAS, pursuant to Chapter 54.06 of the City of DeKalb Municipal Code, as amended, the Mayor and City Council have designated the City Finance Director as the Budget Officer for the City; and

WHEREAS, the Budget Officer has proposed to the corporate authorities a tentative budget for the City's fiscal year commencing January 1, 2018, and ending December 31, 2018 ("2018 Fiscal Year"), as required by Section 8-2-9.3 of the Illinois Municipal Code; and

WHEREAS, after proper notice being given, the Mayor and City Council held a public hearing on November 27, 2017, to obtain public comment on the tentative annual budget for the City for the 2018 Fiscal Year; and

NOW, THEREFORE, BE IT ORDAINED by the Mayor and City Council of the City of DeKalb, DeKalb County, Illinois, as follows:

Section 1: RECITALS.
The foregoing recitals are incorporated into, and made a part of, this Ordinance as the findings of the Mayor and City Council.

Section 2: APPROVAL OF 2018 FISCAL YEAR BUDGET.
The Mayor and City Council hereby approve an annual budget for the City of DeKalb, DeKalb County, Illinois, for the fiscal year beginning January 1, 2018 and ending December 31, 2018, in the total amount of $93,720,356 in the form attached to and, by this reference, made a part of this Ordinance as Exhibit A ("2018 Budget Summary")

Section 3: FILING OF APPROVED BUDGET.
The Finance Director is authorized to update the budget consistent with Exhibit A. The City Clerk is hereby authorized and directed to file a certified copy of this Ordinance, together with a full and complete copy of the 2018 Budget approved pursuant to this Ordinance, with the Office of the DeKalb County Clerk in accordance with the provisions of the statutes of the State of Illinois.

Section 4: Should any provision of this Ordinance be declared invalid by a court of competent jurisdiction, the remaining provisions will remain in full force and affect the same as if the invalid provision had not been a part of this Ordinance.

Section 5: This Ordinance shall be in full force and effect after passage and publication pursuant to law. Publication date: December 12, 2017. Effective date: December 21, 2017.

PASSED BY THE CITY COUNCIL of the City of DeKalb, Illinois at a Regular meeting thereof held on the 11th day of December, 2017 and approved by me as Mayor on the same day.

Passed on First Reading by a 6-2 roll call vote. Aye: Finucane, Marquardt, Fagan, Noreiko, Faivre, Smith. Nay: Jacobson, Verbic. Second Reading waved by a 6-2 roll call vote. Aye: Finucane, Marquardt, Fagan, Noreiko, Faivre, Smith. Nay: Jacobson, Verbic.

Source: DeKalb, Illinois, Ordinances, 2017-051, December 11, 2017, https://www.cityofdekalb.com/DocumentCenter/View/6981/Ord-2017-051-Passed-121117-FY18-Budget-Filed?bidId=

or taxing plan, it most likely will be voiced at the first reading. Prior to one or both readings, the council sets aside time for a public hearing. Sometimes separate hearings are held for the budget and tax proposals; at other times the two are considered at one hearing. Again, state law usually defines the parameters for what local governments can do.

As an aid to council deliberations, the manager's message introducing the proposed budget typically discusses the major initiatives and the cost and changes in personnel for each, organized by strategic area. If economic development is one of the strategic priorities, the manager's message will discuss each of the new initiatives in the proposed budget designed to help promote that priority. The budget office may prepare a similar document summarizing the council's changes to the executive's budget proposal, and the reasons for those changes, to give department heads and other budget preparers insight into the council's thinking so that proposals not funded this time around can be reworked over the next year.

Most local governments adopt one appropriation bill that covers all operating expenditures for the year. If a biennial budget is used, the appropriation bill contains separate amounts for each year in the biennium, or, less commonly, two separate appropriation bills may be approved. If a separate capital budget is prepared, usually a separate appropriation ordinance is drafted and approved for capital expenditures. (The U.S. Congress, which uses a unified budget, adopts twelve separate appropriation bills, one for each subcommittee of the House and Senate Appropriations Committees.)

As the council deliberates on the budget ordinance, members may offer amendments to the proposal modifying the level of funding for a particular area. Each amendment is voted on, and those that receive a majority vote become part of the amended budget ordinance. After all the amendments have been acted upon, the final amended budget is approved and becomes the legally binding spending plan for the fiscal year.

Councils that use a work session prior to council approval may rely on a more informal process to make changes to the manager's proposed budget. These changes are discussed during the work session and, if supported by the majority of the council, are used to modify the final budget. The council then approves the revised budget when it is taken up at the regular council meeting.

If a long-term financial forecast is prepared, the council may give the manager and budget office direction on spending and revenue options when the forecast comes up for discussion, which is usually at the outset of budget preparation. (The council will review the forecast but take no formal action since the forecast serves as an internal planning tool.) In this case, most of the controversial issues will have been resolved well before the budget is presented to the council for action.

Final budget approval

In the system of checks and balances that characterizes American government, the executive usually possesses some veto power over legislative actions. This is also the case with appropriation bills. State governors wield varying degrees of veto power, from **line-item veto** power to no veto power (North Carolina).[5] There are no known cases where an appointed city or county administrator can exercise veto power over a council action. However, mayors in some council-manager and in most mayor-council governments typically possess veto power, including line-item veto of appropriation bills. Councils in these governments can override any vetoes, typically with an extraordinary majority.

Should a local government fail to adopt a budget before the beginning of the fiscal year, state and local laws may provide recourse. In some cases, local charters lay out the way to proceed; in some Texas cities, the city charters dictate that the manager's budget de facto becomes the legally authorized appropriation. In some states, such as New Jersey, a state agency must approve certain local budgets before they become effective. In cases of extreme fiscal distress, states have taken over all executive and legislative operations of a local government, including budget preparation and adoption. Pennsylvania appoints a recovery coordinator to advise elected local officials. Other states, notably Michigan, New Jersey, and Rhode Island, appoint an all-powerful administrator from outside the government to make all decisions in the city in an effort restore financial solvency and avert bankruptcy.

As the fiscal year progresses, major events, such as a sudden drop in revenues or a natural disaster, may require the executive to request amendments to the budget to authorize new expenditures. Most amendments, however, address smaller issues: an unexpected need or a misestimate of the cost of a piece of equipment. In some cases, the council may intentionally underfund an activity or acquisition and ask that the agency return later in the fiscal year for a supplemental appropriation. Governmental accounting rules require that the annual financial report disclose both the original budget as approved and the final budget as amended.

Conflict in budget deliberations

To the average citizen, conflict appears endemic to the budget process, whether at the national, state, or local level. Media coverage of legislative budget deliberations conveys an impression of unending battles. But conflict is inevitable in budget deliberations. It becomes destructive and unproductive only when it is unmanaged. The key is to develop and maintain policies to guide all phases of the budget cycle, and particularly those for budget preparation and legislative adoption.

Budget policies provide a framework for anchoring budget deliberations to the core values that define a city, county, or state. Some governments adopt a written **budget policy statement**; this statement establishes boundaries for budget deliberations that protect the government from actions that might compromise its financial well-being. Thus it may specify the amount and type of budget reserves, regulate the transfer of money across accounts or funds, and impose limits on the amount of debt that the government can incur.

In state and local governments, where most constitutions or statutes require that expenditures not exceed available revenues, the overriding struggle is to curtail proposed spending levels to the level of forecasted revenues. Increases in revenue are considered only after all opportunities for reducing spending and manipulating the accounting system have been exhausted.

The local government manager's task is not to rid the process of conflict, for to do so would strip the budget process of its essential democratic function of airing community concerns and building consensus on government's role in meeting perceived public needs. Rather, the manager's task is to manage conflict so that everyone with a stake in the budget has an opportunity to present information and question recommendations. Figure 8–4 depicts some of the conflicting interests that must be managed. The following discussion examines the sources of conflict commonly encountered during budget preparation, legislative enactment, and executive implementation.

Advocates versus guardians

Within government, and especially during the executive preparation phase of the budget, the conflict between advocates and conservers, or guardians, accounts for much of the debate.[6]

Among the advocates are department heads, who generally request more funding than they know will be approved in the hope of gaining at least some increase in their budget base to meet growing service demands. Other advocates include clients or interest groups who benefit from the department's services, and legislative committees that oversee the agency.

Figure 8–4 Sources of conflict in the budget process

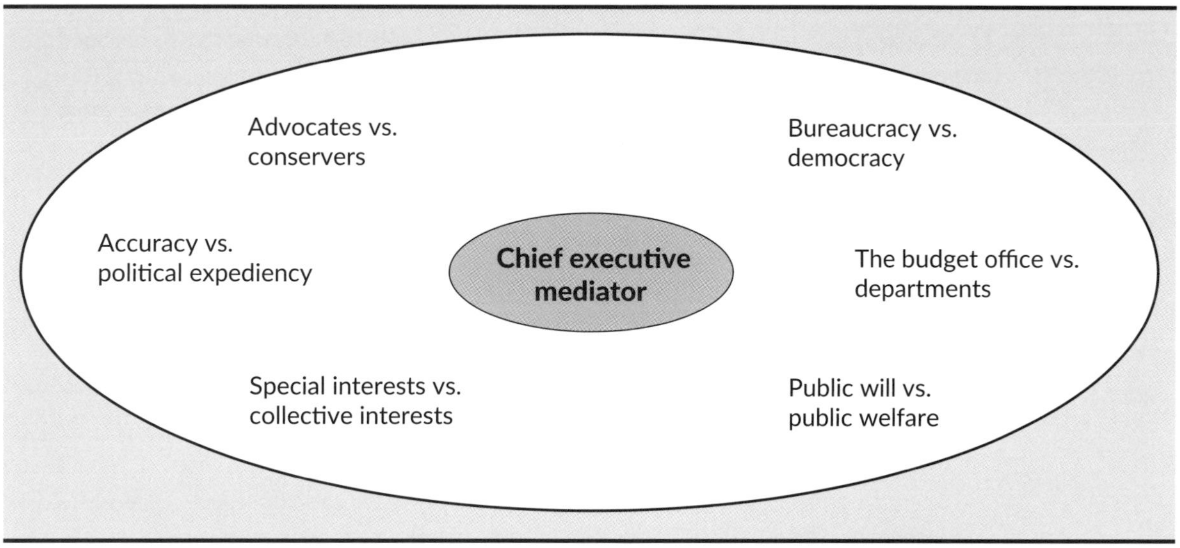

Together these three groups form what political scientists call an "iron triangle"—the mutually reinforcing relationship that exists among an agency, its clients or beneficiaries, and the legislative committee exercising oversight.[7] Each group in the triangle needs the other, and they all benefit from increased funding, especially if the costs are borne by a broad-based tax. Members of a library board have a vested interest in promoting the public library system, in partnership with the patrons of the library, and together they use their influence with the full council to pressure for more funding or even a dedicated source of revenue.

Conservers, on the other hand, are the neck in the hourglass when it comes to spending proposals. The budget office must defend budgetary limits, which are defined by available revenues, and this places them at odds with departmental advocates. In particular, departments funded from general tax sources such as the property, general sales, and income taxes have little incentive to consider revenue availability. The budget office must bear the onus of that task. In essence, the conflict between conservers and advocates involves those who are responsible for the whole versus those who are responsible for a part.[8]

One strategy that executives use to moderate this conflict is to inform departments early in the budget preparation phase about the government's forecasted revenue condition and its implications for each department. Some executives specify a target budget for each department. But for an enterprise fund agency such as a water department, the operating budget is determined by level of consumer demand for the service; thus, allocation of funding is driven more by market considerations than by the political criteria that determine the public goods and services that general fund agencies produce. For these producers of private goods and services, the interests of conservers and advocates converge, and conflict is less apparent.

The budget office versus departments

Another source of conflict is information. A budget analyst must have accurate and timely documentation in order to make fair and responsible budget recommendations. Thus, the budget office constantly scans for information on departmental operations, especially their efficiency and effectiveness. But the more information a department discloses to the budget office, the more control the budget office can exert over the department, especially during budget implementation, so department heads vigilantly scrutinize information, leaving the organization to ensure that it conveys a positive picture of the department and its operations.

This struggle over information is one reason why zero-base budgeting (ZBB) declined in popularity. ZBB requires that departments (or their decision units) submit at least three spending packages: one that provides for minimum services (only the department's most urgent needs), one that continues spending at current levels, and one that provides for enhanced services. If funding falls below the minimum level, the program or agency will not be able to continue operating. Understandably, department heads resist disclosing a package of minimum services: to do so gives the budget office valuable information should spending need to be reduced. Department heads typically contend that their departments are already at the minimum level and that any further reduction in funding would be catastrophic.

Finally, as noted in the previous chapter, the cost of requests for additional information is largely borne by departments that have to devote additional staff time to complete the analysis.

To moderate this conflict, the chief executive should

- Make clear what information is essential to decision making
- Recruit a professional staff of budget examiners who have good interpersonal as well as analytical skills
- Promote automation of the budget preparation process
- Annually examine the instructions and forms contained in the budget manual for redundancy and obsolescence.

In short, the chief executive should recognize that the budget office tends to ask for more information than it needs and that departments tend to resist disclosing more than they must.

Accuracy versus political expediency

The quest for budget accuracy can also find itself at odds with political expediency. Public administrators' preoccupation with budget realities and exactitude often clashes with politicians' attention to image and concern that the budget picture be positive. In the case of revenue forecasts, budget offices generally provide conservative estimates, while legislators pressure forecasters to raise their estimates in order to ease the task of balancing the budget. An imbalance in either direction can be disastrous.

Overly optimistic revenue forecasts contribute significantly to local governments' financial crises, especially in large central cities that are facing long-term economic decline. Lawmakers will often authorize an accelerated payment of taxes in order to increase revenues for the forthcoming year. Conversely, they may defer payments to another year—for example, rolling ahead the last pay period to the next fiscal year—in order to reduce spending for the current fiscal year. Accounting sleight of hand is used all too often to balance expenditures with revenues, especially when revenues are scarce. At one point, after trying vainly to resolve a budget imbalance, the Texas legislature authorized the state comptroller to temporarily transfer more than $1 billion from various special funds to the general fund on the last day of the fiscal year; this allowed the comptroller to certify that the proposed budget for the next fiscal year was indeed balanced—at least on the first day of the new year. The money then reverted to the funds of origin on the following day.

During the past four decades the conflict between accuracy and political expediency has been particularly apparent at the national level, where both the president and Congress have been frustrated by an inability to control the size of the budget deficit except for a brief time between 1998 and 2001. As the deficit has grown, so too has the pressure on both branches of government to adopt a balanced budget. To make the deficit appear less egregious, they have resorted to manipulating budget totals through interfund borrowing from the Social Security

Budget stalemates and government shutdowns

Partisan brawling in Congress routinely erupts over the federal government's annual budget. Unfortunately, the involuntary pawns in these exercises of brinkmanship have been federal civilian employees and contractors, who face repeated threats of being furloughed or having their contracts suspended because funding has not been approved.

Under the U.S. Constitution, Congress is responsible for funding government operations through appropriation legislation: "No money shall be drawn from the Treasury, but in consequence of appropriations made by law" (Article I, Section 9). Congress annually appropriates budget authority to all three branches of government. Subsequent statutes have established the role of the president in preparing an annual budget and of Congress in reviewing the proposed budget and passing appropriation bills before the start of the fiscal year on October 1. Without an appropriation, agencies cannot enter into obligations and federal operations cease—at least in theory.

The Constitution also empowers Congress to borrow funds, which legislators do by setting the maximum amount of debt that the U.S. Treasury may issue. As that debt ceiling is approached, Congress must enact legislation to raise that ceiling—now in excess of $15 trillion—or risk defaulting on its debt service obligations.

Congress has rarely been able to complete work on all elements of the budget before the start of the fiscal year, necessitating passage of a continuing resolution to grant temporary budget authority while it completes work on the appropriation bills. Occasionally, agencies have had to operate for the full fiscal year on a continuing resolution.

The Antideficiency Act of 1982 governs how the president must respond to funding gaps. In the absence of the timely adoption of an appropriation or its substitute (a continuing resolution), the act requires the furloughing of all federal employees except

- Those performing emergency work affecting the safety of human life or the protection of property
- The president, members of Congress, presidential appointees, and certain appointees of Congress
- Federal employees paid from restricted sources not subject to the annual appropriation (e.g., U.S. Postal Service, Federal Reserve, Tennessee Valley Authority, and Amtrak).

The law gives the president, working through the Office of Management and Budget, some latitude in defining "excepted" employees. Some estimates put the number as high as one-quarter of the current federal workforce of 2.8 million civilian employees. In the past, Congress has retroactively paid all employees—excepted and nonexcepted—for the furloughed days, and evidence from these experiences shows no salary savings from a government shutdown.

Nevertheless, federal employees, whether in uniform or not, are victims when they are held hostage to conflicts in the budget process. We as a nation depend on these fellow citizens—experts in their fields—for protection, security, commerce, justice, and economic stability. Our elected leaders would do well to display the same level of professionalism that we have come to rely on from these public servants.

Source: Information for this sidebar is drawn from Clinton T. Brass, *Shutdown of the Federal Government: Causes, Processes, and Effects*, RL34680 (Washington, D.C.: Congressional Research Service, April 13, 2013), fas.org/sgp/crs/misc/RL34680.pdf.

Trust Fund, making overly optimistic economic forecasts, and accelerating tax collections, among other things.

Pressure to avoid tax increases or to make difficult spending reductions tempts legislators to use these deceptive measures. Although state and local governments generally lack the option of incurring deficits in successive years, they, too, have succumbed to budget manipulation. With few exceptions, however, such measures can be used only once. The chief executive must serve as the conscience of the organization and ensure that budget accuracy is not sacrificed for the benefit of short-term political expediency.

Bureaucracy versus democracy

At a more philosophical level, the budget process features conflict between the goals of democracy (equality and accountability) and those of bureaucracy (centralization of power and control). Since the earliest days of democracy in ancient Greece, political theorists have sought to devise strategies to keep the bureaucratic (the executive branch) accountable to the democratic (the people and their elected representatives).[9] The introduction of governmental budgeting in the United States in 1906, when New York City became the first major government in the country to adopt a formal budget process, represented a significant innovation in this quest for democratic control of the bureaucracy. Jesse Burkhead, a leading scholar in the field, observed that

> the budget was conceived as a major weapon for instilling responsibility in the governmental structure: the budget system rests on popular control; the budget will publicize what government is doing and make for an informed and alert citizenry; the budget will destroy the rule of invisible government—the party bosses who are responsible to no one.[10]

By the mid-1920s, most major cities in the United States had established budgeting systems. States also began developing formal budget procedures, Wisconsin being one of the pioneers. Although a formal budget process had been proposed more than a decade earlier, it was not until 1921 that Congress passed the Budget and Accounting Act giving the president responsibility for preparing an executive budget—a document that presents the chief executive's spending proposals for review and action by Congress. The act established a Bureau of the Budget in the Treasury Department to assist the president in budget preparation, and it created the General Accounting Office (now the Government Accountability Office, or GAO) as an investigative arm of Congress charged with auditing the financial reports and management performance of each agency. Thus, in the first two decades of the last century, the budget became the premier tool for achieving accountability to those being governed and, thus, greater control over the bureaucracy.

This quest to elevate democracy through greater citizen involvement in government has since proceeded unabated. Outsourcing, privatization, the National Performance Review, budgeting for outcomes, and priority-based budgeting have all become common parlance in budget deliberations as managers seek innovative ways to demonstrate accountability to councils and citizens. Increasingly, managers are experimenting with social media as a way to engage residents in budget deliberations.[11]

The Internet has given public managers another venue for creatively engaging citizens in budget decision making. For example, Austin, Texas, has developed a "budget in a box" exercise that uses facilitated small groups of citizens to role-play their preferences for spending on each of eight service areas.[12] Boulder, Colorado, invites citizens to share their cost-saving suggestions as part of its priority-based budget process.[13] Citizen satisfaction surveys, focus groups, and input from citizen groups and advisory boards are other methods that local governments use to obtain a valid measure of citizens' budgetary preferences.

Special interests versus collective interests

Budgeting also places special interests at odds with the community as a whole. Interest groups both within and outside government try to garner funding for their particular causes, whether a city's recreation program, state highway construction, or military hardware. Because spending decisions for the general fund agencies are not linked with revenue decisions, interest groups rarely see their requests in terms of cost to the community.

Politically, it is difficult for members of a council or governing board to refuse the requests of special interests, especially well-organized groups. If funding comes from the general fund, the costs for a group's proposal are borne by all taxpayers (the collective interest) at a negligible and presumably unnoticeable cost to any one taxpayer. If legislators oppose the group's request, they risk losing the group's support or, worse, incurring its opposition in the next election. On the other hand, because of the negligible cost to the nonvocal and usually unorganized collective interest, that sector's support is uncertain if legislators oppose the interest group's request. Thus, in a democracy, budgets characteristically contain an ever-widening variety of programs and services as legislators seek to appease the wishes of interest groups—or at least reduce the risk of kindling their opposition.

Occasionally, taxpayers who are politically uninvolved and generally indifferent become sufficiently irritated that they revolt, precipitating tax limitation actions like Proposition 13 in California and the Taxpayer Bill of Rights in Colorado. Onerous and visible taxes such as the property tax provide a focal point for rallying the collective interest into action. Most research indicates that these revolts are more a reaction to perceived government inefficiency than a demand for fewer services, with the possible exception of welfare services.

Public will versus public welfare

Budget conflict may also involve perceptions of public will versus public welfare—a struggle between what the public wants and what is in its long-term best interest. On the one hand, administrators and lawmakers must be attuned to public opinion and the will of the majority. Effective leadership depends on the manager's ability to accurately read public attitudes on sensitive issues facing the government.

Yet the long-term well-being of the community may not be served by what opinion polls indicate to be the public will. Chief executives and other administrators have access to information on the ramifications of a policy that may suggest a detrimental effect to the community's long-term economic and social welfare. For example, public opinion may favor a county government extending a tax abatement for a local manufacturer to expand its existing facilities, but it may be in the county's best interest to use the abatement to attract other types of industries and thus diversify the local economy.

Public managers are educators. Nowhere is that more apparent than in the budgeting process. As leaders, managers must educate lawmakers, the media, department heads, and citizens about what they perceive as being in the public interest. And they must be willing to be educated themselves about what others perceive as being in the public interest. In the budget process, effective management of the conflict between public will and public welfare means being able to both lead and follow while never being too far ahead of or too far behind public opinion.

Managing conflict through a budget policy

How can managers balance the ever-present tensions inherent in the budget cycle and keep deliberations from being sidetracked into endless maneuvering and one-upmanship? As noted above, a budget policy statement provides one mechanism for institutionalizing responsible dialogue within a government's decision-making framework as it establishes the financial standards that guide budget deliberations for both the executive and legislative branches.

In fact, every government has some type of budget policy, although often it is unwritten and thus more vulnerable to being compromised. Past precedent largely frames governmental budget policy, whether written or unwritten. The principal benefit of a written policy is that it provides a standard of budgetary performance that both branches of government have endorsed. If, as a matter of policy, a government will not incur a GO debt burden that exceeds 15 percent of its assessed value of property, then any proposal to exceed that limit places the burden of proof on those making the proposal. The written policy becomes the conscience of the organization by reducing, although never eliminating, the incentives for making imprudent financial decisions in the interest of political expediency. The more specific the policy statement, the more effective it will be in promoting financially responsible budget actions.

A formal statement also provides continuity in budget decision making. It reinforces the core financial values of the organization and preserves them for successive legislatures and administrations. Of course, future legislatures and executives may choose to amend those policies as community needs or standards of financial prudence change. However, any amendment requires deliberation by the leadership on its merits before it becomes effective.

A budget policy may also reduce the number of issues open to debate during budget preparation and adoption. In so doing, it will expedite budget deliberations, a prospect that is normally greeted warmly by anyone who has ever prepared a budget. Noted budgeting scholar Michael White has observed that "budget policy becomes a means for managing participation in the budget process and moving that process along its calendar. Questions not debated mean participants not needed."[14]

A budget policy may have as its overarching goal the preservation of a claim to distinction. For example, the board of supervisors for Fairfax County, Virginia, relies on "Ten Principles of Sound Financial Management" that are "designed to contribute to the County's fiscal management and maintain the County's 'triple A' bond rating."[15] A few local governments, such as Charlotte, North Carolina, now use the balanced scorecard that ties citywide goals to departmental performance measures. As described in the previous chapter, Fort Collins, Colorado, has taken an even more radical approach—budgeting for outcomes—that "focuses on results and priorities, not on cost. The budget process shifts from paying for costs to buying results."[16] This approach has radically altered the ways in which the city evaluates departmental budgets and spending plans are presented to the city council.

A virtually sacrosanct assumption about tax rates or bond ratings often develops within a community's psyche and holds sway over budget deliberations. A number of local governments that have received an Aaa/AAA bond rating from Moody's, Standard and Poor's, and/or Fitch's—Salt Lake City, for example—take great pains not to make any tax or expenditure decisions that could tarnish their exemplary credit ratings.[17] Managers in fiscally conservative regions of the country may have to undertake budget preparations in a city or county where the property tax rate has remained constant for decades, and no manager wants to be the one to break such a record. An even more conservative position is that revenue received from the tax will not increase, so that any increase in the assessed value of taxable property (the tax base) will be offset by a reduction in the tax rate in order to hold revenue yield constant.

Budget deliberations are sometimes tempered by the need to preserve a particular strength of the community. States hard hit by a recession may give special consideration in budget deliberations to preserving a favorable business environment. A city with a reputation for excellence in its recreation and park services may protect these services from budget cuts during tight fiscal periods. These underlying assumptions can become so deeply ingrained in a government that they assume a mystique of their own. Challenging them often ends in failure and in the challenger's loss of credibility in the organization. Only a major crisis will budge the organization from these unwritten but deeply cherished marks of distinction.

The following four sections provide recommendations on policies for the operating budget, revenues, budget implementation, and debt. The accompanying sidebar summarizes the items that a policy statement on the budget should address.

Elements of a budget policy statement

As part of the criteria used in recognizing governments with distinguished budgets, the National Advisory Council on State and Local Budgeting recommends that "a government should develop a comprehensive set of financial policies. [These] policies should be consistent with the broad government goals and should be the outcome of sound analysis."[1] A policy statement on the budget should address the following elements:

1. Operating budget policies
   a. Is the budget document comprehensive? Does it include all operating and capital expenditures? What funds should be included in the operating budget? Should the operating and capital budgets be prepared concurrently or separately?
   b. What constitutes a balanced budget?
   c. In what funds should budget reserves be maintained? How much money should be maintained in each? What is the source of funding for the reserves? Under what conditions should money be withdrawn?
   d. What guidelines should govern budget preparation?
   e. Who is responsible for budget preparation, and what are the critical tasks for which they are responsible?
2. Revenue policies
   a. How much change in the property tax rate is acceptable in a given year?
   b. How will one-time revenues, such as grants or tax windfalls, be used?
   c. How frequently should service charges and fees be reviewed? Should they recover indirect costs?
   d. What policies should govern collection of delinquent taxes and charges?
3. Budget implementation policies
   a. What policies should govern the transfer of money across accounts or funds?
   b. Under what conditions should governments authorize interfund borrowing or interfund payments in lieu of taxes?
   c. When should the chief executive be empowered to encumber budget authority?
   d. Who should be held responsible for expenditures exceeding appropriated amounts?
   e. What standards should govern accounting, financial reporting, and auditing?
   f. How frequently should management prepare a report to council on compliance with financial policies?
4. Debt policies
   a. What is the maximum long-term debt burden that the government will incur (expressed in total dollar amounts, as a percentage of the property tax base, or as a percentage of the property tax rate)?
   b. What mix of long-term debt and current revenues, if any, will be the basis for financing capital improvements?
   c. How will bond proceeds be used?
   d. Under what conditions will short-term debt be issued?

Source: Information for this sidebar is drawn from Clinton T. Brass, *Shutdown of the Federal Government: Causes, Processes, and Effects*, RL34680 (Washington, D.C.: Congressional Research Service, April 13, 2013), fas.org/sgp/crs/misc/RL34680.pdf.

Operating budget policies

Operating policies address the basic philosophical questions of the budget's scope and preparation. Whereas a policy statement should not include a detailed description of the budget cycle, operating policies should address the key issues in budget preparation, including

- How comprehensive is the budget (budget coverage or scope)?
- What constitutes a balanced budget?
- What types of budget reserves should be maintained?
- What general guidelines should govern budget preparation and amendment?
- Who are responsible for budget preparation, and what are their duties?

Budget coverage The comprehensiveness of the operating budget has been debated since the inception of the formal budgeting process in government. The issue is twofold: to what extent should the operating and capital budgets be integrated, and what activities should be reported in the operating budget? Activities or projects not included in either budget constitute **off-budget transactions**: they are evaluated on a case-by-case basis and are not subject to the usual scrutiny given to spending proposals in the regular budget cycle. Off-budget transactions can occur any time after budget adoption. Some governments routinely defer decisions on new initiatives to a midyear budget review to ensure that revenues will be sufficient to cover the continuing services already in the budget.

Coordinating operating and capital budgets Municipalities and counties usually prepare an operating budget separate from the capital budget because the planning and financing sources for each are different. First, capital projects require a much longer planning period because of their large, up-front investment and because any errors in design are costly to correct once construction has begun. Second, although practice varies among governments, capital improvements are usually financed with long-term debt from the sale of GO or **revenue bonds**, whereas operating budgets are financed from current taxes, grants, and service charges.

Although the operating and capital budgets are usually prepared as two separate documents, it is quite common for governments to prepare them concurrently. One benefit of this is that the manager can better assess the impact of a capital improvement on annual operating costs. For example, the acquisition of new computer hardware may reduce operating costs to the extent that they increase worker productivity or decrease the need for personnel; however, the addition of a fire station or a new library will increase operating costs as additional personnel and utilities are needed to staff the new facilities. A second benefit is that concurrent preparation concentrates budget deliberations. Budget preparation is time-consuming and stressful, and no one likes to do it—least of all department heads. Concentrating the budget debate helps keeps tempers under control and discussion focused on the issues at hand.

Other local governments, however, choose to separate deliberations by first preparing an operating budget and later preparing the capital budget. The primary advantage of this approach is that it reduces the workload by spreading budget deliberations out over a longer period. More careful deliberation may reduce errors in judgment and provide a better opportunity to educate participants on the merits of each proposal.

The operating budget policy should specify whether the two budget cycles will proceed concurrently or separately and should briefly explain the reasons for the choice.

Funds to include An operating budget policy should specify the types of funds included in the operating and capital budgets. Governments account for their money in one of eleven types of funds:

- Governmental group: General fund, special revenue funds, debt service funds, capital projects funds, and permanent funds
- Proprietary (or business-type) group: Enterprise funds and internal service funds

- Fiduciary group: Investment funds, private-purpose funds, pension funds, and agency funds.

Governmental funds are generally supported by tax or grant revenues that go to the delivery of public goods and services. Proprietary funds account for the sale of private goods and services, such as water or parking, so they function more typically like business-type ventures of a local government. Fiduciary funds are used by local governments to hold money in trust for other governments (agency funds) or persons (pensions, private-purpose funds). These funds are the least likely to be included in the budget because their activities are typically defined by contract or by state or federal law.

For purposes of understanding the issues in budget coverage, the operating budget covers the recurring expenditures and revenues in all three categories of funds. Capital budgets, however, usually cover projects accounted for in capital projects funds and, to a lesser extent, in special revenue funds and the general fund.

Preferably, the budget policy should call for a comprehensive inclusion of all fund types in the annual budget process. Some governments, such as Birmingham, Alabama, limit the operating budget coverage to transactions in the general fund.[18] In its budget policy statement, Olympia, Washington, provides a detailed list of each of the city's funds and indicates whether the fund is in the annual appropriation with budget authority lapsing at the end of the year or a continuing appropriation.[19] The table also lists those fiduciary funds not included in the annual budget such as the Firemen's Pension, Municipal Court Trust Fund, and a trust fund for an interlocal law enforcement records management system.

At a minimum, the operating budget should include all general fund activities. The issue of budget coverage centers on whether special revenue, debt service, enterprise, and trust funds should also be included. Excluding these funds from the budget planning process may be politically expedient because it gives the appearance of a smaller government. But spending that is not subject to the scrutiny of lawmakers and the rigor of comparative analysis with other spending options undermines accountability and government leaders' control over spending. As a matter of policy, budget scholars advise that all spending be covered in the operating and capital budgets.

One other issue concerns how governments budget for internal services. Governments set up internal service funds as a tool to control costs. For example, a motor vehicles pool may be accounted for as an internal service fund, in which case each department (internal user) is charged for the use of city or county vehicles. From a budgeting perspective, the question is how to budget for this internal service: as a line-item expenditure for each department, or as a lump-sum appropriation to the motor vehicles department that is then allocated to each departmental user? The first method is much preferred. Each department has an incentive to ration its use of the internal service in accordance with the funds it has available for the activity. Occasionally, an internal service may require a subsidy from the operating budget because usage does not provide the level of funding needed to sustain the desired quality of service. For example, the motor vehicles department may not have a sufficient volume of activity to cover its annual direct and indirect operating costs, in which case a subsidy will be needed if the jurisdiction decides to retain the service rather than outsource it to a private provider.

Pension obligations Pension liabilities have become a major issue for many local governments, particularly those that have failed to adequately fund their obligations as they are incurred. Failure to include pension obligations incurred in the current year in the operating budget shifts the liability to future taxpayers and creates what accountants call an unfunded liability. The Governmental Accounting Standards Board (GASB) has issued guidelines for reporting pension obligations as well as for the failure to fully fund those obligations as the liability is incurred.[20]

Promises of more generous pension payouts gave candidates for elected office an easy means of garnering more votes from city employees who, if they vote as a block, can swing the outcome of a local election. Once in office, the elected official then had to press for the promised pension benefits. Pensions usually involve the employee contributing a fixed percentage, for example 5 percent from their wages, with the employer matching that amount by two or more times. But annual revenues were insufficient to meet the employer's accrued obligation. For cities, counties and school districts that did not have a financial policy requiring that they fund obligations like pensions as they were incurred, it became politically expedient to defer that liability until it came due. Credible estimates put the gap in unfunded public pension obligations in the range of $1.4 trillion to $3 trillion.

Complicating the pension crisis has been longer lifespans for retirees creating a greater draw on the pension fund than actuaries had anticipated. Also, increases in medical expenses have added to the strain on these funds. Third, recessions wreak havoc on the earnings of pension funds. In the early 2000s, the Dallas Police and Fire System invested heavily in luxury properties in California's Napa County and Hawaii only to see their value plummet during the Great Recession. Combined with overly optimistic projections for investment returns, the fund teetered on bankruptcy. Ultimately, a long-term solution of institutional reforms in the fund's management, changing the way benefits are paid out, and increasing contributions averted a disaster.

A number of cities from Rhode Island to California have turned to the federal bankruptcy courts, in those states that permit cities to file for Chapter 9 bankruptcy protection, to seek

Figure 8–5 FY 2019 operating budget summary, Cambridge, Massachusetts

Operating Budget

Financing Plan by Source	FY17 Actual	FY18 Projected	FY19 Budget
Charges For Services	$87,909,960	$91,130,295	**$88,816,015**
Fines & Forfeits	$10,779,885	$10,662,085	**$10,626,735**
Intergovernmental Revenue	$47,402,600	$50,475,320	**$48,869,010**
Licenses & Permits	$30,597,260	$32,028,695	**$20,253,100**
Miscellaneous Revenue	$16,342,000	$15,403,170	**$18,755,525**
Taxes	$431,451,210	$424,732,665	**$449,130,725**
Total Revenue	$624,482,915	$624,432,230	**$636,451,110**
Program Expenditures			
General Government	$52,623,625	$48,023,990	**$65,880,850**
Public Safety	$128,727,440	$134,123,455	**$139,391,205**
Community Maintenance and Development	$123,531,940	$129,352,875	**$134,952,840**
Human Resource Development	$38,864,520	$43,029,765	**$46,940,590**
Education	$172,141,330	$182,702,620	**$191,069,505**
Intergovernmental	$53,426,740	$57,171,010	**$58,216,120**
Total Expenditures	$569,315,595	$594,403,715	**$636,451,110**

Source: City of Cambridge, Massachusetts, *Annual Budget 2018-19*, IV-2. https://www.cambridgema.gov/~/media/Files/budgetdepartment/FinancePDFs/fy19adoptedbudget.pdf restructuring of their pension obligations. The result has generally been unfavorable to retirees in lower retirement benefits and to new hires who see reduced future benefits and higher contributions. The City of Fort Worth, for example, closed its $1.6-billion gap in unfunded pension liabilities by increasing contributions from both employees and the city and significantly reducing the cost of living allowance (COLA) for retirees.

Another related long-term liability are the health care benefits that local governments typically extend to their retirees—what accountants have labeled **other post-employment benefits (OPEB)**. In the past, local governments typically did not include funding for these liabilities in their operating budgets and are now having to pay for past OPEBs from current revenues while also setting aside funds for future retirees. The GASB has issued guidelines as well for reporting OPEB.[21]

Budgetary balance At first glance, the definition of a balanced budget may appear obvious. If current revenues equal current expenditures, the budget is balanced; thus, a deficit budget occurs when revenues fall short of expenditures, which requires the government to borrow money or draw on fund balances carried over from previous years in order to cover current expenditures. But as noted earlier in the chapter, political gamesmanship has made even something as simple as defining a balanced budget enormously complex. Questions arise over whether the balance test applies to only the executive's proposed budget or also to the budget adopted by the legislature or to the year-end balance remaining in the budget. There is also the question of how the balance should be measured—on a cash basis or an accrual basis? (These terms are defined and discussed in Chapter 10).

Occasionally, a local government will want to draw down its fund balance—the accumulated year-end surpluses available for reappropriation. In this case, it will intentionally adopt a budget in which estimated current revenues are less than appropriations, with the difference made up by drawing down the fund balance:

Estimated revenues + fund balance = appropriations.

The budget policy should specify the expectation for a balanced budget and the amount of money to be retained in the fund balance as a reserve for contingencies. Figure 8–5, a summary of all funds from the Cambridge, Massachusetts, budget comparing total revenues with expenditures, shows not only a balanced budget but also the budget's comprehensiveness.

Budget reserves Although policies on budget coverage and a balanced budget are not always clearly articulated, many governments have adopted explicit policy guidelines for budget reserves. To accumulate money for future purposes or unforeseen events, governments establish reserve accounts in most governmental funds and then earmark the money for that purpose. In proprietary funds, governments monitor working capital—defined as the difference between **current assets** and current liabilities—to cover operating uncertainties. GFOA recommends that for enterprise funds local governments have as a policy that this difference is no less than forty-five days of operating expenses.[22] The more common types of reserves are for

- Cash flow requirements
- Revenue stabilization (or rainy day funds)
- Unforeseen contingencies
- Equipment replacement
- Repair of buildings or other improvements
- Debt service.

Cash flow requirements Because revenue inflow never coincides with the outflow of payments, governments must maintain sufficient cash on hand to satisfy cash flow needs. The amount of reserve for this purpose—sometimes called operating reserves—depends on the timing of tax and utility payments. For example, most cities in Texas begin their fiscal year on October 1, yet property taxes are not due until the following January 31. Sufficient cash must be reserved in a fund balance to cover disbursements during that period.

For general fund services, one rule of thumb is that there should be enough cash on hand to cover disbursements for sixty days. A government should first examine its cash flow needs and the margin of protection required, and then specify in its budget policy the size of cash flow reserve it wishes to maintain. Some funds may require higher levels of operating reserves than others because of the cyclicality of their revenue stream. For example, enterprise funds such as a water fund may require a higher operating reserve because of the uneven flow of revenues, which peak during the dry summer months.

Revenue stabilization Following the bitter impact of recessions over the past three decades, many state and local governments established **revenue stabilization reserves**, or rainy day accounts, usually maintained in the general fund, to provide resources when revenues decline because of an economic slowdown. While the timing of slowdowns and even recessions can be anticipated somewhat accurately using an inverted yield curve as a harbinger, their severity and length are much more difficult to forecast. And their impact on local communities varies widely, depending on their cause and on the local economy's link to the broader economic cycle. Consequently, state and local governments risk misestimating revenues whenever their assumptions about the economy's future are inaccurate.[23]

While revenues fluctuate with the economy, expenditures usually display a countercyclical trend. During economic downturns, demand for government services such as unemployment compensation, education, and police protection may increase. A revenue stabilization reserve enables governments to insulate their spending and taxing policies from the vagaries of the economy.[24]

Two policy issues that a government must resolve when creating a revenue stabilization reserve are the size of the reserve and the way in which it can be tapped. One approach is to set the reserve equal to a percentage of the operating expenditures; another is to set it according to the maximum change in the property tax rate that the government is willing to adopt. In the final analysis, the appropriate size of the reserve depends on the stability of a government's revenue stream and on its political resolve to protect against budget instability.

Most budget policies leave the question of when to tap the reserve to the discretion of the council on the recommendation of the chief executive. Some governments, such as Milwaukee, Wisconsin, require an extraordinary (three-fourths) majority of the council before money can be transferred from the reserve to the operating budget. An alternative approach pegs accessing the reserve to an economic indicator, such as a decline in the gross state product or an increase in the regional unemployment rate. Whatever mechanism is used, the budget policy should specify the benchmark measure, or "trigger point," for accessing the reserve.

Unforeseen contingencies State and local governments also establish reserves for unforeseen contingencies to provide funding in times of emergencies or disasters. Article X, Section 20, of the Colorado Constitution requires all cities to maintain a restricted reserve in all city funds, which can be tapped only for declared emergencies.[25] A contingency reserve provides a readily available pool of funding to ensure continuation of city operations during an emergency, and it buys time while the city or county assesses the impact of the emergency. Many governments establish a separate contingency reserve in each major fund, such as one for each enterprise fund (water, sewer, sanitation, etc.). In cases where the disaster has a long-term impact, however, as has occurred with Hurricanes Katrina and Sandy, no amount of local contingency funding can provide adequate preparation.

Equipment replacement and building improvements Two other types of reserve that state and local governments use occasionally are for equipment replacement and building improvements. The advantage of an equipment replacement reserve is that money is available for purchasing operating equipment and vehicles as they become obsolete or unusable. Some governments set up a revolving fund that departments can borrow from to replace equipment before the next funding cycle or before the next lease-purchase agreement is approved. Sometimes governments establish a separate reserve that accumulates funds for deferred maintenance, renovations, and repairs to government-owned facilities. Funding for both types of reserves usually comes from surcharges assessed to each department on the basis of its pro rata share of equipment used or building space occupied.

Local governments that pursue a pay-as-you-go policy for capital improvements will likely set up a similar reserve fund to finance new construction, particularly construction for general government activities. Contributions to the reserve may be an annual fee assessed on all general fund activities, a fixed percentage of the annual operating budget, or some combination. Unfortunately, governments that fund their activities using this strategy rarely accumulate sufficient reserves to keep pace with new or replacement construction.

Debt service Lastly, governments establish reserves for debt service payments, usually as a condition, called a covenant, of their bond agreements with private investors. Debt service is the annual or semiannual payment of principal and interest that governments must make on outstanding indebtedness. For GO bonds, a debt service fund is created to account for the taxes levied and payments made to service this type of debt. For revenue bonds, separate accounts are created in an enterprise fund to track revenues and payments for debt service. In the case of revenue bonds, reserves of 10–25 percent of the annual debt service payment may be required by a rate covenant in the bond ordinance that protects bondholders against default. The size of the reserve varies, depending on the instability of the revenue stream from the project financed by the bonds. Less frequently, governments may establish a small reserve for their GO payments, but this is usually more for cash flow purposes than to fulfill a requirement of the bond covenant.

Budget preparation and amendment A budget policy statement should make clear certain critical aspects of budget preparation: the duration of appropriations, the process for amending the budget during the fiscal year, the type and frequency of budget performance reports, and what funds, if any, will be self-supporting.

Duration of appropriation authority For the operating budget, appropriation authority usually lapses at the end of the fiscal year (or biennium for governments on a two-year cycle). Such requirements are often specified in law. Any unspent or unencumbered balances remaining at the end of the year lapse into the fund balance and become available for reappropriation for the next fiscal year. Obviously, department heads have a powerful incentive to spend their full appropriation as they risk having their budgets reduced the next year by an amount equal to the unspent balance. Exceptions to year-end lapsing of authority include appropriations for capital projects, which usually do not lapse until the project is completed, and state and federal grants, which lapse once the grant expires or the grant-funded project is completed.

Amending the budget A budget policy statement should specify the procedures for amending the budget during the fiscal year. Because revenue forecasts must be developed several months before the fiscal year begins, revenue collections may deviate substantially from those on which the budget is based, and the operating budget may need to be amended. In Georgia, as in many state and local governments, revenue forecasts are conservative, leading to a surplus of revenue available for appropriation by the fiscal year's midpoint. Each year the Georgia legislature passes a midyear supplemental appropriation that allocates any revenue surplus to state agencies.[26]

A policy should specify the circumstances under which the legislative body may amend the budget. For example, Fort Collins amends the budget (1) to pay for encumbrances (purchase orders) carried over from the preceding fiscal year; (2) to allocate unanticipated revenues, such as a grant or bond issue; or (3) to allocate reserves where the balances are greater than required by budget policy or where an emergency or unusual circumstance has occurred.[27] Legislatures also amend budgets to transfer money across funds or to retroactively approve a transfer made by the chief executive. Such amendments align the operating budget with the actual levels of spending that are occurring.

Budget status reports A government's budget policy should specify the types of budget status reports to be prepared and their frequency. Governments prepare interim financial reports that compare budgeted with actual amounts of revenues and expenditures to date. These reports, now available in real time with web-based financial management systems, provide decision makers with an important early warning of impending overruns in expenditures or shortfalls in revenues. For governments that rely on legacy data management systems, reports should be prepared quarterly or, preferably, monthly.

Self-supporting funds Finally, the policy statement for the operating budget should specify which enterprise funds will be self-supporting. In general, enterprise and internal service funds should be self-supporting if (1) the benefits largely accrue to users of the service, (2) it is administratively feasible to collect a fee from users, and (3) pricing the service at its full cost will not result in actions by users that are more costly than the revenue raised from the charge. For example, charging full cost for residential use of a landfill may increase illegal dumping of trash along roads and in vacant lots. In such cases, subsidizing the service with general tax revenues is more efficient than trying to make it self-supporting.

Fort Collins has the following policy with respect to this issue. The city currently has five enterprise funds: golf, light and power, wastewater, storm drainage, and water.[28] The goal is for all these funds to be self-sufficient—that is, to recover 100 percent of their costs. If an activity is unable to generate sufficient revenues from its fees over a five-year period so as to achieve self-sufficiency, as a matter of policy it should no longer be considered an enterprise fund but instead be accounted for in the general fund.

A related issue concerns the recovery of indirect as well as direct costs by enterprise funds. Indirect costs (or overhead) are the cost of services that are provided to all units of a government, such as the budget office or human resources, but that are not set up as internal service funds. Full cost recovery requires that enterprise funds bear a pro rata share of the cost of these support services. San Luis Obispo, California, states in its policy that its enterprise funds will "fully cover the total direct and indirect costs—including operations, capital outlay, and debt service"—of its water, sewer, and parking enterprises.[29]

Assigned responsibilities in the budget process A budget policy should specify the broad outlines of key duties in budget preparation and adoption. For example, it should specify the officer responsible for budget preparation—either the finance officer or, if a separate budget office exists, the budget officer. It should describe in general terms the duties of this officer, such as his or her authority to standardize budget documentation, prepare the budget calendar, and review departmental budget requests for accuracy and conformance to budget guidelines. It should also specify who is responsible for preparing revenue forecasts and the frequency with which such forecasts are prepared. Finally, the policy should clearly assign responsibility for overseeing the budget's implementation to the chief budget officer. The duties in this phase include preparing and reviewing budget status reports, monitoring revenues, reviewing agency expenditure requests for conformance with the budget, authorizing transfers across accounts or departments, and reviewing requests for supplementary appropriations.

Revenue policies

As with policies governing the operating budget, revenue policies provide continuity in the procedures and assumptions guiding the funding decisions of government. A revenue policy also increases the efficiency of deliberations on taxes and service charges by establishing a basis for addressing these sensitive political issues. A policy discourages exceptions by making those seeking an exception explain why it should be granted.

Governments typically prepare revenue manuals that provide extensive detail on the legal basis, administration, and yield history of every source of revenue they collect. However, the policies of concern here are those that directly affect funding of the operating and capital budgets: stability of tax rates, use of one-time revenue sources, review of service charges and fees, and collection of delinquent revenues.

Tax rate stability Local leaders can promote revenue stability through a diversified revenue structure. With respect to fluctuations in the property tax rate, a common policy among local governments that have discretion in the property tax rate being levied is to limit increases in the annual levy to the rate of inflation. Since GO bonds are usually repaid with property taxes, local governments often have to increase tax rates to meet annual debt service requirements. In those states that require voter approval to issue GO bonds, governments look to growth in the tax base for the revenue to repay the bonds while holding tax rates constant. Research has found a substitution effect between property taxes levied to repay debt and those levied to fund general government operations, which suggests that as the property taxes dedicated to debt service go up, the latitude for increasing the tax rate for operating purposes goes down.

Use of one-time or temporary revenue Political leaders can easily become lulled into thinking that a temporary revenue windfall, such as a block grant, will continue into the future, and they then use the money for ongoing operations. Public finance experts call this a **flypaper effect** because each dollar of such funding tends to increase local spending by more than a dollar of personal income. To protect against developing a dependency on one-time or temporary revenue, some governments have a policy of using windfall revenues to finance the purchase of capital assets (equipment, buildings, land) or other nonrecurring purchases. This, too, poses risks if governments defer much-needed capital projects in anticipation of receiving a grant. An alternative strategy is to earmark windfall revenues for deposit in the revenue stabilization account. But, in fact, it is impossible not to develop some dependency on such resources. If the capital item is needed and the one-time revenue windfall is not present, other resources will be used. Ideally, a policy should target transitory revenues to purposes that will minimize the risk of dependency.

Review of service charges and fees As local governments have reduced their dependence on the property tax over the past decade, and as both state and local governments have scrambled to find new sources of funding, their dependence on service charges and fees has significantly increased. However, the tendency has been to review and update these levies only in the event of a budgetary crisis precipitated by a shortfall in taxes. Characteristically, state legislatures review university tuition rates only when other state revenues are tight.

As governments depend more on charges and fees, they must review rates annually and adjust them to reflect the cost of service delivery. A number of governments have formalized this practice into their budget policies. For example, San Luis Obispo's extensive policy on user fees classifies the city's recreational services into three categories based on the percentage of cost recovered through the charge: (1) high-range cost recovery activities (60–100 percent of cost recovered), (2) midrange cost recovery activities (30–60 percent of cost recovered), and (3) low-range cost recovery activities (0–30 percent of cost recovered).[30] The policy then lists the recreational programs in each category. Part of the budget preparation process includes examining each program for compliance with the fee policy.

Collection of delinquent revenues While a budget policy statement is not the appropriate forum for a full explication of delinquent revenue collection policies, it should include the level of performance that the government seeks to achieve. For instance, it may prescribe that delinquencies will not exceed 5 percent of the levy for the year and provide that, if they do, management will increase the productivity of the unit responsible for delinquent accounts receivable.

Budget implementation policies

The budget policy should cover issues pertaining to budget implementation, including procedures for transferring money across accounts or funds, interfund borrowing or payments, budget impoundments, and assignment of responsibility for expenditures. The following discussion covers the more salient issues for inclusion in a budget policy statement.

Transferring money After the council has adopted the budget through an appropriation ordinance (or an act at the state level), department heads enter into obligations through the approval of contracts and purchase orders that result in the expenditure of money once the goods or services have been delivered. When departments' spending needs change, the manager may authorize the transfer of budget authority from one department or fund to another in order to bring the budget into line with the departments' actual spending needs. The budget policy should specify the types of transfers that can be made and the authorization required to make them.

A typical budget policy may authorize transfers as follows:

1. Budget transfers across accounts within a department or agency require only the city or county manager's (or finance director's) authorization.
2. Budget transfers across departments but within the same fund require the city manager's recommendation and the city council's approval. Such transfers may be made only in the last three months of the fiscal year.
3. Budget transfers across funds (e.g., from the general fund to a capital projects fund) require city council approval.

In addition, legislative approval is almost always required to transfer appropriations between capital project funds and sometimes even across accounts within these funds.

A related issue concerns interfund payments in lieu of taxes (PILOTs). Transfers of these types are usually governed by legislation that requires, for example, an enterprise fund to annually make a payment to the general fund for property taxes that otherwise would have been received had the service been provided by a private firm. In Fort Collins, the water, wastewater, and light and power funds transfer 6 percent of their operating revenue each year to the general fund as a PILOT. Occasionally, these transfers are characterized as returns on investment or as overhead charges assessed to the enterprise activity for the indirect costs incurred by the general fund in administering the activity.

Interfund borrowing and payments By contrast, interfund borrowing occurs when a temporary revenue shortfall in one fund is offset by a surplus in another. Such borrowing often occurs during the budget year as a cash management measure. However, governments also use interfund borrowing to balance operating budgets across fiscal years, as the federal government does when it borrows from the Social Security Trust Fund to lessen the deficit. Such practices are usually unsustainable for the long term. San Luis Obispo's policy distinguishes between interfund transfers and interfund borrowing. Interfund borrowing may be done by the finance director only for cash management purposes if repaid in forty-five days.[31]

Impoundments Another issue that should be addressed in a budget policy is impoundments. If revenues fail to keep pace with spending or if budgeted expenditures are no longer needed, the chief executive should have the authority to impound or restrict spending. At the federal level, the Congressional Budget and Impoundment Control Act of 1974 clarified the president's impoundment authority by creating two categories: a **deferral**, whereby the president recommends delaying spending on a program for a period of time, and a **recision**, whereby the president recommends cancellation of budget authority for a particular program or line item.

Local governments may grant impoundment authority through a policy statement. Fort Collins gives the city manager authority to direct "budget reductions," but the council must be informed. This policy also obviates the issue of an appointed executive acting without the express approval of an elected council by providing that "while the appropriation amount is not changed, expenditures shall not exceed the reduced amount recommended by the City Manager."[32]

Responsibility for expenditures A related issue concerns responsibility for expenditures that exceed appropriations. An appropriation represents a legal limit on commitments in spending that the executive may incur for the fiscal period. Control is further exercised by the budget office through a process of apportioning the appropriation over the fiscal year and by the line-item detail provided in the budget document, which limits the amount of spending that each department head can incur and implicitly holds those with authority to spend money accountable for not exceeding the appropriated amounts. Fiscal prudence would suggest that this implicit authority should be formalized as part of the budget policy. Such a policy should state that each department or agency head is liable for expenditures exceeding those appropriated to the department, and that each is responsible for keeping spending within appropriated amounts.

Debt policies

A fourth area typically included in a budget policy concerns debt issuance and administration. Provisions addressing these issues specify the maximum long-term debt burden the government will incur, the mix of debt with current revenues in financing capital improvements, the use of bond proceeds, and the conditions under which short-term debt will be issued.

Long-term debt burden One of the most common provisions in a budget policy statement places limits on the amount of debt a government can incur. These limitations are on both the percentage of operating revenue spent for debt service and the amount of outstanding direct debt as a percentage of the full value of assessed property. For example, Fort Collin's policy differs by type of fund. For the Governmental Funds, annual debt service cannot exceed five percent of annual revenues; San Luis Obispo limits debt service to 10 percent of general fund revenues. State law in Utah limits GO debt to 4 percent of a city's adjusted taxable property value.[33] Percentages will vary among governments depending on the composition of their property tax base and the rate of growth in population. More rapidly growing communities that have a larger proportion of residential property set higher limits.

Capital improvement financing San Luis Obispo stipulates that capital improvements will be financed with a maximum of 60 percent debt and a minimum of 40 percent current revenues. The benefit of such a policy is the fiscal discipline it imposes on governments to accumulate enough money, possibly in a building or equipment replacement fund, and then to carefully prioritize capital projects before construction begins. The disadvantage is that it may impose costly delays on the construction of capital improvements that, when completed, would improve operational efficiencies in the city or county.

Use of bond proceeds Another common provision in budget policy statements is a stipulation on how bond proceeds can be used. For example, San Luis Obispo uses debt "only for one-time capital improvement projects and only under the following circumstances:

a. When the project's useful life will exceed the term of the financing.
b. When project revenues or specific resources will be sufficient to service the long term debt."[34]

Short-term debt A final issue concerns the use of short-term debt. For example, governments may limit such debt to bond anticipation notes, or they may allow the issuance of notes for a broader range of purposes, such as to meet cash flow needs. Olympia, Washington's policy states that **tax anticipation notes**, issued to cover short-term cash flow needs, cannot exceed 60 percent of expected appropriations and must mature during the current fiscal year.[35] Governments that issue short-term debt should carefully assess their needs and then develop a policy that protects them from abuse of short-term debt without undermining their ability to meet cash flow needs.

Conclusion

Preparation of the executive budget engages department heads in intense, time-consuming deliberations over their departments' activities, their role in the government's overall strategic plan, and the measures being used to assess their progress toward achieving goals and objectives. Long-term forecasts into at least the next five years provide the context in which budget deliberations occur by projecting the full impact of past commitments on future expenditures and fund balances. As budget deliberations commence, regular updates of revenue forecasts for the current budget period are a key feature of budget preparation and adoption. The final step in this phase is the executive-level hearings, out of which comes the manager's proposed spending plan for the next fiscal year or biennium. The proposed budget must conform with the local government's definition of a balanced budget.

The locus of deliberations then moves to the legislative branch, where the council reviews and modifies the proposed spending plan. Most of the legislature's deliberations usually center on the tax-supported as opposed to fee-supported activities found in the enterprise funds.

Both the preparation and legislative approval phases are infused with conflict. Conflicts, the products of opposing needs and goals, are most likely to arise between advocates and conservers, the budget office and departments, accuracy and political expediency, bureaucracy and democracy, special interests and collective interests, and public will and public welfare. The challenge for the local manager is to create an environment that uses the conflict in a constructive manner and to keep budget deliberations on track and focused on finding solutions that serve the long-term interests of the community.

A primary tool for managing conflict is a formal statement of budget policies that explicitly establish financial standards to guide deliberations. Such policies can be written or unwritten, but a formal statement provides a standard of budgetary performance that participants have agreed upon and that provides a framework within which both the executive and the legislative branches can engage in constructive dialogue through the budget cycle.

Notes

1 Shayne C. Kavanagh and Daniel W. Williams, *Informed Decision-Making Through Forecasting: A Practitioner's Guide to Government Revenue Analysis* (Chicago: Government Finance Officers Association, 2016): 189.

2 Office of Management and Budget, Navajo Nation, *Fiscal Year 2018 Budget Instructions Manual,* July 14, 2017, 21.

3 The Office of Management and Budget, Escambia County, Florida, *FY 2018/2019 Budget Preparation Manual.*

4 City of Fort Worth, Texas, *FY 2018 Adopted Annual Budget and Program Objectives,* 23, http://fortworthtexas.gov/performance/budget/FY2018/pdf/FY2018-budget.pdf.

5 Glenn Abney and Thomas P. Lauth, "Gubernatorial Use of the Item Veto for Narrative Deletion," *Public Administration Review* 62 (July/August 2002): 492–501.

6 Anthony Downs, *Inside Bureaucracy* (Boston: Little, Brown, 1967), 96–103.

7 Robert B. Denhardt and Janet V. Denhardt, *Public Administration: An Action Orientation,* 5th ed. (Belmost, Calif.: Thomson Wadsworth, 2006), 53.

8 Lance T. LeLoup, "From Microbudgeting to Macrobudgeting: Evolution in Theory and Practice," in *New Directions in Budget Theory,* ed. Irene S. Rubin (Albany: State University of New York Press, 1988), 33.

9 Dwight Waldo, *The Enterprise of Public Administration* (Novato, Calif.: Chandler and Sharp, 1980), 81–98.

10 Jesse Burkhead, *Government Budgeting* (New York: John Wiley & Sons, 1956), 14.

11 Victoria Gordon, *Participatory Budgeting, Ten Actions to Engage Citizens via Social Media* (IBM Center for The Business of Government, September 2014).

12 City of Austin, Texas, "Budget in a Box" (August 2018), http://www.austintexas.gov/online-form/budget-box.

13 City of Boulder, Colorado, "Priority Based Budgeting" (August 2018), https://bouldercolorado.gov/budget/priority-based-budgeting.

14 Michael J. White, "Budget Policy: Where Does It Begin and End?" *Government Finance* 7 (August 1978).

15 Fairfax County, Virginia, "Ten Principles of Sound Financial Management as of April 21, 2015," https://www.fairfaxcounty.gov/finance/sites/finance/files/assets/documents/miscdocs/2017/tenprinciplesofsoundfinancialmanagement.pdf.

16 City of Fort Collins, Colorado, "Budgeting for Outcomes," https://www.fcgov.com/bfo/.

17 City of Salt Lake City, Utah, "Financial Policies," *FY 2018-19 Mayor's Recommended Budget,* C-1, http://www.slcdocs.com/budget/mayor19.pdf.

18 City of Birmingham, Alabama, Finance Department, *2018 Annual Operating Budget,* https://data.birminghamal.gov/dataset/annual-operating-budgets/resource/7b3a7187-3343-4c01-910a-97aa13326260.

19 City of Olympia, Washington, *2018 Adopted Operating Budget,* 14, http://olympiawa.gov/city-government/budget-financial-reports.aspx.

20 Governmental Accounting Standards Board, Statement No. 5 *Disclosure of Pension Information by Public Employee Retirement Systems and State and Local Governmental Employers* (Norwalk, Conn.: Governmental Accounting Standards Board, November 1986).

21 Governmental Accounting Standards Board, Summary of Statement No. 45 *Accounting and Financial Reporting by Employers for Postemployment Benefits Other Than Pensions* (Norwalk, Conn.: Governmental Accounting Standards Board, June 2004).

22 Government Finance Officers Association, *Working Capital Targets for Enterprise Funds,* February 2011, http://www.gfoa.org/print/425

23 La Shonda M. Stewart, John A. Hamman, and Stephanie A. Pink-Harper, "The Stabilization Effect of Local Government Savings: The Case of Illinois Counties," *Public Budgeting & Finance* 38 (Summer 2018): 23-39.

24 Yilin Hou, "Budgeting for Fiscal Stability over the Business Cycle: A Countercyclical Fiscal Policy and the Multiyear Perspective on Budgeting," *Public Administration Review* 66 (September/October 2006): 730-741.

25 City of Fort Collins, "Financial Management Policy 5, Fund Balance Minimums," (November 11, 22017), 2, https://www.fcgov.com/finance/pdf/FinancePolicyFundBalance2017.pdf?1511370529.

26 Thomas P. Lauth, "Mid-Year Appropriations in Georgia: Allocating the 'Surplus,"' *International Journal of Public Administration* 11 (1988): 535.

27 City of Fort Collins, "Financial Management Policy 1, Budget Policy" 6-7.

28 City of Fort Collins, "Financial Management Policy 3, General Financial Policies" 5-6.

29 City of San Luis Obispo, California, "Section B, Budget and Fiscal Policies," *2017-19 Financial Plan,* B1-8. http://www.slocity.org/Home/ShowDocument?id=15625.

30 Ibid., B1-6.

31 Ibid., B1-3.

32 City of Fort Collins, "Financial Management Policy 1, Budget Policy," 7.

33 City of Salt Lake City, *Mayor's Recommended Budget, Fiscal Year 2018-19,* C-1.

34 City of San Luis Obispo, "Section B, Budget and Fiscal Policies," B1-15.

35 City of Olympia, *2018 Adopted Operating Budget,* 33.

EXCEL EXERCISES

Microsoft's Excel is a widely used tool by budget analysts. The following Excel exercises introduce readers to the preparation of a departmental budget request and the preparation of revenue forecasts.

1. This Excel exercise requires analyzing the line-item budget for a city's development department, which has responsibility for issuing building permits and inspecting residential and commercial construction. This city has a policy goal that development fees will cover operating expenditures of this department. The assignment is to develop a budget request for FY 2014–2015 for this department and to determine whether this department will have sufficient revenues to meet its expenditures. Detailed instructions and data for this exercise are available at https://icma.org/documents/budgeting-guide-chapter-8-exercise-1

2. This exercise introduces several features in Excel that aid in developing revenue projections using trend analysis and a moving average. The first task involves correcting the historical data on sales tax collections for inflation. The dataset is actual sales tax collections by month from October 1992 through February 2013. The corresponding consumer price index (CPI) for each month is provided. The data can be used to evaluate current-year trends as well as to project revenue for the next budget year. The assignment is to develop a moving average trend for the inflation-adjusted sales tax collections, compute the month-to-month percentage change in collections, and graphically display those percentage changes. Detailed instructions and data for this exercise are available at https://icma.org/documents/budgeting-guide-chapter-8-exercise-2

CHAPTER 9

The budget cycle: Executive implementation

The best laid schemes o' mice an' men
Gang aft agley.

—Robert Burns

This chapter provides the following takeaways:

- How to effectively communicate budget information with stakeholders.
- Know what software is available for budget preparation and implementation and its limitations.
- Put in place the controls needed to ensure compliance with the approved budget.
- Know what policies should be adopted to facilitate adjustments to the budget as needed.
- Identify the methods for progressively mediating a budget crisis.

Budgets represent a government's best estimate of the actions it intends to take during the fiscal year and the revenues it expects to receive to finance those actions. But plans never go exactly as intended, and budgets are no exception. A major taxpayer may file for bankruptcy, reducing the amount of expected tax revenue. A natural disaster or, worse, a terrorist attack may strike the community, throwing the budget and the economy that it nurtures into a tailspin. For this reason, budgets contain financial controls, which provide local governments with a series of overlapping warning systems that alert managers to impending financial problems and equip them with the tools they need to take corrective action.

Financial controls in local government

The last two phases in the budget cycle account for the three distinctive levels of financial control: executive implementation, accounting, and reporting (Figure 9–1). These three levels of control provide a system of checks and balances on the financial integrity of a local government. That there are multiple levels of financial control is indicative of its importance to political leaders and managers: local governments that lose control of their finances quickly find themselves mired in political and legal difficulties.

Executive implementation occurs after a council adopts the budget into law, effectively empowering those with spending responsibility to enter into legal obligations that result in the future disbursement of funds; submit purchase requests; and otherwise make commitments that will eventually involve the exchange of money for services, materials, or other assets. It begins with an interpretation of the appropriation legislation, which can be complicated by the presence of **budget riders**—special provisions (often unfunded) that are attached to the legislation and that mandate executive actions. The budget office takes responsibility for making certain that agencies comply with the law's provisions. Implementation ends with the lapse of budget authority at the end of the fiscal year and the closing of all appropriation and revenue accounts.

While the budget office is mostly concerned with procedural matters in budget implementation, the accounting office is responsible for the second level of control: maintaining records on all transactions unleashed by the budget's adoption. The accounting system records, reconciles, and reports the results of budget transactions using uniform procedures that have been approved by the accounting profession.

Figure 9–1 Financial control systems and participants

Sources of financial control	Key participants	Tools of financial control
Budget implementation	Budget office	• Encumbrance approval • Position controls • Apportionment and allotment • Transfer and reprogramming approval • Budget amendments and impoundments • Budget reserves • Termination of budget authority
Accounting/financial reporting	Accounting unit	• Recording transactions • Creating and closing funds • Chart of accounts • Reconciling accounting records with budget
Auditing	Internal and external auditors	• Interim financial reports • Internal controls • Annual financial report • External audit

Finally, financial reporting provides the third level of control. The comptroller's office, working closely with accounting and budgeting, prepares a year-end financial report that summarizes the results of operations to produce a tally of the cumulative effect of those transactions on the local government's financial position for the preceding fiscal year. Quite often, the comptroller is located in the accounting unit and reports to the chief financial officer.

While these three financial controls complement one another, budgeting and accounting have evolved, by and large, independent of one another. Innovations in budgeting, including implementation by the executive branch, have evolved in response to management innovations that originated in the political environment. Accounting and financial reporting, on the other hand, have evolved in response to accountants' quest for accuracy, reliability, and comparability in reporting financial results.

Moreover, these three levels of financial control serve different stakeholder groups. Accounting and financial reporting satisfy the informational needs of investors, bond-rating firms, banks, and other levels of government that provide grants. Budget implementation, by contrast, responds to the informational needs of internal users such as managers and lawmakers, providing them with assurance that the budget is being implemented as intended and relying on the financial environment to identify events that might throw the budget out of balance.

This chapter examines the first level of control, implementation of the approved budget. (The second and third levels are discussed in the next chapter.) Budget implementation is a broad umbrella that entails the following functions:

- Communicating budget information to stakeholders both inside and outside of government
- Maintaining budget compliance by monitoring the financial actions of departments and agencies
- Altering budget authority during the year to take corrective action if events require it
- Putting into place budget policies for times of fiscal crisis, whether precipitated by economic circumstances, such as mounting budget deficits, or by noneconomic events, such as a natural disaster or rising sea levels due to global warming.

Each of these topics is discussed below.

Communicating budget information

Financial accountability is at the heart of democratic governance. Those responsible for implementing the budget have an obligation to keep citizens and other stakeholders informed about budget decisions. Nowadays, this is done by posting the operating budget (and capital budget, if separate) on the local government's website.

The Internet has greatly facilitated the dissemination and accessibility of budget information, concurrently simplifying the budget office's task of updating that information as the budget progresses through preparation, adoption, and implementation. Typically, the budget is first made available to the public when the manager's proposed budget is presented to council; the next update comes when the council approves the final budget. Some local governments update the budget website whenever the budget is amended during the year. The Internet has also enabled local governments to post related financial information, such as performance reports, long-term financial forecasts, and the year-end comprehensive annual financial report.

Publicizing the budget

Not only do internal processes for preparing budgets vary widely among local governments but the documents themselves bear no resemblance to each other across cities, towns, and counties.[1] The budget document is as unique to the government that issues it as the process

Effective budget communication

The local manager is not only the point person on budget deliberations but also the primary communicator to the community on budget matters. In council-manager governments, the manager's voice stands out from all the others for its authoritativeness and credibility. How does the manager effectively communicate budget matters to the community?

Effective communication begins at the outset of the budget process with agreed-upon policies to guide deliberations (P), insistence on assembling accurate information (A), and the timely progression of budget deliberations (T)—PAT for short. An investment in these three elements at the outset of the budget process facilitates the effective communication of the results.

Policies. Conflict is inherent in the budget process, and tough economic times only intensify that conflict. Budget policies approved by the council provide the manager with the formal tools to manage any conflict that arises by establishing the boundaries for deliberations on the operating budget, revenues, budget implementation, and debt. The policies should also specify how citizens and other stakeholders are to be informed of budget decisions.

Accurate information With all the talk about deficits, political spinning and manipulation of budget information have left many citizens skeptical about what and who to believe. It is the professional manager who provides the key to ensuring the integrity of the information that is produced and disseminated throughout deliberations on the budget.

When financial crises actually occur, they tend to rivet the public's attention on budget deliberations. Will taxes be increased? Will employees be furloughed or positions eliminated? Will vacancies remain unfilled? Will public facilities be closed or hours reduced? Recessions elevate public angst over the possible ramifications, making effective communication on budget matters especially important to citizens' understanding of how these issues are resolved.

In such situations, managers are best served by providing citizens with an accurate estimate of the expected budget deficit as early as possible. As budget deliberations progress, such an estimate will serve the budget office well, elevating its reputation and reassuring citizens about the veracity of its assessments and solutions, especially when competing scenarios for resolving the deficit are offered.

Timely progression of deliberations The third component of effective communication is the timely progression of the budget process. Ultimate responsibility for the timely adoption of an appropriation ordinance rests with the council, and it is the manager's responsibility to submit to the council an executive budget that can provide a framework for discussion. Before this can happen, however, a calendar needs to be published that identifies the tasks to be completed and the deadlines and individuals responsible for completing them; department heads must have the instructions they need to make decisions and prepare their budget requests; and the budget office needs to provide an update of revenue forecasts. Even in the worst economic times, timely completion of this complex process conveys a message of accountability and administrative discipline to citizens.

that gave rise to its contents. (On the other hand, as noted in the following chapter, the year-end financial reports are highly standardized across state and local governments—a result of the accounting profession's adoption and enforcement of rules for recording and reporting accounting information.)

The Government Finance Officers Association (GFOA) has been at the vanguard of promoting better budget communication. Since 1984, GFOA has sponsored the Distinguished Budget Presentation Awards program,[2] inviting states, provinces, and local governments to submit their budget documents for evaluation on twenty-seven criteria in the areas of

- The budget as a policy document
- The budget as a financial plan
- The budget as an operations guide
- The budget as a communications device.[3]

The first category—the budget as a policy document—tacitly acknowledges the central role that budgets play in shaping policy choices. Among the criteria in this category are a statement of the short-term initiatives that shaped the current budget choices, a statement of the government's priorities and of the policy issues it faced as it prepared its current budget, and an accounting of the goals and objectives of each department in the jurisdiction as well as a demonstration of their link to the overall goals of that government. And because they recognize not only that budgets shape the policies of local governments but also that budget and financial policies shape budget deliberations, the GFOA criteria call for the inclusion of budget and financial policies in the budget document.

The second category—the budget as a financial plan—focuses on the historical role of the budget as a tool for financial management. Specifically, budget documents should contain a description of the fund structure used to make appropriations in the operating and capital budgets, a summary of the major revenues and expenditures for all operations, a comparison of revenues with expenditures for at least a three-year period (last year, current year, and proposed budget year), a description of the major revenue sources, and an explanation of the basis for the forecast for the budget period. The GFOA guidelines also specify that budgets should provide information on the projected changes in the fund balances, detailed information on capital spending (either as part of the operating budget or as a separate capital budget), a discussion of the impact of capital improvements on the operating budget, and information on debt service and its effect on the operating budget.

Criteria for an award in the third category—the budget as an operations guide—include an organizational chart; information describing the government's organizational units; performance measures at the departmental level; the impact of those measures on the goals and objectives of that unit and on the government's mission; and a summary table of personnel or full-time equivalents (FTEs) for the past, current, and proposed budget periods.

The final award category focuses on the budget as a medium of communication with stakeholders, especially those outside government. The criteria specify that the document shows significant trends affecting the budget; the impact of other planning processes, such as the strategic plan or a long-range financial plan, on the operating and capital budgets; the process for preparing and approving the budget (including a budget calendar); and figures such as pie charts and histograms that present important information in a user-friendly format.

Applications are reviewed by three anonymous reviewers, usually budget officials in jurisdictions of comparable size. Reviewers assign a rating of outstanding, proficient, or not proficient to each criterion in the four evaluation areas. Budget reviewers rate only the published documentation, not the preparation process that produced it or how effectively the information within it is used to make budget decisions. The award is valid for only one year, and governments must reapply for it annually. Recipients display the one-page citation in their budget for the following year. As noted on the GFOA website, a few governments have received the Distinguished Budget Award every year since the program's inception.

The real value of the GFOA awards program is the attention it brings to improving the budget document's communication value, especially to those outside of government. It also provides a forum for identifying innovative practices among budget offices as well as among governments with particularly good budget reporting practices. However, the absence of an

Technological support for budgeting

The complexity of the budget process creates significant challenges for developers of software to support budget preparation. In *Budgeting Technology Solutions,* the Government Finance Officers Association's Shayne Kavanagh and colleagues have undertaken the most comprehensive study to date documenting the development and state of affairs in budgeting technology.[1] The following summarizes their research.

The challenge for software developers is that every local government approaches budget preparation differently, and the unique processes and information needs of each make conventional off-the-shelf solutions unsatisfactory. This challenge grows exponentially as local governments add such specialized functions as measuring, monitoring, and analyzing performance indicators, or preparing and monitoring the capital budget. Several vendors have taken software applications developed for the private sector and tried to adapt them to the budgeting needs of local governments, especially larger local governments that have the financial capacity and economies of scale to justify more versatile applications.

For budget implementation, the software commonly used is referred to generically as enterprise resource planning (ERP) systems.[2] ERP systems are integrated financial and personnel management systems whose primary function is to process day-to-day transactions in such areas as accounting and payroll. A key feature of ERP software is a consolidated database that serves the needs of a number of subsystems

Because ERP systems are focused on transaction processing, budget preparation and adoption capabilities have tended to be underdeveloped in ERP solutions. Some of the capabilities that are typically lacking include

- **Forecasting:** Projecting both revenues and expenditures beyond the current year
- **Collaboration:** Allowing multiple users access to the same database and building a budget database that integrates their requests into a meta-database
- **Formulation:** Adapting software capabilities to the local government's budget workflow so that users can evaluate different budget scenarios on the basis of assumptions about expected revenues, expenditures, salaries, employee benefit packages, capital decisions, and any other factors that could affect budget totals
- **Analysis:** Analyzing financial and nonfinancial data to help users make decisions on the optimal allocation of resources
- **Performance measures:** Allowing integration of a strategic plan to map goals, objectives, outputs, and outcomes to monitor and report progress
- **Publication:** Providing information in a format that is user-friendly and capable of being exported to other venues, such as the accounting or personnel system as well as a website.

Although local governments have customized the software for budget preparation and implementation, there is currently no silver bullet, "no particular product that commands an overwhelming share of the stand-alone budget system market."[3]

The software used most widely for budget preparation is Microsoft's Excel, an Office productivity spreadsheet program that can be supplemented with add-on capabilities to enhance collaboration among users throughout the preparation phase. The advantages of Excel add-ons include the familiarity of the spreadsheet format to users and, not unimportantly, the fact that Excel requires minimal technical support. Excel's greatest limitation is that it was designed for individual use, not for the consultative interaction that must occur during budget preparation and adoption. It has limited drill-down capabilities, which are essential aids to departments and budget analysts seeking to identify problematic trends. Newer

continued

versions of Excel have greatly expanded its data management capacity, and the software has been modified to allow some drill-down capabilities. But there will always be the problem of keeping multiple spreadsheets linked so that the information they contain can be rolled up into a single file.

A large number of vendors have developed budgeting software for business applications, but only a few of these are adaptable for use by local governments. For example, Questica's cloud-based option has a visually appealing dashboard. For smaller local governments, a lower cost option is a vendor-hosted service, referred to as software-as-a-service (SaaS). It lowers costs by using the economies of scale from multiple subscribers. Its advantage over on-site software is lowering or eliminating the cost of hiring or contracting out technology support, lower hardware costs, and more timely upgrades to the software. The disadvantages are the data reside with the vendor and the limitations on customizing the software. SaaS vendors typically offer options to customize the configuration (or parameters) of the software to fit the local government's preferences for collecting, analyzing, and displaying budget data. But the SaaS options lack flexibility beyond modifying a set of vendor-determined parameters.

1 Shayne Kavanagh et al., *Budgeting Technology Solutions* (Chicago: Government Finance Officers Association, 2006), http://gfoa.org/sites/default/files/BudgetTechnologyReport.pdf.

2 David Melbye, ed., *The ERP Book, Financial Management Technology from A to Z* (Chicago: Government Finance Officers Association, 2010).

3 Kavanagh et al., 6.

objective evaluation of the preparation process underlying the final document means that a government may have a quality document but lack a process that promotes such desirable features as citizen participation, objective analysis of alternatives, and financial controls that ensure budget compliance.

Levels of budget detail

Budget information exists in a hierarchy, and the document that appears on a local government's website generally aggregates that information at the highest level. For most users of the budget, this summary information is usually sufficient. The budget office typically maintains much more detailed information than what is contained in the published document. If trends in spending or revenues begin to deviate significantly from what is in the budget, the more detailed information may be useful to the budget office for identifying the source of the problem, as well as to the accounting office for monitoring costs and identifying errors in coding transactions.

The important point is that "the budget" is in fact a compilation of increasingly more detailed line items, each of which has its own account number and is monitored throughout implementation. As discussed in the accompanying sidebar, web-based budget systems break down the summary information, usually in a line-item format, enabling users to drill down to increasingly more precise levels of detail. The details enable the budget office and departments to know how much of each type of spending has been authorized and to track that spending throughout the fiscal year. They also help departments prepare more accurate budget requests in subsequent years.

Maintaining budget compliance

The myriad and seemingly duplicative financial controls imposed on government serve the distinctive information needs of multiple stakeholders with varying expectations for financial accountability. For example, lawmakers typically authorize appropriations using line items (a control measure) and require a report at the end of the fiscal year showing how actual spending compared with the amount approved in the budget. However, this information is of less interest to investors in municipal bonds and their representatives in the bond-rating firms, who are instead interested in how successful the government has been over time in keeping its total expenditures within available revenues and in how frequently the budget is amended during the fiscal year.

Meanwhile, managers are concerned that expenditures not exceed the limits set by appropriations and that revenue collections keep pace with budget expectations. The interim financial report, usually available online in most local governments and continuously updated by the accounting office, allows managers to monitor progress toward meeting these objectives.

Council approval of the budget takes the form of one or more appropriation ordinances. An appropriation does not grant money; rather, it grants budget authority—authorization for administrators to enter into binding agreements, such as contracts and purchase orders (POs), that will necessitate the future disbursement of funds once the goods or services are delivered. Managers who incur financial obligations greater than the amount authorized by the appropriation are liable for such excesses unless the budget is amended or other alterations to budget authority are made.

Implementation involves fine-tuning the financial plan to fit reality while not negating the intent of the council. In performing this function, the budget office wields considerable influence. Largely as a result of adaptations required by past experience, a number of tools, listed in Figure 9–2, have been developed to aid the budget office in this politically sensitive but fiscally critical task.

Encumbrances

A distinguishing feature of government finance is its use of encumbrances (or "obligations" in federal jargon). An encumbrance occurs when a request for the purchase of goods or services is approved and forwarded to an outside vendor. As a sort of pending expenditure, an encumbrance reduces the amount of budget authority available for other expenditures.

Figure 9–2 Budget controls flowchart

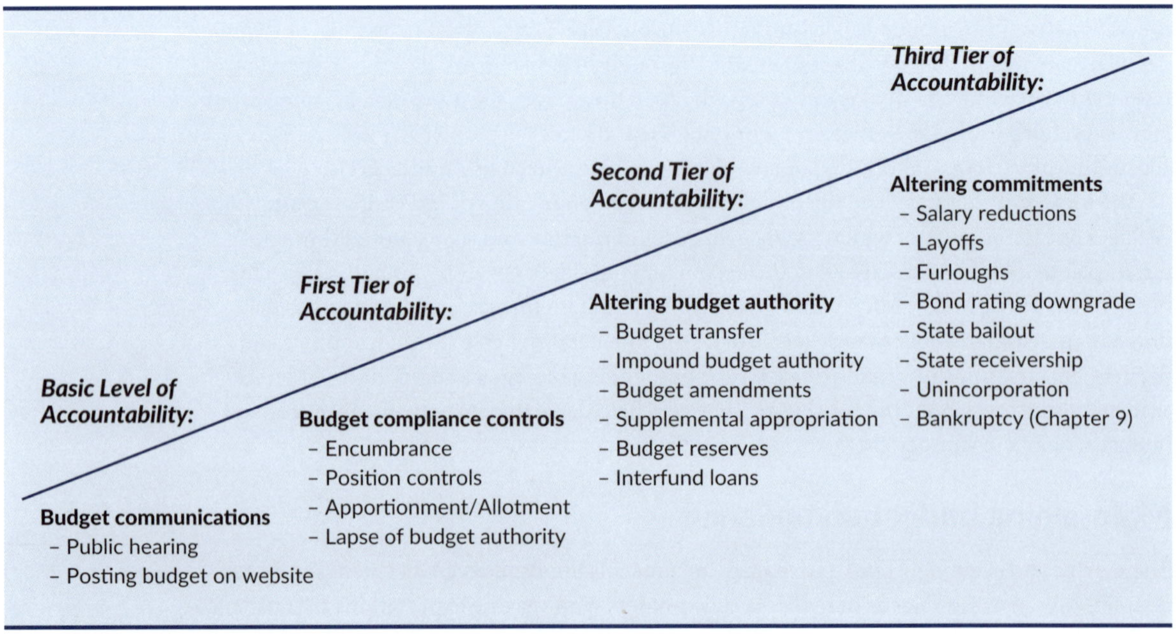

Encumbrances link budget authority with the purchasing and accounting systems. A department originates the request by completing a **purchase requisition**, an online form that includes a description of the item or service to be provided; this requisition must be authorized by the purchasing department, which, with ERP systems, can verify the availability of budget authority and enter the requisition into the accounting records in one step. Although the rules vary by government, typically a purchasing department requires two or three bids from potential vendors; requisitions for less costly items, however, may often require only a single bid from a preapproved vendor. (In some cases, less costly items may be purchased on a government-issued credit card, and no requisition is submitted.) The requisition lists the vendors from whom bids have been received.

Once approved by purchasing, the requisition goes to the budget office for verification that sufficient budget authority is available in the agency's appropriation and that the purchase is consistent with legislative intent. It next goes to accounting, where it becomes a PO and the estimated cost of the purchase is encumbered, or set aside, pending delivery of the good or service. The PO is then forwarded to the vendor, who is now authorized to deliver the item or service.

In an accounting sense, an encumbrance represents a contingent liability: the government's liability for payment is contingent upon delivery of the goods or services described on the PO. An encumbrance is a temporary account, so that once the item is delivered, the encumbrance entry is removed from the accounting records and changed to an expenditure. (This process is explained more fully in Chapter 10.)

POs that are outstanding at the end of the fiscal year present a complication. That is when appropriation authority lapses (unless it has been granted for a longer period of time), and if the item has not yet been delivered, the agency placing the PO no longer has legal budget authority to pay the vendor. This situation is usually handled by establishing a reserve account that sets aside a portion of the fund balance for outstanding encumbrances. The appropriation approved by the council for the following fiscal year includes sufficient funding for these outstanding orders, thus renewing the department's authority to pay the vendors once the orders are fulfilled.

Position controls

The appropriation ordinance approved by the council may stipulate the number and level of positions authorized for each department and program. Such details are most likely to be found in local governments where personnel expenditures can represent as much as 80 percent of the costs for general operations, although the percentage is usually less. More common is the inclusion of FTE positions in the budget document, which provides a better comparison across departments, especially those that rely heavily on part-time employees. The budget office will be responsible for approving new hires as well as for reclassifying existing positions.

Here the budget links with the human resource information system so that a manager who seeks to hire a new employee can verify that sufficient budget authority exists in the account(s) being charged for the position and that the action does not violate the council's intent. Given the long-term budget implications of a newly created or a reclassified position, the budget office carefully scrutinizes any requests for staffing changes. In smaller governments, the council or commission will have considered such requests as part of its budget deliberations and included sufficient funding in the budget should the requests be approved.

When a position becomes vacant, salary savings accumulate until it is filled. The budget office monitors salary savings closely and often includes an estimate of the aggregate level of savings in the proposed budget. In governments with high employee turnover rates, or during favorable economic times when salaries and job opportunities are plentiful, salary savings may become quite substantial. As a general rule, governments should treat salary savings as funds available for reappropriation rather than risk spending them before they materialize.

Apportionment and allotment

Among the oldest forms of budget control are apportionment and allotment. Although some confusion exists in the literature on their definitions, according to the U.S. Government Accountability Office (GAO), apportionment divides appropriations into specific time periods, usually quarters, or among projects or activities.[4] The appropriation is not necessarily divided into four equal amounts; rather, it reflects the unique schedule of each agency. The practice is designed to prevent the premature depletion of budget authority by agencies.

Allotment, on the other hand, involves the distribution of budget authority among units of the agency. Whereas the appropriation is for a department, such as a department of health, the department will allot budget authority for its appropriation to its various programs, regional offices, and other units in accordance with its internal budget plan. Allotting budget authority is a common practice for subdividing appropriation authority.

Lapse in budget authority

Included in the ordinance approving an appropriation is language stating that the authority to enter into obligations terminates on the last day of the fiscal year (or biennium if authority is given for two years). All unencumbered account balances then revert to the general fund and become part of the fund balance available for reappropriation in the subsequent fiscal year.

As it precludes departments from accumulating large unencumbered balances to be carried over year after year, the lapse in budget authority compels managers to encumber the full amount of budget authority they have been given for the fiscal year. It also compels department heads and managers to spend expeditiously the funds that have been appropriated for the purposes intended by lawmakers and to do so during the time period specified. In other words, the appropriation becomes a mandate for the department to provide a particular level of service during the fiscal year—not more and not less.

One of the adverse consequences of the lapse in budget authority is the rush to commit funds at the end of the fiscal year—a phenomenon often lampooned in the media. In fact, year-end spending may be quite responsible, especially if managers delay making commitments as a way to hold back funds for contingencies or as a strategy for finding the best bargain for their purchases. Although the practice continues, apportionment of budget authority reduces this behavior, as does the continuous updating of financial reports and their online availability.

Altering budget authority

The previous section described the more common tools used in budget implementation as the first line of defense for maintaining financial control. The second line of defense is taking corrective action once a problem has been identified. The more quickly such action can be taken, the more options a manager has and the less the potential damage to government operations.

Local governments can take corrective action by altering budget authority, if need be, after the fiscal year has commenced. One way this can be done is by transferring budget authority (appropriations) across departments or among the eleven types of funds identified in Chapter 8. Another way is by amending a department's budget authority during the fiscal year. For example, the cost of a repair or of a large piece of equipment may exceed the estimate made for the original budget, in which case the department would seek an amendment to increase its budget authority so it could acquire the equipment or make the repair. A third way is for the council or, in some cases, the manager to tap budget reserves for purposes sanctioned by the legislation creating the reserves. Some of these tools require only the department head's approval; others require approval of the budget office; and still others require the recommendation of the manager and final approval of the council.

Budget transfers

The budget office holds a pivotal role in monitoring the movement of appropriations. One common approach that local governments use to realign the approved budget with actual revenues and expenditures is to shift budget authority between departments or the funds used to track transactions. At the local level, the manager's discretion to make interdepartmental transfers of budget authority is typically specified in the charter or in an ordinance of the council. Some managers may enjoy latitude in making such transfers; however, their doing so is rare.

The GAO distinguishes between budget transfers and reprogramming.[5] Transfers involve moving funds from one budget account to another. Reprogramming refers to moving funding within a budget account from one line item to another.

The more common type of transfer reimburses one department or fund for services provided or materials used. For example, if the inventory for office supplies is maintained as an internal service fund, requests from departments for supplies will require an interdepartmental (and interfund) transfer of resources. Initiation of such a transfer occurs when the requesting department prepares an interdepartmental order, which typically requires the approval of only the department head placing the order.

Transfers that are not reimbursements may occur as a result of changing priorities or unexpected needs. For example, the city manager may have a discretionary account from which to shift budget authority to a department that has incurred unexpected salary expenditures, such as for overtime. Transfers of this type are more likely to be subject to council oversight, or at least to the expectation that the manager will notify the council whenever they are made.

Managers also have the authority to move appropriated funds within a department or, more likely, to reprogram funds—that is, to move them from one line item to another within a department. Reprograms are more common than interdepartmental transfers, but both tools provide administrators with much needed discretion to respond to changing conditions and expectations. For a large local government, such actions may occur hundreds or even thousands of times during the fiscal year. While most transfers involve relatively small amounts of funds, the budget office reviews every transfer for compliance with policy and statutory specifications.

Impound budget authority

At the federal level, the president, working with the Office of Management and Budget (OMB), may order part of an agency's appropriation **impounded**, making it temporarily unavailable for use. At the local level, the question may emerge as to whether the manager can impose budget reductions during the fiscal year. Generally, reductions in spending are precipitated by an unexpected drop in revenues, and in order to maintain a balanced budget, quick action is required. In such cases, the manager may take impoundment-like action by imposing a spending freeze—leaving unfilled all but the most essential vacancies, delaying large purchases, restricting travel, or taking other measures to bring about a rapid reduction in spending. For the appointed local manager, the decision to impound an appropriation or to freeze spending is less volatile than it is for an elected chief executive since, regardless of the manager's authority under law, the council will be kept informed and, where required by law, involved in making budget adjustments as conditions warrant.

Budget amendments

If the required budget correction is of sufficient magnitude, the council may amend the original budget to redirect existing budget authority, increase total budget authority, or reduce that authority. Budget amendments usually follow the same deliberative process used in the regular budget cycle: the manager first proposes a package of amendments, the council's appropriate committee holds hearings and marks up the legislation, and the full council then considers and acts upon the proposal.

Too many budget amendments may raise concerns among bond raters and other external stakeholders with a financial interest in the local government. The rule of thumb is that three amendments during the fiscal year—one at the midpoint, one at the end of the fiscal year to resolve all lingering budget issues, and another as a contingency should a major event alter the local economy—will raise no alarms. More than three becomes a "canary in the mine," alerting stakeholders that a serious defect may exist in budget preparation and possibly in implementation. Amending the budget more than five times in a fiscal year suggests (1) poor budget forecasting procedures, (2) inadequate controls on expenditures, or (3) unsatisfactory technological support for budget and financial management services.

In some cases, such as in the state of Georgia, the legislature routinely adopts a midyear budget amendment, to which all spending increases for the fiscal year are deferred and funded, depending on the growth in revenues.[6] Budget amendments may also occur with a change in leadership, such as the appointment of a new city or county manager early in the budget year. The new executive may want to redirect certain spending priorities as part of a new leadership philosophy.

Supplemental appropriation

A supplemental appropriation, which is found most often at the federal level, provides additional budget authority to a department or program during the current fiscal year for an unexpected event, such as natural disaster relief administered by the Federal Emergency Management Agency. It may also be made because the legislature appropriated enough budget authority for only part of the year and wants an agency to return midyear for additional budget authority—possibly as a compromise to gain initial approval of a new program or project whose costs are difficult to predict.

Another budget term that has garnered attention in recent years is **sequestration**, which is used to describe a backdoor process for reducing the federal budget by withholding previously appropriated budget authority.[7] The term has found its way into local and state budgeting, too, although most uses are better characterized as impoundment of budget authority. While an impoundment is an executive-level withholding of budget authority, sequestration involves the legislature (Congress) withholding budget authority ex post facto.

The process works as follows. Congress begins its budget process by setting targets for total spending, taxation, deficit, and public debt. The target legislation may include instructions to OMB to withhold (sequester) budget authority should the final appropriations by Congress, passed in thirteen separate bills, exceed the targeted level of spending. Congress then passes appropriation bills granting budget authority to the various federal agencies. Sequestration kicks in if the sum of these appropriations exceeds the target level. Sequestration involves across-the-board cuts to federal programs and is proportionately divided between defense and domestic programs; entitlement programs, such as Social Security and Medicare, are usually excluded. Although sequestration has been mandated on several occasions, Congress had repeatedly chosen to raise the target spending level at the last minute rather than impose across-the-board cuts—until 2013, when for the first time it let stand a sequestration order that had been adopted two years earlier.

Budget reserves

Another tool available for adjusting budget authority during implementation is a budget reserve (also called an economic stabilization fund or rainy day fund), which has been previously set aside for contingencies. In most cases, tapping local budget reserves requires an appropriation by the council. The local government should have in its budget policy a provision on the creation and use of reserves and the conditions under which they can be tapped.

In discussions on the creation of a budget reserve, several issues surface, including why one is needed, how resources for the reserves should be allocated, how large a reserve to maintain, whether a separate fund is needed, and under what circumstances the reserve should be tapped.

Purpose of reserves One reason that local governments establish budget reserves is to create a cushion against the vagaries of the economy. As local governments have increased their dependence on such revenue sources as sales and excise taxes, their budgets have become more vulnerable to economic cycles—particularly the contraction of sales tax revenue during recessions. Thus, as a hedge against revenue shortfalls created by economic cycles, most state and local governments have established rainy day funds.

A second reason that municipal governments have long maintained budget reserves is that the bond-rating agencies place considerable emphasis on the use of a reserve to ensure the timely payment of debt service (principal and interest). Governments that fail to demonstrate such a reserve will certainly suffer a lower bond rating as a result.

Third, local governments maintain budget reserves to manage cash flow. For example, if the fiscal year begins July 1 and property taxes are not due until the following January 1, the government will need cash reserves to cover that six-month lag. If it does not have the cash reserves, it must borrow money in anticipation of the payment of current taxes (using so-called tax anticipation notes) to finance operations during that period.

Finally, local governments maintain reserves for a host of contingencies, including a natural or technological disaster, pending litigation, an unanticipated delay in receiving state or federal aid, or the need to replace a large piece of equipment or a building. Whatever the reason, budget reserves provide an option for cushioning the impact of external events on local government operations.

Allocation, sources, and size of reserves In his discussion of budget reserves, public finance expert Ian J. Allan identifies three methods that governments use to allocate resources to reserve accounts: formula, use of a predetermined portion of operating surpluses, and dedication of revenues from a particular source. State governments in particular dedicate year-end surpluses for their budget stabilization funds, whereas local governments appear to rely more heavily on a formula to determine the appropriate size of the reserves. This may be because of the emphasis that Moody's and Standard & Poor's, the two most influential bond-rating firms, give to formulae: bond-rating firms use a rule of thumb of at least 5 percent of annual operating expenditures.[9] Some governments use from sixty to ninety days of operating expenditures as an acceptable level for reserves. The more unstable a government's revenue base, the larger its reserves should be. Thus, governments that rely on cycle-sensitive revenues, such as sales and excise taxes, should maintain a higher level of reserves in order to ensure a more stable level of budget expenditures.

Location of reserves Lawmakers must decide whether to retain reserves in a separate fund or as an account within an existing fund. The preference among states is to create a separate budget stabilization fund because its purpose can be explicitly defined in law and the procedures for using its financial resources clearly dictated.

Budget reserve accounts in Dallas, Texas

In its financial management policies, the City of Dallas, Texas, specifies five reserve accounts that it will maintain.

The Contingency Reserve provides for unanticipated needs that emerge during the year, such as a new health or public safety need, revenue shortfalls, or opportunities for cost savings. This reserve is maintained at a level ranging from 0.5 percent to 1 percent of the general fund budget.

The second line of defense is an Emergency Reserve, tapped after the Contingency Reserve has been depleted and used for more extraordinary events, such as a disaster or an unexpected liability created by the federal or state government. The Emergency and Contingency Reserves together must be maintained at a level of at least 5 percent of the General Fund operating expenditures.

The city's policy calls for three other reserves for more specialized purposes: The Risk Reserve covers the city's deductible expense for insured losses. The General Fund maintains a **liability account** that provides a reserve for covering legal claims against the city. The Landfill Closure/Post-Closure Reserve exists to collect funds for the anticipated cost of complying with state and federal requirements to maintain landfills in perpetuity following their closure.

Source: City of Dallas, *Annual Budget for Fiscal Year 2017–2018* (September 2017), 590–592, https://dallascityhall.com/departments/budget/financialtransparency/AnnualBudget/FY-2017-18-Adopted-Budget.pdf.

One disadvantage of a separate fund is the attention it attracts, especially from the media. It is difficult for lawmakers to explain why a government will ask taxpayers to approve a tax rate increase when it has accumulated two or three months' worth of operating expenditures in reserves. The preference among local governments would appear to be setting up separate accounts within existing funds for various contingencies. This keeps the number of funds to a minimum and reduces the visibility of reserves while providing adequate safeguards on the proper use of the resources.

Interfund loans

In certain cases, the manager may recommend that council approve an interfund loan—the transfer of money from one fund to another with the stipulation that the transfer be repaid at an agreed-upon future time and possibly even at an agreed-upon rate of interest. Particularly problematic are transfers involving state and federal grants: local governments must give particular attention to statutory as well as grant guidelines when transferring balances from these revenue sources.

Budgeting in times of fiscal crisis

Prudent leaders in local government know that a balanced budget is a moving target. Sometimes budget plans go awry, even when a local government has vigilantly pursued all the right financial management practices. Economies go through cycles brought on by recessions, inflation, or overexpansion. They also go through sectoral shifts brought on by changes in technology, economic development, and competition from domestic and international sources. Then there are the imponderables: natural disasters, epidemics, weather events, and acts of terror.

As noted in the sidebar on page 220, a fiscal crisis complicates the manager's task of preparing and keeping a balanced budget, and a prolonged recession makes that task even harder. With each budget cycle, the options for reconciling available revenues with expenditures

Figure 9–3 The life cycle of a budget crisis

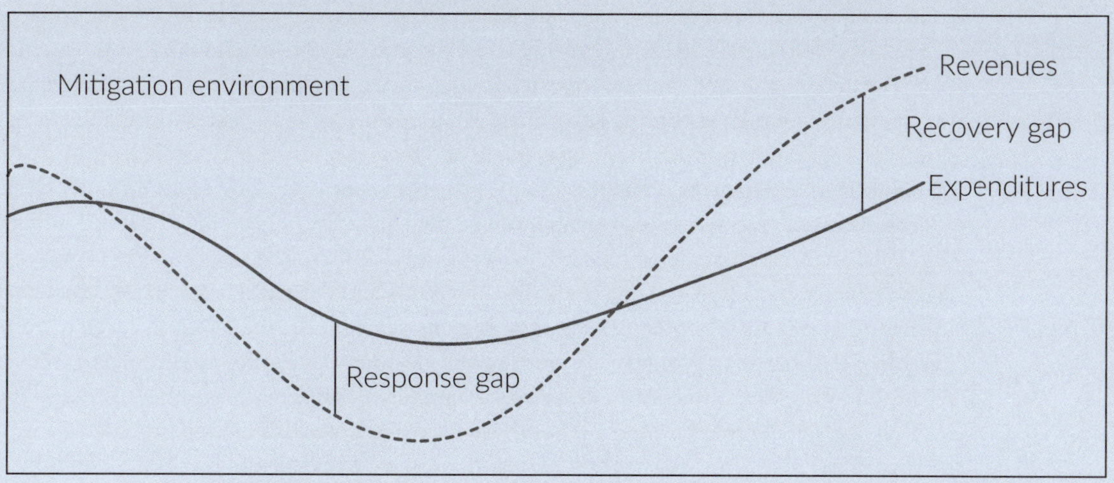

become more politically painful. The key to effectively managing a budget in such conditions is to assess the magnitude of the deficit early and to take preemptive action that keeps spending in check. The more quickly a manager gets ahead of a budget crisis, the more options the manager will have to ride out the crisis.

The model used by scholars in emergency management to describe the cycle of a disaster provides a useful framework for understanding budget crises. In a sense, budget crises are a type of disaster (Figure 9–3). There is a response followed by a recovery phase, both of which occur within the context of mitigation—policies designed to reduce the adverse effects of the disaster.

One of the more common measures managers take to mitigate unforeseen events is the creation of budget reserves or rainy day funds. Another is the use of long-term forecasts that project revenue and expenditure trends for up to five years into the future. These forecasts, updated annually, provide early warnings of impending gaps and give managers an opportunity to take corrective actions to mitigate adverse trends. Developing a strategic plan and targeting economic development initiatives to that plan is yet a third way for managers to mitigate the effects of fiscal crises. Finally, a manager may opt to introduce more market-like procedures, such as budgeting for outcomes, into budget deliberations.

Once a crisis develops—a recession, the loss of a major employer, or a more prolonged sectoral shift—the response phase begins. Initially, revenues drop more quickly—and thus become less—than expenditures, creating a response gap (Figure 9–3). Because most local governments must maintain a balanced budget, they must close the gap through reduced spending, increased revenues, or both. The more quickly they respond to the crisis, the more likely they can avert a serious response gap, at least in the short term. In 2018, the four million residents of Cape Town, South Africa, faced the unthinkable—dry reservoirs. For the preceding decade, city leaders had ignored the warnings that the city's pace of population growth and development could not be sustained with existing water supplies. Considering that water development projects take two to three decades to complete from design to delivery, a crisis was highly likely. Then in 2018, after three successive years of global warming–induced drought, the city had nearly exhausted its available water. Denial has now been replaced by a scramble to find new sources of water.

The experience of cities and counties during the Great Recession shows a wide divergence in response gaps. Because the recession was driven by a collapse in housing prices that began in 2006, the effect on local budgets varied depending on the local government's dependence on the property tax; its dependence on state and federal aid, both of which have declined in relative importance; and the level of overvaluation of the housing market prior to the collapse. In a study of California's 482 cities, Jeremy Goldberg and Max Neiman found that those cities that prepared long-term financial forecasts, that aggressively managed their expenditures, and that built up their reserves during good times experienced less fiscal distress during the recession.[10] They also noted that citizen engagement and budget transparency, while helpful, do not eliminate the need to make difficult decisions once the scope of the downturn becomes clear.

The effects of recessions also vary in terms of how quickly local revenues respond—that is, the lag effect. A study of the nation's 109 largest central cities found that property tax revenues lagged behind changes in housing prices by three years and behind changes in local personal income by two years.[11] In other words, it takes three years for the full effect of a drop in housing prices to show up in property tax revenue and another year for the tax revenue to recover. As a result of the Great Recession, there was a significant uptick in the number of cities filing for Chapter 9 bankruptcy protection or otherwise seeking state protection from defaulting on their debts. Every recession is different, and every local budget will respond differently to a recession. But Figure 9–3 suggests one general rule: the deeper and more protracted the response gap, the longer until a recovery begins and the less robust that recovery gap will be.

As the recovery continues, expenditures may return to precrisis levels or even ratchet higher, generating funding for delayed maintenance (street, bridge, or building repairs) and new capital projects. As is the case with most other budgeting relationships, the interplay between revenues and expenditures throughout the response and recovery cycles is unique to every community and depends on that community's economic, political, and managerial characteristics.

While politically a response gap may be explained by too many expenditures compared with revenues, it is really a much more complex interplay between the revenue and expenditure streams. The rate at which the response gap develops depends on the differences in elasticities between the two streams. The more elastic—or sensitive—the revenue stream is to changes in the economy, the faster the response gap develops and the wider it will probably be. Local governments with less sensitive revenue streams will experience less of a budget crisis as a result of economic changes. For a manager, the challenge is to estimate accurately the relationship between these two streams for the jurisdiction—a part of the mitigation phase. Understanding the revenue-expenditure interplay and having tools available for mitigating the response gap are key to effectively managing that gap.

Noted public administration scholar Charles Levine developed one of the more useful typologies for how local governments deal with fiscal crises.[12] He segmented budget crises by their duration (short term versus long term) and intensity (low versus high). As depicted in Figure 2-4, a short-term crisis of low intensity is a budget *crunch*. A long-term crisis of high intensity is a budget *crush*. Building on Levine's typology adapted in Figure 2-4, Figure 9–4 displays the progression of actions that a local government may take as it rides out a budget crisis. This figure provides a dynamic profile of the strategies—reducing expenditures and increasing revenues—that local governments use to deal with budget crises.

Initially, managers look to expenditure reductions to realign revenues with expenditures. Actions that reduce spending innocuously (at least for the short term) include reducing or eliminating overtime, making productivity improvements, reducing operating hours, imposing a hiring or spending freeze, delaying maintenance or capital expenditures, and imposing city- or county-wide furlough days. During the Great Recession, many larger local governments managed the budget crisis by mandating furlough days, such as extending a three-day weekend to four days and requiring employees to take an extra vacation day or unpaid leave. Revenue initiatives may include selectively raising fees, particularly for activities in the general

Figure 9-4 Strategies for responding to a budget crisis

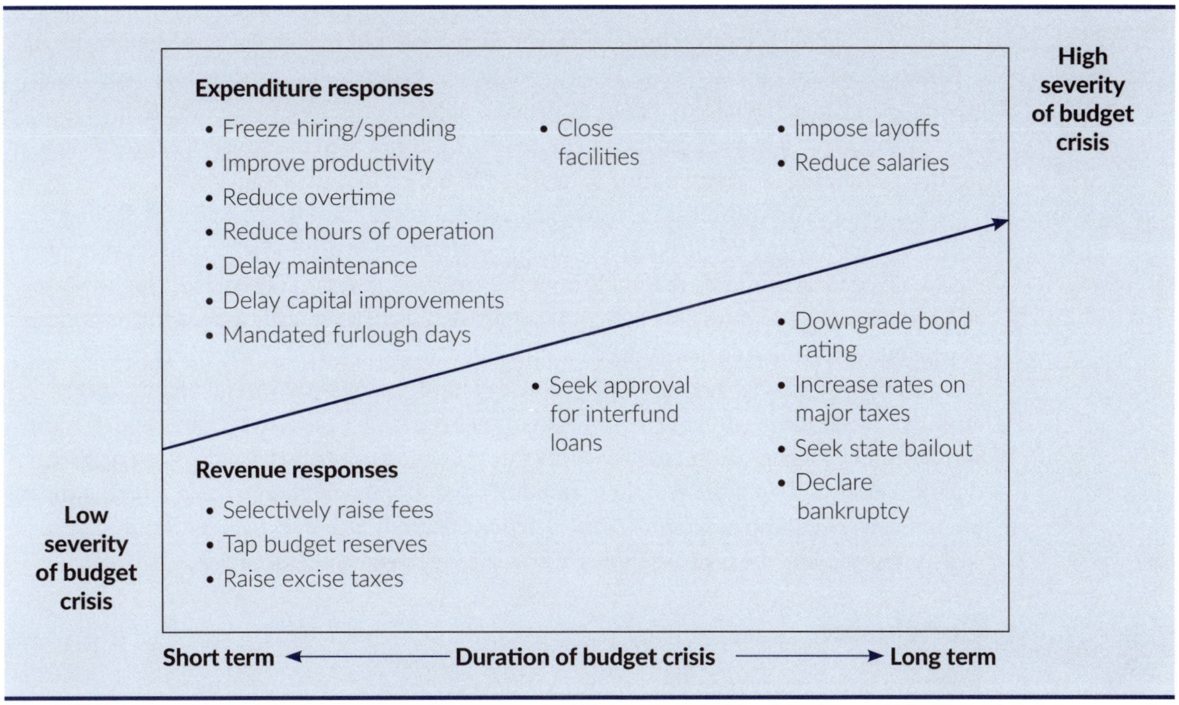

fund that receive a tax subsidy, such as recreation; tapping budget reserves; or, more proactively, increasing selected excise taxes.

If the crisis continues or worsens, the options for closing the response gap become fewer and more painful: increasing taxes, reducing salaries, reducing the workforce, and closing facilities. The local government may seek relief from the state, if such assistance exists. Alternatively, it may seek approval for interfund borrowing or acquiring debt, particularly if the budget crisis was caused by a natural disaster or episodic event. Chances are that the bond-rating agencies have already reevaluated the local government's creditworthiness and may have decided to downgrade the bond rating if long-term prospects for resolving the crisis appear dim. If the rating falls below investment grade (less than Baa for Moody's and BBB for Standard & Poor's), it will be impossible for the local government to borrow money in the open market. Should that occur, the local government may work out a long-term loan with a major bank or with the state if legislation allows for such relief.

The ultimate recourse for a local government—cities, counties, school districts, and special districts, but not states—is to file for bankruptcy.[13] Chapter 9 of the U.S. Bankruptcy Code provides the statutory basis for local governments to petition the federal bankruptcy court to reschedule payment of their debts, including municipal bonds, accounts payable, and even salaries and pensions payable. Chapter 9 provides a last-resort measure of relief for local governments. However, only twenty-four states allow their local governments to seek federal bankruptcy protection; the remaining states prohibit seeking such relief but offer a state-mandated remedy.

Chapter 9 bankruptcy does not allow liquidation of a local government's assets or the dissolution of the local government. However, those options may be possible under state law, depending on the state. Under Chapter 9, the federal court cannot dictate the terms of restructuring the obligation. The local government, in consultation with creditors or other stakeholders, must propose a plan that the bankruptcy court then acts upon.

Local governments use a Chapter 9 filing to reorganize their obligations for different reasons. For example, following a major loss of its investment portfolio in 1994, Orange County, California, filed for Chapter 9 protection while it worked out repayment agreements with its creditors. Westlake, Texas, filed in 1997 to nullify a decision to disincorporate; Central Falls, Rhode Island, filed in 2011 to reduce its pension obligations; Hillview, Kentucky, filed in 2015 to reduce an adverse legal judgment; in 2013, Detroit filed the largest Chapter 9 claim in history petitioning for restructuring of its $18-$20 billion in outstanding debt.

While budget professionals have given considerable attention to strategies for dealing with the response gap, they have given much less attention to dealing with the recovery gap. Again, as the local economy rebounds from the crisis—and especially if it has a highly elastic revenue stream—revenues flow into local coffers at rates that typically exceed the resumption of expenditures, resulting in a budget surplus. A few strategies have emerged for dealing with this surplus—diverting revenues to the rainy day fund, giving taxpayers dividends, accelerating debt repayment—but much more attention needs to be given to this situation. Budget surpluses inevitably give rise to calls for tax rate reductions, tax refunds, and other revenue-reducing measures. Depending on the community and its vulnerability to crisis, a more prudent use of the recovery gap may be to invest in actions that mitigate the effects of future crises, such as diversifying the tax base through strategically targeted tax incentives.

Conclusion

Executive implementation of the approved budget is the first of three pillars of financial control. The first task in implementing the budget is to communicate budget information to stakeholders, such as citizens, creditors, and state and federal grantors. Most local governments now use their websites to post and update their operating and capital budgets. Budget information is organized in a hierarchy of increasing detail, with highly detailed line items at the lowest level.

Budget implementation is a two-sided coin: on one side are procedures designed to maintain budget compliance; on the other are procedures and policies designed to alter the budget as circumstances warrant. To maintain budget compliance, nearly all governments use encumbrances. Budget offices also approve the creation of new positions or the reclassification of existing positions as part of the budget control process. Two of the oldest controls are apportionment and allotment. Finally, councils grant budget authority for a fixed period of time, whether the fiscal year or the biennium. When that period ends, budget authority lapses, and any unused funds are no longer available for spending.

Budget authority can be altered to realign the budget with the actual amount of revenues coming in and expenditures flowing out. Budget offices review and approve the transfer of budget authority across accounts and even agencies. As a result of changes in economic or political conditions, the council's budget may be amended during the fiscal year, or the chief executive may impound (freeze) budget authority in order to avert a year-end deficit. Budget reserves are maintained as short-term solutions for meeting contingencies.

The onset of a budget crisis precipitates a response gap, as revenues fall more quickly than expenditures. Local governments can use a number of measures to mitigate a short-term gap and return the budget to balance, but if the crisis continues and intensifies, the options for restoring budget balance become politically more difficult.

Notes

1 Justin Marlowe, "The Budget as a Communication Tool," *IQ Report* 37, no. 4 (2005).

2 Government Finance Officers Association, *Distinguished Budget Presentation Award Program* (Chicago: GFOA, 2018). http://www.gfoa.org/budgetaward

3 Government Finance Officers Association, *Distinguished Budget Presentation Award Program, Electronic Vote Page* (Chicago: GFOA, 2018).

4 U.S. Government Accountability Office, *A Glossary of Terms Used in the Federal Budget Process,* GAO-05-743SP (Washington, D.C.: September 2005), 12.

5 Ibid., 85, 95–96.

6 Thomas P. Lauth, "Georgia: Shared Power and Fiscal Conservatism," Chapter 3 in *Budgeting in the States: Institutions, Processes, and Politics,* ed. Edward J. Clynch and Thomas P. Lauth (Westport, Conn.: Praeger Publishers, 2006): 33-53.

7 Philip G. Joyce, *The Costs of Budgetary Uncertainty: Analyzing the Impact of Late Appropriations* (Washington, D.C.: IBM Center for the Business of Government, 2012), 18.

8 Ian J. Allan, "Unreserved Fund Balance and Local Government Finance," *Research Bulletin* (GFOA), (November 1990): 4.

9 Ibid., 5–6.

10 Jeremy M. Goldberg and Max Neiman, *Managing Budgets During Fiscal Stress: Lessons for Local; Government Officials* (Washington, D.C.: IBM Center for the Business of Government, 2014): 21-22.

11 Howard Chernick, Adam H. Langley, and Andrew Reschovsky, "Central City Revenues after the Great Recession," *Land Lines* (July 2012): 1–6.

12 Charles H. Levine, "Police Management in the 1980s: From Decrementalism to Strategic Thinking," *Public Administration Review* 45 (November 1985): 695.

13 Jane Beckett-Camarata and Cleopatra Grizzle, "The Financial Crisis in Harrisburg, Pennsylvania," *Public Finance and Management* 14 (2014): 5-29.

EXCEL EXERCISES

Microsoft's Excel is a widely used tool by budget analysts. The following Excel exercise introduces readers to monitoring budget compliance through executive implementation.

Excel Exercise #3: Monitoring budget compliance. Once the operating budget is approved, the focus then is on budget implementation. One of the most important tasks in this third phase of the budget cycle is monitoring actual revenues and expenditures with the purpose of anticipating unfavorable trends. For this exercise, the analysis returns to the line-item budget for a city's Development Department. This Excel exercise involves projecting year-end expenditures (1) for each line item, (2) for total departmental expenditures, (3) for each revenue source, and (4) then comparing trends in actual expenditures and revenues with the totals in the adopted budget. Using these projections, not only can comparisons be made to the adopted and revised budgets, but projected revenues can be compared to projected expenditures to evaluate the potential impact on fund balance. Data for this exercise are available at https://icma.org/documents/budgeting-guide-chapter-9-exercise-3

CHAPTER
10

The budget cycle: Accounting and auditing

> But what is government itself, but the greatest of all reflections on human nature? If men were angels, no government would be necessary. If angels were to govern men, neither external nor internal controls on government would be necessary.
>
> —*James Madison*

This chapter provides the following takeaways:

- Understand the exchange of information between the budget and accounting systems.
- See how fund accounting works and how it complicates the budgeting process.
- Know how the information that is in the online and year-end financial reports is produced and how to use it to make management decisions.
- Understand the role of the external auditor and the information they produce.
- What to look for in effective internal controls and why they are important.

Chapter 9 introduced the three interdependent levels of financial control—executive implementation, accounting, and auditing—and Figure 9–1 summarized the tools commonly used by each. Chapter 9 also discussed the first of these three levels in depth. This chapter explores the second and third.

The accounting system provides the information needed for making corrections to the budget during the year if revenues are lower than anticipated or unforeseen costs push spending beyond what was authorized. Accounting information is organized around departments and programs so that responsibility for budget decisions can be established, and it includes line items showing in detail the amount of budget authority authorized for specific purposes.

The comptroller's office or chief accountant, working closely with the budget office, prepares periodic financial reports that summarize the accounting information, disclose the results of operations to that point in the fiscal year, and give those with oversight responsibility the information they need to monitor unexpected trends that emerge during the year. For example, if a fund balance is drawn down, suggesting that revenues have not covered expenditures, this appears in the interim financial reports, usually available online with continuous updates. At the end of the fiscal year, the comptroller prepares the CAFR, which aggregates financial information for all operations and reports on the financial position of the local government.

While the budget is the preeminent financial planning document in government, the accounting system provides the framework for maintaining the financial integrity of the organization. And the check on the integrity of the accounting system is the external auditor's verification of the accuracy of the CAFR and the internal controls that govern how financial data are collected, processed, and documented.

The budgeting-accounting interface

To the casual observer, budgeting may appear to be a mere extension of accounting. Accountants track the flow of money into and out of the organization and periodically prepare reports on the organization's financial condition. But appearances are deceptive. In government, the budgeting and accounting systems function independently of one another, although each supports the other. Much like a Venn diagram, functionally they represent two independent circles that intersect. And it is at the point of intersection that the more interesting dynamics occur.

For example, the accounting system provides input into the budgeting cycle in such areas as year-end fund balance, under- or overage in revenues and expenditures, and historical information for each account used by department heads in preparing their budget requests. In essence, the accounting system provides the budget with a reality check as the fiscal year progresses. Once the fiscal year ends, the actual balances from the accounting system are compared against the approved amounts in the budget to assess the management team's effectiveness in maintaining compliance with the approved budget.

On the other side, the budget system produces information used as input by the accounting system. For example, at the outset of the fiscal year, after the budget has been approved, the accounting system enters the approved amount for each budgetary account as its beginning balance. The approved budget instructs the accounting system on how much to set aside in the fund balance for reserves and what interfund transfers to make. And the budget provides the accounting system with information on the amount and type of revenue to accrue.

The accounting framework

The accounting framework enables a local government to log the thousands of transactions authorized by the budget into accounting records. This framework is standardized for all local and state governments, regardless of the size of their budgets.

Accounting and the financial reports that it produces provide information about where the government is financially at any time, how much money has been spent, and what the money has been spent on. Accounting helps identify trouble spots—where spending is getting out of control or where revenues lag behind budgeted expectations. To do this successfully, accounting must be accurate: its reports must be timely, must be formatted to answer the key financial control questions, and must track actual revenues and expenditures against the budget as it is implemented. Without this continual flow of reliable information, the government would not know if the budget is balanced and could not take timely corrective action when necessary.

At about this point the astute observer asks, "How do accountants keep all of this straight?" While budgeting remains individualized (each organization develops its own processes and rules and compiles them into a budget policy statement and budget manual), accounting relies on a common set of rules to govern its procedures.

Generally accepted accounting principles

Beyond maintaining accuracy, it is essential that an accounting system adhere to a common set of standards to ensure that the same types of transactions are recorded in the same way over time and across each type of local government. Taxes receivable and salaries payable must be recorded and reported, year in and year out, in the same way and under the same set of rules by all local governments. Such consistency makes it possible to compare financial reports across time and with those from other local governments. It also helps those who oversee the government's finances to understand and interpret what they are reading. Auditors, state officials, bond-rating firms, banks, and federal agencies providing grants are among the primary external users of financial accounting data.

Summary of the thirteen generally accepted accounting principles (GAAP)

Principle 1. Accounts be maintained on a GAAP basis and demonstrate compliance with finance-related legal requirements.

Principle 2. Funds be the basis for maintaining accounting records.

Principle 3. Eleven basic types of funds are used in governmental accounting.

Principle 4. Governments maintain a minimum number of funds and only those required by law.

Principle 5. Accounting records maintain a distinction among the capital assets of proprietary funds, fiduciary funds, and governmental funds.

Principle 6. The historical cost of capital assets (land, buildings, equipment, infrastructure) and long-term debt be maintained in the accounting records.

Principle 7. Depreciation of capital assets be recorded in the accounting records.

Principle 8. Accounting records maintain a clear distinction between long-term liabilities attributable to a specific fund and those attributable to the general government.

Principle 9. The accrual basis of accounting be used for government-wide financial statements and for proprietary and fiduciary funds, and that the modified accrual basis of accounting be used for fund-specific financial statements.

Principle 10. An annual budget be adopted, budgetary control be provided by the accounting system, and the budget be compared annually with actual results of operations.

Principle 11. Interfund transfers be recognized and reported depending on whether the transfer involves reciprocity.

Principle 12. A common terminology and classification system be used throughout all financial records.

Principle 13. Interim financial reports be prepared and that the format of the comprehensive annual financial report (CAFR) follow a specified format.

Source: Adapted from GASB *Codification of Governmental Accounting and Financial Reporting Standards* (Norwalk, Conn: Governmental Accounting Standards Board [GASB], 2010). © Financial Accounting Foundation, 401 Merritt 7, Norwalk, CT 06856, USA. Used with permission.

The accounting system must provide financial information that is understandable, reliable, relevant, comparable, consistent, and timely.[1] These six goals form the conceptual basis for the thirteen standards—called generally accepted accounting principles (GAAP)—adopted by the accounting profession to guide the recording and reconciling of transactions for all state and local governments. Because these principles are generally accepted among governments, accounting information is much more standardized than is budgeting information.

The accompanying sidebar summarizes the thirteen accounting principles adopted by the Governmental Accounting Standards Board (GASB), the seven-person body of accounting professionals that was created in 1984 and is widely recognized as the official source of accounting standards for state and local governments. Because GASB principles and guidelines carry great weight with the financial community, considerable controversy surrounds the GASB's role in—and the influences that its actions have on—public budgeting. In 1999, the GASB adopted Statement No. 34, *Basic Financial Statements—and Management's Discussion and Analysis—for State and Local Governments*,[2] which introduced sweeping changes in the structure of the basic financial statements for state and local governments and in the way that accounting information is recorded and reconciled. These changes are discussed throughout this chapter.

The use of separate funds, along with the use of three different bases of accounting, makes accounting in government much more complex than its private sector counterpart. Because of these differences in perspective, totals in the budget and in the annual financial reports based on the accounting data often differ. GASB 34 requires that the accounting office prepare a separate column in the CAFR that adjusts the year-end revenues and expenditures using the same basis as the budget in order to accurately compare the actual results with what was budgeted.

Fund structure

Whereas a business combines the results of the operations of all its subsidiaries into one consolidated report, a local government disaggregates its operations into funds and creates a separate report for each type of fund (see Figure 10–1). A fund is defined as an accounting entity with a self-balancing set of accounts. Each fund functions independently under the aegis of the city or county council; each receives revenue from a different source, each spends money for different purposes, and each maintains its own set of accounts and financial reports. The expenditures from each fund have to be covered by the revenues from that fund, plus any transfers of money from other funds. Because of the fund structure, governments do not have a single bottom line but many bottom lines, one for each fund. The sum of all activities recorded in the funds represents the full scope of a government's services for that period of time.

Funds are almost always created by law—either by the state, as a charter provision for home rule local governments, or through ordinances approved by the local governing body. The fundamental purpose of the fund structure is fiscal control: the revenue coming into a fund must be used for purposes authorized by the law that created the fund. If a fund receives more in revenue than it spends, the fund balance increases. Conversely, if revenues fail to keep pace with spending, the fund balance declines. A fund, like a business, cannot continue to exist if its balance drops below zero (i.e., if its liabilities exceed its assets, meaning that it has negative value). Strict rules also govern the relationships among funds. For example, a surplus balance in one fund may not be available to offset a shortfall in another, which greatly complicates budgeting in the public sector.

A local government may have fewer than a dozen funds or may have several hundred, depending on its size and on the complexity of its funding sources. Figure 10–2 identifies the eleven basic types of funds required by GASB 34 and the three broad categories into which they are grouped: governmental, proprietary, and fiduciary.[3] While local governments may

Figure 10-1 Budget Summary page, Coral Gables, Florida

CITY OF CORAL GABLES
SUMMARY OF REVENUES, EXPENDITURES AND CHANGES IN FUND BALANCE
2017-2018 BUDGET
(BUDGETED FUNDS ONLY)

	GENERAL FUND	DEBT SERVICE FUND	CAPITAL PROJECTS FUNDS	ENTERPRISE FUNDS	TOTAL
0	$ 49,254,593	$ 2,782,052	$ 25,601,237	$ 1,738,713	$ 79,376,595
Fiscal Year 2016-2017 (Estimated)					
Revenues	147,349,584	5,492,514	57,850,913	40,978,074	251,671,085
Expenditures	149,092,488	6,489,514	68,379,545	40,727,722	264,689,269
FY 2017 Change in Fund Balance	**(1,742,904)**	**(997,000)**	**(10,528,632)**	**250,352**	**(13,018,184)**
Fund Balance @ 09/30/17 (Estimated)	**47,511,689**	**1,785,052**	**15,072,605**	**1,989,065**	**66,358,411**
Fiscal Year 2017-2018 Budget					
Revenues:					
Taxes	98,379,165	-	3,095,045	-	101,474,210
Licenses	3,518,750	-	-	-	3,518,750
Permits	7,299,000	-	-	-	7,299,000
Fines & Forfeitures	1,890,000	-	-	-	1,890,000
Intergovernmental	5,545,000	-	-	-	5,545,000
Use Charges	9,494,000	-	-	28,226,500	37,720,500
Recreation Fees	2,498,000	-	-	1,735,500	4,233,500
Rentals & Concessions	3,587,115	-	-	2,713,022	6,300,137
Investment Earnings	350,000	8,000	305,000	85,000	748,000
Other	5,729,500	330,000	-	-	6,059,500
Transfers In	12,241,432	5,953,993	7,598,056	277,326	26,070,807
Total Revenues	150,531,962	6,291,993	10,998,101	33,037,348	200,859,404
Expenditures:					
General Government	33,842,501	-	3,054,258	-	36,896,759
Economic Environment	1,291,564	-			
Public Safety	73,629,640	-	1,623,689	-	75,253,329
Physical Environment	21,016,672	-	75,000	14,860,119	35,951,791
Transportation	3,178,477	-	8,868,045	6,764,566	18,811,088
Culture & Recreation	8,933,372	-	3,380,214	1,917,249	14,230,835
Debt Service	-	6,679,497	-	1,636,116	8,315,613
Transfers Out	13,574,696	750,000	-	8,982,679	23,307,375
Total Expenditures	155,466,922	7,429,497	17,001,206	34,160,729	212,766,790
FY 2018 Change in Fund Balance	**(4,934,960)**	**(1,137,504)**	**(6,003,105)**	**(1,123,381)**	**(11,907,386)**
Fund Balance @ 09/30/18	**$ 42,576,729**	**$ 647,548**	**$ 9,069,500**	**$ 865,684**	**$ 54,451,025**

Signifcant changes in Fund Balance are primarily due to the following:
In the General Fund - For FY17 - Reappropriation (Rollover) of prior year purchase orders
In the General Fund - For FY18 - Planned use of fund balance for one-time operating expenditures

In the Capital Projects Funds - For FY17 - Planned use of fund balance for capital projects and reappropriation (rollover) of prior year project balances.
In the Capital Projects Funds - For FY18 - Planned use of fund balance for capital projects.

In the Enterprise Funds - For FY17 - Planned use of fund balance for capital projects and reappropriation (rollover) of prior year project balances.
In the Enterprise Funds - For FY18 - Planned use of fund balance for capital projects.

Source: City of Coral Gables, Florida, *2017-18 Budget*, 92. http://www.coralgables.com/modules/showdocument.aspx?documentid=22732

have dozens of funds (states even have hundreds), the funds can all be categorized into one of these eleven types.

Governmental funds There are five types of governmental funds.

General fund The general fund, usually the largest and most important of the governmental funds, is the primary operating fund and the most important in terms of the operating budget.

Figure 10–2 The eleven basic fund types

Funds	Examples
Governmental funds	
General fund	
Special revenue funds	Hotel/Motel Tax Fund
Debt service funds	2002 Series Debt Service Fund
Capital projects funds	Eagle Street Improvement Fund
Permanent funds	Oaklawn Cemetery Perpetual Care Fund
Proprietary (business-type) funds	
Enterprise funds	Water/Wastewater Fund
Internal service funds	Motor Vehicle Pool Fund
Fiduciary funds	
Investment trust funds	Countywide Cash Investment Fund
Private-purpose trust funds	Employees' Tuition Savings Fund
Pension trust funds	Municipal Employees Retirement Fund
Agency funds	Local Sales Tax Fund

It is "general" because any transaction that cannot be accounted for in another fund must be recorded in the general fund. In most cases, governments will refer to it as the general fund in their budget and financial reports, although Texas, for example, calls it the General Revenue Fund.

Special revenue funds While a government will have only one general fund, it may have several special revenue funds, each with a particular name, such as the Hotel/Motel Tax Fund. Such funds are established to account for the proceeds of revenue sources, typically an excise tax, earmarked or restricted by law for particular purposes. For example, the use of revenues from a hotel/motel occupancy tax may be restricted to historic preservation, economic development, and the promotion of tourism. Local governments often use special revenue funds to account for grants used for operating purposes, both to segregate revenues with restricted uses from those used for general operations and to provide a means of verifying that the revenue was used for the legally specified purposes.

Debt service funds Debt service funds account for resources used to pay the principal and interest on long-term general debt—for example, the annual debt service required on a general obligation (GO) bond. The purpose of establishing a separate fund for bond repayment is to demonstrate that money to pay back the debt has been set aside and will not be used for anything else. (Debt service funds were formerly called "sinking funds," in reference to the process of sinking [retiring] a debt obligation.) Governments may have one or more such funds, depending on their accounting preferences; sometimes, for example, they establish a separate fund for each GO bond series.

Capital projects funds Capital projects funds account for the financial resources used to construct or acquire capital facilities. For example, the council may create the Eagle Street Improvement Fund for the reconstruction of this thoroughfare. Revenues flowing into the fund may include GO bond proceeds that were authorized for the project, state and federal grants, and current taxes. Expenditures flowing out of the fund are usually payments to contractors for project design and construction. Once the project is complete, the fund is closed and the remaining balance is transferred elsewhere.

Capital projects funds help not only to account for but also to control the cost of large capital projects. Because accounting within the general fund is not project oriented, attempting to keep a detailed record of project costs within the general fund would be difficult, if not impossible. By creating a separate fund, the local government makes more visible the total actual cost as well as the amount of money flowing into the project as it progresses.

Permanent funds The final governmental fund type, permanent funds, constitutes endowments in which the principal is protected from use (and is therefore nonexpendable) and only the income is available for expenditure—for example, a fund established for the perpetual care of a city cemetery or an endowed scholarship fund. GASB 34 introduced endowment funds to report on outflows that are legally restricted to whatever the fund earns. The earnings made from investing the fund's principal are restricted to uses that benefit the government or its citizens.

Proprietary funds There are two kinds of proprietary funds: enterprise and internal service.

Enterprise funds Enterprise funds account for services that are substantially supported by customer fees—for example, water and wastewater services, other public utilities, and a range of governmental, quasi-business activities (toll roads, airports, public transit, docks, golf courses, and government-owned radio and television stations). Tracking these services in separate funds makes it easier to see whether each enterprise is bringing in enough revenue to cover all its costs. The local government can then decide whether to increase fees or subsidize the service costs with a transfer from general revenues.

GASB 34 requires that an activity be accounted for in an enterprise fund if it is financed with debt that is backed by fees generated by that activity.[4] (Activities that are backed by the government's full-faith-and-credit pledge in addition to the activity's revenue stream are not required to be accounted for in an enterprise fund.) This expanded rule for the use of enterprise funds means that more activities previously accounted for in the general fund will be moved into an enterprise fund.

Some enterprise funds generate revenues that exceed operating costs. For example, cities that own the electric utility and have a large state or federal presence, such as a state university, commonly shift some of the cost of local services to these otherwise tax-exempt properties by setting electric rates high enough to generate a "profit." The excess is returned to the city's general fund to subsidize the activities it finances.

One final point concerns the distinction between enterprise and special revenue funds. Enterprise funds receive revenue from service charges levied on customers of a public service. Special revenue funds may also receive some service charge revenue, but it is not used as collateral for revenue bonds to finance the fee-for-service activity. For example, a city-owned cable television service should be accounted for through an enterprise fund since user fees support the service. However, the gross receipts tax levied on a private cable company is accounted for in a special revenue fund (if the tax is dedicated to a particular purpose) because the revenue does not support the cable service.

Internal service funds Internal service funds are similar to enterprise funds except that they account for the activities of government departments that do work for (or provide equipment to) other government departments rather than for the public. For example, a motor pool, which provides vehicles for various departments and agencies, may be fully funded by the charges levied on other agencies. Its rates may include both operating and capital costs (e.g., the cost of replacing vehicles). Other government agencies or departments include in their operating budgets a line item for the rental charge to use motor pool vehicles.

One advantage of an internal service fund is that it encourages efficiency: if data processing is financed through the general fund and provided at no charge to departments, departments are more likely to overuse this "free" service. However, if the service is accounted for in an internal service fund and departments are charged on the basis of use, they are more likely to limit their data processing costs.

Fiduciary funds The four types of fiduciary funds account for resources that governments hold in trust for individuals or other governments.[5] At the federal level, the Social Security Trust Fund represents one of the largest in the federal budget. Fiduciary funds are typically excluded from the operating and capital budgets of governments.

Investment trust funds Investment trust funds, such as a Countywide Cash Investment Fund, account for resources that are commingled by several governments and held in trust for investment by a sponsor, such as a county.

Private-purpose trust funds Private-purpose trust funds are similarly fiduciary in nature, but in this case, the resources are held in trust by a government on behalf of individuals, private organizations, or even other governments.

Pension trust funds Pension trust funds are held in trust by a local government for payment of employee retirement benefits.

Agency funds With agency funds, governments can act as custodians of resources on behalf of other governments. For example, a state may collect sales taxes on behalf of its cities, in which case the taxes are held in an agency fund and periodically remitted to the local governments.

Interfund activity One of the potential trouble spots in financial accountability concerns the treatment of interfund activities. GASB 34 classifies such activities as either reciprocal or nonreciprocal.[6] Reciprocal interfund activities are loans and reimbursable services provided by one fund to another. In both cases, one fund reimburses another for benefits received, much as if it had purchased a service or incurred a loan from a source outside the government. Payment from the general fund to the water utility fund for the use of water from fire hydrants represents a reciprocal activity.

Nonreciprocal interfund activities are interfund transfers and reimbursements that do not require "payback" of any kind. An interfund transfer appears as an item in the operating budget and is authorized when the budget is approved. For example, a government might transfer money from the general fund to a newly created internal service fund to provide start-up capital for the new venture, and there is no expectation that the transfer will ever be repaid. The transfer may be required by charter or by an ordinance of council. An interfund reimbursement—for example, from a utility fund to the general fund for overhead—reimburses one fund for payments it made that are to be charged to another fund.

Accounts: The building blocks of funds

While funds are the basic building blocks of governmental accounting, they are themselves made up of accounts. An account is defined as "a separate financial reporting unit for budget, management, and/or accounting purposes."[7] Each account is given a unique number (or account string) that identifies the fund in which it is found and the type of account it is (cash, supplies, taxes receivable, accounts payable, etc.).

In the budget, there are two kinds of accounts: estimated revenues and appropriations. Each source of revenue (e.g., each taxpayer) and each type of appropriation is also given a separate account number. These budgetary accounts are also entries in the accounting records. The two

Figure 10–3 Common types of asset and liability accounts

Assets	Liabilities
Current assets	Current liabilities
Cash and cash equivalents	Accounts payable
Investments at fair market value	Claims payable
Taxes receivable, net of allowances	Salaries payable
Accounts receivable, net of allowances	Compensated absences payable
Unbilled utility service	Interfund payables
Interfund receivables	Accrued interest
Due from other governments	Deferred revenues
Merchandise inventory	Payables from restricted assets
Prepaid items	Total current liabilities
Deferred charges	
Total current assets	Noncurrent liabilities
	Leases payable
Noncurrent assets	General obligation bonds payable
Restricted assets	Revenue bonds payable
Capital assets, net of accumulated depreciation	Notes payable
Total noncurrent assets	Compensated absences payable
Total assets	Landfill closure/postclosure costs
	Total noncurrent liabilities
	Total liabilities

types of accounts link the budget and accounting system and form the cornerstone for the accounting records. All other accounts derive their balances from these budgetary accounts. Once the council approves the budget, the line-item information from the budget is entered into the accounting records and tracked by the accounting system.

Components of the basic accounting equation While revisions to the budget made during the fiscal year—budget transfers, budget amendments, supplemental appropriations—are recorded in the budgetary accounts, the vast majority of transactions recorded in the accounting system are in three additional types of accounts, which form the basic accounting equation: assets = liabilities + fund balance.

Asset accounts **Asset accounts**, such as cash or taxes receivable, represent things of value. A fund accumulates assets through its transactions. The levying of a property tax creates an asset in the form of taxes receivable (the amount of which can be measured and is available to pay liabilities in the current fiscal year). Once the taxes are paid, the receivable becomes cash, a more liquid form of the asset. In a typical classification, assets are ranked according to their liquidity—how easily they can be converted into cash—with the most liquid ranked first. Current assets represent those assets that can be converted into cash within the current year. Fixed assets, on the other hand, represent the least liquid assets, such as land, buildings, equipment, and other improvements that are recorded on the basis of their historical cost. Figure 10–3 shows the types of asset accounts in a typical local government.

Liability accounts **Liability accounts** represent legal obligations that require the eventual transfer of assets. Liabilities are ranked in order of when they are due: current liabilities, such as accounts payable or wages payable, are ranked first because they are due within the current year, and long-term liabilities, such as outstanding revenue bonds, are ranked last. The delivery

Figure 10–4 Components of fund balance for a government fund

	General Fund	Major Special Revenue Funds: Highway Fund	Major Special Revenue Funds: School Aid Fund	Major Debt Service Fund	Major Capital Projects Fund	Other Funds	Total
Fund balances:							
Nonspendable:							
Inventory	$ 125,000	$ 108,000	$ 16,000	—	—	—	$ 249,000
Permanent fund principal		—	—	—	—	$ 164,000	164,000
Restricted for:							
Social services	240,000	—	—	—	—	—	240,000
Parks and recreation	80,000	—	—	—	—	—	80,000
Education	55,000	—	—	—	—	—	55,000
Highways	—	—	—	—	$ 444,000	—	444,000
Road surface repairs	—	24,000	—	—	—	—	24,000
Debt service reserve	—	—	—	$ 206,000	—	—	206,000
School construction	—	—	—	—	301,000	—	301,000
Law enforcement	—	—	—	—	—	214,000	214,000
Other capital projects	—	—	—	—	51,000	—	51,000
Other purposes	30,000	—	—	—	—	—	30,000
Committed to:							
Zoning board	16,000	—	—	—	—	—	16,000
Economic stablization	210,000	—	—	—	—	—	210,000
Homeland security	110,000	—	—	—	—	—	110,000
Education	50,000	—	103,000	—	—	—	153,000
Health and welfare	75,000	—	—	—	—	—	75,000
Assigned to:							
Parks and recreation	50,000	—	—	—	—	—	50,000
Library acquisitions	50,000	—	—	—	—	—	50,000
Highway resurfacing	—	258,000	—	—	—	—	258,000
Debt service	—	—	—	306,000	—	—	306,000
Public pool	—	—	—	—	121,000	—	121,000
City Hall renovation	—	—	—	—	60,000	—	60,000
Other capital projects	50,000	—	—	—	471,000	—	521,000
Other purposes	80,000	—	73,000	—	—	176,000	329,000
Unassigned:	525,000	—	—	—	—	—	525,000
Total fund balances	$ 1,746,000	$ 390,000	$ 192,000	$ 512,000	$ 1,448,000	$ 554,000	$ 4,842,000

This level of detail is not required for display on the face of the balance sheet. Fund balance categories and classifications may be presented in detail or in the aggregate if sufficient detail is provided in the notes to the financial statements.

Source: Governmental Accounting Standards Board, Statement No. 54, Fund Balance Reporting and Governmental Fund Type Definitions (Norwalk, Conn.: GASB, February 2009): 71. © Financial Accounting Foundation, 401 Merritt 7, Norwalk, CT 06856, USA. Used with permission.

of a piece of equipment or the service of an employee for a day creates a liability for the fund that at some point must be paid with an asset, usually cash.

An encumbrance creates a contingent liability—a budget implementation tool—but the accounting system, while tracking encumbrances, only recognizes the expenditure and corresponding liability it creates once the equipment is delivered. Delivery of the piece of equipment creates a fixed asset on the left-hand side of the accounting equation and an account payable on the right-hand side. In the case of salaries, most governments encumber salaries automatically at the outset of the fiscal year and then create the liability (salaries payable) at the end of each pay period. Figure 10–3 also shows the types of liability accounts in a typical local government.

Fund balance In an accounting context, the difference between assets and liabilities in proprietary and fiduciary funds represents **net assets**, analogous to the wealth that a business accumulates through its operations. However, in the case of governmental funds—which exist to deliver services, not to accumulate wealth—this difference is known as fund balance. GASB 54 breaks the fund balance into five components, ranked below by the degree to which each is available for the council's discretionary use (see Figure 10–4):[8]

- *Nonspendable* fund balance is made up of (1) contractual or other legal obligations, such as the principal of an endowment, or (2) resources that cannot be converted into cash, such as prepaid insurance.[9] This portion of the fund balance is the least accessible to the council for its discretionary use.

- *Restricted* fund balance contains resources (1) available for purposes stipulated in law (statutory or constitutional) or (2) from external resource providers such as federal or state grantors.
- *Committed* fund balance comprises amounts designated for purposes determined by formal action of the council or board of directors.
- *Assigned* fund balance is intended to be used for specific purposes but does not meet the criteria to be classified as restricted or committed. In governmental funds other than the general fund, assigned fund balance represents the remaining amount that is not restricted or committed.
- *Unassigned* fund balance is the residual classification for the government's general fund and includes all spendable resources not included in the other categories. This portion of fund balance is available for the most discretionary use by the council.

The objective of this classification is to provide local government leaders with an accurate measure of the amount of resources they can reapportion in future budgets; sometimes lawmakers mistakenly assume that it is simply the cash balance. The unassigned balance is particularly critical to the budget office as it prepares revenue projections for the forthcoming year.

Whereas governmental funds account for only current assets and liabilities, proprietary and fiduciary funds account for current and fixed assets and current and long-term liabilities. Thus, the difference between liabilities and assets encompasses more economic activity, as reflected in the term *net assets.*

Chart of accounts To facilitate the use of common terminology as required by GAAP, the accounting department maintains a **chart of accounts**, which assigns a number to each fund, each department or agency account, and each object of expenditure. A chart of accounts provides a common framework that brings consistency to the budget as well as to the accounting system and enables information to be moved efficiently from the budget to the accounting system and back again. One source for such a chart is Governmental Accounting, Auditing, and Financial Reporting, or GAAFR, the Government Finance Officers Association's authoritative guide on state and local government accounting practices.[10]

A simplified version of a chart of accounts gives each fund and department a three-digit code, each unit below the department level a four-digit code, and each object of expenditure a four-digit code. The combination of these codes makes up the account number for a particu-

Figure 10–5 Chart of accounts

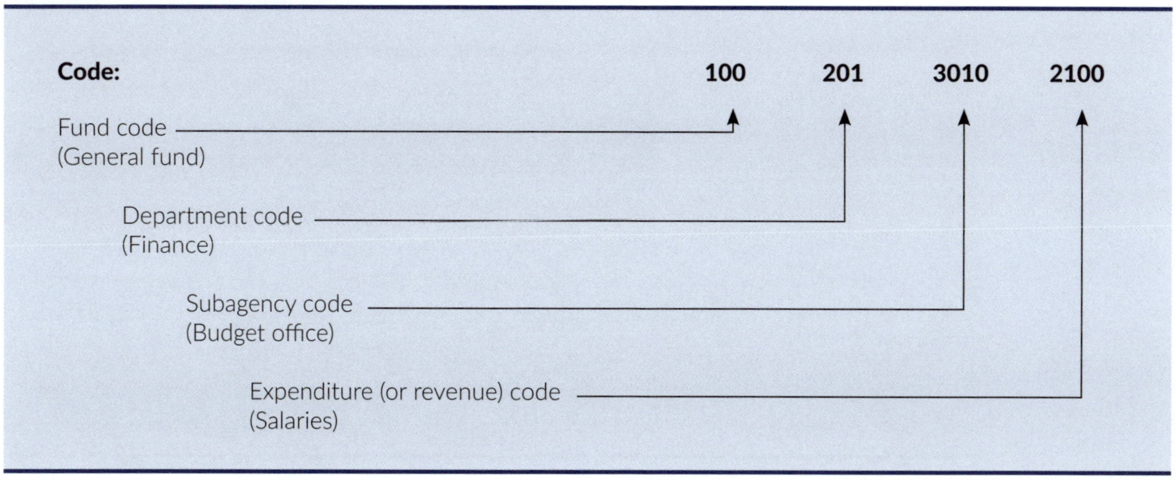

lar type of transaction. For example, salary expenditures by the city manager's office from the general fund might have an account number of 100-201-3010-2100 (see Figure 10–5).

The system for numbering accounts varies across local governments, and typically the chart of accounts reflects the peculiarities of a particular city. For county governments, however, states typically mandate a standard chart of accounts to facilitate state and county coordination of financial practices. In Washington State, the state auditor conducts the year-end financial and compliance audit of all municipalities and counties and so has established a universal chart of accounts applicable to all local governments to facilitate that task.

The accounting process

The heart of the accounting process is the recording and reconciling of transactions into accounts in the appropriate fund or funds and the reporting of the effect of these transactions on account balances. Figure 10–6 shows the steps in the accounting cycle, beginning with a transaction and ending with the preparation of interim and year-end financial statements. Some characterize these tasks as the "3 R's" of accounting: recording, reconciling, and reporting. Accounting software has become sufficiently inexpensive and user-friendly that most local governments maintain at least their accounting records in an electronic format. Once the transaction is entered into the database, the recording, reconciling, and reporting functions are performed automatically.

The recording function

In the *recording* function, every financial transaction, whether a bank deposit, a receipt of property taxes, or the payment of overtime to a police officer, is recorded in an account. These transactions are then aggregated into interim financial reports that are made available to managers throughout the year. These reports, which most local governments post online, help maintain compliance with the budget throughout the year. At year-end, all the transactions are

Figure 10–6 The accounting cycle

Posted to... (Journal → Ledger)

Journal	Ledger	Reports
transactions	accounts	funds
recorded chronologically	A, L, FB, R, E, encumbrances	11 types

Step 1. Business transaction occurs – taxes levied, budget adopted Payroll approved, check issued, check deposited, transfer made.

Step 2. Transactions chronologically recorded in General Journal (i.e., Book of Original Entry).

Step 3. Posting transactions from Journal to General Ledger and subsidiary ledgers (Revenue Subsidiary Ledger, Expenditure Subsidiary Ledger, etc.).

Step 4. Online statements updated daily.

Step 5. Closing entries recorded in Journal and posted to Ledger at year end.

Step 6. Comprehensive Annual Financial Report (CAFR) prepared.

Step 7. CAFR audited by external auditor.

compiled into a standardized format in the CAFR, which summarizes the actual results from all the transactions during the year and reveals how close the results are to the budget as amended.

Every transaction, whether the levying of taxes or disbursement of the payroll, generates some type of documentation. In the case of a property tax levy, invoices are mailed to property owners in the city or county. This documentation provides the accounting system with evidence of a transaction, which is then logged chronologically into a journal or book of original entry. Governments may maintain several specialized journals, such as a cash receipts journal or a purchases journal, in which to log transactions.

The recording function uses an ingenious device developed during the Middle Ages—double-entry bookkeeping—to enter every transaction into a journal. Each transaction has at least one debit entry and one credit entry (ergo, "double entry"). For any given transaction, the sum of the debits must always equal the sum of the credits. However, as anyone who has ever slogged through an accounting problem knows, human error always has a way of working its way into the process. Invariably at the end of a long string of transactions, debits and credits do not balance, and the remainder of the night is spent trying to find the mistake.

Standardizing the recording of accounting information

Many of the standards that guide accounting practices, especially those in GASB 34, originated in the private sector, where the **accrual basis** of accounting is the rule. Accrual accounting works well for businesses that sell a product or service. Investors want to know how profitable a business is, so businesses need an accounting system that accurately matches revenues earned from the sale of products with the expenses incurred in producing them. In accrual accounting, revenues from the sale of products are recognized when they are both earned and measurable, and expenses for the raw materials and labor are recorded when they are used in the production process. (One important expense is **depreciation**, or the decrease in the value of fixed assets—buildings and equipment—used to produce those products.) **Net income** is the difference between the revenue stream and the expense stream. The more profitable the business, the more efficient it is at converting raw materials and labor into finished goods for which there is a market.

For governmental funds, accrual accounting is not as useful. Tax-supported activities do not earn revenue, and there is no direct link between their cost and tax revenue; the cost of responding to a fire alarm, for example, has little connection to the amount of taxes paid by the caller. Since governmental funds produce goods or services that serve citizens, the concern is with expenditures—the cost of labor and *supplies delivered during the fiscal period,* as opposed to expenses, which are the cost of labor and supplies *used during a period of time*—and with determining whether revenues received from taxes and other sources during a given fiscal period are sufficient to cover the expenditures for that fiscal period. For this reason, governments use the modified accrual basis of accounting for governmental funds. As discussed in the next section, however, the accrual basis is used for proprietary and fiduciary funds since they involve the sale of goods and services to customers of government.

Under the modified accrual basis, local governments wait until revenue is *available* and *measurable* (they know approximately when and how much revenue will be received) before recording it. The accounting system then compares revenues with expenditures to show lawmakers and managers whether taxes and fees were sufficient to cover budgeted expenditures. It also compares the actual revenues with those estimated in the budget and the actual expenditures with those appropriated in the budget to determine how well each unit in the executive branch adhered to the budget.

A third basis of accounting—the cash basis—recognizes a transaction only when cash is exchanged. While government budgets often use a cash basis, GAAP requires that accounting and financial reporting be on an accrual or modified accrual basis, depending on the type of fund. As a result, the accounting system works under one set of rules while budget reporting proceeds under another.

Obviously, some tension exists between the assumptions that underlie the budget, the standards that guide the accounting system, and the reports that system generates. Budgets reflect the need to meet legal obligations (payrolls, vendor invoices, debt service) incurred during the budget period. Accounting for a governmental fund focuses on its financial condition: whether a fund's current assets equal or exceed its current liabilities. For proprietary and fiduciary funds, the focus broadens to include the fund's economic condition—that is, its current and fixed assets and its current and long-term liabilities.

Reconciling accounting data

Reconciling involves a separate set of tasks that posts the journal entries to a ledger—a spreadsheet that reorganizes the journal information by accounts. For example, all the journal entries that involve the receipt or disbursement of cash are posted to the cash account. All journal entries that involve creating or paying liabilities to vendors for their services are posted to accounts payable. Accounts, in turn, are grouped in the ledger by type: assets, liabilities, fund balance, revenues, and expenditures/expenses.

One significant wrinkle in governmental accounting (there are actually many wrinkles, but this one is major) is that, as has been noted, activities and their accounts are grouped into funds. The accounts associated with police and fire protection are in the general fund—at least most of them. The accounts associated with a street-widening project are in a capital projects fund. Each fund has its own set of accounts in each of the basic categories: assets, liabilities, and fund balance. Most also have accounts for revenues and expenditures (or expenses for the business type of funds).

Journal entries are entered chronologically and always involve at least two entries (see Figure 10–7). By convention, the first line is the debit or left-hand entry, and the second line is the credit or right-hand entry, which is indented. (It is possible to have more than one debit or credit entry, in which case the debit entries are listed first followed by the credit entries, which are indented.) The sum of the debits must always equal the sum of the credits. These entries are followed by a brief explanation of the nature of the transaction—as shown in Figure 10–7, for example, "to record property tax levy."

As organized in the journal, the information is not particularly useful. It is impossible to know the cumulative effect of these transactions on the cash balance of a fund, for example. Thus, the next step in the accounting cycle depicted in Figure 10–6 is the *posting* of this information to the general ledger, which organizes information by accounts and contains the control accounts for each of the subsidiary ledgers. For example, the general ledger would

Figure 10–7 Journal entry for recording a property tax levy

Date	Account title	Debit	Credit
January 16	Taxes Receivable	$500,000	
	Revenues		$500,000
	To record property tax levy.		

contain an entry under "taxes receivable" for $500,000, which is the sum of all the property tax liabilities contained in the property tax subsidiary ledger.

The adoption of the budget constitutes a transaction that is first journalized and then posted to the ledgers. In this transaction, the control accounts are estimated revenues and appropriations, with the more detailed individual accounts posted to the appropriate subsidiary ledger.

Reporting accounting results

The culmination of the accounting cycle is the *reporting* of the results of all transactions. The culmination of financial control is the preparation of interim and annual financial reports. Financial reports are of two types. The first type, interim reports, provides users within government with real-time information on the balance of each account for each fund. Information technology has made online interim reporting feasible and affordable for most governments and nonprofits. The second type of report, the CAFR, provides external constituencies (citizens, bond raters, investors, grantors) with critical information on the financial condition of each fund and of the organization overall. This report, at least the basic, most aggregated information, is subject to an examination by an external auditor, who issues a written statement on the report's accuracy (the audit opinion).

Interim financial reports For managers, the interim reports are more important than the CAFR. Interim financial reports compare the budgeted amount for each account—both estimated revenues and appropriations—with the actual amount—revenues and expenditures to date. This comparison is central to ensuring that actual receipts for each revenue source are keeping pace with estimates, and that expenditures and encumbrances for each account do not exceed the amounts authorized in the budget.

Interim reports, which are generally published online, reproduce the expenditure and revenue ledgers for each fund and show the proportion of the total budget that has been expended to date (see Figure 10–8); this information may also be summarized graphically to give council members a visual representation of the trends in actual revenues and expenditures. These reports enable the budget office to monitor the budget status of each department—and of each line-item appropriation within the department—and to identify potential areas of concern.

If a city government adopts a budget in which estimated revenues exactly equal appropriations, then during the year, if revenues exceed estimated revenues, the fund balance increases. Similarly, if expenditures plus encumbrances are less than appropriations, the fund balance does not decrease as much as anticipated. However, if the trends in expenditures and revenues suggest that revenues are falling seriously short and are not being made up by unexpected increases in revenues from other sources, the budget office will recommend corrective action.

The challenge from a budget control perspective is monitoring the interaction of the four temporary accounts—assets, liabilities, expenditures, and appropriations—during the

Figure 10–8 A line item from an interim financial report

Account name	Budget for current year	Actual revenue for		Percentage of budget
		Current period	Year-to-date	
MPA scholarships	$500,000	$25,000	$275,000	55.0%

fiscal year and their net effect on the fifth account, fund balance. Algebraically, this can be represented as

$$\text{assets} = \text{liabilities} + \text{fund balance} + \underbrace{\text{estimated revenues} - \text{revenues} + \text{expenditures} - \text{appropriations \& encumbrances}}_{\text{(accounts closed at end of year)}}$$

As the final step in the accounting cycle, the budgetary accounts to the right of fund balance in the above equation must be closed at the end of the fiscal year, and any residual resources must be transferred to the fund balance. For governmental funds, this action reduces the information in the accounting records to the basic accounting equation identified previously—assets = liabilities + fund balance—and is reported in the financial statements as the balance sheet. (For proprietary and fiduciary funds that use the accrual basis of accounting, this is the statement of net assets.) Once again, if actual revenues are greater than expenditures, the year-end fund balance will increase, and obviously, if the reverse is the case, the year-end balance will decline.

Although the four temporary accounts are closed, the information they contain is not lost. As discussed in the next section, this information is used to prepare an important report for each fund—the statement of revenues, expenditures, and changes in fund balance (or, colloquially, the operating statement), which compares the budget with actual revenues and expenditures and provides management as well as the council with critical information on overall budget compliance and on the changes in each fund's balance as a result of the prior year's operations.

With electronic financial management systems, once the original transaction is entered into the accounting database, the subsequent steps of journalizing, posting to the appropriate subsidiary ledger, aggregating information in control accounts in the general ledger, preparing interim statements, and, finally, closing the temporary accounts to the fund balance are completed with minimal intervention. For purposes of internal control, a separate approval may be required to post journal entries to the ledger and another to authorize disbursement of cash to pay liabilities.

Annual financial report One purpose of the CAFR is to ensure that funds were spent in compliance with the budget as approved and amended by the council. A second purpose is to ensure that revenues covered expenditures—that is, that the budget was balanced at the end of the fiscal year. Deviations from law or from balance are reported to the council.

GAAP does not address the content or design of information in interim reports, but it says a great deal about such matters for the CAFR—in particular, for the basic financial statements, management's discussion and analysis (MD&A), notes to the financial statement, and required supplementary information (RSI).[11] Prepared primarily for use by external stakeholders, the CAFR provides a report on all funds managed by a government for the preceding fiscal year.

Unlike interim reports, that portion of the CAFR covered by GAAP is subject to examination by an external auditor, who reports on its accuracy and is accountable to the elected lawmakers—the council or commission. Because the CAFR is prepared by management, a system of checks and balances requires such independent verification. Once the audit is completed, a copy of the auditor's opinion, usually one to two pages in length on the firm's letterhead, is included in the CAFR.

An annual report prepared in compliance with GAAP will also include an estimate of unfunded liabilities: amounts that the government owes or is likely to owe in the future for which it has not put any money aside. Although these numbers do not appear in the budget, they are relevant to financial control because they indicate the cumulative effect of such liabilities and the amount of funding needed to handle the anticipated demands. For example, if employees are accumulating sick days, is the local government setting money aside to pay this benefit? Is the government putting enough money into its self-insurance fund and into its pension trust funds?

For governmental funds, the CAFR contains a statement of revenues, expenditures, and changes in fund balance comparing the budget with actual revenues and expenditures. GASB 34 requires that such a budget comparison statement be prepared for the general fund and for each major special revenue fund that has an annually approved budget. It also requires the budget comparison to report (1) the original approved budget; (2) the final amended budget, which represents the ultimate appropriation authority for the fiscal year; and (3) the actual amounts (on a budgetary basis) for the same period, and to provide a column showing the variance between the actual and final budgets.

One more important piece of information shows up in the CAFR that is useful for financial control: a list of interfund activities, both reciprocal and nonreciprocal. While it is not easy to tell what was transferred from which fund to which fund, the totals of transfers in and transfers out of each fund are listed somewhere in the report. These figures allow the reader inside or outside the government to see at a glance which funds are receiving a subsidy and what proportion of the fund is accounted for by interfund activity. By comparing these figures between CAFRs, an analyst can figure out whether the level of transfers is going up as a proportion of the budget, and if so, where the increases are occurring.

GASB does not specify a time frame for completing the year-end financial report and submitting it to an external auditor.[12] Some states may set a deadline, such as sixty days after the end of the fiscal year. The longer the delay in completing the report, the less timely the data are to users, both within and outside government. On the other hand, the finance officer typically wears multiple hats and may have to give priority to completing other tasks, such as completing the annual budget, before turning to prepare the annual financial report. As a general rule, the CAFR should be available to the external auditor within sixty days after the end of the fiscal year.

Auditing

About three to four months after the close of the fiscal year, the comptroller prepares the CAFR, and the council or commission then retains an auditing firm to undertake a financial and compliance audit of that report. The external auditor, working under the guidelines of generally accepted auditing standards (GAAS), determines whether (1) the CAFR was prepared in accordance with GAAP, (2) the government complied with internal and external policies and procedures, and (3) the government's internal controls provide adequate protection of its assets and reasonable assurances against errors or fraud.

To accomplish these goals, the auditing firm dispatches a team of auditors—usually lower-ranking members of the firm—to undertake various field tests. The audit team sets up operations in the local government's finance department for a few days to several weeks. It begins by testing the internal controls. For example, it may track a purchase requisition through the approval and data entry process to ensure that all steps have been followed. The team then uses statistical sampling procedures and confidence intervals to verify within a reasonable range of error the accuracy of the account balances in the CAFR. (The accompanying sidebar elaborates on the importance of internal controls.)

Once the auditing firm has satisfied the criteria in GAAS, its top management reviews the findings of the field team and issues an opinion. An unqualified opinion—the much preferred

Internal controls

The integrity and accuracy of information produced by the accounting and financial reporting systems depend on the trustworthiness and reliability of those persons who authorize, record, reconcile, and ultimately report the financial data. Internal controls represent the network of policies and procedures that govern how financial data, and the assets they produce, are collected, processed, and documented. In larger local governments, an internal auditor, who typically reports to the manager, oversees and monitors this network.

Internal controls exist in every organization, small or large, public, for-profit, or not-for-profit. Maintaining and periodically verifying an inventory of personal computers (PCs), for example, is part of internal control. When a new PC arrives, a property label with an inventory number is attached. That documentation is used to track the PC's location, and an annual inventory review will verify that location and the current user.

Internal controls provide managers, accountants, and auditors with the assurance that procedures are being followed; that those procedures provide reasonable protection from fraud and theft of assets; and that if weaknesses in internal controls are identified, remedial action will be taken.

Internal control begins at the top, with the example set by the manager. How important is integrity to the manager? Does the manager model compliance with policies and procedures? Does the manager regularly communicate the importance of internal checks to department heads and other lower-level administrators? How does the manager handle violations of internal controls? No system is foolproof; every organization has vulnerabilities that enable the determined person "to beat the system." But a culture of compliance and integrity is foremost in any efforts to minimize the risk of such vulnerabilities.

Internal control has five components through which policies and procedures are most closely monitored and evaluated. The first component is *authorization:* internal policies must make clear who can authorize a transaction, whether that transaction is the initiation of a purchase requisition, the issuance of a check, or the approval of a contract. Every document should have at least two signatures, at least one of which is from a supervisor of the person initiating the transaction.

The second component is the *design of documentation*, such as sequentially numbered purchase orders and checks. The destination of duplicate copies of documentation should be indicated on each form to ensure proper distribution.

The third component concerns the *proper security of assets and records*, such as inventory controls, custody of investment securities, and backup procedures for financial and personnel records.

The fourth component of an effective internal control system is the *segregation of sequential duties*. For example, the person who is responsible for opening utility payments received by mail or over the counter should not be the same person who records the payments in the accounting system, and neither of these persons should be the one responsible for making the daily deposit to the bank or reconciling the monthly bank statement with the cash ledger. In a smaller local government with a limited staff, segregation of duties becomes more difficult but just as essential; here, the manager may need to assume responsibility for verifying bank statements and other externally generated documentation against internal records.

The fifth component is *reconciliation and verification* of actual balances with those reported in the accounting records. Monthly bank statements should be reconciled with the cash balance reported in the general ledger. Inventory records should be verified at least annually by visual inspection of equipment and materials held in inventory. Personnel records need to be periodically verified with employees and their supervisors.

Internal controls provide a system of checks and balances that helps to ensure but cannot guarantee that transactions are being accurately recorded, that assets are protected from fraud, and that financial information is reliable.

Source: Adapted from Stephen J. Gauthier, *Governmental Accounting, Auditing, and Financial Reporting* (Chicago: Government Finance Officers Association, 2012), 733–749. Used with GFOA permission.

audit outcome—means that the CAFR *presents fairly* the financial position of the government. If the CAFR lacks accuracy or if the internal controls were found to be unsatisfactory, the auditor issues a qualified opinion, meaning the CAFR *presents fairly, except for . . .* , and proceeds to explain the reasons for the qualification. (In the private sector, anything less than an unqualified opinion means the certain demise of the firm as stockholders lose confidence in management's capacity to sustain the firm's profitability.) In rare cases, the auditor may issue an adverse opinion *(does not present fairly)* or no opinion because information is insufficient to form a judgment.

One other report prepared by the audit firm that is relevant to financial control is the management letter. While the audit opinion is prepared for lawmakers and other external users, the management letter addresses matters that fall within the purview of the executive branch. The letter may provide recommendations on improving internal controls, accounting procedures, data processing of financial activities, or cash management and investment. It is always prudent for the manager to give careful attention to these recommendations since the auditor will look the following year to see what actions, if any, have been taken to correct the deficiencies identified in the letter.

Conclusion

Accounting and auditing are two of the three systems that provide financial control in local government. While the budget is the preeminent financial document in government, financial reporting alerts local government leaders to impending financial problems. Financial reports also verify to external stakeholders that the local government has control of its finances and is capable of adapting to changing circumstances. An external audit verifies the accuracy of the balances reported in the CAFR, the local government's compliance with state and local laws and internal policies, and the integrity of the government's internal controls.

Unlike the budgeting system, accounting is guided by GAAP, the generally accepted principles that form the foundation for standardizing the way that local governments in the United States record, reconcile, and report financial information.

The end result of the accounting process is the preparation of financial reports—interim reports that provide managers and council members with a continuous progress report on the status of revenues and expenditures relative to the budget, and the year-end CAFR, which provides a final reconciliation of all transactions and shows their cumulative effect on account balances. While interim reports, which are now generally available online for managers, provide managers with an early warning system should revenues or expenditures deviate substantially from the budget, the CAFR provides lawmakers with a final reckoning of actual revenues and expenditures with the budget, as amended by the council.

Notes

1 Stephen J. Gauthier, *Governmental Accounting, Auditing, and Financial Reporting* (GAAFR) (Chicago: Government Finance Officers Association [GFOA], 2012), 6.

2 Governmental Accounting Standards Board, Statement No. 34, *Basic Financial Statements—and Management's Discussion and Analysis—for State and Local Governments* (Norwalk, Conn.: Governmental Accounting Standards Board, June 1999).

3 Gauthier, *Governmental Accounting, Auditing, and Financial Reporting*, 39–48.

4 Ibid., 44.

5 Ibid., 46–49.

6 Robert J. Freeman and Craig D. Shoulders, *Governmental and Nonprofit Accounting* (Upper Saddle River, N.J.: Prentice Hall, 2003), 49.

7 U.S. Government Accountability Office, *A Glossary of Terms Used in the Federal Budget Process*, GAO-05-734SP (Washington, D.C.: U.S. Government Accountability Office, September 2005), 2.

8 Governmental Accounting Standards Board, *Fact Sheet about Fund Balance Reporting and Government Fund Type Definitions* (Norwalk, Conn.: GASB, February 2009).

9 Governmental Accounting Standards Board, Statement No. 54, *Fund Balance Reporting and Governmental Fund Type Definitions* (Norwalk, Conn.: GASB, February 2009).

10 Gauthier, *Governmental Accounting, Auditing, and Financial Reporting*, 933–984.

11 Management's discussion and analysis (MD&A), which is supplementary information required by the GASB, is an introductory narrative prepared by the finance director that identifies the key issues affecting the unit of government's financial well-being and the financial trends influencing its well-being. The notes to the financial statements provide more detail on specific items in the financial statements; they also disclose important accounting policies that guided the unit of government in reporting its financial information. The GASB considers this component to be integral to the basic financial reports, and they are in the scope of the external audit. Required supplementary information (RSI), such as MD&A, may also include reports comparing budget amounts with actual, infrastructure condition, trends in postemployment benefits, and the employer's pension liabilities.

12 Governmental Accounting Standards Board, *The Timeliness of Financial Reporting by State and Local Governments Compared with the Needs of Users* (Norwalk, Conn.: Governmental Accounting Standards Board, March 2011).

EXCEL EXERCISES

Microsoft Excel is a tool widely used by budget analysts. The following Excel exercise introduces readers to the task of determining the annual debt service requirements for a general obligation (GO) bond issue and the impact of the annual cost on the operating budget.

Excel Exercise #4. Budgeting for annual debt service. This Excel exercise involves costing out the annual debt service requirements for a general obligation bond issue and an analysis of the effect of those annual payments on the operating budget. The dataset is actual annual payments of principal and interest for a twenty-year bond issue. The data can be used to determine the annual cost of debt service and the required tax rate needed to produce the revenue for the debt service fund. Data for this exercise are available at https://icma.org/documents/budgeting-guide-chapter-10-exercise-4

CHAPTER 11

Planning and budgeting for capital improvements

Every noble work is at first impossible.

—*Thomas Carlyle*

This chapter provides the following takeaways:

- How best to organize the location, scope, and timing of the capital budget process.
- What to include in a capital budgeting policy.
- What criteria to include in a metric for ranking proposals for the capital improvement plan.
- What revenue sources are appropriate for financing the capital budget.
- What strategies are being used to develop a technology-enhanced community (i.e., a smart community) and what are the implications of each for the capital budget.

Investment in capital improvements—those long-lived fixed assets that are essential to economic and social well-being—entails a substantial commitment of financial and human resources by government. For purposes of this chapter, public capital improvements represent a government's fixed assets in its accounting ledgers and are of four types:

- *Infrastructure:* Includes such general-purpose assets as streets, storm drainage, water and sewer lines, other utility lines, wastewater treatment facilities, streetlights, and sidewalks. In most municipal budgets, these capital improvements constitute the largest capital outlay. While some analysts categorize all public improvements as infrastructure, this chapter differentiates infrastructure from the other types of capital improvements.
- *Public buildings:* Government offices, courthouses, warehouses, police and fire stations, jails, school facilities, airport facilities, community centers, and other public-purpose structures.

- *Equipment:* Items that are large or costly, such as computers, vehicles (e.g., police and fire), communications (e.g., telephones and emergency communications), and machinery. Some governments consider computer software to be equipment for budgeting purposes.
- *Land acquisition:* Includes the cost of purchasing and preparing land for construction or for use as parkland or even a landfill.

The importance of these four types of public improvements to the economic and social well-being of a nation is indisputable. This is obvious simply in terms of public infrastructure, for example. The highway system provides both direct and indirect benefits to business by making the production and delivery of private goods and services more efficient.[1] The direct benefits for interstate commerce are obvious: expediting the delivery of goods to points around the country. But the indirect economic and social benefits may be even more significant: widespread mobility of the population, jobs created in the private and nonprofit sectors, and tourism. Public improvements are widely recognized as key to the economic vitality and continued prosperity of developed as well as developing nations.

Public capital improvements are selected, prioritized, and funded usually in the capital budget. This chapter discusses the management of the capital planning process and the preparation of the capital budget, as well as the linkage between the capital budget and the operating budget. It also examines financing issues in capital budgeting—specifically, the choice between using current revenues and incurring debt—and the management of debt financing. The chapter concludes by discussing the unique challenges to capital planning for local governments contemplating becoming a technology-enhanced community (TEC), otherwise known as a smart community. The short lifespan of the technology combined with the substantial upfront cost for infrastructure to support a TEC requires specialized planning expertise and a long-term commitment by the local government.

As Chapter 8 made clear, conflict is inherent in the budgeting cycle, and the capital budgeting cycle is no exception. Many of the conflicts described in that chapter apply to the capital budgeting process and require negotiation and occasional intervention by the local govern-

Figure 11–1 Sources of conflict in the capital budgeting process

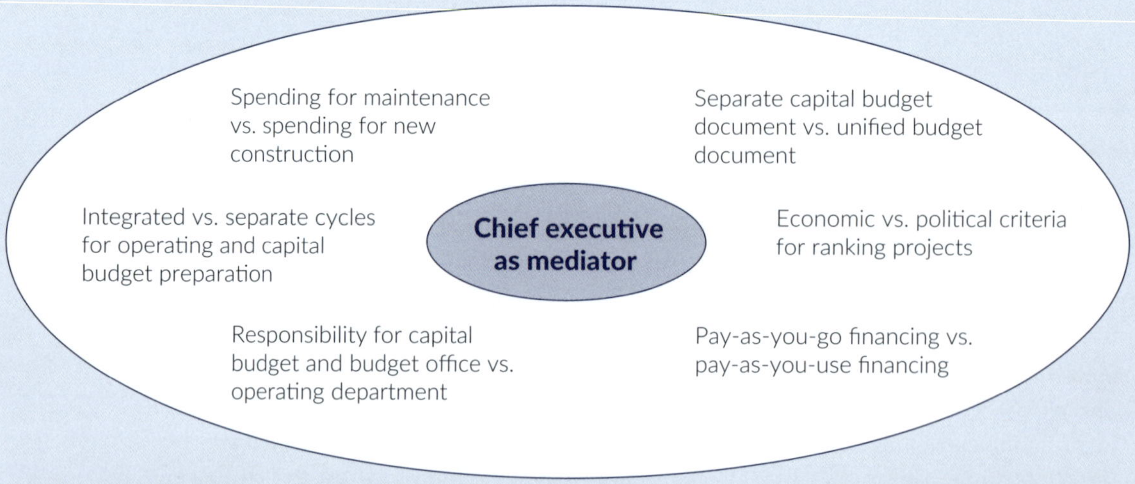

Source: Adapted from Robert L. Bland and Wes Clarke, "Budgeting for Capital Improvements," in *Handbook of Government Budgeting*, ed. Roy T. Meyers (San Francisco: Jossey-Bass, 1999), 659. © John Wiley and Sons. Creative Commons Attribution License (CC-BY) 4550300943255.

ment manager. However, the capital budgeting cycle also generates unique conflicts, which are summarized in Figure 11–1 and discussed where relevant throughout this chapter.

The context of capital budgeting

For capital acquisitions, careful planning is essential in order to avoid costly and embarrassing mistakes.

Defining capital expenditures

Whereas operating expenditures are for the recurring services of government, such as personnel, supplies, and maintenance, **capital expenditure**s are used to acquire fixed assets that have significant value and a life expectancy of more than one year.

Two things about the capital budget are worth noting. First, unlike the operating budget with its focus on the annual (or biennial) renewal of spending by categories (e.g., salaries, supplies), the capital budget focuses on spending for projects usually for a multiyear period. Second, not all capital expenditures are reported in the capital budget; this is especially true of expenditures for less expensive items such as office equipment. Typically the budget office or governing body sets a minimum dollar value—for example, $20,000—for items to include in the capital budget. The minimum value will vary depending on the size of the budget and the policy preferences of the chief executive and governing body. Items costing less than the minimum must be requested through the operating budget.

One other issue pertains to the term *capital budgeting* itself. In the business world, capital budgeting means the analytical techniques, such as net present value (NPV) and cost-benefit analysis, used to evaluate the financial merits of alternative investment proposals and the proper mix of debt and equity to fund those projects with the greatest return on investment.[2] NPV is the difference between a project's future costs and benefits, discounted for the time value of money; normally, the alternative with the highest NPV will be selected since it will yield the greatest net benefits. Cost-benefit analysis does the same sort of thing but compares alternatives using a ratio of total costs to benefits. Much of the literature in business finance addresses the theory and application of these techniques to investment decisions.

In public financial management, capital budgeting encompasses a much broader function, including the process of reviewing projects and ranking them in the capital budget document. As is discussed later in this chapter, capital budgeting also entails preparing an inventory of capital assets owned by government, evaluating the condition of those assets, estimating their cost of replacement, and preparing a multiyear capital improvement plan (CIP), the first year of which constitutes the capital budget. Figure 11–2, which is taken from the CIP for the City of Virginia Beach, Virginia, illustrates a common approach to budgeting for capital expenditures.

Organizing the capital budget process

In organizing the capital budget process and document, three issues must be resolved:

- Within the city or county, where should responsibility for preparing the capital budget be located?
- What is the scope of the capital budget process?
- Should preparation of the capital budget be timed concurrently with that of the operating budget?

Location Responsibility for preparing the capital budget can be located in the finance department, the budget office (if separate from finance), the planning department, or even

Figure 11-2 Excerpt from the Capital Improvement Program for Virginia Beach, Virginia

City of Virginia Beach, Virginia
Fiscal Years 2019 through 2024 Capital Improvement Program
Appropriation and Financing Plan

			Un-Appropriated Subsequent Years					
Appropriation/Financing	**Appropriated to Date**	**FY 2019 Budget**	**FY 2020 Budget**	**FY 2021 Budget**	**FY 2022 Budget**	**FY 2023 Budget**	**FY 2024 Budget**	**CIP Total**
Capital Improvement Program By Business Area/Category								
Capital Projects								
Buildings and Assets	119,472,238	80,625,157	20,329,673	25,655,273	21,286,328	12,538,273	32,538,273	312,445,215
Coastal	66,244,970	12,675,000	18,220,000	11,420,000	11,651,000	15,598,156	13,809,777	149,618,903
Economic and Tourism Development	135,858,973	89,664,831	103,079,615	5,281,407	5,233,833	5,187,211	5,141,521	349,447,391
Information Technology	46,204,756	14,145,028	17,843,657	16,393,725	18,296,540	17,573,702	12,641,731	143,099,139
Parks and Recreation	63,891,276	9,538,033	8,877,055	8,952,362	9,279,772	9,359,344	9,441,124	119,338,966
Roadways	506,738,326	59,742,704	60,952,254	51,994,783	48,244,323	47,819,512	33,447,052	808,938,954
Schools	102,294,000	47,461,000	63,871,000	42,391,000	42,891,000	38,891,000	40,891,000	378,690,000
Sewer Utility	209,403,963	19,655,000	26,335,000	25,527,500	27,435,000	26,985,000	25,785,000	361,126,463
Storm Water	197,415,358	48,153,514	45,253,514	47,653,514	45,253,514	46,253,514	47,553,230	477,536,158
Water Utility	36,559,576	13,085,000	9,960,000	12,097,500	13,415,000	15,960,000	14,030,000	115,107,076
Total Capital Projects	1,484,083,436	394,745,267	374,721,768	247,367,064	242,986,310	236,165,712	235,278,708	3,215,348,265
Total Capital Improvement Program	1,484,083,436	394,745,267	374,721,768	247,367,064	242,986,310	236,165,712	235,278,708	3,215,348,265

Source: City of Virginia Beach, Virginia, *Adopted Capital. Improvement Program, Resource Management Plan FY 2018-19*, 16. https://www.vbgov.com/government/departments/budget-office-management-services/budget-archives/SiteAssets/Pages/default/FY%202018-19%20Adopted%20CIP%20-%20FINAL.pdf

the public works department. In smaller local governments, public works may be responsible for utility operations (water, wastewater, and storm drainage) in addition to its regular duties of street maintenance. The most logical locus, however, is the budget office, especially if it is separate from the finance department.

While preparation of the capital budget differs substantively from preparation of the operating budget, the technical aspects are similar. Both require timely and accurate revenue projections, a timetable, forms and supporting documentation, executive-level budget hearings, and final budget documents. Both also require close coordination with other departments; for capital budgeting, coordination with planning, engineering, utilities, and public works is essential. In larger governments where the capital budget unit is assigned responsibility for overseeing project construction and implementation, a contract administrator may be added.

Related to the location of responsibility for capital budget preparation is the question of who participates in selecting projects and what criteria should be used to decide on their inclusion in the CIP and capital budget. Because capital improvements are mostly public goods, political as well as financial and economic criteria inevitably influence project selection. The way a city or county council is elected, for example, has a significant bearing on the choice of projects included in a CIP. At-large council members are more inclined to support improvements for the good of the whole community, whereas district representatives are more preoccupied with the ensuring that their districts receive an equitable share of funding for capital projects. Thus, who participates in the capital planning process greatly influences the outcome.

Many jurisdictions use an interdepartmental capital allocation committee to review and rank proposals for inclusion in the CIP and capital budget. One common approach is to appoint a citizens task force to make recommendations to the council. Involving citizens in the evaluation phase allows for their meaningful participation in the process and may provide the foundation for public support if a bond referendum is necessary. Public finance scholar Jane Beckett-Camarata found evidence that when cities use a strategic planning process that assesses citizen priorities in conjunction with a capital budgeting process, they see a positive effect on per capita long-term debt, own-source revenue, and the general fund balance.[3]

Scope of duties In principle, the government unit that is responsible for capital budgeting should have responsibility for the full range of capital improvements funded from general revenues or general obligation (GO) debt—from planning to construction or acquisition to inventorying and monitoring their condition. In reality, duties will depend on the chief executive's preferences, the abilities of the director of the capital budgeting unit, and the number of staff members available to perform the tasks.

Not all capital projects are included in the CIP process. For example, because the projects in a tax increment financing (TIF) district are financed from dedicated tax revenues and debt, they are typically not integrated into the CIP; instead, each TIF district has its own planning process and capital budget. Large enterprise activities, such as a municipal electric department or other utility operations, may have separate capital planning processes because of their scope and dedicated sources of revenue. However, it is essential that these specialized planning processes be coordinated with the tax-supported CIP process in order to ensure that projects are coordinated (e.g., repaving of a street occurs after, not before, replacement of water lines) and that the full financial and operating impact of a project is determined.

Timing The final organizational issue is the timing of the capital budget cycle. Preparing the capital and operating budgets concurrently has the advantage of limiting the time spent on budget preparation, a boon to department heads. Presumably, the impact of capital spending on the operating budget (and vice versa) will be recognized more readily when the two cycles are concurrent.

On the other hand, one advantage of preparing the capital budget in the operating budget off-season (countercyclical to the operating budget cycle) is that it distributes the workload for staff more evenly throughout the year. Even under the best of circumstances, preparing an operating budget requires enormous amounts of energy and time; adding to this workload the task of drafting a capital budget may jeopardize the quality of deliberations on both budgets. Another advantage is that it reduces the amount of information that must be processed by lawmakers at one time. If, however, a government has a separate staff dedicated exclusively to capital budget matters, then preparing the two budgets concurrently is not just more feasible but actually preferable.

The timing decision is also affected by the source of funding. If a significant portion of the funding for capital improvements comes from dedicated (or earmarked) sources or from GO debt, a separate preparation and approval cycle is appropriate. But if a significant portion of that funding comes from current revenues in the general fund, concurrent preparation is preferable. Capital and operational priorities need to be evaluated together if they are competing for the same pool of funding.

A related timing issue involves using distinctive fiscal years for the operating and capital budgets. Some local governments have found it advantageous for internal control purposes to use an October 1 to September 30 fiscal year for their operating budgets, the same as the federal government, thereby reducing the complexity of reporting compliance with federal grants. They then use a calendar year for their capital budgets to better match the accounting cycles of private contractors.

The merits of a separate capital budget cycle

While the federal government and some states use a unified budget in which no distinction is made between the two classes of expenditures, most state and local governments segregate capital and operating expenditures into two distinct cycles and documents. The reasons for doing this are several.

Different types of expenditures The most obvious reason is that capital expenditures are fundamentally different from operating outlays. Capital spending is project specific whereas operating expenditures finance recurring programs, most of which have at least an implicit commitment from government for their continued provision.

Different funding sources In most cases, capital outlays originate from one-time sources, such as debt proceeds and grants from other levels of government that are earmarked for particular projects. Operating outlays primarily rely on recurring revenues, such as current taxes and service charges.

Different levels of risk Capital investment decisions carry much greater risk than operating decisions. Large sums of money are usually at stake in a capital project, and an error in the design or location of the project can result in disastrous political and economic consequences. For example, for a short distance the interstate highway through downtown Pittsburgh drops below the water level of the Monongahela River, which it parallels. During high-water periods, the highway must be closed because of flooding, and traffic must be diverted onto congested downtown streets. To prevent such costly and embarrassing mistakes, careful planning on all levels—federal, state, and local—is necessary prior to project implementation. In addition, the planning and design of capital facilities have long-term implications for the operating budget. For example, designing a public housing complex for energy efficiency and spending additional money up front for top-grade insulation will mean lower utility costs over the life of the structure.

Whereas an error in an operating budget can be revised the following year or even amended during the current year, errors made in planning and budgeting for a capital improvement can be corrected only at considerable expense—which in most cases is prohibitive. Capital projects, especially for infrastructure, tend to be interlinked, requiring careful attention to their sequencing. For example, a street resurfacing project may be preceded by the replacement of the water and sewer lines, depending on their condition. The planning and review period for capital projects, especially major construction projects, must be sufficiently long to evaluate the projects, assess their impact on the community, and acquire the funding for their completion. Often, the time needed for project design, permitting, and construction does not coincide with the terms of office of the elected officials who may have championed the project. Changes in the composition of a council or management may alter past priorities for capital projects.

Timing requirements At the local level, the uneven distribution of capital projects requires careful timing in order to maintain a stable property tax rate. Infrastructure improvements typically occur in cycles as a community experiences periods of growth. As the infrastructure ages, replacement costs begin to occur, and the cycle repeats itself. If debt financing is used, capital projects must be spaced so that bonds can be sold at intervals and debt service is maintained at a fairly stable level commensurate with the growth in the tax base. Governments pressed by economic and political considerations may accelerate capital spending to stimulate their economy in the expectation that moderately higher tax rates in the near term will be offset by future economic development.

State and local governments that choose not to issue debt must give even more careful attention to the timing of project initiation in order to keep tax rates stable. These governments rely on current revenues, especially earmarked taxes, plus money set aside in capital reserves to finance new construction or renovations. Whether they issue debt or use revenues, governments wishing to maintain stable tax rates will find separating capital and operating decisions into two distinct but complementary cycles to be a useful planning and management aid.

Monitoring A separate capital budget cycle provides for more careful monitoring of project implementation. Once the capital budget is approved by the governing body, spending can begin on the authorized projects, subject to the availability of funds. In larger governments, the capital budget unit not only will prepare the budget but also may help departments oversee the acquisition of capital improvements. A central capital budgeting staff can bring greater continuity and consistency to project implementation than can departments working alone. Continuity and consistency, in turn, lead to better management of government resources.

1 Gerald Seeber, personal communication with author, March 2007.

Developing a capital planning and budget policy

Just as a budget policy statement can be an effective managerial tool for institutionalizing good budget practices and channeling conflict in constructive directions, so too can a capital planning and budgeting policy statement. Such a statement provides the financial standards to guide deliberations for both the executive and legislative branches and thus becomes the conscience of the organization in budget deliberations. It also helps resolve many of the conflicts identified in Figure 11–1. The sidebar below lists possible elements for inclusion in a state or local government's capital planning and budgeting policy.

As a matter of policy, every government should prepare a CIP, even if it integrates capital and operating outlays into one unified budget. A CIP provides an invaluable tool for systematically reviewing all projects, comparing proposed new projects with those already in the plan, and then repeating the cycle annually as the proposed project moves closer to inclusion in the capital budget and, ultimately, acquisition. If a CIP is used, all proposals for capital investment must go through that process in order to ensure integrity in the CIP. Figure 11–3 is an example of a sample policy statement from the City of San Luis Obispo, California.

The capital budgeting process

The demand for capital acquisitions far exceeds a government's capacity to finance them, which makes it necessary to ration funding to those acquisitions with the highest priority. How governments rank and select projects is the crux of the preparation phase of a capital budget.

The capital budgeting process, like its counterpart on the operating side, must screen the myriad proposals, which is done through a series of reviews in which advocates must justify their spending requests. And like the operating budget cycle, the cycle for capital spending is information-intensive, relying on data collected throughout the process to justify each

Recommended elements of a capital planning and budgeting policy statement

1. The capital improvement plan (CIP)
    a. What is the planning period?
    b. How inclusive should the CIP be?
    c. Will expenditures for maintenance and/or renovation be included in the capital budget?
2. Organizational issues
    a. What unit will be responsible for preparing the CIP and capital budget?
    b. Should the capital budget be prepared concurrently with the operating budget or during the off-season?
    c. Will a capital allocation committee be used to evaluate and recommend a ranking of proposed projects? Will the committee include citizens?
3. Project evaluation
    a. What procedures will be used to evaluate and rank proposed projects?
    b. What criteria will be used to evaluate and rank proposed projects?
4. Funding sources
    a. Will debt be used for capital projects, and under what circumstances?
    b What type of bond (GO or revenue) will be used, and under what circumstances?
    c. How much debt, if any, can be incurred?
    d. Under what conditions will grant money be used?
    e. How will unused balances in the capital project funds be used?

Figure 11–3 Sample policy statement, San Luis Obispo, California

Capital improvement management

A. **CIP Projects: $15,000 or More.** Construction projects and equipment purchases which cost $25,000 or more will be included in the Capital Improvement Plan (CIP); minor capital outlays of less than $25,000 will be included with the operating program budgets. Such projects are accounted for in the Capital Outlay Fund.

B. **CIP Purpose.** The purpose of the CIP is to systematically plan, schedule, and finance capital projects to ensure cost-effectiveness as well as conformance with established policies. The CIP is a five-year plan organized into the same functional groupings used for the operating programs. The CIP will reflect a balance between capital replacement projects that repair, replace or enhance existing facilities, equipment or infrastructure; and capital facility projects that significantly expand or add to the City's existing fixed assets.

C. **Project Manager.** Every CIP project will have a project manager who will prepare the project proposal, ensure that required phases are completed on schedule, authorize all project expenditures, ensure that all regulations and laws are observed, and periodically report project status.

D. **CIP Review Committee.** Headed by the City Manager or designee, this Committee will review project proposals, determine project phasing, recommend project managers, review and evaluate the draft CIP budget document, and report CIP project progress on an ongoing basis.

E. **CIP Phases.** The CIP will emphasize project planning, with projects progressing through at least two and up to ten of the following phases:

1. ***Designate.*** Appropriates funds based on projects designated for funding by the Council through adoption of the Financial Plan.
2. ***Study.*** Concept design, site selection, feasibility analysis, schematic design, environmental determination, property appraisals, scheduling, grant application, grant approval, specification preparation for equipment purchases.
3. ***Environmental Review.*** EIR preparation, other environmental studies.
4. ***Real Property Acquisitions.*** Property acquisition for projects, if necessary.
5. ***Site Preparation.*** Demolition, hazardous materials abatements, other pre-construction work.
6. ***Design.*** Final design, plan and specification preparation and construction cost estimation.
7. ***Construction.*** Construction contracts.
8. ***Construction Management.*** Contract project management and inspection, soils and material tests, other support services during construction.
9. ***Equipment Acquisitions.*** Vehicles, heavy machinery, computers, office furnishings, other equipment items acquired and installed independently from construction contracts.
10. ***Debt Service.*** Installment payments of principal and interest for completed projects funded through debt financings. Expenditures for this project phase are included in the Debt Service section of the Financial Plan.

Generally, it will become more difficult for a project to move from one phase to the next. As such, more projects will be studied than will be designed, and more projects will be designed than will be constructed or purchased during the term of the CIP.

proposal's inclusion in the final budget. The process has three stages: planning, budgeting and financing, and implementation.

Planning for capital improvements

Because of the long-lived nature of capital assets, the planning phase is the most critical. During planning, proposed projects are identified, evaluated, costed, and ranked. Unlike the allocation process in the operating budget cycle, the allocation process for capital items closely links budgeting with land use planning. In fact, a city's or county's master plan for land use should provide the direction for most of the decisions on infrastructure spending.

Figure 11–3 Sample policy statement, San Luis Obispo, California, *continued*

F. **Insurance Benefit Fund.** The City will establish an Insurance Benefit Fund for the purpose of setting funds aside to manage the fluctuations in liability and worker's compensation insurance programs. A reserve within the Insurance Benefit Fund for the Liability Excess Insurance Program will be maintained at approximately 75% funded confidence level based on the prior five-year average claims experience.

G. **CIP Budget Carryover.** The City's annual CIP appropriation for study, design, acquisition and/or construction is based on the projects designated by the Council through adoption of the Financial Plan. Adoption of the Financial Plan CIP appropriation does not automatically authorize funding for specific project phases. This authorization generally occurs only after the preceding project phase has been completed and approved by the Council and costs for the succeeding phases have been fully developed. Accordingly, project appropriations are generally made when contracts are awarded. If project costs at the time of bid award are less than the budgeted amount, the balance will be unappropriated and returned to fund balance or allocated to another project. If project costs at the time of bid award are greater than budget amounts, five basic options are available:

1. Eliminate the project.
2. Defer the project for consideration to the next Financial Plan period.
3. Rescope or change the phasing of the project to meet the existing budget.
4. Transfer funding from another specified, lower priority project.
5. Appropriate additional resources as necessary from fund balance.

H. **CIP Budget Carryover.** Appropriations for CIP projects lapse three years after budget adoption. Projects which lapse from lack of project account appropriations may be resubmitted for inclusion in a subsequent CIP. Project accounts, which have been appropriated, will not lapse until completion of the project phase.

I. **Program Objectives.** Project phases will be listed as objectives in the program narratives of the programs, which manage the projects..

J. **Public Art.** CIP projects will be evaluated during the budget process and prior to each phase for conformance with the City's public art policy, which generally requires that 1% of eligible project construction costs be set aside for public art. Excluded from this requirement are underground projects, utility infrastructure projects, funding from outside agencies, and costs other than construction such as study, environmental review, design, site preparation, land acquisition and equipment purchases.

It is generally preferred that public art be incorporated directly into the project, but this is not practical or desirable for all projects; in this case, an in-lieu contribution to public art will be made. To ensure that funds are adequately budgeted for this purpose regardless of whether public art will be directly incorporated into the project, funds for public art will be identified separately in the CIP.

K. **General Plan Consistency Review.** The Planning Commission will review the Preliminary CIP for consistency with the General Plan and provide is findings to the Council prior to adoption.

Source: City of San Luis Obispo, California, 2017-19 Financial Plan, B1-13-B1-15. http://www.slocity.org/Home/ShowDocument?id=15625

Who participates in the selection and ranking of capital requests greatly affects the outcome. Regardless of the chief executive's style of management, use of an interdepartmental capital allocation committee to examine and rank each proposal is advisable, especially where individual projects compete for a limited amount of available funding. The committee's recommendations should then be forwarded to the chief executive, who makes a final recommendation to the council.

Inventorying existing capital assets An effective capital budgeting process begins with an inventory of the government's existing stock of capital investments and an evaluation of their current condition.

Public administrators know firsthand the difficulty of obtaining funding for maintenance and repair. One reason for this difficulty is the absence of any public interest group to lobby for such funding. Politically, new construction possesses much greater appeal than the renovation or even repair of existing assets, and so it receives priority in the funding process and squeezes out funding for maintenance projects. One of the sources of conflict illustrated in Figure 11–1 is this competition between outlays for maintenance and funding for new construction. As Michael Pagano has noted, it is far easier for decision makers to eliminate funding for maintenance and repair because such investments are less visible and less politically sensitive and, unlike other budget reductions, have no immediate repercussions on service delivery.[4] Yet investing in maintenance may provide returns that greatly exceed comparable investment in new acquisitions. Thus, a capital budget policy statement should clarify the priority of maintenance investment over new construction.

Pagano calls for local governments to link the capital budget to maintenance items in the operating budget and to fund maintenance through the capital budget, using long-term debt if the benefits accrue to more than one year.[5] In this way, a government can forestall the premature deterioration of its public facilities and increase their useful life. In regions where populations are stable or declining, investing in maintenance and renovation makes much more financial sense than investing in new construction. Unfortunately, federal policy, especially in the area of highway construction, has generally favored new construction over maintenance.

One approach managers use to encourage investment in maintenance and repair is the preparation of a comprehensive inventory of **fixed assets** including infrastructure. In the past, governments made little effort to maintain an inventory of their assets, the original cost of those assets, their current condition, or the cost of replacement. However, now that Governmental Accounting Standards Board Statement No. 34 (GASB 34), *Basic Financial Statements—and Management's Discussion and Analysis—for State and Local Governments,* requires state and local governments to better account for these assets, such an inventory has the additional benefit of providing the data needed to comply with those reporting requirements.

Information on the condition of existing capital assets helps illustrate to citizens and lawmakers whether previous investment in maintenance and repair is paying off. It also reduces the "squeaky wheel" phenomenon in the allocation of limited funding for capital improvements. It can be an indispensable managerial aid in building consensus on spending priorities. Most important, an inventory and condition assessment give legitimacy to investing in maintenance and repair.

The capital improvement plan (CIP) Most state and local governments prepare a rolling CIP that spans a multiyear period and provides itemized details on projects they wish to undertake during those years. Some governments plan for as few as three years, others for as many as ten years; five years is a common time frame. The first year of the CIP becomes the proposed capital budget for the forthcoming year.

For multiyear projects, such as major road construction, the CIP identifies the year in which the project is to begin, the expected cost for each year of the project, the sources of funding, and the expected completion date. Because organizations rarely have enough money to meet all their capital needs, a CIP allows decision makers to schedule the most pressing needs. Each year, the CIP is updated, revenue and expenditure estimates for the outlying years are revised, new projects may be added to the five-year time frame, and projects already in the plan may be dropped or delayed as other, more pressing requests take priority. Annual repetition forces administrators and legislators to reevaluate each project more than once and to judge the merits and urgency of new capital requests against those already in the CIP. While the governing body must adopt the capital budget as an appropriation, it does not necessarily endorse or even review the CIP. If it does endorse the CIP, implementation will depend on the availability of funding and is subject to revision in subsequent years.

A few requests may require immediate approval for funding because of their urgency, and so they may move to the current year without going through the multiyear review process. However, if this happens repeatedly, the CIP loses much of its value as a planning device. The primary benefit of the CIP is that it forces decision makers to examine the full range of projects and rank them according to priority and urgency. It also forces the finance office to identify revenue sources and, if debt is used, to schedule the sale of a sufficient but not excessive number of bonds.

While casual observation may suggest that preparing the CIP proceeds rather mechanically, in fact it is a highly political process. The capital budgeting cycle formally begins with a call for project proposals by the budget office, followed by deliberations on project selection.[6] Proposals come from both within and outside the organization, but most originate from departments and agencies—most particularly, public works (street improvements), utilities (water, wastewater, sanitation), and planning (as part of the master plan). Citizen complaints are another source of requests for capital spending, although these requests are likely to be funneled through city agencies. A third source is the campaign promises of elected officials. Community-based interest groups are also an important source of proposals. One fact is certain: the number of proposals will greatly exceed the ability of the government to finance them all.

Selecting projects for the CIP A lot is at stake when it comes to funding a project. The location of a new highway and its major intersections can mean a windfall in increased values to property owners whose property abuts the project. The bid specifications for an expensive fire truck or a fleet of police vehicles can determine which manufacturer will be selected to provide the equipment. Having in place a well-managed project selection process that considers the impact on long-term community needs and not just political priorities helps to sustain economic growth and benefits the quality of life.[7]

Establishing priorities In a democracy, the political process, through the election of candidates, helps define a community's values and priorities. In the context of capital planning, these values are reflected in the priorities of the chief executive who, in consultation with the governing body, initially establishes the broad priorities for capital allocation. For example, an older city or county with a shrinking employment base may link capital planning to redevelopment projects designed to attract new industries. A mayor in another city may focus on neighborhood revitalization centered around the construction or renovation of school buildings.

Every government has its own protocol for selecting capital projects. The leadership in one community may specify several service areas (streets, storm drainage, and parkland) that will receive capital funding, while the leadership in another community may target investment for broad categories, such as disaster preparedness. The important point is that it is up to a local government's political leadership to specify the general capital spending priorities of that government.

Ranking proposals The next stage in the project selection process, ranking proposals, begins with the identification of possible projects for inclusion in the CIP. It is essential that all requests for inclusion be submitted on standardized forms.

Once the budget office has received all the requests, the capital allocation committee begins the critical task of ranking the proposals. Every local government uses stated or unstated criteria—political, economic, or administrative—to evaluate the projects being con-

Capital Project Priority Ranking System, Washington County, Maryland

During the review process the CIP Committee prioritizes projects based on the County's broad goals, department priorities, anticipated funding sources, and the priority-ranking matrix. The priority-ranking matrix is composed of fourteen scored and weighted criteria, which is the basis for assigning projects into one of the five priority-ranking categories.

The fourteen scored and weighted ranking criteria used by Washington County are:[1]

1. Legal Mandates
2. Public Health and Safety
3. Environmental Impact
4. Conformity to County Commissioners Goals and Plans
5. Conformity to Agency, Department, and Jurisdictional Plans
6. Community Support
7. Project Cost
8. Funding
9. Operating Budget Impact: Cost/Benefit.
10. Preservation of Facility
11. Project Life
12. Economic Impact
13. Recreational, Cultural, or Aesthetic Value
14. Percent of Population Benefiting

After the projects are scored and weighted using the above criteria, the projects are then categorized based on the score into Priority 1 through Priority 5. The priority category definitions are as follows:

Priority 1 - Projects needed to comply with a court order or legislative mandate, and/or projects that are critical to the health, safety, and general welfare of County citizens.

Priority 2 - Projects essential to the general welfare of the community, operating or maintaining of a physical facility, but not critical relative to other projects.

Priority 3 - Projects that provide a public operational improvement or are important in relation to County financial capabilities, needs, or other program requirements.

Priority 4 - Projects that provide for necessary maintenance or replacement, but where deferral will not result in significantly increased cost to the County.

Priority 5 - Projects that conflict with the master plan and/or projects for which there are concerns related to serious need, cost, justification, or timing.

After all proposed projects are prioritized using these criteria, the CIP Committee (1) reviews the project ranking report for reasonableness; (2) checks for any projects that appear out of order; (3) determines if there are any linkages between projects; (4) evaluates if there are any advantages to having projects done concurrently; (5) ascertains if there are any projects dependent on one another; and (6) reviews the project's impact on the operating budget. Adjustments to the final ranking may be necessary based on this extensive Capital Improvement Plan prioritization process.

The CIP Committee provides an enterprise-wide view and prioritizes proposed projects while balancing project requests against known County objectives. After their review is complete, the CIP Committee presents the Ten-Year Capital Improvement Plan to the Board of County Commissioners. The County Commissioners review the recommended Ten-Year Capital Improvement Plan during budget workshops and at a public hearing prior to budget adoption.

1 The following list of criteria omits the details provided by the source document.

Source: Washington County, Maryland, *Fiscal Year 2018 Ten Year Capital Improvement Plan*, 16-18, http://washco-md.net/budget_finance/pdf/2018-2027CapImprovPlan.pdf.

sidered for funding. The accompanying sidebar lists eleven commonly used criteria. Ideally, the criteria are clearly specified in a capital planning policy statement. Using selection criteria to make decisions requires that specific indicators be developed.

Many proposals will emerge out of a local government's various planning processes—plans for land use, utilities installation, facilities, information technology, and transportation. Because these proposals have already undergone extensive deliberations, they often find their way more quickly into the CIP.

When prioritizing proposed projects, governments may choose to use a weighted ranking system to give more weight to those projects that address the preferences and priorities of lawmakers or the community. Communities wishing to stress economic development will give greater weight to economic factors; communities wishing to promote quality of life will give relatively greater weight to recreational, cultural, and aesthetic values. The weights may even be altered periodically as the priorities of the community and lawmakers change. In still other cases, communities may want to leverage local funds with state or federal grants or private funding. While using external funds enables local governments to lower their cost for the improvements, such an approach to project selection skews priorities to favor those of the state or federal agencies providing the funds over those of the community.

Finalizing the CIP The final step in the planning phase is preparing the final CIP. Citizens should have an opportunity to provide input, be it in a public hearing, on a citizen advisory committee, and/or through citizen representation on the capital allocation committee. It is also advisable that the CIP be submitted to the governing body for review and approval. Approval does not authorize money for any of the projects in the plan, but it adds credibility to the planning process, involves the council in the process, and legitimizes the work of the capital allocation committee and chief executive on the CIP.

Budgeting for capital improvements

While the CIP provides a multiyear inventory of proposed projects that a government anticipates undertaking and proposed sources of financing, the capital budget provides detailed information on the actual design, cost, and financing of projects recommended for the forthcoming year. The appropriation adopting the capital budget gives the executive branch the same authorization for capital improvement expenditures that the appropriation adopting the operating budget gives for the recurring expenditures in the delivery of government services.

Preparing the capital budget Preparing the capital budget document includes the following tasks:

- Putting together a capital budget manual that contains a calendar or flowchart of the process (see, e.g., Figure 11–4, a flowchart of the process used by Fairfax County, Virginia, for preparing and approving its capital projects), instructions, and forms for departments to use when completing their requests
- Determining the exact costs of each project
- Providing a detailed estimate of the revenues, both recurring and from bond sales, that will be available for the budget period
- Bundling debt needs and scheduling a voter referendum, where necessary, to authorize debt funding; obtaining voter approval on any bond sales, if required
- Holding a public hearing on the proposed capital budget before it is approved.

Capital budget manual The capital budget manual, like its counterpart on the operating budget side, provides departments with detailed instructions and the required forms for completing their capital spending requests. It also contains a calendar outlining the timetable

Figure 11–4 Flowchart of the preparation and approval of capital projects, Fairfax County, Virginia

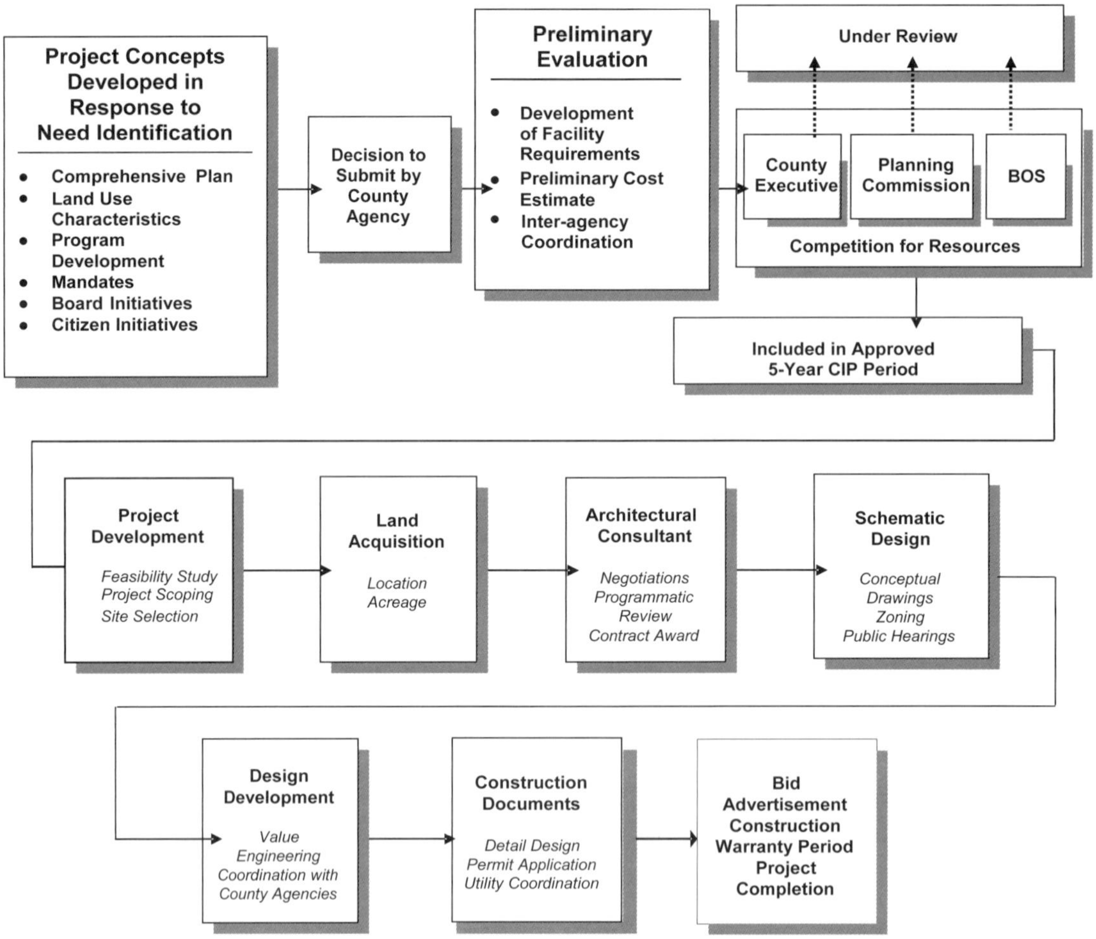

Source: Fairfax County, Virginia, *FY 2019–FY 2023 Advertised Capital Improvement Program*, 10, https://www.fairfaxcounty.gov/budget/capital-improvement-program-cip.

for budget preparation. As was the case with the operating budget, the calendar includes a call for proposals, a review of those proposals by the budget office, executive-level review and hearings, and a budget workshop for legislators prior to adoption.

Cost projections Initially, requests for inclusion in the CIP are ranked by the capital allocation committee for each year in the planning period. Of course, because of limited revenues, only a few requests will be funded. Up to this point, the estimates of project costs used in the CIP have likely been based on departmental projections prepared in consultation with the budget office or on preliminary engineering studies. As a proposal becomes a firm candidate for funding, the government seeks detailed cost estimates, often by contracting with a private consultant who prepares a detailed cost projection.

If the project involves the construction of a new building or the renovation of an existing one, an architectural firm will first be employed to prepare drawings of the facility, and an engineering firm will then prepare specifications for the project and an estimate of the costs.

Figure 11–5 Capital project request, Garland, Texas

PAGE NO: P08	*Continuing Project*	CITY OF GARLAND - 2018 CAPITAL PROJECT REQUEST	*Amounts in 000's $	COUNCIL DISTRICT(S): All
DEPARTMENT: PARKS & RECREATION		PROJECT TITLE: SKATING/SKATEBOARD FACILITY	PROJECT NO(S). 18330	ACCOUNT NO(S). 614-2499-1833004

PROJECT DESCRIPTION

This funding provides for design and construction of a skate park at Central Park.

FUNDING SOURCE(S)

2004 Bond Fund	$ 500,000
2018 Certificates of Oblig.	590,000
TOTAL FUNDED	$ 1,090,000
UNFUNDED	$ 60,000
PROJECT TOTAL	$ 1,150,000

IMPACT ON OPERATING BUDGET

✔ Will Impact
☐ Will Not Impact
# of Positions ____

Annual Cost/(Savings):	
Personnel	
Operations	7,500
Capital	
Total	$7,500

IMPACT EXPLANATION

The Skating/Skateboard facility will impact the Operating Budget by approximately $7,500 per year starting in 2019-20. This project will require funding for additional turf and trim maintenance, litter pickup, facility repairs, and site furnishings.

STRIP MAP

*PROJECT COSTS	Thru 12-2017	2018	2019	2020	2021	2022	2023 to Completion	Total
Design	16	124						140
Land/Right-of-Way								
Construction	48	902	60					1,010
Landscaping								
Equip. & Furnish.								
Other								
TOTAL COSTS	64	1,026	60					1,150

*SOURCE OF FUNDS	Thru 12-2017	2018	2019	2020	2021	2022	2023 to Completion	Total
Current Funds								
GO's/Com Paper Issued	450							450
GO's Unissued		50						50
RB's/Com Paper								
Certificates of Obligation		590						590
Other								
Unfunded			60					60
TOTAL SOURCES	450	640	60					1,150

PROJECT SCHEDULE	START	FINISH
Design	12/2015	2/2018
Land/Right-of-Way		
Construction	11/2017	6/2019
Finish Out		
Other		
TOTAL SCHEDULE	12/2015	6/2019

Source: City of Garland, Texas, *2018 Capital Improvement Program,* P08. http://garland-prod.civica.granicusops.com/civicax/filebank/blobdload.aspx?BlobID=30664

On non-income-producing projects, such as street improvements or building renovations, the evaluation is confined to a detailed estimate of the costs. For income-producing projects, such as utility improvements or a parking garage, the government must determine their economic viability. One widely used technique is the **payback period**—that is, the number of years required before the project pays back in net earnings the initial capital investment. The longer the payback period, the less economically viable the project. Other, more sophisticated techniques, such as NPV and cost-benefit analysis, may also be used.

In the City of Garland, Texas, each capital project request shows the project schedule: the beginning and completion dates for project design, right-of-way or land acquisition, construction, landscaping, and equipment or other furnishings (Figure 11–5). In addition, the Garland budget includes an assessment of the project's impact on the operating budget, if any. For multiyear projects, the form shows the project cost by year; the amount of money, if any, spent thus far on the project; and summary information on funding sources.

Revenue estimations State and local governments usually rely on a variety of revenue sources to fund each capital project. As seen in Figure 11–5, these sources can include current revenues. During the budget preparation phase, detailed estimates of expected revenues must be made. The budget office likely has been making such estimates all along and has a reasonably good idea of the amount of money available from current funds (taxes, fund balances, grants, special assessments, and service charges). As the budget office begins to finalize the capital budget request for legislative consideration, the accuracy of these estimates increases in importance; this is because capital budgets at the state and local levels, like operating budgets, are revenue driven. The revenue forecasts prepared for the operating budget affect the capital budget to the extent that current revenues are used to finance at least part of the capital budget. For utility system or public housing improvements, accurate estimates of consumer demand are also essential to accurate estimates of the revenue stream that will service future debt obligations as they come due.

Debt planning The budget office must determine early in the cycle how much money must be borrowed to fund capital projects in the forthcoming year. For most local governments, debt for all general fund projects planned for that year should be bundled into one GO bond issue. As a rule, the cost of preparing the documentation needed to support each sale makes it uneconomical to enter the bond market more often than necessary; smaller governments may go several years between bond sales. In the case of enterprise fund projects, a revenue bond will usually be sold once the project's financial viability has been determined, to be paid off using the future revenues brought in by the finished project. Usually, revenue bond issues are not bundled but are sold separately for each project. (More discussion on planning the sale of debt follows later in this chapter.)

Public hearing The final step in the capital budgeting cycle is a public hearing on the proposed spending plan. This hearing is usually combined with the hearing on the CIP so that citizens have an opportunity to comment not only on the projects being proposed for the budget year but also on those being considered for future years, as listed in the CIP.

Appropriating for capital outlays The governing body must approve the capital budget before implementation can begin. A. John Vogt describes three methods for adopting the capital budget.[8] In the first method, the governing body adopts the capital budget as part of the annual or (biennial) operating budget; under this approach, multiyear projects are funded only one year at a time, creating potential uncertainty in project financing. In the second method, the governing body adopts a separate capital budget and appropriates sufficient budget authority to see the projects through to completion (also known as a sum-sufficient basis). In the third method, the governing body approves a bond referendum, although a separate appropriation for each project is usually still required by law.

For larger improvements, appropriations are often made in three phases: planning and design, construction, and close-out.

Capital spending's impact on the operating budget Capital investment decisions made today have long-term impacts on operating costs. Managers must carefully assess those impacts as part of the evaluation of each capital improvement. Will the improvement increase operating costs and, if so, by how much? Will the operating budget be able to absorb the additional costs? Experienced managers know that while a proposed project may have sufficient funding for construction or acquisition, it may be delayed because the operating budget is unable to absorb the additional cost once the improvement has been implemented. Again, Garland, Texas, requires departments proposing a project to include an estimate of the impact on the operating budget. That impact may be an increase in operating costs, as in the example in Figure 11–5, or a decrease through reduced maintenance or other savings.

The effect of capital spending on the operating budget varies across public services, depending on the extent to which the service is labor- or capital-intensive. Capital purchases that replace staff or older facilities reduce future operating costs. New automated garbage trucks may reduce the number of sanitation workers needed. But capital purchases that add new facilities or services will also increase operating costs. Labor-intensive services such as police protection will be more sensitive to capital expenditures that expand capacity than will capital-intensive services such as highway maintenance. A new police substation must be staffed and operated, whereas a repaired road will require little further attention, at least in the short term, and may in fact result in lower maintenance costs in the operating budget. Labor-intensive services such as the police station will also require immediate operating expenditures, while capital-intensive services such as a new road may require operating expenditures (for maintenance) only after the passage of time.

While its effect on the operating budget may vary by project, capital spending is never inversely related to operating expenditures. In other words, in the aggregate, capital outlays mean higher future operating costs, especially for labor-intensive services.[9]

Financing capital improvements

The CIP includes a projection of the sources of revenue for financing scheduled capital improvements. The capital project requests in the CIP for Garland (Figure 11-5) include a section for "sources of funds," which lists the revenues that will be used to fund this particular project.

State and local governments pursue either a **pay-as-you-go** or a **pay-as-you-use** strategy. Governments that use a pay-as-you-go approach issue no debt; they rely instead on the current revenues described in the accompanying sidebar to fund all improvements. However, when the need for public improvements outstrips the current revenues available to fund them, as often happens in rapidly growing jurisdictions, governments have no choice but to pursue a pay-as-you-use strategy. They issue debt through such devices as municipal bonds in order to raise the needed funding, and they repay the debt over the life of the asset as the asset is used.

Under pay-as-you-go financing, current taxpayers bear the full cost of a facility that will benefit current as well as future residents. Under pay-as-you-use financing, taxpayers who benefit from the improvement (e.g., a major highway) are also the ones paying the debt service. By matching users with payment, debt financing promotes **intergenerational equity.** Another advantage of debt financing is that interest on state and local municipal bonds issued for a public purpose as defined by the federal tax code is exempt from federal income taxation.

Strategies and revenues used for financing capital improvements

Pay-as-you-go financing

- Current taxes, especially those linked to a particular service, such as gasoline taxes earmarked for highway improvements
- Other own-source revenues, such as utility charges
- Grants from the state or federal government
- Reserves accumulated over time in a replacement fund or as retained earnings in a utility fund
- Development impact fees

Pay-as-you-use financing

- Bonds or other government-issued debt instruments
- Special assessments on property owners benefiting from the improvement
- Grants from the state or federal government

This exemption constitutes an in-kind cash subsidy from the federal government to state and local governments because investors are willing to loan them money at lower interest rates. As long as the repayment of the debt does not exceed the life of the asset, pay-as-you-use financing is recommended.

Financing for a capital project typically comes from a number of sources, including debt. Improvements to utility services (water, wastewater, heat, and solid-waste collection) should be financed through service charges levied on users or through impact fees on new development for projects that expand the system's capacity to accommodate growth. Bonds may be issued to acquire funds for construction and then be repaid with fees and charges levied on users as the bonds come due.

Using debt Debt financing allows a government to spread out payment over the life of the asset, thereby shifting the cost of servicing the debt to those who use the asset. At the same time, however, it raises several issues: accountability for the debt, term of the debt, and amount of the debt. Thus, if a state or local government chooses to use debt, it should adopt a debt policy statement spelling out the procedures for issuing debt, the purposes for which debt may be used, the role of citizens in approving the uses of debt proceeds, and the maximum amount of debt (or debt service) the government will incur. A policy statement reassures investors that the government is committed to honoring its obligations and will protect citizens from too large a tax burden.

Accountability Repayment of outstanding debt must have priority in the operating budget. Annual debt service obligations (principal and interest) must be met before all other obligations, including the payroll. Failure to make a debt payment constitutes a **default** on that debt, and a government that defaults loses the confidence of investors and will find it difficult to issue any debt in the future.

To promote accountability in the repayment of tax-supported debt, governments usually establish debt service funds, in which they deposit money from tax levies that will be used to pay interest and principal as the debt comes due. Annually, as part of the operating budget process, sufficient taxes or service charges are levied so that money can be put into the debt service fund to cover the obligations for that year.

Term of debt Governments occasionally fall into the trap of using debt to cover a shortfall in current revenues, hoping that the next fiscal year will bring better economic times and an increase in operating revenues. However, long-term debt should never be used to cover revenue shortfalls. The rule of thumb is that long-term debt should be used only to acquire assets with a lifetime longer than one year, and repayment of the debt should not extend beyond the life of the asset. If a resurfaced city street is expected to last ten years, the bonds used to finance that project should be paid off in ten years or less. (To cover cash flow needs, local governments do routinely issue short-term notes and **commercial paper**, which are tools for treasury management, not debt financing.)

The longer the life of the debt (i.e., the longer the maturity), the more costly it becomes for the government to borrow. This is because investors demand higher interest rates to compensate for the greater uncertainty of future market developments. Moreover, few investors are willing to commit their money for longer periods, regardless of the life of the asset. Thus, most state and local debt does not exceed a maturity of twenty-five years.

Amount of debt Although debt can be a powerful stimulus to economic development, overburdening a community with long-term obligations can easily defuse that stimulus. As a rule of thumb, the annual cost of servicing GO debt (principal and interest) should not exceed 20 percent of the operating budget—a guideline that is reportedly used by the credit-rating industry. Research suggests that a substitution effect exists between taxes for debt service and those for general operations: when a jurisdiction must increase the amount of tax revenues spent for debt service rather than increasing taxes, it decreases the amount of money spent on other services.[10] If a government is experiencing rapid population growth, it may need to temporarily exceed the 20-percent limit, but if it is experiencing no growth or a shrinking tax base, it should reduce its debt service obligation to 15 percent or less of the operating budget.

Debt capacity for revenue bonds is a more complex issue because it depends on the revenue-producing capabilities of each project. Obviously, the annual debt service for any particular project must not exceed what the project is capable of generating in revenue in excess of operating costs. Several cities faced bankruptcy during the Great Recession of 2007–2009 because of their inability to repay debt on overly optimistic expectations from revenue-producing ventures. For facilities in which the government acts as a monopolist, such as water and wastewater, prices can be set to produce enough revenue to cover annual operating costs and debt service, although political pressure is strong to keep utility rates low. But other types of facilities—parking garages and recreational facilities, for example—may have to compete with nongovernmental providers, and the local government may not control the market. In such cases the government must carefully analyze the market, users' willingness to pay, estimated revenues, and the amount of debt those revenues will cover.

Revenue vs. GO bonds Municipal debt is classified according to the type of revenue pledged as the source of repayment. A GO bond represents an unlimited pledge by the government to use all available sources of revenue and taxing powers—its "full faith and credit"—to repay the obligation. Often, state law requires governments to first obtain voter approval through a referendum before issuing GO bonds.

By contrast, a revenue bond represents a limited pledge of revenue sources to the repayment of qualifying bonds. Usually, revenue bonds are used to finance a revenue-producing project, such as a public housing complex, public hospital, toll road, water or utility facilities and lines, or a parking garage. Only revenue earned from the project can be used to repay the bonds used to build it. The government does not pledge its full faith and credit to the repayment of these bonds, although it may subsidize the project with general tax revenues, especially during the development phase. Because of the more limited pledge, voter approval is usually not required, and the bonds incur slightly higher interest rates because of the higher risk of default. However, investors can see a clear link between the use of the debt and the repayment of the bonds, which normally increases their confidence that the government will repay the debt.

Although most governments could incur more GO than revenue debt because of their greater capacity to repay GO bonds, GO debt constitutes only one-third of the total municipal debt burden across the nation.[11] One reason for this is that GO bonds are only used for public facilities that have no revenue-producing capabilities—for example, streets, school buildings, storm drainage, and general-purposes equipment such as public safety vehicles. Especially among cities, these facilities represent a smaller portion of the budget than revenue-producing facilities such as housing, utilities, and public transit. Another reason that revenue bonds are used more often than GO bonds is that they do not require voter approval.

Occasionally, governments must cover not a budget shortfall but a temporary cash shortfall, which is created by the mismatch between the inflow of revenues and the outflow of disbursements. For such purposes, governments usually issue short-term notes or commercial paper, which have a life of less than a year and are almost always repaid from revenues received in the current year.

Planning the sale of debt When planning the sale of debt, the finance officer must decide on the type of debt to issue, the amount and maturity structure of the issue, and the method for selling the securities. The goal in this phase is to negotiate terms for the sale that are the least burdensome for the government but still appealing to investors. Whether the debt is acquired from a number of private investors and investment firms or directly from a bank, the government will issue bonds that specify the terms of the agreement between the lender and borrower (the type of revenue pledged by the government to repay the bond, the interest rate, maturity date, and par or face value). The larger the debt being acquired, the less likely that the government will acquire it from one single bank or other lender.

Municipal bonds are almost always sold with serial maturities. That is, the bonds mature, or come due, in a series over the life of the debt. A basic rule in debt financing is that the higher the demand for municipal bonds, the lower the interest rate. By issuing bonds in serial form, with smaller par values (e.g., $5,000) and with relatively short maturities, local governments can broaden the pool of potential investors and thereby increase demand for their bonds.

Selling the bond issue Prospective investors expect full disclosure of the issuer's financial condition, all the pertinent facts on the project being financed by the debt issue, and the local government's legal pledge of revenue to repay the bonds. To increase investor interest, this information is prepared and distributed in an official statement four to six weeks prior to the bond sale. Governments often contract with a professional financial adviser to assist in the preparation of the official statement. Once the bonds have been sold, the terms of the sale (interest rates, maturities) are incorporated into the final official statement.

Local governments may try to increase investor interest in their bonds by obtaining **credit enhancement**. For instance, they may purchase the backing of a third party for the bond issue, which means that, should the local government default on some or all of its debt, the third party assumes responsibility for repaying the obligation. Third-party backing reassures investors that their money will be repaid. Unfortunately, during the Great Recession the volume of defaults caused a collapse in the industry that has, as yet, not recovered. Kenneth Kriz and Marc Joffe found evidence that municipal bond insurance was not beneficial to most issuers and that lower-rated issues were the most likely to benefit but the least likely to afford the cost of insurance.[12]

A more common form of credit backing is the purchase of a letter of credit (LOC) from a bank. In the event that the local government cannot pay its debt service, the bank extends it a line of credit on which the government can draw to make its debt service payments. As with any other line of credit, the borrowed funds must be repaid. An alternative approach is for the state government to extend its credit backing to municipal bonds. With this backing, which occurs in only a few cases, the state guarantees repayment on qualifying debt should the local government be unable to make its payments. The objective of any credit enhancement is to make municipal bonds more attractive to investors, especially for issuers that are new to the market and have not established credit with investors.

Repaying outstanding debt In the final phase of the debt cycle, the finance officer ensures the timely repayment of debt obligations to investors. This is done by establishing a debt service fund through which to account for the receipt and disbursement of money in payment of GO debt, and by contracting with a bank to handle the processing of interest and principal payments as they come due. Interest is paid semiannually, and principal is paid annually on the anniversary of the date of sale for bonds maturing that year. The budget office determines the amount of principal and interest coming due each year and includes this obligation in the annual operating budget. To provide a dedicated source of funding for GO debt service, the council will often adopt a property tax rate that is separate from that for operating purposes.

In the case of revenue bonds, a separate restricted account is set up in the accounting ledger for the utility or other enterprise fund to track revenues committed to their repayment as they mature. A separate reserve account is also maintained, often specified as a covenant in the bond prospectus, for a portion of the service charges paid by users to be set aside to cover debt service in the event of an unexpected drop in revenues.

Project implementation

Once the governing body adopts the capital budget appropriation, departments in the executive branch can begin awarding contracts for the various projects in the budget. However, as with the operating budget, spending must be carefully coordinated with available revenues. The central budget office, working in conjunction with the finance department, will monitor incoming revenues to ensure that they are consistent with projections in the budget. If for some reason actual receipts fall below projections, spending must be curtailed in order to maintain a balanced budget.

The central budget office also plays an important role in reviewing contracts before they are signed to make certain that they are consistent with the appropriation ordinance. The planning office will review contracts for their adherence to the comprehensive plan. And the engineering office may review contracts for their technical content, ensuring that they meet the local government's needs.

Technology-enhanced communities (TEC)

First, there was smart growth, then smart buildings, then came smart phones, and now smart cities. With the development of technology to acquire, archive, and analyze large amounts of data has come the recognition that it can be used to improve local government operations, better engage citizens in governance, increase transparency, and promote economic development. But these new capabilities also raise old questions of accountability, accessibility, privacy, and fairness that are at the core of public administration. Local governments are on the cusp of innovation by adapting this new technology to provide better services.[13] The unique planning and capital investment demands of TEC pose new challenges to local governments as they undertake the capital planning and budgeting processes.

Pushing the smart community agenda are the major players in the technology industry who see in local governments a sizeable market for the use of their technology.[14] But local governments have been slow to embrace the vision promoted by proponents. Their concern is motivated, in part, by the lack of evidence demonstrating the tangible benefits from acquiring the costly technology. The ever shorter life spans of that technology, for example the progression of wireless phones from the rollout of 3G in 2003 to 4G in 2013 to 5G in 2019, add to their cautiousness. These uncertain life spans have a chilling effect on a local government's willingness to make a major investment in the infrastructure to support digitalization of public services.

More broadly, adopting these technologies for use in local public services requires vision, money, and an understanding of the strengths and limitations of the technology. Many new innovations in government start with an entrepreneurial local government and then spread to other communities that copy the successful elements. Unfortunately, adoption of these technologies has been generally customized to the needs of each local government, giving other potential users no standard policy to copy. Even if the vision for a smart city project exists, money and tech-savvy staff are in short supply. An ICMA survey found that budget limitations, internal capacity shortcomings, lack of supporting infrastructure, and lack of technical expertise posed the primary barriers to adopting smart-city technologies.[15]

But underlying these concerns are more basic questions about the role of local government in an increasingly technology-infused world. The first concerns what to call this era. Smart cities has morphed into smart communities as planners realized that some applications may work best at the neighborhood level while others at a county or even regional level. But "smart" carries a not-so-subtle implication as being "better" than those communities that choose not to increase their investment in technology. The "smart" label creates a presumption of the merits of a technology application that is difficult to defend in the capital planning process, a position no manager would espouse. A preferable label not geographically bounded, and one used here, is technology-enhanced communities.

Another management concern is whether local governments should provide technology to their residents and businesses, or is that best left to industry? For example, should a city finance, construct, and operate a fiber optic network? By undertaking a full-scale application of technology, a local government assumes responsibility for the risks that it poses to users—cyberattacks, loss of privacy, legal liability for erroneous or malicious information, obsolescence, and misuse of data, among a host of other issues.

Managers may have concerns with the lack of hard data on the benefits from investment in technology beyond the basic inhouse services. Nor has evidence been produced showing that those local governments that have made a more aggressive investment in TEC have an advantage in luring and retaining business development. Inevitably, the question of who pays for the cost of technology works its way into the conversation. It becomes more politically charged when the cost is borne through general revenues but access to the technology, such as a fiber optic network, is not available to all neighborhoods.

Another concern facing managers is privacy. Open data, or data collected and then made publicly available by government entities, is an important policy issue for local governments that want to increase transparency and citizen trust. Unfortunately, open data can be used for nefarious or criminal purposes. For example, a realistic TEC application arrays cameras on every stoplight to optimize traffic flow, increase pedestrian safety, and decrease congestion. But access to these data, either through open forums or an open records request, could be used to track drivers. TEC communities collect massive amounts of data that necessitate determining the balance between open data and privacy. The Health Insurance Portability and Accountability Act provides an excellent example of how private data can be collected and publicly shared without compromising privacy of information.

Local governments considering a TEC initiative face a wide range of possibilities for building a community of tomorrow. In their evaluation of digital planning by eight large cities, Anthony Townsend and Stephen Lorimer found that each pursued a different emphasis, or strategy, that shaped its digital plans.[16] Different emphases require decisions on whether the beneficiaries of digitalization will be internal to the local government or include the community (households and businesses). They involve decisions on whether the scale of digitalization will be confined to users internal to the local government or extend to users in the community. Figure 11-6 displays the four strategies, arranged progressively by the difficulty of the policy and planning decisions each requires, from a basic data collection strategy, to an e-government strategy, to a public engagement strategy, and the most ambitious a technology-intensive neighborhood strategy.

Basic data collection strategy (G2G)

A basic strategy taken by local governments is to primarily confine technology development and its benefits internally to its employees (G2G). While the community may benefit from the availability of more data, such as websites with the government's CAFR and budgets, the primary purpose of technology is investing mostly in digitizing internal processes.

Figure 11-6 Four strategies for planning for a technology-enhanced community

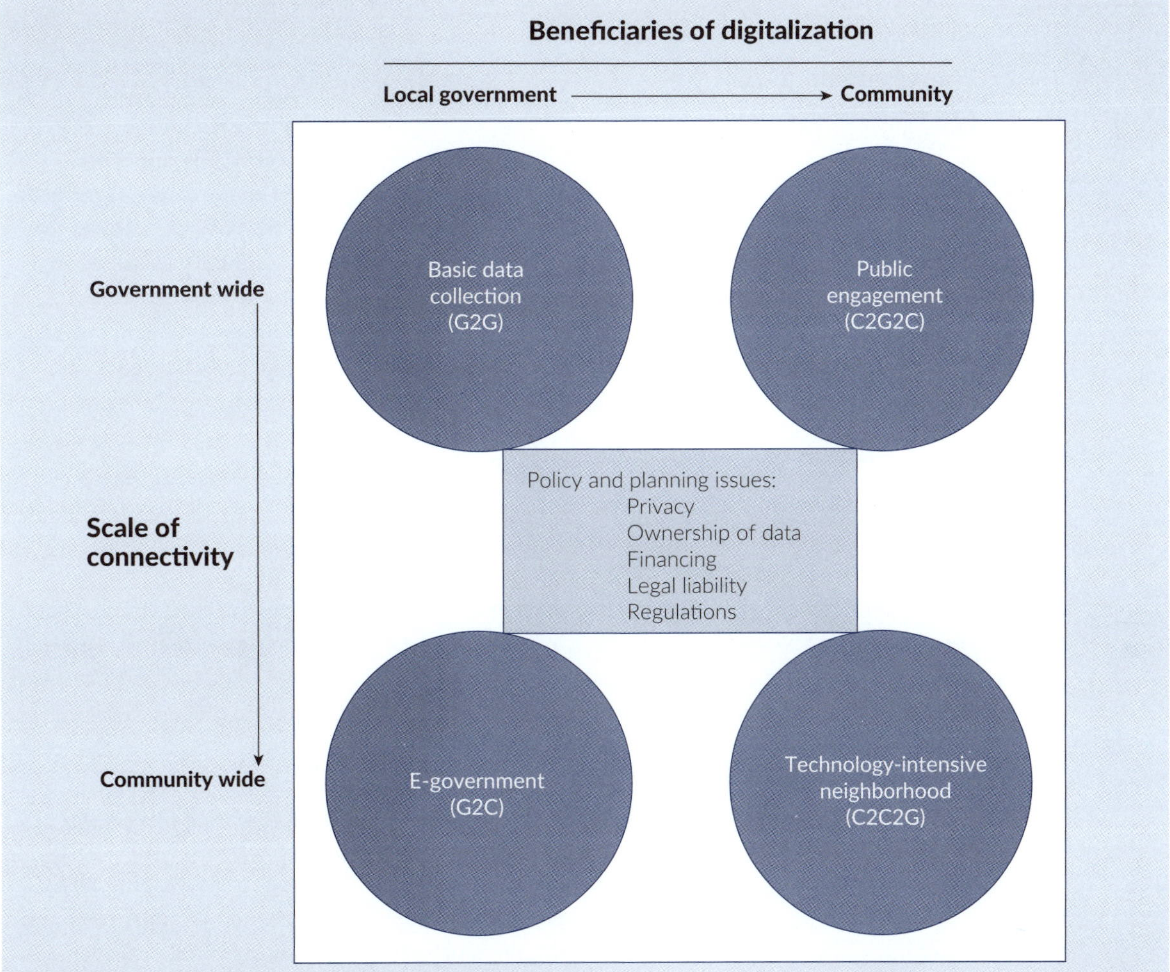

Local governments using this default strategy may add technology to existing infrastructure, such as wireless electric and water meters or motion-sensitive sensors for street lighting, as a way to control costs of technology, increase operating efficiency, and reduce the risk of overpromising benefits from the capital investment. In addition to the data generated from their enterprise resource systems for human resources, the budget, and purchasing, local governments using this strategy may collect data from additional sources such as drones (unmanned aerial vehicles or UAVs), body cameras on public safety officers, closed circuit TV (CCTV), and in the near future robots that use artificial intelligence (AI) to deliver parcels. Some governments may integrate real time data using GIS scans, such as police or fire calls, into their dashboards.

The local government's capital investment is confined to upgrades of hardware and software to manage the data. Using inhouse experts or consultants, the government may develop a dashboard for displaying real time and static data. It may use the data in evaluating performance, identifying understaffed areas, and managing peak demand periods. And data analytics may be performed by budget personnel to evaluate policy initiatives.

The primary benefits of this basic strategy are the minimization of risk to loss of privacy, lower likelihood of legal issues involving open record requests and liability, moderate demand on technology staff to develop and maintain information systems, lower capital and operating costs by building on existing capacity, better capacity to deflect cybersecurity attacks, and a reduced time horizon for digital planning.

E-government (G2C)

Local governments pursuing a more ambitious strategy seek to extend their connectivity to the community mostly through developing interactive websites (G2C). While there is community-to-government interaction, this strategy is distinguished by the local government taking the initiative to connect with the community through online portals: applications for employment, tax and utility invoices and payments, street closings, and utility usage reports. E-government also includes the numerous types of alerts provided by government to the community: Amber Alert, Silver Alert, weather alerts using sirens, and wireless emergency alerts.

Governments using this strategy likely archive and report real time and static data on a dashboard. Unlike the first strategy, a local government pursuing e-government may make available downloadable data through its dashboard, enabling users to analyze the data independently. This increases the risk that third parties use data for unintended purposes, that they use data to harm the local government, or they use it to harm others. At the same time, making the data available in downloadable form elevates the transparency of a local government and its engagement with the community.

An e-government gains internal processing efficiency by reducing staff time to collect and process data that is now generated externally. Supporting the technology, however, requires greater investment in expertise to design and maintain the online templates and greater investment in the hardware and software to support it.

Public engagement (C2G2C)

Local governments opting to become direct providers of digital services to residents and businesses enter uncharted terrain that typically necessitates partnering with a third-party technology provider. These local governments are on the cutting edge of developing a TEC.

Governments pursuing a public engagement strategy likely have a well-established record of providing e-government and basic data collection services. Moving to public engagement, in which citizens now become coproducers of information with the local government, necessitates longer-term planning and more coordination with the CIP. The data may be produced by the community or government, but once in the local government's possession it is made available to the community (C2G2C). Devices such as sentiment analyses or pop-up polls provide a nonscientific but quick indication of trending public opinion on local policy issues. Virtual town hall meetings provide a forum for engaging community members in more substantive discussions of those issues. Crowdsourcing offers yet another tool local governments may use to garner public input in shaping policy solutions.[17] Partnering with third-party vendors, such as Waze, provides a venue for the local government to provide real time data on street and road closures or construction projects that enhance traffic flow.

Local governments contemplating pursuing a public engagement strategy must consider a major investment in universal fiber optic service and providing WiFi accessibility in public areas. The prohibitive cost of universal installation of fiber optic along with limitations in state law, in some cases, forces most local governments to seek a private vendor to install and operate the network. Public-private partnerships open a new set of issues that require resolution before launching the initiative, including ownership of the data, protection of personal information, restrictions on partnerships with other vendors, cost sharing of upgrades, and the approval process for changes in rates or service quality.

In fact, home builders have already entered this arena. New housing developments increasingly feature top-to-bottom Internet services that enable remote control of all amenities from exterior and interior lighting to room temperatures to appliance controls. These housing developments provide fiber optic and WiFi services in combination with other amenities such as a community garden or a water park. However, their success may be limited by concerns of owners with the developer's access to and use of personal data generated through the digital networks. As such, private developers may benefit from partnering with a local government, with its credibility and accountability to residents, as much as the local government benefits from partnering with the developer, with its access to financing and capability to administer a digitized neighborhood.

Technology-intensive neighborhood (C2C2G)

The most ambitious TEC initiatives involve designing and developing a technology-intensive neighborhood (TIN) from the ground up and connecting residents to each other and to local government (C2C2G) in almost every aspect of their lives. A host of initiatives are underway in medium to large cities pilot testing this strategy. Toronto, Canada, has partnered with Sidewalk Labs, a subsidiary of Google, to rebuild a twelve-acre section of the city's waterfront with virtually everything digitally connected and monitored.[18] Denver, Colorado, has partnered with Panasonic to develop a new neighborhood, Pena Station NEXT, that features "smart technology, community, clean energy, and mobility."[19] Frisco, Texas, has partnered with AT&T to install "from the ground up" 5G wireless capability in a new mixed-use development, Frisco Station.[20] The city has also partnered with California-based Drive.ai to pilot test on demand self-driving vehicles to shuttle commuters. Songdo, South Korea, is furthest along in the quest for a technology-centric city, although population growth and business investment have fallen well short of expectations.

Financing these ambitious initiatives lurks as a limitation on their potential. While PPPs offer a means for using private capital for start-up costs, the revenue stream from such initiatives remains unclear and unrealized at this point. One possibility is a public improvement district (PID) in which tech-intensive neighborhoods incur an additional dedicated tax to cover the public benefits from the technology, much like an HOA fee.

These four strategies pose increasingly difficult and complex policy issues that require resolution before undertaking the project. The last two strategies that push the TEC to new plateaus require long-term planning, separate from the CIP process, that carefully assesses both the costs and benefits to the local government.

Conclusion

Because of the sizeable investment public improvements require, decisions on their timing and design carry much greater risk than decisions regarding operating expenditures. Large sums of money are usually at stake in a capital project, and an error in the design or location of the project can result in disastrous political and economic consequences. Thus, the identification, prioritization, and funding of public improvements require a separate process from that of the operating budget. The cornerstone for the process is the CIP, which identifies the capital improvements that the local government wishes to undertake, typically over the next five years. The first year of the CIP becomes the capital budget, the financing plan for the projects that the government will undertake in the forthcoming year.

Initially, the priorities for capital allocation must come from elected leaders, who articulate the capital needs of the government through the campaign process and through their role as representatives of the electorate. What projects are selected for funding is also greatly influenced by who participates in the capital planning process.

An inventory and condition assessment of existing physical assets should precede the preparation of the CIP.

The CIP provides not only a year-by-year inventory of proposed projects, but also a plan for lawmakers for financing those projects. Local governments rely on shared taxes, grants, municipal bonds, special assessments, and local own-source revenue to fund capital acquisitions. Municipal bonds provide local governments with a flexible means of financing capital improvements while promoting intergenerational equity.

Preparation of the capital budget requires budget staff to determine the exact cost of each project through an engineering study and to make a detailed estimate of revenues including bond sale proceeds. Budget staff must identify the amount of bonds to be sold in order to provide financing for the projects. The analysis also involves assessing the impact of capital projects on future operating costs. Most all capital projects, particularly those more labor-intensive services (fire or police station, library), eventually lead to higher operating costs in subsequent years.

During the actual construction of capital projects, the budget office must carefully coordinate spending with available revenues. If debt is used, care must be used in accounting and budgeting for the debt service.

The emergence of smart cities, or the preferred term technology-enhanced communities, introduces new challenges in capital planning and budgeting. Should such initiatives be deferred to private firms that have greater access to venture capital and to the costly expertise needed to support digitalization of local governments? Who should pay for this technology and how should those costs be recouped? Does a TEC have an advantage in attracting and retaining business investment? And the most politically charged issue—how is privacy protected once data are collected and retained by a local government?

Four strategies were identified that profiled the beneficiaries of digitalization (government wide versus community wide) with the scale of users of the data (internal users versus community users). The most basic strategy confines technology development and its benefits to employees in local government (G2G). An e-government strategy seeks to connect the community to the local government mostly through interactive websites (G2C). A public engagement strategy puts local governments in the role as providers of digital services to businesses and residents. Data may be produced by both community users and the local government, creating a two-way interaction (C2G2C). The technology-enhanced neighborhood provides for the most aggressive strategy by connecting community residents with each other and with their local government (C2C2G). Prior to initiating any of these strategies, a manager must address the key issues of privacy, ownership of data, how to pay for the technology, and the local government's level of commitment to supporting the digitalization initiative.

Notes

1 Benedict S. Jimenez and Michael A. Pagano, "What Factors Affect Management Quality? State Infrastructure Management and the Government Performance Project," *Public Works Management & Policy* 17 (March 2012): 124–151.

2 Eugene L. Grant, W. Grant Ireson, and Richard S. Leavenworth, *Principles of Engineering Economy,* 6th ed. (New York: John Wiley & Sons, 1976), 510.

3 Jane Beckett-Camarata, "An Examination of the Relationship between the Municipal Strategic Plan and the Capital Budget and Its Effect on Financial Performance," *Journal of Public Budgeting, Accounting & Financial Management* 15 (Spring 2003): 23–40.

4 Michael A. Pagano, "Notes on Capital Budgeting," *Public Budgeting & Finance* 4 (Autumn 1984): 31–40.

5 Ibid.

6 Beverly S. Bunch, "Capital Planning and Budgeting," in *Management Policies in Local Government Finance* 6th edition, ed. Justin R. Bartle, W. Bartley Hildreth, and Justin Marlowe (Washington, D.C.: International City/County Management Association 2013):

7 Arwiphawee Srithongrung, "The Impacts of State Capital Management Programs on State Economic Performance," *Public Budgeting & Finance* 28 (Fall 2008): 83–107.

8 A. John Vogt, *Capital Budgeting and Finance: A Guide for Local Governments* (Washington, D.C.: ICMA, 2004).

9 Robert L. Bland and Samuel Nunn, "The Impact of Capital Spending on Municipal Operating Budgets," *Public Budgeting & Finance* 12 (Summer 1992): 32–47.

10 Robert L. Bland and Phanit Laosirirat, "Tax Limitations to Reduce Municipal Property Taxes: Truth in Taxation in Texas," *Journal of Urban Affairs* 19 (Spring 1997): 45–58.

11 Neil O'Hara, *The Fundamentals of Municipal Bonds,* 6th ed. (New York: John Wiley & Sons, 2012), 62.

12 Kenneth A. Kriz and Marc D. Joffe, "Municipal Bond Insurance After the Financial Crisis: Can It Help Reduce Borrowing Costs for Local Governments?" (Arlington, Va.: Mercatus Center at George Mason University, 2017).

13 International City/County Management Association and the Institute for Building Technology and Safety, *Smart Solutions: Technology Serving Communities* (Washington, D.C.: International City/County Management Association, August 2017).

14 Brookings Institution/ESADE, "Getting Smarter About Smart Cities," April 2014, 3.

15 International City/County Management Association and Smart Cities Council, "2016 Smart Cities Survey, Summary Report of Survey Results," https://icma.org/sites/default/files/308555_2016%20smart%20cities%20survey_summary%20report_final.pdf.

16 Anthony Townsend and Stephen Lorimer, "Digital Master Planning: An Emerging Strategic Practice in Global Cities," NYU Marron Institute Working Paper #25, June 2015, https://marroninstitute.nyu.edu/uploads/content/Working_Paper_25_Digital_Master_Planning.pdf.

17 Helen K. Liu, "Crowdsourcing Government: Lessons from Multiple Disciplines," *Public Administration Review* 77 (September/October 2017): 656-667.

18 Waterfront Toronto, 2016/17 *Annual Report,* June 13, 2017, https://waterfrontoronto.ca/nbe/wcm/connect/waterfront/c9e7aaec-ed75-4320-84f1-e4d06875e0d5/2016-17+Annual+Report+-+June+13%2C+2017+%28for+posting%29.pdf?MOD=AJPERES.

19 City of Denver, *Pena Station NEXT,* http://www.penastationnext.com/.

20 "Frisco Station and AT&T to Create 5G Evolution Connected Community from the Ground Up," *Business Wire,* August 9, 2018, https://www.businesswire.com/news/home/20180809005098/en/.

CHAPTER 12

Budgeting for improved performance

> If you can't measure it, you can't manage it.
>
> —*Peter Drucker*

This chapter provides the following takeaways:

- An understanding of the types of performance measures available to managers.
- How to design measures that serve the needs of both community residents and a local government's leaders.
- A more holistic approach that conceptually measures performance gaps—performance drag, performance deficit, performance dividend, and performance legacy.
- The utility of benchmarking.
- The limitations to performance measurement and how managers can overcome them.

Improving government productivity has been a matter of discussion among budget gurus since the inception of modern budgeting in 1906, when the New York Bureau of Municipal Research required the city's departments to adopt budget procedures. The topic resurfaced in the early 1950s after the second Hoover Commission Report called for all federal agencies to use performance measures as a way to control costs.[1] Four decades later, then–Vice President Al Gore led the National Performance Review (NPR) initiative; launched in 1993 when Congress passed the Government Performance and Results Act, the NPR refocused attention on monitoring agency activities for improving performance, promoting customer-friendly service, and increasing cost savings through improved productivity. Then during the George W. Bush administration, NPR morphed into the Program Assessment Rating Tool. These efforts have

Figure 12–1 Alternative strategies to productivity improvement in local government

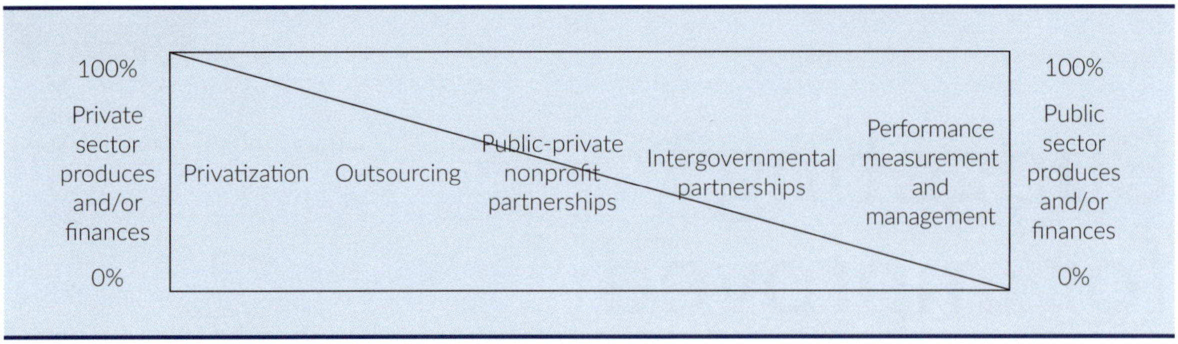

all sought to reduce costs through competition (or some surrogate, such as measuring and reporting performance), to better align services with agency mission, and to increase administrative accountability for the use of resources (both personnel and money) and what is accomplished with those resources.

This chapter explores the development of **performance measurement** in local government, where many of the innovations adapted at the state and federal levels were first developed. The renewed interest in performance improvement that began in the early 1990s is part of a broader quest, propelled by the New Public Management movement's push to improve government productivity by interjecting market forces into the public sector.

Figure 12–1 shows the various tools that governments use to increase efficiency in the production, financing, and delivery of public goods and services. Figure 1–1 and the accompanying discussion in Chapter 1 distinguished between privatization and outsourcing, the productivity improvement strategies that rely the most on investment by the private sector. This chapter examines the other end of the spectrum: the use of performance measures to improve productivity and accountability in government-produced and financed services.

Context of performance measures

In the private market, producers must offer services that consumers want at prices that consumers find acceptable. This is also true to some extent in the public sector, but the political process is an imperfect and unreliable means of determining what services citizens want and at what price. Performance measurement introduces another mechanism that managers and their councils can use to help make their budget priorities better reflect citizen preferences and to more efficiently provide the goods and services that citizens want.

Not only have public managers led the effort to introduce more market-like forces into the public arena, but organizations such as ICMA and the Governmental Accounting Standards Board (GASB) have launched initiatives to make performance measurement a more effective management and budgeting tool. ICMA sponsors a Certificate in Performance Measurement to recognize local governments that instill "a culture of performance management, pursuing comparative analysis and data-informed decision making, and promoting transparency."[2] The program recognizes three levels of proficiency in performance reporting and management—certificate of excellence, certificate of distinction, and certificate of achievement.

In the last decade, the GASB has ventured beyond its mission of establishing accounting standards to develop criteria for reporting performance indicators. Those criteria call for the preparation of an annual performance report—a separate document from the comprehensive annual financial report—that can provide "information to assist users in assessing the service efforts, costs, and accomplishments of the governmental entity."[3] Several local governments—

Figure 12–2 Basic performance measures

Type of measure	Definition	Other terms commonly used
Inputs	The quantity of resources (e.g., full-time equivalents, dollars, number of hours) used to produce goods and services	Efforts (GASB)
Outputs	The amount of goods and services produced and usually reported as a number of units	Accomplishments (GASB) Workload measures
Outcomes	A measure of the impact of inputs on an objective or goal The change in conditions (e.g., crime rate) as a result of the inputs	Effectiveness measures Results measures Impact measures

Bellevue, Washington, for example—maintain a performance dashboard using what the GASB calls service efforts and accomplishments, or SEA, as measures of performance at the program and departmental levels.

Measures of performance

The use of performance measures has gained widespread acceptance among local governments, especially the larger ones. While the three commonly used types of performance measures are inputs, outputs, and outcomes (Figure 12–2), there is no standard nomenclature, and every government tailors its measures and definitions to its own purposes.[4] As noted in the next section, many measures that are meaningful to managers responsible for operations may not be particularly useful to citizens or to customers of government services. Even more fundamentally, perceptions of performance held by those within a local government may be dramatically at odds with perceptions held by those outside the government.

Input measures Input measures, such as full-time equivalent employees or number of hours devoted to a task, are the easiest to identify and measure. Most of these data are already available at the departmental level. Unless the budget office places a limit on the number of measures, however, the tendency is for departments to generate multiple input measures, which can eventually become unwieldy.

Output measures Output measures are the next easiest to identify and track. These are workload measures—the amount of goods or services produced—which department heads generally collect as part of their efforts to justify the need for additional funding during budget preparation and adoption. (Some department heads try to identify the unmet demand for a public good or service—a demand measure; however, documenting such a measure has usually proven elusive.)

Outcome measures Outcome measures are the most difficult to articulate and measure, but they are also the most useful to managers during budget preparation and to legislators during budget adoption. Demonstrating the impact of a proposed spending change on organizational or community conditions provides those responsible for budget decisions with valuable information when evaluating the relative merits of a proposal. As discussed in Chapter 8, the problem is that the link between changes in spending and outcomes is rarely understood.[5]

An increase in spending on police patrol may not necessarily reduce crime, particularly if the increased investment occurs concurrently with an increase in unemployment or in the law enforcement efforts by surrounding local governments.

These three basic measures may be combined to create additional indicators of performance. For example, the ratio of inputs to outputs provides a measure of the efficiency with which a good or service has been produced. During budget implementation, **efficiency measures** are most useful in monitoring trends in the cost of producing goods and services. Governments with advanced cost accounting capabilities, such as Sunnyvale, California, can allocate both direct and indirect costs to each program or activity—from collecting property taxes to investigating a crime—and thereby identify upticks in the full cost per property tax account administered or per crime investigated.

Measures of performance in budgeting

Since the 1990s there has been an explosion of experimentation in the use of performance measures to improve analysis in budget decision making as well as delivery of public services at the lowest cost. With this increased experimentation has come a new set of terms to describe performance innovations. Figure 12–3 provides a typology of the tools used to improve government performance.[6]

Performance measures Performance measures are metrics that administrators use to monitor an organization's use of resources (inputs), the results of its efforts (outputs), and the impact of those efforts on the community (outcomes). In the past decade, the use of performance measures by local, state, and federal governments has mushroomed. These measures are often reported in the budget document, although that document seldom makes clear the connection between performance measures and budget decisions.

Performance budgeting Performance budgeting involves the use of performance measures to make budget decisions. Here governments have encountered significant obstacles because of the causal linkage problem described in Chapter 8. Donald Moynihan and Stéphane Lavertu studied the use of performance reforms in federal agencies and concluded that while they "promoted performance measurement," they did not promote the use of performance data for making budget or operational decisions.[7] And when performance measures are used in budget deliberations, the question inevitably arises as to what those measures really mean. Should programs that have exemplary performance be given more funding? Should underperforming units be penalized? If a program is underperforming, could it be because it lacks the funding to perform at a higher level? Should a city reduce funding to its police department if it failed to reach a crime reduction target? Because of the discomfort in answering these causal linkage questions, performance measures have, at best, informed budget deliberations.[8]

Performance management Performance management integrates performance measures into the day-to-day operations of a program or department. It usually begins with the development of a strategic plan at the departmental level that establishes a five-year window as to the department's goals and objectives, and the strategies that the department intends to pursue to

Figure 12–3 Typology of tools to improve government performance

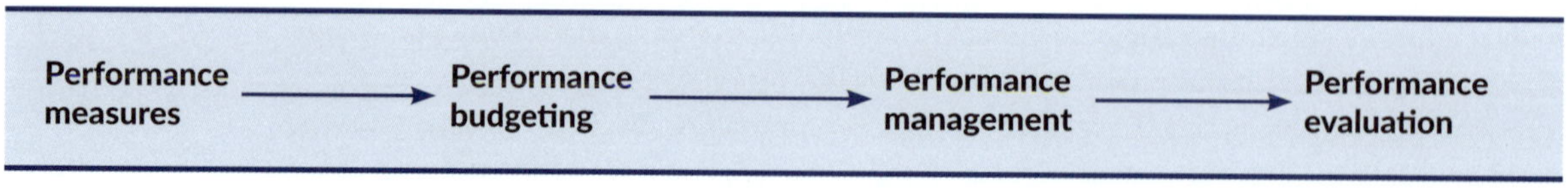

Figure 12–4 Performance evaluation model, Sheriff's Department, Marathon County, Wisconsin

SHERIFF'S DEPARTMENT – PROGRAM MODEL

Contact Name: Randall Hoenisch, Sheriff **Standing Committee:** Public Safety Committee
Working Committee: Public Safety Committee
Program Customer: Marathon County Citizens; Persons Passing Through; Other Emergency Service Agencies; Other State/Federal Agencies

COMMITMENTS (Inputs)		ACTIVITIES		PURPOSE (Outcomes)		
Programs	Resources	"Work"	"Result" – Output	Immediate (0-10 years)	Long-Term Vision (10+ years)	County Overarching Goals
1.Communications • Dispatch for all Emergency Services • 911 Phone Center • CAD/TIME System	Staff: 34 FTE Tax Levy: $2,564,804 Revenue: $65,576	Dispatch of all Emergency Services	Provide vital information about emergency scene	Understand and apply lifesaving techniques	Increased safety and effectiveness	People receive an immediate response from the right public safety professional during emergencies.
2.Corrections • Jail Management • Adult Basic Education • Alternative Programs • Secure Detention	Staff: 73 FTE Tax Levy: $5,818,892 Revenue: $1,029,103	Operate a secure corrections facility	Number of inmates served by the County Jail	Decrease in the average daily jail bed days by seeking alternative sentencing methods	Continued budget adjustments to meet the demands of jail and citizen safety	People receive a real response to crime. People are rehabilitated, so they do re-offend. Offenders receive punishment commensurate with the crime.
3.Investigations • Criminal Investigations • Evidence Control • Special Investigations Unit	Staff: 19 FTE Tax Levy: $1,856,770 Revenue: $38,299	Investigate criminal activity Identify criminal trends and behavior	Number and types of crimes investigated and closed successfully Accuracy of statistical data	Citizens believe if they commit crime they will be identified and arrested	Citizens and businesses are not targets of criminal behavior	
4.Patrol • 24 Hour Patrol Service • Traffic Enforcement • Special Teams	Staff: 50 FTE/ 9 PTE Tax Levy: $5,377,255 Revenue: $114,200	24 hour patrol service Accident investigation	Number of arrests, citations, warnings, accidents investigated	Motorists believe they will be caught if violating traffic laws Provide a more visible presence increasing responsiveness and enhancing the safety of the community Maintaining special teams to secure the safety of the community	Drivers become more aware, cautious, and begin to self police Continued efforts to reduce traffic fatalities by promoting defensive driving education	Criminal activity is deterred and culturally unacceptable. People are protected from crime and are safe.
5.Emergency Management • Preparedness • Special Teams Liaison	Staff: 2 FTE Tax Levy: $134,083 Revenue: $15,000	Identification and assessment of high risk areas	Educate community on role they play in emergency management	Continued improvement of plans involving hazard mitigation, flood insurance, etc	Become a more knowledgeable source to the community on emergency preparedness	Marathon County maintains a safe and reasonable standard of transportation infrastructure.

Source: *2011 Budget: Financial Plan and Information Summary for Marathon County, Wisconsin*, C-5, co.marathon.wi.us/Portals/0/Departments/MCF/Documents/final2011budgetbook.pdf.

achieve its goals. The strategic plan is guided by the city's or county's overall strategic goals or outcomes. For example, Bellevue, Washington, tracks seven community-wide outcomes that guide budget deliberations: responsive government; improved mobility; quality neighborhoods; safe community; healthy and sustainable environment; innovative, vibrant, and caring community; and economic growth and competitiveness.[9]

Performance management involves the periodic review of the department's progress toward achieving its goals and objectives and of how each person in the unit contributes to those results. In some cases, salary increases are linked to how well individuals and the department have performed in this regard. Coral Spring, Florida, has a well-developed strategic planning process that links performance measures with departmental strategic plans and operating budgets.[10] The Austin, Texas, performance management team reports city performance using dashboards that it collectively calls "Performance ATX."[11] Lewisville, Texas, uses dashboards to report performance metrics using both static and live data and, for some measures, provides drop-down boxes that display historical trends.[12]

Performance evaluation The final tool—performance evaluation—is the newest and least familiar tool in the performance improvement arsenal. The evaluation component uses information from past performance as feedback into the strategic planning and budgeting process to better inform the future development of performance measures and outcomes. Performance evaluation also involves reviewing a department's operations to determine what processes inhibit the department from achieving its objectives. Until 2013, Marathon County, Wisconsin, reported in its budget a well-articulated linkage between inputs, activities, initial outputs (results), and intermediate and long-term vision, as evidenced in Figure 12–4. This process forced department heads to evaluate the immediate as well as long-term consequences of their choices, both budgetary and managerial.

Performance expectations and perceptions

One of the most notable findings in a 2005 report prepared by New York City's Center on Municipal Government Performance is that "people judge government performance in ways that often differ markedly from the standard measures that governments use to evaluate themselves."[13] The discrepancy is partly attributable to whether those doing the judging are insiders or outsiders. Figure 12–5 provides a way to classify the different types of performance measures and tools according to who they benefit—internal or external users.

Insiders, such as department heads who craft the performance measures, see the organization as a series of silos—semiautonomous departments, programs, and activities that compete for scarce budget resources and public approval and that have little in common with other departments, programs, and activities.[14] Outsiders (citizens and even legislators) see government more holistically and often do not even distinguish among overlapping units of local government.[15] Rather, they are more inclined to base their evaluation of a program or service on their overall evaluation of the local government—a halo effect that can result in a favorable or unfavorable assessment of government performance. In an insightful article that contends that governments fall into the rut of measuring the wrong things, Kevin Baum wrote, "If the difference you're making makes no difference, what's the difference? . . . If we can't demonstrate through concrete metrics of performance, metrics that show the results of our efforts, outcomes our customers care about, then in the eyes of the citizens, we didn't make a difference."[16]

Essentially, citizens' expectations of local government performance are based on intuition—what they know or believe that their local government should be capable of doing. Whether those expectations are met has little to do with the performance measures reported by departments per se: rarely do citizens have the interest, let alone the time, to scrutinize and comprehend program-specific performance measures. Rather, their expectations are met or not met according to what they perceive, and their perceptions are shaped by personal experiences, word of mouth, and the media.

The three-factor model of performance measurement

A beginning point for addressing the disconnect between citizen expectations and the way local governments assess their performance is to decide for whom performance is being mea-

Figure 12–5 A typology of performance measures

	Departmental outcomes	City/county outcomes
Internal users	Workload measures Output measures Full-time equivalents Efficiency measures Management by objectives Departmental goals/objectives	Community goals Strategic goals Budgeting for outcomes (BFO) Balanced scorecard
External users	Citizen satisfaction Customer ratings Response times	Holistic indices Price of government (BFO) Urban livability measure

Figure 12–6 Sources of performance expectations, deficits, and surpluses

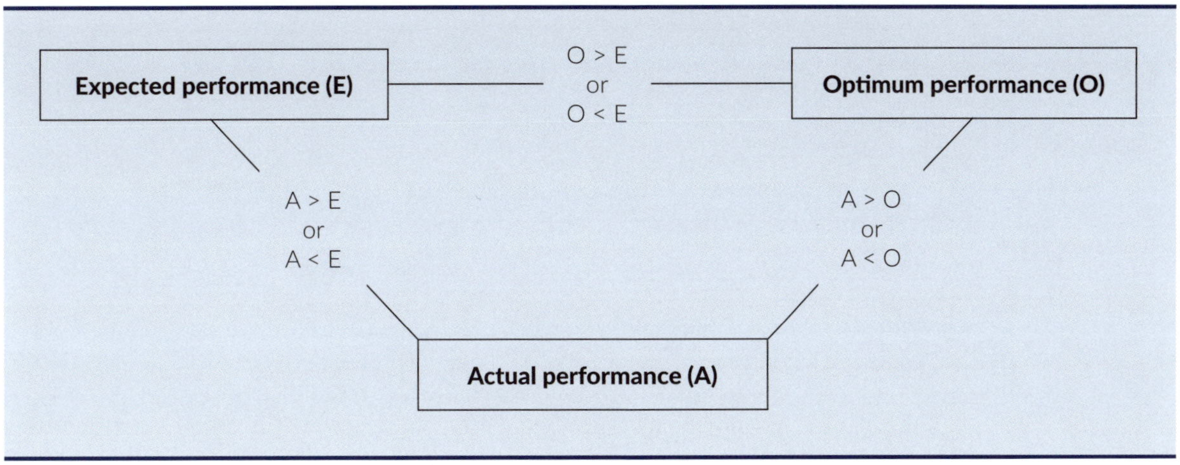

sured—for program and department heads, for managers and elected officials, or for external stakeholders such as residents and businesses.

At the macro level, a government's performance can be viewed from three independent but interacting perspectives: expected performance (E), optimum performance (O), and actual performance (A). Figure 12–6 depicts the relationship among these three perspectives.[17]

Expected performance represents that level of service that executives, legislators, and external constituencies reasonably expect to receive given their knowledge and available information about the services the government provides. Performance expectations may be established by the campaign promises of elected leaders, strategic plans, industry benchmarks, accreditation standards, or best practices. Mission and vision statements express an organization's expectations of itself, which find more detailed expression in the goals and objectives that make up its strategic plan. But those self-described expectations do not always align with what citizens and other constituencies expect.

Optimum performance represents that level of service that managers and council members assume to be achievable, the true potential, given the resources they appropriate in the final budget. (These assumptions are not always explicitly stated or agreed upon.) A good department or program administrator leverages resources (labor and capital) to achieve more than what was optimally assumed possible. An increase in funding, the introduction of new technology, a reorganization, or any kind of alteration in the way a service is delivered carries with it an assumption that actual performance will increase. For example, outsourcing is usually justified as a way to bring actual performance up to or even beyond optimum performance.

Actual performance represents the observed level of service produced given available funding and administrative capabilities. Actual performance differs from the optimum for a range of reasons, including managerial capabilities, the quality of the workforce, shortages of qualified labor or essential materials, and unforeseen events that affect overall performance.

In a perfect world with perfect knowledge and good management, an organization is at the top of its game when E = O = A—that is, when expected outcomes align with what is optimally achievable given its resources, and the organization's actual level of performance meets both expectations and the optimum. A manager of such a city, department, or program would be considered highly effective.

In the public sector where the causal connections among inputs, outputs, and outcomes are poorly understood and often misrepresented for political gain, the ideal equilibrium rarely occurs and—when it does—rarely lasts. Gaps between A, O, and E are of two general types

Figure 12–7 Types of performance gaps

(E ≥ O) > A Performance drag	A > (O ≥ E) Performance legacy
(E ≥ A) > O Performance dividend	O > (A ≥ E) Performance deficit

(represented by the lower inequality of each pair in Figure 12–6): gaps in expectations (O < E or A < E) and gaps in performance (A < O). Bridging these gaps requires a different set of strategies for each. It is an unfortunate commentary on our times that little is said or written about the upper inequalities in each pair. Most managers would probably contend that their organizations perform, at a minimum, with actual outputs and outcomes exceeding the optimum (A > O) and possibly even expectations (A > E).

Managers spend most of their professional careers dealing with three of the four types of gaps shown in Figure 12–7: (1) performance drag, in which actual performance lags what is capable of being achieved or what is expected [(E ≥ O) > A]; (2) performance deficit, in which actual performance exceeds or at least meets expectations but lags what is optimally achievable [O > (A ≥ E)]; or (3) performance dividend, in which actual performance exceeds the optimum but lags or at least meets expectations [(E ≥ A) > O]. A fourth gap—performance legacy—[A > (O ≥ E)]—is that occasional case when a program's performance exceeds, at least momentarily, both its optimal level and what stakeholders expect.

Performance drag This case involves actual performance falling short of both expectations (E > A) and optimal performance (O > A). Raising expectations or increasing funding (O) will likely have little effect on productivity (A). To correct for the performance gap, the manager may change administrators if there is reason to believe that the drag is due to poor administration. In Texas, for example, a persistently poor-performing school district may be taken over by the state's education agency, which brings in an administrative team of its choosing to remedy the poor performance. City councils may do the same if they believe that a new manager will produce more satisfactory results—that is, move performance toward E = O = A. Other times, an executive may seek to reorganize a unit. If the lack of training or automation is thought to be the source of the gap, appropriate remedies may be tested. Departments and programs in this category are prime candidates for outsourcing.

An organization experiencing performance drag also suffers from unrealistic expectations by its external constituents. The widespread reductions in state and local funding precipitated by the Great Recession lowered the optimum service capacity of state and local governments, but citizen expectations did not decline commensurately. Reduced funding for public schools led to larger classes and less specialized instructional services, but parents maintained the same expectations for educational achievements. Elected officials are particularly loath to suggest that their constituents reduce their expectations in accordance with reduced funding. In fact, they often artificially inflate citizens' expectations by suggesting that actual service levels will not be affected by budget reductions because of the excess capacity in agency budgets.

Performance deficit Local governments and programs in this category perform at or above expectations but below their optimum given their funding (O > A). Persistently poor-performing programs may fit this profile. Because their citizens have grown accustomed to poor service and expect no more, changing performance in these organizations begins by raising expectations in hopes of stimulating improvements in actual performance (A). A persistently low-performing school, for example, experiences a turnaround when a new principal motivates parents to demand improvements in the educational services provided to their children. Additional corrective actions include those identified to remedy the performance drag gap. Departments and programs in the performance deficit category are also prime candidates for outsourcing, especially if all other attempts to improve actual performance fail.

Performance dividend Departments and programs in this category are performing above the optimum level (A > O) because a good administrator is effectively leveraging appropriations into surplus outputs and outcomes. Here is an administrator who merits commendation. Unfortunately, no good deed goes unpunished, and actual performance still lags or at best meets expectations—possibly as a result of unreasonable campaign promises or other external factors such as a tax limitation.

In theory, organizations in this category should be good candidates for increased funding. However, they probably will not receive increased funding because outputs and/or outcomes exceed what the budget allocation would imply is the optimum level. Administrators in this situation often find their budgets held constant. Programs or activities in this category should not be candidates for outsourcing, although they may be put on the auction block because of the income dividend they can provide a private operator. However, they are prime candidates for constituents' efforts to mobilize and pressure the council for more funding.

Performance legacy Public organizations in this category, such as the fire and police departments of New York City after 9/11, not only perform above their optimum capacity but also exceed their constituents' expectations. Of course, those expectations may well migrate upward if actual performance remains above optimum performance. But while public organizations are rarely rewarded with increased funding because they leveraged their resources to accomplish more than the optimum, organizations in the legacy category provide a standard of excellence for us to appreciate and applaud. Their best practices merit further research, and those practices that can be transferred should be emulated. Moreover, citizens should be made aware of those organizations that achieve performance excellence and the administrative leadership that made it possible.

For over a century now, scholars and practitioners have tried to integrate performance measures and performance management into the public budgeting process with unsatisfactory results. Most of those efforts have been at measuring discrete activities and then assessing whether performance meets expectations. The foregoing discussion approaches the issue from a broader perspective. It also exposes a gap in the past use of performance measures, which has focused on bridging the performance gap while failing to take into account the expectations of constituents. The foregoing suggests that managers must also recognize citizens' expectations as an essential factor in improving the performance of public organizations.

Benchmarking

Another tool to help establish thresholds of performance expectations is benchmarking. Benchmarks can be established internally on the basis of historical trends; for example, the chief of police may decide on a target number of crimes to use in referencing changes in the county's crime rate index. Or benchmarks may be adapted from external sources, such as the best practices of other local governments. Benchmarks may even be formulated by independent professional associations or by federal and state agencies—for example, targets for water quality or for student performance on a standardized exam. In any case, benchmarks provide a standard of expected performance to compare against actual performance. If a performance deficit occurs and there is reason to assume that insufficient funding is the reason for it, the administrator can use the budget process to appeal for additional funding to bring true performance potential into alignment with expectations.

The three-factor model of performance measurement

The widespread practice of measuring inputs, outputs, and outcomes focuses attention on the production side of the equation. The implicit assumption is that productivity in public organizations and their employees is less than optimal. By measuring performance and setting benchmarks, their productivity can be improved. When effectively used, so goes the assumption, performance measurement provides the incentives needed for public organizations and their employees to achieve greater results.

By contrast, the three-factor model of performance measurement described in this chapter and summarized in Figure 12–6 proposes a more holistic framework for evaluating the performance of public organizations. The implicit assumption behind this model is that improved performance of public organizations may be achieved not only on the production side but also on the demand side by bringing stakeholder expectations into better alignment with what is possible with given resources. The model proposes that the assessment of public sector performance entails a complex interaction between expected performance (E), optimum performance (O), and actual performance (A). In ideal conditions, the three factors are in equilibrium: the city government provides the level and quality of services (A) that citizens expect (E) with the optimal use of resources (O). Under these conditions, outsourcing or privatizing services provides no added benefits. Actual outputs and outcomes vary commensurate with any change in O ($\Delta A = \Delta O$).

The following discussion, which draws from the analytical tools of economics, ventures rather audaciously into a theoretical examination of the implications of budget changes on the three-factor performance model. It is exploratory and, as such, detached from the city or county administrator's daily struggle to hold things together. But the theoretical constructs provide a fresh framework for understanding and predicting organizational performance, and it relies on a more balanced set of assumptions in terms of the productivity of public employees.

Connecting budgets to performance

For the chief executive, gaps in expectations pose ongoing administrative challenges. Citizens or council members may have unrealistic expectations of what can be accomplished with the resources available to the organization. A successful candidate for elected office may have promised results that cannot be achieved without significant changes in funding or the addition of new technology. A city council's decision to add resources to a program (increase optimum performance) may have come with a promise of results that exceeds what is possible. For example, a decision to hire additional police officers may have come with expectations for reductions in crime rates that are unattainable, at least with the current mix of labor, capital, departmental administration, and economic conditions.

In a budgeting context, changes in funding levels provide managers with a means to assess the administrative effectiveness of a program. A program or department that leverages additional funds into even greater outputs and outcomes ($\Delta A > \Delta O$) will be seen as highly effective. Nowadays, when soliciting proposals for internally competitive awards, universities typically ask for an analysis of the estimated return on investment for each proposal. The assumption is that additional funding will go to those programs that demonstrate, at least on paper, that they can leverage additional resources into even greater outputs or outcomes.

The relationship between changes in optimum performance (ΔO) and changes in actual results (ΔA) is illustrated in the figure below. An increase in funding carries with it a change in optimum performance. When a city council allocates more funding to the library, it assumes that the optimum performance of the library will also change. What actually happens to the library's performance depends on how well its administrators can leverage the additional resources into increased outputs and outcomes. A good library director will try to achieve a performance elasticity (e_p) that equals or exceeds 1.0 ($\Delta A / \Delta O \geq 1.0$).

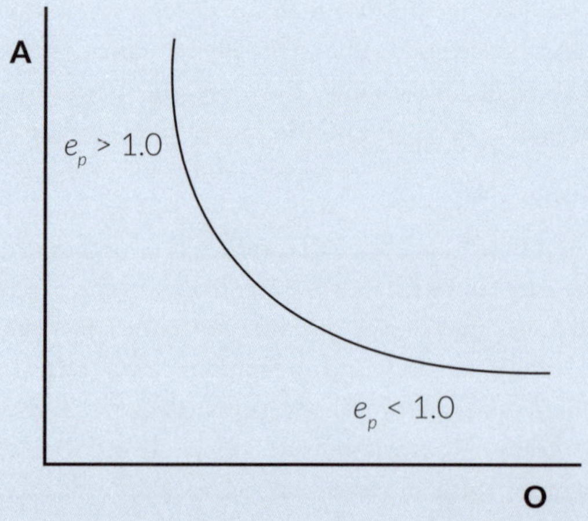

Increased optimum performance

Changes in optimum performance occur whenever budget authority is altered. If budget authority is increased but actual performance remains unchanged, then $e_p = 0$ ($\Delta A / \Delta O = 0$). This program or department director was unable, for whatever reason, to increase outputs or outcomes as a result of the increased investment. An expectations gap almost certainly will emerge ($\Delta E > \Delta A$), most likely as a performance drag. If the gap persists, it may become a performance deficit as citizens and council members lower their expectations of the program's performance.

On the other hand, if the increase in budget authority is accompanied by an even greater increase in actual performance (a program director leverages additional funding into relatively greater results), then $e_p > 1.0$ ($\Delta A / \Delta O > 1.0$). No expectations gap will develop in this case. The library director has succeeded in producing results from the increased funding that exceeded what was optimally possible. The library's results constitute a performance dividend.

However, if an increase in budget authority is accompanied by an anemic increase in actual performance, then $e_p < 1.0$ ($\Delta A / \Delta O < 1.0$) and an expectations gap will likely emerge. The library administration did increase productivity but the increase was less than the optimum given the new level of resources available. As in the first scenario, the gap may begin as a performance drag but may morph into a performance deficit if the expectations gap persists. The library administration is not at the top of its game. If the city manager allows the subpar performance to continue, the library's constituents most likely will complain about the disappointing performance and eventually adjust their expectations accordingly.

Decreased optimum performance

If budget authority is *reduced*, optimum performance also declines. As was the case with increases in budget authority, changes in actual performance will respond in one of three ways given the mix of labor, capital, and program administration. If budget authority is decreased but the actual level of productivity remains unchanged, then $e_p = 0$ ($\Delta A / \Delta O = 0$). In this case, no expectations gap is likely to develop. The reduction in state funding for public schools in Texas during the Great Recession has reduced the optimum level of performance, but school administrators have risen to the challenge. They have reorganized their instructional staffs and taken creative measures to maintain the quality of educational services. If they are successful and standardized test scores remain steady (the coin of the realm), they may achieve a performance dividend. An expectations gap will develop only if parents lack good information on the link between state funding for public schools and student performance.

On the other hand, if the decrease in budget authority and thus the optimal level of performance result in an even greater relative decline in actual performance, then $e_p > 1.0$ ($\Delta A / \Delta O > 1.0$). Program resources have shrunk, but the productivity of the program has declined even more. Rather than rise to the challenge, this program and its administration have regressed. An expectations gap will almost certainly develop among the program's constituents. It may begin as a performance drag, and if changes are not made in the program (new leadership, reorganizing, outsourcing), those expectations may morph into a performance deficit.

Finally, if the disinvestment in a program leads to a decline in actual outputs and outcomes but that decline is relatively less that the loss of resources, then $e_p < 1.0$ ($\Delta A / \Delta O < 1.0$). Productivity has dropped but the drop has been relatively less than the decline in funding. While performing above the optimum, the program still experiences a decline in productivity. Although an expectations gap could develop among stakeholders if they lack accurate information about how the loss of funding has affected the program's outputs, this likely constitutes a performance dividend as program administrators have clearly adapted somewhat to the new level of optimality.

Once again, the preceding examination is theoretical rather than practical. There are unresolved issues. For example, how can stakeholder expectations be measured? Some of the concepts also need to be fine-tuned. But if we are able to better understand the factors that shape the performance of public organizations and their employees and the expectations of stakeholders, we can better manage that performance and, most importantly, set realistic expectations with citizens for what local government can accomplish.

Strategic planning

An alternative approach is for local governments to use their strategic planning process to set performance standards that take into consideration the unit of government's unique circumstances. Any true performance deficit or surplus that develops is then evaluated against the goals and objectives stipulated in the strategic plan. Performance deficits are inevitable given limited funding and managerial talent, but if a particular program is important to the local government's strategic priorities, the manager may decide to devote additional resources to closing the performance gap. Strategic plans developed by every level in the organization can help managers and department heads sort out their priorities and target efforts to programs whose improved performance is of strategic importance.

In this approach, performance measurement begins with a strategic plan.[18] That plan, when developed with input from stakeholders both inside and outside the local government, provides department heads with guidance on how their departments can best contribute to the strategic priorities of the local government and on how those contributions can be measured. This information is invaluable for budget decision making.

A strategic plan includes a mission statement for the unit of government, as well as for each department and even each program, that articulates the reason for that entity's existence. Departments and programs should be encouraged to prepare their own strategic plans, drawing their priorities from those articulated in the local government's more comprehensive plan. The strategic planning process periodically brings stakeholders together to review and update the mission statement. The process usually includes an assessment of the local government's internal strengths and weaknesses and external opportunities and threats (a SWOT analysis).

The next step in developing a strategic plan is the identification of goals, objectives, and strategies. A goal is a one-sentence statement of a desired result or state of affairs that guides much of the work of the unit during the planning period, usually three to five years. Depending on the size of the department or program, a maximum of five goals is a reasonable number for the planning period. Each goal has several objectives, which provide more specific and measurable targets that guide the unit's efforts to achieve the goal (see Figure 12–8). Some-

Figure 12–8 Excerpt of performance indicators, Treasurer's Office, Manassas, Virginia

SERVICE EFFORTS AND MEASURES

Measure	FY 2015 Actual	FY 2016 Actual	FY 2017 Budget	FY 2017 Projected	FY 2018 Budget
Output					
% of total tax collection to tax levy / % of delinquent taxes to tax levy	99.22% / 3.16%	98.66% / 3.47%	99.00% / 4.00%	98.00% / 4.00%	99.00% / 3.50%
Input (Workload)					
# of payments processed / % of processed payments that are taxes	133,737 / 75.27%	139,984 / 71.50%	123,000 / 75.00%	125,000 / 70.00%	130,000 / 70.00%
Outcome (Effectiveness)					
Rate of Return on investments (PFM, SNAP, LGIP)		1.06% / .56% / 1.16%	.05% / .56% / 1.16%	.05% / .56% / 1.16%	.05% / .56% / 1.16%
Outcome (Effectiveness)					
% of time City funds are deposited and invested within 24 hours of receipt	99.7%	99.9%	99.8%	99.9%	99.9%

Source: City of Manassas, Virginia, *FY2018 Adopted Budget*, 258. http://manassascity.org/DocumentCenter/View/30963/FY-2018-Adopted-Budget?bidId=

times objectives can be staggered so that as one is completed, the next is undertaken, and once the last one is completed, the unit has achieved the goal. Each objective, in turn, has specific strategies for achieving the goal and its objectives, and specific performance measures against which the department can measure its success.

Department heads can use the goals and objectives to develop performance measures that will guide each program through the planning period and provide a basis for evaluating administrators' success in achieving those results. Where progress lags, the leadership can use the budget process to assess the need for additional funding, make changes in the program's mission or leadership, or reassess the objectives and the strategies for achieving those objectives. The strategic plan and its implementation—including tracking performance through input, output, and outcome measures—thus inform the budget-making process. Noted budget scholar Philip Joyce calls this a "performance-informed budget system."[19] Performance measures do not replace the judgment required for making difficult allocation choices between complex and interdependent services, but they can supplement and inform that judgment.

Limitations to performance measurement

That performance measures can be useful tools in budgeting and in improving the management of public agencies is fairly easy to demonstrate. The more difficult hurdle has been finding effective and meaningful ways to integrate the growing archive of data on program and department performance into management decision processes. A study by public finance scholars Julia Melkers and Katherine Willoughby reported the following:

> Local administrators and budgeters are surprisingly positive about their experience with developing performance-measurement systems and employing measures for a variety of activities and decisions. Not surprisingly, the same respondents are much less enthusiastic about the effectiveness of using performance measures to influence budgeting processes and outcomes in particular.[20]

Burt Perrin, a consultant in evaluation, concluded from his research that measuring outcomes has an important role in informing budget deliberations, but it can never be applied mechanically to make those decisions.[21]

Local and state governments' experience with measuring performance has encountered several obstacles, most notably dissatisfaction with the use of performance data. Three factors—informational, organizational, and managerial—help explain the reasons for this dissatisfaction.

Information obstacles

Three types of information are needed to strengthen the link between performance measures and budgeting: information about what citizens want from government, information about the impact of funding levels on performance, and information about the costs of government.

What citizens want from government As noted above, citizens view local government more holistically whereas department heads and managers see the organization as a series of separate entities, each with its own programs and activities competing for resources and public approval. Since program administrators develop the measures used to evaluate their programs' performance, it is not surprising that the measures they develop tend to reflect their own informational needs, particularly inputs and outputs and ratios of the two. But performance measures designed by and for insiders will not have much meaning for those whose assessment of government performance is based on their experiences with local government, such as citizens and the media.

One approach is to develop **meta measures**, indicators of community-wide conditions that better serve the more holistic information needs of citizens.[22] Bellevue, Washington, for example, contracts with a private firm to annually conduct a performance survey to gauge citizen satisfaction with its services.[23] The consulting firm uses a five-star rating based on the composite scores of five community indicators. Much like the familiar five-star ratings used for hotels and investments, the city's rating scale provides a quick and understandable guide to Bellevue's overall performance as seen by its citizens.

Impact of funding levels on performance Lack of knowledge about the effect of funding levels on performance is another obstacle to the use of performance measurement.[24] As has been noted throughout this book, budgeting is about discovering probable linkages—the connection between changes in funding levels and outputs or preferably outcomes. A reasonable assumption is that an increase in funding for police protection will reduce the crime rate. But that is not always the case. Moreover, funding decisions can have unintended consequences. Philip Joyce calls for the development of "logic models" that connect funding levels with performance outcomes.[25]

Costs to government Finally, in order to use performance measurement effectively, local governments need much better information about costs. Unlike their counterparts in the private sector, where costs are monitored closely as integral to maximizing profits, governments operate with little concern for allocating specific costs to specific services or tasks. The budget process determines the level of spending on a program or service and, consequently, the quantity of services provided. To ration demand, governments create queues by classifying service requests (high priority, low priority), reduce service times or amounts of the good or service, or reduce the quality of service provided (larger classes, slower response times, less frequent maintenance).

Costs include both those directly connected to the service or program's delivery (direct costs) and those associated with supporting activities, such as management, human resources, accounting, and purchasing (indirect costs). A good cost accounting system allocates both types of costs to each program or activity. That information is used to evaluate trends in the cost of producing the service and opportunities for improved productivity through a merger with other services or a reduction in inputs.

Organizational obstacles

Organizationally, departments and programs measure their performance as though they act in isolation from other programs or overlapping governments. Management consultants have long lamented the devolution of large organizations into silos of departments and programs, each focusing on its own priorities and needs with relatively little interaction across internal boundaries.[26] The larger the local government, the more apparent this phenomenon becomes. Yet the problems that face communities (and large corporations for that matter) do not follow organizational boundaries. The most meaningful measures of performance, especially those assessing outcomes, capture the multifaceted nature of public policy issues.

A goal of reducing crime may involve an after-school program sponsored by the parks and recreation department, a gang intervention program sponsored by the police department, a job fair sponsored by the community development department, and a teen court sponsored by the municipal or county court. This does not consider the additional initiatives of overlapping governments, such as a school district or public transit agency. Performance measures that consider only one program's or one department's activity reinforce this insular mindset.

The same can be said for almost any issue that a community faces. Internally, executives in government struggle to promote interdepartmental initiatives to tackle these messy problems. But the hierarchical need for clear lines of authority and accountability, in performance monitoring as in all other functions, collides with the quest for more holistic responses to community problems. The three-factor model of performance measurement described earlier offers a strategy for rethinking performance measurement, taking into consideration the more holistic interests of citizens and the multifaceted dimensions of community needs.

Managerial obstacles

The underlying assumption of performance measurement, as Allen Schick noted, is predicated on the belief that organizations can be changed by measuring and reporting their performance.[27] There are several ways in which performance measures can inform decision making in a local government. Unfortunately, these measures also have limitations. Performance measures bring to the forefront of budget deliberations our imperfect knowledge of the causal linkage between inputs and outcomes. This imperfect knowledge creates a slippery slope for managers trying to decide whether to increase, hold constant, or reduce funding for programs on the basis of their performance.

Simply creating and reporting inputs, outputs, and outcomes does not change the quantity or quality of work completed. Nor does the use of performance measures necessarily distinguish exemplary from poor performance, an implicit assumption that will have a major impact on budget deliberations. Inadequate funding or understaffing may explain why a program did not meet its target level of performance, but perhaps other factors are involved. Education leaders continually struggle with this issue when evaluating underperforming schools: Should they invest more money or hire more staff, or are there factors beyond the government's "inputs" that can ultimately change the outcomes? Is the solution to sanction the underperforming school by reducing the inputs of money and qualified teachers?

A related issue concerns the relative priority of different outcomes. Not all outcomes are of equal importance. A strategic plan can articulate the government's priorities for the fiscal year or biennium. Asking department heads to prioritize their outcomes provides the manager with some guidance, but those prioritizations cannot be relied on alone. Department-level administrators naturally emphasize the measures that reflect most favorably on their department or program's performance and downplay those that reflect less favorably. (One benefit of having a large number of performance indicators is that it increases the odds that at least some of them will show favorable trends.) Managers can provide leadership by clarifying the government's priorities, directing funding where necessary to achieve them, and holding department and program managers accountable for their contribution to those priorities.

Yet another issue concerns the integration of performance measures into the budget process. Legislatures, from councils to Congress, make relatively little use of departmental measures of performance.[28] From their research, Melkers and Willoughby conclude that local government budget decisions show "limited consideration of performance measures."[29] There are two reasons for this lack of integration between performance measures and budget decisions.

First, performance measures focus on the "ends" of government: what is produced and what is accomplished. Yet budgeting has an important "means" component whereby communities sort out their values. What goods and services should a local government provide and at what level of effort? In Verne Lewis's classic article (and as noted in Chapter 7), budgeting is about how much to allocate to activity A as opposed to activity B.[30] Performance measures help managers assess how well the ends of government are being achieved, but they do not answer the more basic value questions of what ends government *should* be pursuing,[31] which is the focus of budget deliberations, especially as budget decisions progress up the chain of command.

Second, performance measures focus attention on productivity improvement, but governments, especially in a democracy, pursue other important purposes, such as citizen participation and fair treatment. For example, citizen involvement in budget deliberations,

Figure 12–9 Price of government[a] for Fort Collins, Colorado

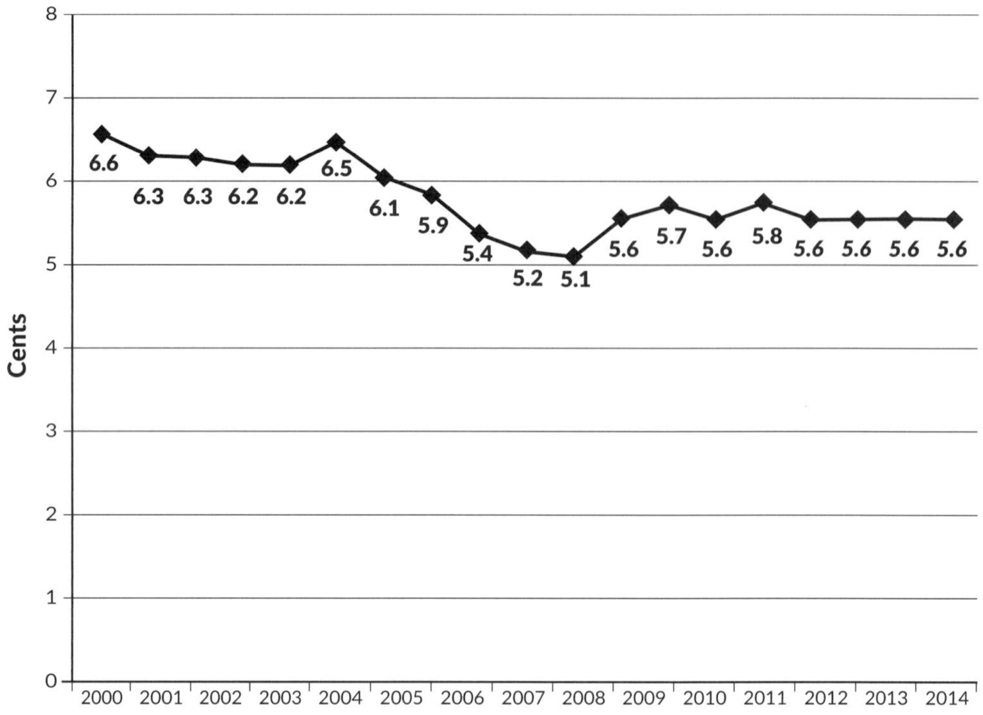

Source: City of Fort Collins, Colorado, *2017-2018 Biennial Budget*, 17, https://www.fcgov.com/citymanager/pdf/budget-2017-2018.pdf.

a As measured by cents of every dollar earned going to pay for city services, including utilities and golf.

including developing and evaluating community-wide measures of performance, is of growing importance in the postmodern world, especially as the Internet has made information more accessible and online dialogue more feasible. The budget process provides a venue for building consensus among community leaders and citizens. Budget decisions also concern the distribution of resources, such as across neighborhoods and socioeconomic groups. Budgets have an important function that extends beyond the productivity improvement focus of performance measures.

Meta measures of performance

Given the limitations to performance measurement and the obstacles that have been identified, it seems justified to assume that the information needs of citizens are shaped by factors largely ignored by most performance measures used internally by managers. Earlier, the idea of a meta measure was introduced—a measure of the overall performance of a city or county. One such measure is the price of government. This measure, which the budgeting for outcomes approach recommends be included in the annual budget document, is the ratio of the total taxes and fees paid by a city's residents to their total personal income. Figure 12–9, which depicts the price of government for Fort Collins, shows a downward sloping price for the city's costs, decreasing from 6.6 percent of personal income in 2000 then settling at 5.6 percent for the past four years.

The national media have entered the arena using a single measure to rank cities on their quality of life. For example, *Money Magazine* annually ranks the ten best places to live. Since 1949, the National Civic League has annually awarded the All-America City designation to ten communities that epitomize the league's values of promoting civic engagement, community involvement and self-governance reflective of the diversity of the community, and collaboration by all sectors of the community—public, private, and nonprofit.

The Milken Institute, a nonpartisan think tank, annually prepares a report on the "Best Performing Cities, Where America's Jobs Are Created and Sustained."[32] The composite index is a weighted average of nine economic measures, with job and wage growth receiving the greatest weights.

As local governments continue to experiment with composite measures of their performance, Bellevue, Washington's, serves as a good model. The more standardized these meta measures can be, the more useful the interlocal comparisons become. Using a third party to obtain the data and compute the measures adds credibility to the process and results.

Conclusion

Managers have long recognized the need to improve productivity in local governments. The past three decades have seen an impressive array of innovations intended to provide managers and their councils with the tools to accomplish this goal. But integration of performance measurement into budget and management decision making faces several obstacles. First is the challenge of measuring what matters to citizens. In measuring progress toward internal management objectives, a local government may miss the opportunity to relate budget decisions to broader objectives. The organization of governments into insular departments and programs limits the capacity of staff to see community problems holistically, yet that is how citizens and lawmakers view government and government performance. A gap typically exists between citizens' expectations of what that government is capable of delivering, which are shaped by the media and the promises of elected officials, and their perceptions of local government performance, which largely result from their personal encounters with local government.

Second, although local governments do not fully understand the impact of changes in inputs on outputs and outcomes, managers have recognized that data and the technical capacity to analyze them are essential to improving their organization's overall performance, as perceived by their citizens, and few have the capacity to collect adequate cost data.

Finally, most performance measures fail to reflect the complex interrelatedness of community issues and the need for interaction among departments and programs when addressing those issues.

While performance measures focus on the ends of government services (outputs and outcomes), the budget process is preoccupied with questions of value and the relative worth of alternatives. Using performance measurement to improve budget decisions thus requires a recognition of this tension and the development of measures that are relevant to questions of value and worth.

To this end, a new framework for measuring performance balances actual performance with what is optimal, given the resources provided and the expectations of stakeholders. Ideally these three indicators should be in equilibrium. Managers spend much of their time, however, addressing gaps between the three measures: performance drag, performance dividend, performance deficit, and performance legacy.

A more productive approach would be the use of meta measures—more holistic measures of performance that serve the needs of citizens better than the measures commonly used to guide day-to-day management. In sum, performance measures ideally should

- Convey information useful not only to users internal to government but also to citizens who assess local government's performance holistically
- Help managers link inputs to outputs and the effects of those outputs to desired outcomes
- Facilitate a better understanding of the interconnectedness of local government programs and services
- Aid budget participants in allocating resources so that perceived and true performance deficits are reduced.

Each local government operates in a unique environment with its own mix of outputs that will achieve an optimum level of community well-being. The challenge for local leaders is to allocate resources to achieve that outcome.

Notes

1 Geert Bouckaert, "The History of the Productivity Movement," *Public Productivity & Management Review* 14 (Fall 1990): 53–89.

2 Information on ICMA's Certificate of Performance Management can be found at https://icma.org/documents/icma-certificates-performance-management-criteria.

3 Governmental Accounting Standards Board, *Service Efforts and Accomplishments, Concepts Statement No. 5* (Norwalk, Conn: Governmental Accounting Standards Board, November 2008), 3.

4 A useful discussion of the application of performance measurements is Anne Spray Kinney and Michael J. Mucha, eds., *The State and Local Government Performance Management Sourcebook* (Chicago: Government Finance Officers Association, 2010).

5 Paul L. Posner and Denise M. Fantone, "Performance Budgeting, Prospects for Sustainability," in *Performance Management and Budgeting: How Governments Can Learn from Experience,* ed. F. Stevens Redburn, Robert J. Shea, and Terry F. Buss (Armonk, N.Y.: M.E. Sharpe, 2008), 92–113.

6 Adapted from National Performance Management Advisory Commission, *A Performance Management Framework for State and Local Government: From Measurement and Reporting to Management and Improving* (Chicago: National Performance Advisory Commission, 2010), 21–43.

7 Donald Moynihan and Stéphane Lavertu, "Federal Managers and Performance Reforms," *La Follette Policy Report* 22 (Fall 2012): 13.

8 Philip G. Joyce, "Linking Performance and Budgeting Opportunities for Federal Executives," in Redburn, Shea, and Buss, *Performance Management and Budgeting,* 49–66.

9 City of Bellevue, Washington, "Performance Dashboard, 2018," https://bellevuewa.gov/city-government/departments/finance/budget-and-performance/performance-reports/performance-dashboard

10 Anne Spray Kinney and Michael J. Mucha, "Performance Budgeting: Linking Funding to Results," in Kinney and Mucha, *State and Local Government Performance Management Sourcebook,* 47.

11 City of Austin, Texas, "Performance.AustinTexas.gov," https://cityofaustin.github.io/PerformanceATX/.

12 City of Lewisville, "Performance Metrics, 2018," http://metrics.cityoflewisville.com/.

13 Barbara J. Cohn Berman, *Listening to the Public: Adding the Voices of the People to Government Performance Measurement* (New York: Fund for the City of New York, 2005), 5. See also Barbara J. Cohn Berman, *When Governments Listen: Moving toward Publicly Engaged Governing* (New York: Fund for the City of New York, 2012).

14 Kevin Baum, "Getting in a Rut: Why Performance Management Fails," *Government Finance Review* 22 (June 2006): 46–47.

15 Jan Hawn and Rich Siegel, "Communicating Performance: Working with Bellevue's Residents to Develop Meaningful Measures," *Government Finance Review* 22 (June 2006): 24.

16 Baum, "Getting in a Rut," 44–45.

17 An intriguing conceptual parallel exists in psychology's three elements that make up a person's sense of self: actual self, ideal self, and ought self. Shai Davidai and Thomas Gilovich, "The Ideal Road Not Taken: The Self-discrepancies Involved in People's Most Enduring Regrets," *Emotion* 18 (2018): 439-452; E. Tory Higgins, "Self-discrepancy: A Theory Relating Self and Affect," *Psychological Review* 94 (July 1987): 319-340.

18 John J. DiIulio Jr., Gerald Garvey, and Donald F. Kettl, *Improving Government Performance: An Owner's Manual* (Washington, D.C.: Brookings Institution, 1993), 9.

19 Joyce, "Linking Performance and Budgeting Opportunities for Federal Executives," 64.

20 Julia Melkers and Katherine Willoughby, "Models of Performance-Measurement Use in Local Governments: Understanding Budgeting, Communication, and Lasting Effects," *Public Administration Review* 65 (March/April 2005): 188.

21 Burt Perrin, *Moving from Outputs to Outcomes: Practical Advice from Governments around the World* (Washington, D.C.: IBM Center for the Business of Government and The World Bank, 2006).

22 Harry P. Hatry et al., *How Effective Are Your Community Services?*, 3rd ed. (Washington, D.C.: ICMA, 2006).

23 Northwest Research Group, "2017 Bellevue Performance Measures," July 2017, https://bellevuewa.gov/UserFiles/Servers/Server_4779004/File/Finance/Performance/BEL_2017_PM_Final_Report_Final_07-31-2017.pdf.

24 Hatry, *How Effective Are Your Community Services?*, 3.

25 Joyce, "Linking Performance and Budgeting," 63–64.

26 Baum, "Getting in a Rut," 46–47.

27 John B. Gilmour, "Implementing OMB's Program Assessment Rating Tool," in Redburn, Shea, and Buss, *Performance Management and Budgeting*, 23.

28 Joyce, "Linking Performance and Budgeting," 54–55.

29 Melkers and Willoughby, "Models of Performance-Measurement Use," 184.

30 Verne B. Lewis, "Toward a Theory of Budgeting," *Public Administration Review* 12 (Winter 1952): 43–54.

31 John Nalbandian, "Context, Challenge, Ethics, and Opportunity," in *Management Policies in Local Government Finance*, 6th ed., ed. John R. Bartle, W. Bartley Hildreth, and Justin Marlowe (Washington, D.C.: ICMA Press, 2012): 3–14.

32 Jessica Jackson, Joe Lee, Michael C.Y. Lin, and Minoli Ratnatunga, *Best Performing Cities 2017: Where America's Jobs are Created and Sustained* (Santa Monica, Calif.: Milken Institute, January 2018), https://www.milkeninstitute.org/publications/view/897.

Glossary

Ability-to-pay principle A basis for distributing the tax burden. According to this principle, on which the progressive rate structure used by the federal and many state personal income taxes is based, those with a greater capacity, as measured by annual household income or wealth, should bear a greater relative share of the burden. As household income increases, a higher rate of taxation applies for each additional bracket of income.

Accrual basis A method of accounting in which revenues are recorded when measurable and earned, and expenses are recognized when a good or service is used. *See also* **cash basis, modified accrual basis.**

Adjusted gross income The sum of all taxable income, less income excluded from the tax base, less adjustments for income already taxed or for the cost incurred in earning that income (e.g., the cost of an employer-mandated relocation) or certain other adjustments (e.g., contributions to individual retirement accounts).

Adjustment A reduction in gross income designed to reduce or eliminate double taxation, such as with alimony payments, the cost of earning income, or job-related moving expenses. An adjustment is also made for standard and itemized deductions and personal exemptions, which reduce taxable income, and for credits, which reduce tax liability.

Agglomeration economies Reductions in operating costs that result when firms in the same industry locate in proximity to each other in order to benefit from the savings that come from sharing the costs of specialized services or accessing a specialized pool of labor. Such concentrations of industries may be driven by natural forces or fortuitous historical events.

Amnesty A controversial revenue enforcement measure used to collect delinquent taxes, fines, and charges. As a one-time incentive, the penalty is reduced or eliminated in reward for payment during the amnesty period. Amnesty programs provide a one-time infusion of revenue for local governments and are always accompanied by a promise from the local government to elevate enforcement efforts following the amnesty period.

Apportionment The release of funds on a quarterly or project basis by the budget office. Designed to prevent the premature depletion of a unit's appropriation, apportionment is more common at the state and federal levels than at the local level.

Appropriation Adoption of an ordinance or other statute by a local legislature authorizing administrators to make expenditures or enter into obligations for specific purposes.

Assessment cap A statutory provision, usually statewide, that limits annual increases in property assessments to the cost of living or a specified percentage, whichever is less. Assessment caps are intended to limit extraordinary increases in taxable values and the revenue windfalls to local governments that such increases produce. Unfortunately, these caps introduce significant horizontal inequities into the distribution of the property tax burden since lower-valued properties tend to increase in value at a lower rate than higher-valued properties.

Asset account A type of account that records information on things of value to a fund. Asset accounts are of two general types: current assets, such as cash or things that can be converted into cash fairly quickly (e.g., investments, receivables, and inventory); and noncurrent assets, such as fixed assets or things of value with a life expectancy of more than one year (e.g., land, buildings, and equipment). *See also* **liability account.**

Balanced budget A budget in which current revenues equal current expenditures. After expenditures have been pared, budgets may be balanced by adjusting taxes and fees to generate total current revenues, by drawing down fund balances accumulated from prior years, or by short-term borrowing to make up the difference between revenues from taxes and other income and current expenditures. The legal requirements for a balanced budget may be set by the state or the local government.

Balanced scorecard An approach to budgeting that uses a local government's mission and strategic plan to develop ten to fifteen key measures of success by which the city or county will judge its overall performance. One key measure of success is citizen satisfaction with a local government's performance. Budget decisions are made on the basis of strategic priorities, and a scorecard is kept on how effectively performance improves in the key performance areas.

Base budget A budget that provides an estimate of the spending authority needed to continue current levels of service with no changes in the level of effort. A base budget provides a benchmark for evaluating the effect of any proposed spending or revenue changes on the budget. It nets out one-time expenditures or other special appropriations to provide managers with an accurate estimate of the true cost of continuing operations at the existing level of effort.

Benefits-received principle A defensible basis for tax equity that states that those who benefit from a public service should bear a pro rata share of its cost. The more private the benefits from the service, the greater the proportion of its cost that should be recovered from beneficiaries through either direct charges or taxes. The most widespread application of this principle is in the use of charges for public services, such as toll roads and utility services. Benefits-based taxes are also an example of the application of this principle of equity.

Biennial budget A budget that covers a two-year period.

Block rate A service charge that changes across levels of consumption. A block-rate pricing strategy segments consumption into blocks and then prices each block separately according to the per unit variable costs for providing service for each level of consumption.

Border-city/county effects The negative economic consequences that occur when tax rates or service charges differ substantially among local governments within a region, thereby violating the principle of tax neutrality. Households and businesses make economic decisions on the basis of tax (or service charge) considerations. Such behavior creates a net drain on the productive output of the local economy. States have a responsibility to promote neutrality through policies that encourage broader-based, flatter-rate taxes, especially at the local level of government.

Bounded benefits Policies or laws that allow the creation of a restricted area within a local government, such as a tax increment financing district (TIF) or home owners association (HOA), that captures the benefits of a tax policy or public service. These benefits are capitalized into property values that accrue to current property owners. For example, an HOA that restricts ownership to residents at least 65 years old will accrue bounded benefits from a property tax freeze for senior homeowners.

Budget authority Authority provided through an appropriation act approved by the council to enter into financial commitments, such as contracts and purchase orders, that will result in the eventual disbursement of cash. In the case of the operating budget, most budget authority lapses at the end of the fiscal year if the authority has not been committed at that point. In the case of the capital budget, authority may not lapse until construction of the project is completed.

Budget deficit The result of current expenditures exceeding current revenues. The difference must be covered through either borrowing or tapping other resources, such as budget reserves or the budget stabilization fund.

Budget manual A booklet prepared by the budget office that includes, at a minimum, the budget calendar, the forms that departments need to prepare their budget requests, and a description of the budget process. It also contains instructions on entering information into the budget database if the database is online, and procedures for submitting requests that are new initiatives.

Budget policy statement A written statement, ideally endorsed formally by the council, providing standards of financial performance that guide budget deliberations. Such a statement provides guidance on the scope of the operating (and capital) budget, the definition of a balanced budget, the types and terms for maintaining reserves, and the entity responsible for budget preparation. It expedites budget deliberations and brings continuity to budget decision making.

Budget reserves Money accumulated in special accounts for future purposes—for example, to deal with unforeseen circumstances or to replace buildings or equipment. *See also* **rainy day fund.**

Budget rider A statutory provision attached to an appropriation act or other type of legislation that modifies the appropriation for certain agencies, groups of citizens, or revenue sources. A rider may be attached to win the support of a key legislator, to limit a particular type of expenditure, or to mandate particular procedures on agencies as a condition for receiving their appropriation.

Budget transfer The shifting of budget authority from one account or fund to another after the council has adopted the budget. Authority to make such transfers is granted either explicitly in charter or law, or implicitly by agreement between the council and the manager.

Budgeting for outcomes An entrepreneurial approach to budget preparation that relies on competition among departments and programs to contain costs and promote innovative solutions to community problems. Units inside and outside the city government submit offers to meet the requested service results. All spending requests must be part of an offer, and each offer includes quantifiable and verifiable measures of the results to be delivered.

Capital budget A spending plan for improvements to or acquisition of land, facilities, equipment, and infrastructure. The capital budget (1) balances revenues and expenditures, (2) specifies the sources of revenues, (3) lists each project or acquisition, and (4) must ordinarily be approved through adoption of an appropriation by the legislative body. *See also* **operating budget.**

Capital improvement plan (CIP) A list of capital projects for a period of time, usually five years, by department. The CIP may list anticipated revenues to pay for the projects.

Capitalization The backward shifting of changes in property taxes and impact fees to landowners in the form of lower prices for their land. A tax increase reduces the value of the land; that is, the tax burden has been capitalized into land values, and the cost of the tax increase is borne by the landowner. The reverse occurs for tax (or fee) decreases.

Cash basis A method of accounting in which revenues are recorded only when cash is received, and expenditures are recorded only when payment is made. Since payments for goods and services can be delayed to the next fiscal year, cash on hand can result in an inaccurate picture of the financial condition of a fund. To be in conformance with generally accepted accounting principles, local governments must use the accrual or modified accrual basis (depending on the type of fund), rather than the cash basis, of accounting. *See also* **accrual basis.**

Chart of accounts A chart that assigns a unique number to each type of account (e.g., salaries or property taxes) and to each budgetary unit in the organization. The chart of accounts provides a system for recording revenues and expenditures that fits the organizational structure.

Circuit breaker A state-funded property tax relief program, usually to low-income homeowners or renters or both, through a tax credit or rebate on the state personal income tax. Such programs have the advantage of targeting tax relief to the most needy property owners; however, they are more administratively costly than across-the-board exemptions and can adversely affect state budgets during economic downturns.

Classification of property A tax relief measure whereby states classify property by use, applying a different tax rate or level of assessment to each class. Property classification schemes generally favor residential over income-producing property and introduce horizontal inequities into the property tax.

Classification of users A pricing strategy that classifies users by type or location of the user or by location of the service. Prices are then stratified by categories so that low-cost users do not subsidize higher-cost users.

Clawback clause A contractual provision that empowers a local government to pursue repayment in the event a contractor fails to meet the terms of a contract. In the case of locally funded incentives for business investment, a clawback provision gives the local government the legal basis to pursue refunding of a portion or all of the incentive in the event the business fails to fulfill the terms of the contract awarding the incentive.

Collaboration A public-private-nonprofit partnership in which financial risk is shared by the parties (both the local government and its partners) and the benefits of the partnership accrue directly to the residents and businesses of a community. *See also* **contracting, outsourcing, and mixed delivery.**

Commercial paper A short-term debt with maturities not exceeding 270 days issued by local governments to meet cash flow needs. Because tax collections and the proceeds from bond sales are received at irregular intervals through the fiscal year, a local government may encounter a cash shortfall to meet its short-term obligations. Commercial paper provides a mechanism for local governments to raise needed cash at competitive interest rates with repayment made once taxes are received or bonds are issued.

Competitive bidding A method for selecting vendors or other providers of services by issuing a request for proposals or call for bids. For larger, more complex projects, the local government may host a bidder's conference in which additional details on the proposed project are provided and prospective bidders can ask questions. On or before the deadline, prospective vendors then submit bids using the bid form or other approved template provided by the local government. After comparing the bids using the same criteria, the lowest price bid submitted by a qualified vendor is selected.

Comprehensive annual financial report (CAFR) A report that summarizes financial data for the previous fiscal year in a standardized format. Usually referred to by its abbreviation, the CAFR is organized by fund types and contains the following documents: (1) an auditor's report; (2) management's discussion and analysis (MD&A); (3) a statement of net assets (or a balance sheet for governmental funds); (4) a statement of activities for all funds; and (5) a statement of revenues, expenditures, and changes in fund balance (an operating statement) for governmental funds. An operating statement comparing the budget with actual amounts will also be prepared for the general fund.

Connection charges A service charge for a household, business, or developer to buy into the existing capacity of public facilities.

Consolidated allocation technique A method for allocating indirect costs that involves summing the cost of all support services (purchasing, personnel, central administration, budget, etc.) and then apportioning those costs to direct services for which a fee is collected. Indirect costs are then allocated on the basis of each chargeable activity's share of the total budget, or share of total salaries and fringe benefits, or a similar measure of relative size. This method ignores the interdependence among support services and thus allocates more of the cost of these support services to chargeable services than is justified.

Contracting A public-private-nonprofit partnership in which financial risk is not shared (the contractor bears the financial risk) and the benefits of the partnership accrue to the local government (and only indirectly to its residents). *See also* **outsourcing, mixed delivery, and collaboration.**

Credit enhancement A term describing the backup pledge for repayment of a debt obligation. Should the debtor default on repayment of either the principal or interest on the loan, repayment of the debt is made by the backup pledge. In the case of municipal bonds, credit enhancement may be provided by an insurer, the state, a bank, or another third party.

Current assets Those assets that can be converted into cash within one year. On the asset side of the ledger, accounts are arranged in order of their liquidity—the speed with which they can be sold for cash. Cash and investments are the most liquid. Other current assets include taxes and accounts receivable, inventory, and prepaid expenses.

Current services budget *See* **base budget.**

Decision package A term originally used with zero-base budgeting (ZBB) to describe the various levels of spending proposals that departments use in submitting their budget requests. Three types of decision packages are used in ZBB: a base-level package, which meets only the most basic service needs; a current services package, which ensures delivery of services at the current level; and an enhanced package, which allows the decision unit to extend its services to currently unmet needs.

Dedicated improvements A method for shifting the cost of new development to developers who must transfer new improvements—such as new streets, lighting, and drainage—to the local government as a condition for local government approval of the new subdivision.

Default Failure to make a debt payment (principal or interest) on time.

Deferral The authority of a chief executive to temporarily suspend budget authority, with reinstatement of that authority before the end of the fiscal year. A chief executive's deferral authority should be clarified in the budget policies. *See also* **recision.**

Depreciation A type of expense associated with the use of fixed assets other than land. The annual depreciation of fixed assets is reported on the financial statements of funds using the accrual basis of accounting.

Deterministic (formula-based) revenue projection One of four methods for forecasting revenues. The deterministic or formula-based method relies on a straightforward mathematical formula to estimate tax yield, such as tax base x tax rate = tax yield. In the case of the property tax, the tax base is set through the appraisal process, making estimations of property tax yield a simple mathematical computation.

Development charges Charges by local governments to compensate for regulating new construction and for the impact of that construction on public services. Impact fees for off-site improvements and building inspection fees are examples.

Direct allocation A method for allocating the cost of support services by summing the costs of these indirect services (payroll, finance, central administration) then allocating them to the utility services based on each service's share of the total budget or share of total salaries and fringe benefits.

Direct costs Expenses that are directly attributable to the production of a service, such as wages, benefits, supplies, and contract services, and that would be eliminated if the service were discontinued.

Disaster resiliency Policies and actions designed to anticipate, withstand, and recover from the consequences of a natural or technological disaster so as to minimize the economic impact and financial cost caused by the disruption. Resiliency conveys the idea of policies and practices that minimize the length of time required by a local community to return to normalcy following a disaster.

Disbursement Payment, usually by check, for goods or services that have been delivered and invoiced.

Earned-income credit An adjustment to tax liability available to low- and moderate-income workers that allows taxpayers to reduce their income tax liability. The credit is usually given on a sliding scale that takes into consideration household income and the number of dependents. Some states allow the earned-income credit to exceed liability, creating a negative income tax by providing a cash subsidy to qualifying households.

Econometric (causal) modeling One of four methods for forecasting revenues. The econometric or causal method relies on multivariate statistical models to predict revenue yield. The models use such economic measures as unemployment rates, inflation, gross state product, bankruptcy rates, population change, and per capita personal income to estimate parameters from historical data. The estimated models are then used to predict revenue yields into future years.

Economies of scale The cost savings that usually occur with increases in output. If the number of units increases, fixed costs are divided among more units, and the ratio of units to fixed costs results in lower costs per unit.

Effective property tax burden A measure of the impact of property tax liability to the market value of a property or, in the aggregate, the ratio of total property tax revenue to the sum of the market values of all taxable property in a taxing jurisdiction.

Efficiency measure A type of performance measure that is the ratio of inputs to outputs. It measures the amount of input required for each unit of output of a good or service that has been produced.

Encumbrance Budget authority that is set aside when a purchase order or contract is approved. An encumbrance (also known as an *obligation*) represents a contingent liability of the fund. It assures suppliers that sufficient funds will be available once the order is fulfilled. *See also* **purchase order.**

Enterprise fund A separate fund used to account for services—for example, water, sewer, golf, and airports—that are supported primarily by service charges paid by users.

Entrepreneurial budgeting Budget preparation procedures that interject market-like measures, such as competition and performance contracting, into budget deliberations. Such procedures include budgeting for outcomes, balanced scorecard, and responsibility-centered management.

Equity The approach to establishing a revenue structure that promotes fairness to all sectors and citizens in the community. Fairness is established by imposing benefits-based levies, minimizing tax favors, balancing the burden on the poor and the wealthy, and recognizing that the perception of fairness varies by community and through time. Equity is evaluated horizontally (across taxpayers in comparable economic status) and vertically (the extent to which taxpayers in different economic situations are treated differently by the tax code).

Escrow account An account with a bank or other third party into which funds are deposited to pay for property taxes and property insurance as they come due. The holders of a mortgage typically require that the borrower establish such an account. The monthly mortgage payment includes additional funds for taxes and insurance, thereby assuring the lender that sufficient finds will be available to meet these obligations.

Excise tax A levy on a specific type of transaction at a rate specific to each type. Excise taxes, also known as *selective sales taxes,* are levied separately from a general sales tax and are usually based on separate statutory authority.

Executive budget A proposed budget put together by the chief executive or his or her designees for review and approval or modification by the legislative branch.

Expenditures An accounting term that refers to the value of goods and services *received* during a period of time, regardless of when they are used (accrual basis) or paid for (cash basis).

Expenses An accounting term that refers to the value of goods and services *used* during a period of time, regardless of when they were received (modified accrual basis) or paid for (cash basis). For example, depreciation is the expense incurred in using up fixed assets for the accounting period.

Fees-for-service A generic term that refers to the wide range of levies imposed by governments on a quid pro quo basis. Fees levied under a government's proprietary powers include services charges or utility charges, whereas fees levied under a government's regulatory powers include license and permit fees or, in some cases, even impact fees on developers.

Fiscal note A statement added to proposed legislation estimating the full cost of the mandate to local governments. By requiring state lawmakers to calculate the costs that mandates impose on local governments, fiscal noting is intended to restrain state lawmakers from initiating unfunded mandates.

Fixed assets A category of noncurrent assets that includes land, buildings, and equipment that are reported in proprietary and fiduciary funds. The annual cost of using buildings and equipment in producing the services provided by the fund is reported as depreciation in the CAFR.

Flat rate A uniform fee based on the average cost of serving all users. While it is simple to administer, a flat fee requires that users whose costs are below average must subsidize those whose costs are above average. Because a flat-rate pricing structure creates no incentive to reduce wasteful consumption, it should be used only when it is administratively infeasible to measure consumption.

Flypaper effect A response by local governments to receiving a state or federal grant or an award from a private foundation such that each dollar of such funding tends to increase local spending by more than a dollar of personal income. Funding from external sources increases local spending by more than a comparable increase in income among community residents. Such funding has a flypaper effect because it tends to stick where it lands.

Fractional assessment The assessment of taxable property at less than full market value. This adjustment to taxable values may be set intentionally at less than 100 percent or may, de facto, be at a fraction of full value.

Freeport exemption A common form of a personal property tax exemption extended to manufacturers for their raw and finished goods that are temporarily held in inventory before being moved across state borders.

Full disclosure A three-step procedure, also called *truth in taxation or truth in millage,* whereby governments (1) determine the tax rate that yields the same tax levy as in the preceding year, (2) publish that tax rate in the local newspaper, and (3) adopt a tax rate to generate sufficient tax revenues to balance the current operating budget. This procedure effectively eliminates the potential for a tax windfall whenever property is reappraised, because it shifts responsibility for increases in the tax levy away from reappraisal and onto the legislative body, which sets the tax rate.

Full-time equivalent (FTE) The number of hours per year that a full-time employee is expected to work. If there are two workers, each of whom works half that number of hours per year, the two workers together equal one FTE. For part-time employees, FTEs are computed as the fraction of hours worked to the total number of hours in the work year (typically, 2,080 hours).

Full-value assessment A legal requirement that appraisals must be set at the estimated market value, with the only adjustments being for partial exemptions such as a homestead exemption. Although at least twenty-one states and the District of Columbia nominally have a full-value assessment standard, relatively few states actually maintain their assessments at this standard.

Fund accounting A term used to describe the use of funds in recording, reconciling, and reporting financial transactions. Governmental accounting information is organized into funds, each with separate revenues, expenditures (or expenses), and fund balances, and each fund is a self-contained set of self-balancing accounts.

General obligation (GO) bond A bond backed by the government's unconditional ability to raise taxes. GO bonds are also known as *full-faith-and-credit* bonds because of a government's unconditional pledge to repay the debt using whatever revenue-raising capabilities are at its disposal. *See also* **revenue bond.**

Graduated tax rate The division of taxable income into brackets, with each increment subject to a separate tax rate. In a graduated rate structure, higher brackets are subject to progressively higher tax rates. Total tax liability equals the sum of each bracket's liability.

Gross income All income subject to taxation, both earned and unearned, except whatever income is excluded by law from the tax base.

Homestead exemption A tax relief measure that permits local governments to exempt from the tax base a portion of the appraised value of qualifying residential property, which lowers the effective tax burden of residential property owners and shifts it onto other types of property. The adjustment may be a fixed dollar amount per residential property or a percentage of value.

Horizontal equity The equal distribution of the revenue burden among persons or businesses in comparable circumstances. In theory, in a perfectly horizontally equitable world, taxpayers in the same income bracket would bear the same income tax liability. Many adjustments to the tax base or tax liability, however, undermine horizontal equity in order to achieve other social or economic goals.

Impact fee A charge to developers for the cost of off-site capital improvements needed to serve a new development. Impact fees provide up-front financing for the expansion of public facilities, such as water and sewer treatment facilities or arterial roads, needed to serve a new development.

Impoundment A restriction on spending, generally imposed at the discretion of the chief executive.

Income elasticity The relationship between revenue yield of a tax and changes in income. When a tax is income elastic, revenue yield increases (decreases) at a greater rate than growth (decline) in the local economy as measured by changes in income. Conversely, when a tax is inelastic, revenue yield is less responsive to economic growth and decline.

Income tax credit *See* **tax credit.**

Independent auditor An accounting firm (or, occasionally, a state or local official not associated with the local government) that reviews the CAFR and compares it with a sample of financial transactions in order to certify that the report accurately represents the fiscal condition of the governmental unit and its funds.

Indirect costs Costs that are incidental to the production of goods and services, such as administration, budgeting, accounting, personnel, purchasing, legal, and similar staff support services. Unlike direct costs, indirect costs do not disappear if the service or good is discontinued. Also known as *overhead.*

Informed (professional) judgment One of four methods for forecasting revenues. The informed (or professional) judgment method relies on prior experience and knowledge of the local economy to adjust forecasted revenues. Informed judgment is an essential estimation method for any revenue forecast, regardless of the level of sophistication of that methodology.

Input measures Performance measures that track the amount of resources (money and FTEs) allocated to a program, department, or other unit of local government.

Intangible property A class of personal property composed of stocks, bonds, bank deposits, and other types of securities. Because of the difficulty in establishing ownership, intangible property has steadily declined in importance in the property tax base.

Intergenerational equity In the case of financing capital improvements, future users (generations) may benefit from the investment as do current users. The use of debt to finance capital improvements (pay-as-you-use), repaid over the life of the asset, distributes the cost across generations more fairly than paying cash for the improvement (pay-as-you-go).

Itemized deduction Qualifying expense that can be deducted from taxable income. Federal law allows deductions from the personal income tax for extraordinary medical expenses, property taxes, sales or income taxes, charitable contributions, and interest payments for a residence among other purposes. Such deductions were designed to increase the horizontal equity of the income tax. *See also* **standard deduction.**

Land write-down A technique used by local governments to sell a redeveloped property in a tax increment district at a cost to the private investor that is lower than the cost to redevelop the property. The predevelopment costs of the land are recouped through the tax increment fund over the life of the project.

Legal liability The person or business entity defined in law as responsible for the tax or fee. State and local laws establish legal liability in order to facilitate tax enforcement.

Liability account A type of account that contains information on claims to the fund's assets, either by other funds of the local government or by external entities. As liabilities come due (accounts payable, bonds payable), cash or other assets are transferred to the claimant to satisfy the claim. *See also* **asset account.**

License An authorization, issued under a government's regulatory powers, for an individual or business to engage in an ongoing activity. Local governments regulate activities, such as various professions, or grant privileges, such as owning a pet, and assess a fee for the license to recover at least a portion of the cost of regulating that activity. Once the license expires, it may be renewed. *Compare with* **permit.**

Line-item budget A budget format in which departmental outlays are grouped according to the items that will be purchased, with one item or group of items on each line. *See also* **object of expenditure.**

Line-item veto A rejection by an elected chief executive of one item or group of items in a line-item appropriation that was approved by the legislative branch. A line-item veto provides a check by the executive branch on the spending decisions of the legislative branch. In most cases, an extraordinary vote of the legislature can override the executive's line-item veto.

Managed competition A method for selecting providers of public services in local government by inviting both administrative units and private firms to bid on contracts for service provision. The assumption is that increased productivity will result when governments are subjected to the same competitive forces as exist in the private sector.

Management by objectives (MBO) A management tool popularized during the 1960s and 1970s that was a top-down process for unifying the organization and its employees. Management developed an action plan for the year with measurable objectives; employees in turn developed individual performance objectives designed to help achieve the organization's priorities. At the end of the year, each employee was evaluated and rewarded on the basis of how well that employee succeeded in meeting his or her performance commitment.

Merit goods and services Goods and services endowed with a public purpose but providing individual benefits that can be denied to those unwilling to pay for them. Some of the benefits from these goods and services accrue to the whole community, such as the improvement of business opportunities or the creation of jobs, and so a portion of their cost should be borne by all taxpayers. The remaining private benefits should be financed by service charges to users.

Meta measures Measures of community-wide conditions that provide residents with a more holistic assessment of the local government's performance.

Mixed delivery A public-private-nonprofit-partnership where financial risk is shared by the partners (both the local government and its partners) and the benefits of the partnership accrue to the local government (and only indirectly to its residents). *See also* **contracting, outsourcing, and collaboration.**

Mixed drinks tax An *ad valorem* tax levied at the retail level on alcoholic beverages consumed in restaurants or comparable venues. The tax is levied separately from the general sales tax or other excise taxes on alcohol, and tax yields have proven relatively immune to economic cycles. In other words, consumption of mixed drinks occurs in good time and bad.

Modified accrual basis A form of accrual accounting in which (1) expenditures are recognized when the goods or services are received and (2) revenues, such as taxes, are recognized when measurable and available to pay expenditures in the current accounting period. *See also* **accrual basis, cash basis.**

Multiplier effect The multiplicative effect of a dollar of new investment in the local economy. Multiplier effects vary by type of investment but are well documented and are an important part of estimating the long-term economic impact of public and private expenditures.

Negotiation A method for selecting vendors or other providers of services, particularly professional services, by identifying one or more qualified providers then entering into discussions with them on the terms of an agreement. The process may begin with a request for qualifications (RFQ) in which prospective vendors submit information, on a form provided by the local government, describing their record of service and competency to provide the desired services. A local government may pursue a sole-source agreement because there is only one qualified supplier or because selecting a vendor through competitive bidding is not feasible.

Net assets Under the accrual basis of accounting, the difference between assets and liabilities. A net assets statement combines all funds and any component units in which the local government has a primary financial interest, such as a school district.

Net income A measure of the profitability of an enterprise fund. Net income is the difference between the revenues earned from the services provided by the fund and the expenses incurred in generating those revenues. It is a measure of the efficiency of the enterprise at leveraging its expenses into profits.

Neutrality The approach to revenue policy that places long-term economic viability over short-term political accommodation. The key to neutrality is selecting tax policies that do not interfere with or hinder market growth. This means (1) relying on flat tax rates levied on broad tax bases, (2) using benefits-based levies where feasible, (3) avoiding interjurisdictional rate differentials, and (4) being attentive to local business taxes to achieve this.

Object of expenditure An item to be purchased in an operating budget. *See also* **line-item budget.**

Off-budget transactions Transactions that are not recorded or reported as part of either the operating or capital budgets. Most local governments rely on a comprehensive budget policy; that is, all transactions are reported as part of a budget. The federal government, however, maintains some activities, such as the U.S. Postal Service, as off-budget accounts.

Operating budget That portion of a budget that deals with recurring expenditures such as salaries, electric bills, postage, printing and duplicating, paper supplies, and gasoline. The operating budget may be a separate document from the capital budget, or a consolidated document may be prepared that has one section devoted to operating expenditures and another to capital expenditures. Taken together, the operating and the capital budgets should equal the total amount of spending for the fiscal period. *See also* **capital budget.**

Other post-employment benefits (OPEB) A commitment to continue providing benefits, such as health and dental insurance, to an employee after retirement. Local governments may not budget for this contingency until the actual expenditure is incurred. The Governmental Accounting Standards Board now requires that local governments fully disclose these long-term liabilities in their CAFRs.

Outcome measures Performance measures that demonstrate the impact of a proposed spending change on organizational or community conditions and that provide those responsible for budget decisions with valuable information on evaluating the relative merits of the proposal.

Output measures Measures the amount of work accomplished, such as the number of citizens served, number of hours expended, or number of emergency calls processed.

Outsourcing A public-private-nonprofit partnership in which financial risk is not shared (the contractor bears the financial risk) and the benefits of the partnership accrue directly to residents and businesses. *See also* **contracting, mixed delivery, and collaboration.**

Pay-as-you-go financing A method of paying for capital projects that relies on current tax and grant revenues rather than on debt.

Pay-as-you-use financing The use of debt rather than current revenues to pay for capital outlays.

Payback period For income-producing ventures, such as a utility service, the length of time required to recover the cost of an investment.

Payments in lieu of taxes (PILOTs) Payments from nonprofit organizations, especially those with large amounts of tax-exempt property, to local governments instead of the property taxes they otherwise would have owed. The federal government provides impact aid to local school districts where federal installations remove a substantial amount of property from the tax base. PILOTs and impact aid are voluntary payments made by the tax-exempt property owner to local governments.

Payroll tax An excise tax that masquerades as a type of income tax in which the tax base is the employer's payroll. Whereas employees are liable for personal income taxes, the employer bears legal liability for the payroll tax. However, except in more competitive employment markets, the incidence of the payroll tax is likely shifted to employees, especially lower-skilled ones, as lower wages.

Peak period The time when usage and demand are at their highest. In cases where a service cannot be stored, peak demand means that production and delivery capacity must be built to satisfy peak usage. A peak-period service charge varies according to when a service is used so that off-peak-period users do not subsidize peak-period users. Peak-period pricing, when it varies by the cycles of service usage, such as by hour, day, or season, approximates the marginal-cost pricing strategy advocated by economists.

Penalty and interest Separate charges imposed for failure to pay a tax or utility charge by the due date. The penalty charge is the punitive assessment for failure to meet the due date, and interest compensates the local government for the lost investment income from revenue. Penalties may be at a fixed amount or they may escalate the longer the debt remains unpaid; interest is assessed as a percentage of the outstanding balance and accrues each month the debt remains unpaid.

Performance budgeting A budget format that includes (1) performance goals and objectives and (2) inputs, outputs, outcomes, efficiency, and effectiveness measures for each governmental program.

Performance measurement An approach to productivity improvement in local governments that focuses on monitoring and reporting inputs, outputs, and outcomes of departments and their subunits. The approach limits productivity improvement to the supply side of local government—encouraging increased work effort by employees by setting expectations for outputs and outcomes and reporting the results over time.

Permit Use of a local government's regulatory powers authorizing an individual or business to undertake a one-time activity or task. Permits usually grant a privilege for a fixed period of time, such as a building permit or a parade permit. Local governments may charge a fee for the permit as compensation for regulating the activity. *Compare with* **license.**

Personal exemption An adjustment to the tax base for each dependent in a household, often granted under personal income tax laws in order to promote horizontal equity. Larger households incur more living expenses, so tax codes often include a fixed dollar amount that is deducted from the adjusted gross income in the process of computing taxable income. Personal exemptions also promote vertical equity.

Personal income Income that is derived from both earnings (wages, salaries, tips, commissions) and unearned sources (interest, dividends, capital gains, rent, royalties).

Personal property Mobile property that is not attached permanently to real estate, including tangible property (e.g., furniture, equipment, inventory, and vehicles) and intangible property (e.g., stocks, taxable bonds, and bank accounts).

Planning, programming, budgeting system (PPBS) A budget reform that links budgeting with planning and evaluation on a program-by-program basis. The aim of PPBS, now generally known as program budgeting, was to introduce more formal economic analysis into budget deliberations: under PPBS, the benefits and costs of each program are determined, and funds are allocated to those programs that provide the greatest net benefits. *See also* **program budgeting.**

Point of sale A basis for determining liability for the general sales tax and, in some cases, excise taxes. If point of sale is used, the city or county in which the transaction occurs receives the tax revenue. A few states give local governments the option of establishing liability on the basis of point of residence. The buyer's jurisdiction of residence receives the revenue from the sales (or excise) tax, rather the jurisdiction in which the transaction occurs.

Priority-based budgeting *See* **budgeting for outcomes.**

Private goods and services Consumer goods and services that are sold in discrete units for a price and whose benefits nonbuyers are effectively excluded from enjoying. Normally, these goods and services are produced by the private market, but local governments assume responsibility for their production if there is no profit incentive for private investors, or because it makes the most sense economically for there to be just one producer, or because there is a historical precedent for government involvement in the production process. Government can finance private goods and services through charges to users or through general revenues. *See also* **Public goods and services.**

Privatization The transfer of all funding and administrative responsibility for a service or program from a local government to a private or nonprofit firm.

Privilege tax A type of excise tax levied on the privilege of conducting a particular type of business or transaction. Examples include occupational privilege taxes levied on particular professions or individual employees, admission taxes, deed transfer taxes, and bank franchise taxes.

Program budgeting Budgeting in which budgetary information and allocated funds are organized along program rather than departmental lines. A program is a set of activities with a common goal. *See also* **planning, programming, budgeting system (PPBS).**

Progressive distribution A measure of the distribution of the burden of a tax or service charge across household income. If that distribution increases *relative to household income,* it is a progressive distribution. If a tax burden *as a percentage of household income* increases as household income increases, it is a progressively distributed.

Property (ad valorem) tax A tax based on the assessed value of a property, either real estate or personal property. Tax liability falls on the owner of record as of the appraisal date. Although its role in local revenue structures has declined over the past three decades, the property tax remains the primary source of revenue for municipalities and counties.

Proportional distribution A distribution of the tax or service charge burden such that the effective tax rate remains flat across the income spectrum. That is, lower-income households incur a tax burden that takes the same percentage of their income (or wealth) as it does higher-income households.

Proprietary income Income that is derived from the ownership of an unincorporated business. Proprietary income may be subject to the personal income tax.

Public choice As a result of government failure, public choice advocates hold that public policy should rely on market choices to more efficiently allocate resources to and within the public sector. Government monopolies are inherently inefficient. Public choice holds that to correct this government failure, the solution is to expand the use of quasi-market mechanisms, such as toll roads, vouchers for public education, the contracting out of public services, and increased privatization of government-provided services. Public choice has been the genesis for the emergence of entrepreneurial budgeting.

Public goods and services Goods and services produced by local government that cannot be sold in units and whose benefits accrue to all citizens. These goods and services are generally accounted for in governmental types of funds and are financed from general taxes. *See also* **private goods and services.**

Public-private partnership An agreement between a local government and a private business or nonprofit organization to provide a good or service to the unit of government or its citizens. Public-private partnerships are classified according to whether the customer is the unit of government or its citizens and whether the financial risk is shared or unshared between the parties to the agreement.

Purchase order (PO) An agreement to buy goods and services from a specific vendor, with a promise to pay once delivery is made. The purchase process begins with a purchase requisition—a formal application which, when completed by the department, initiates the purchase process. Once approved and issued to the vendor, the purchase requisition becomes a purchase order. *See also* **encumbrance.**

Purchase requisition A document initiated at the department level that seeks approval for the purchase of a good or service. Requisitions typically must be approved by the department head, budget office, and purchasing office. Requests above a certain dollar amount set by policy, such as $10,000, may require approval of the chief executive and legislature. Once approved, the requisition becomes a purchase order that authorizes the vendor to proceed with production and delivery of the requested item.

Rainy day fund A type of budget reserve that provides resources when tax revenues temporarily decline (as the result of a recession, the loss of a major taxpayer, or other similar circumstance). A budget policy should establish such a reserve, its source of funding, and the conditions when it can be tapped to supplement current revenues. *See also* **budget reserves.**

Real property A class of tangible property that constitutes land, buildings, and equipment. The role of real property, especially single-family residences, has steadily increased in importance in the property tax base.

Receivables A type of asset account that records revenues that are due but not yet collected. Taxes receivable have been levied but have not yet been paid. Accounts receivable are service charges, such as for utility services, that have been levied but have not yet been paid. The receivables account reports revenues that are measurable but not necessarily available for the current budget year.

Recision The authority of a chief executive to permanently terminate budget authority. A chief executive's authority to rescind budget authority, such as imposing a freeze on hiring, and the role of the council in approving the recision should be clarified in the budget policies. *See also* **deferral.**

Regressive distribution A measure of the distribution of the burden of a tax or service charge across household income. If that distribution declines *relative to household income,* it is a regressive distribution. A regressive distribution may occur if the tax liability actually increases across household income categories. But if that tax burden as *a percentage of household income* declines as household income increases, it is a regressively distributed tax burden.

Relative price effect The result of inflation-driven increases in spending that tend to outpace increases in revenue. This occurs because government is more labor-intensive than the private sector.

Request for proposals *See* **competitive bidding.**

Request for qualifications *See* **negotiation.**

Revenue bond A bond backed by revenues from the project that the borrowed money was used to create, expand, or improve. Also known as a *limited pledge bond* because of the conditional backing given to repayment of the debt. *See also* **general obligation (GO) bond.**

Revenue manual A document that provides details on each source of revenue available to a local government. The document is usually organized alphabetically by revenue source with information on each source's legal basis in state or local law, annual yields and rate history, principal payers, accounting code, and the entity in local government responsible for collection and enforcement.

Revenue stabilization reserve *See* **rainy day fund.**

Revenues The resources that governments derive from taxes, user charges, and other sources of income. Revenues are recognized by local governments in their accounts in one of two ways. For governmental funds using the modified accrual basis of accounting, revenues are recognized when they are measureable and available to pay for expenditures. For proprietary and fiduciary funds, revenues are recognized when they are measurable and earned.

Sales tax holiday A temporary (two- to four-day) moratorium on state and local sales taxes, usually in August, that exempts the sales tax on back-to-school items such as clothing, supplies, and even computer hardware and software.

Security deposit As a tool for enhancing collection of utility charges, a local government often requires new customers to provide a deposit up front before it provides service. Once the user establishes a record of timely payment, the deposit may be refunded with accrued interest.

Selective sales tax *See* **excise tax.**

Sequestration A budget reduction measure used at the federal level of government whereby Congress approves budget authority through an appropriation act but then instructs the Office of Management and Budget to withhold a percentage of that authority from executive agencies. The net effect is to impose an across-the-board reduction in federal spending ex post facto.

Setoff provision A local government's withholding of compensation from contractors who are delinquent in paying their property taxes or utility services charges.

Short-term debt A type of debt issued when a local government encounters a cash flow deficit or wishes to begin a major capital project before bonds are sold. Short-term debt may be issued as tax anticipation notes (TANs) or bond anticipation notes (BANs) to meet short-term cash needs. The anticipated tax or bond revenue provides the collateral for repayment.

Sin tax *See* **sumptuary tax.**

Special assessment A levy on property owners for the increased property value created by the installation of nearby public improvements. Special assessments differ from other benefits-based levies in that the maximum assessment is the increase in property value created by the improvements, regardless of the extent to which the beneficiaries use the facility. Historically, special assessments have been used for street improvements, water and sewer lines, curbs, sidewalks, and storm drainage improvements.

Split tax roll A generic term describing the result of different tax rates being applied to different classes of taxpayers. For example, homeowners may pay one (usually lower) rate on their primary residence, while businesses pay another (usually higher) rate on their property. In more recent incarnations of this concept, a split tax roll or two-tiered rate structure targets tax relief to homeowners and is a tool for bringing equity to education funding.

Standard deduction An adjustment to the personal or corporate income tax base that reduces taxable income. A standard deduction provides a fixed dollar amount for each category of tax filers (single, married filing jointly, married filing separately). *See also* **itemized deduction.**

Step method An indirect costing method that considers the benefits that support services derive from each other. Support services are ranked according to the amount of service each provides to all other support services, and then the benefits of each support service are apportioned to all lower-ranked support services. This approach makes at least some adjustment for the benefits that support services derive from each other before indirect costs are allocated to line activities, including those for which charges are levied.

Strategic plan A type of plan that provides for the goals, objectives, and strategies of a local government or one of its units. Included in the plan is an analysis of the organization's strengths, weaknesses, opportunities, and threats (SWOT); a mission statement; identification of goals, measurable objectives, and strategies to obtain those objectives; measurable benchmarks; and possibly a separate vision statement. The strategic plan also provides overall direction for the major initiatives that an organization plans to pursue and the connection of those initiatives to the organization's mission and purpose.

Sumptuary tax A type of excise tax that is designed to discourage consumption of certain classes of goods, such as tobacco, alcohol, gasoline, and diesel fuel, by rendering their cost prohibitive. The assumption is that the cost of the tax on these sumptuary goods and services is shifted forward to consumers as a higher price. The more price elastic the demand for the taxed item, the greater the impact of the tax on consumption. Also known as a *sin tax*.

Supplemental appropriation Additional budget authority approved through an appropriation act after adoption of the budget. A legislative body may find it necessary during the fiscal year to approve additional budget authority for the local government, particularly for unforeseen contingencies such as a disaster or settlement of a lawsuit

Sustainable economic development Incentives offered by a local government to promote ecofriendly growth using renewable resources. Some local governments have modified their economic development policies to attract ecofriendly industries and provide incentives for existing industries to convert to more resource-efficient technology.

Tangible property A category of personal property, such as furniture, equipment, and inventory, that has physical form and substance, yet is mobile.

Target-base budgeting (TBB) A budget process in which departments are provided with a maximum level for their budget requests. The budget office requires separate justification for proposed spending levels that exceed the target.

Tax abatement A temporary reduction in the property (or sales) tax burden of a business. The purpose of the abatement is to attract new business investment to the community by increasing the business's after-tax profits.

Tax and expenditure limitation (TEL) A state or local law that provides relief to taxpayers by restricting either a local government's taxing powers or its spending discretion. Most TELs target the property tax, although a few restrict the annual increase in spending by the local government or cap the number of employees per 1,000 population.

Tax anticipation note *See* **short-term debt.**

Tax base The objects or transactions to which a tax is applied. State law or local ordinances define the tax base as well as the objects or transactions exempted from taxation.

Tax base sharing An approach to interlocal cooperation in which tax revenue from new business development is shared among municipalities in the metropolitan area. The first and most successful application of this approach for the property tax is in the Minneapolis–St. Paul area. In the case of the sales tax, North Carolina's approach to apportioning revenue between cities and counties is a form of tax base sharing.

Tax competition A generic term that describes the rivalry among local governments, particularly those with overlapping tax bases, for tax revenue. It also describes their rivalry for new business investment.

Tax credit A dollar amount by which a taxpayer's liability may be reduced. Credits are most often associated with personal income taxes and represent an adjustment to tax liability. In the case of an earned-income tax credit, qualifying taxpayers may receive a payment if the credit exceeds the liability. Circuit breakers are a type of tax credit granted on a state income tax for local property tax liability.

Tax deferral A tax relief measure that delays tax payments by homeowners until their property is sold or the estate is settled. A deferral is effectively a loan from the local government, usually at terms favorable to the taxpayer.

Tax expenditures An alternative term for tax breaks or tax loopholes, preferred by economists, that characterizes such measures as expenditures on the revenue side of the budget. Tax expenditures include any targeted reduction in the tax base, tax rate, or tax liability.

Tax exportation The shifting of the tax burden to nonresidents. Local governments export their tax burden through such measures as hotel and motel taxes, entertainment taxes, taxes on the income or purchases of commuters, and taxes on businesses selling their products or services to customers outside the taxing jurisdiction.

Tax freeze A property tax relief measure that freezes property assessments, property tax rates, or property tax liability.

Tax incidence The economic burden of a tax. While the law establishes tax liability, the economic burden can be shifted either forward to consumers in the form of higher prices or backward to owners in the form of lower profits. Understanding the incidence of a tax is a prerequisite to assessing its equity and neutrality.

Tax increment financing (TIF) A tax incentive designed to attract business investment by the dedication of property tax revenue from the redevelopment of an area (tax increment district) to finance development-related costs in that district. Tax increment financing divides tax revenue from the area into two categories: (1) taxes on the predevelopment value of the tax base, which are kept by each taxing body; and (2) taxes from increased property values resulting from redevelopment, which are deposited by each jurisdiction in a tax increment fund and are used to finance public improvements in the redevelopment area.

Tax lien A legal claim on assets, usually real property, that serves as collateral for any outstanding tax liabilities (or sometimes utility charges). A lien remains attached to the title of the property until the liability has been satisfied. Should the taxpayer fail to make payment by the due date, a government may elect to foreclose on the lien by seeking a court order transferring title of the property to that government. The property is then sold at a tax sale, and the proceeds are used to settle outstanding claims by creditors, beginning with delinquent and currently due taxes.

Tax pyramiding A nonneutral consequence of taxes that fall on each stage of a production process. Whenever a product has multiple stages in its production process, any tax (other than a value-added tax) on each stage results in a cascading (or pyramiding) effect, with taxes falling on top of taxes.

Taxable income The tax base for the personal and corporate income tax after all adjustments, including deductions and exemptions, have been applied. Changes in any of these adjustments or in the exclusions from the tax base affect taxable income. In the case of a graduated income tax, taxable income is segmented into brackets.

Taxable nexus A legally defensible connection that must exist between a person or business and the transaction or property being taxed in order to establish tax liability. The U.S. Supreme Court ruled in June 2018 in the case of *South Dakota v. Wayfair, Inc.* that states can compel out-of-state vendors that lack a taxable nexus to collect the sales tax. However, in the case of wage and personal income taxes on professional athletes, state and federal laws require a taxable nexus.

Time-series (trend) analysis One of four methods for forecasting revenues. The time-series or trend method relies on yields of a revenue source in prior years to estimate yield for the coming year. Trend analysis may use data for as much as the past ten years. It assumes that the past yields from a revenue source are the best predictors for the budget year, although the validity of that assumption suffers as a result of significant events such as recessions, the loss (or addition) of a major employer, or a change in population.

Total quality management (TQM) An approach to management improvement that strives to create a culture of quality in the organization whereby all employees continuously seek ways to improve outputs. Driven by customer satisfaction, TQM relies on employee-based quality circles to generate ideas for improving service outputs and, ultimately, outcomes.

Truth in budgeting An organizational culture that ensures that the budget office is a dependable and credible source of analyses, independent of the influence of special interests, and staffed by qualified budget analysts who have access to the technology and data needed to provide informed judgments of the probable linkages among inputs, outputs, and outcomes.

Truth in millage *See* **full disclosure.**

Truth in taxation *See* **full disclosure.**

Unearned income The portion of the income tax base generally from returns on capital as opposed to labor. Sources of unearned income include interest, dividends, realized capital gains, royalties, and rent.

Uniformity clause A provision in many state constitutions that compels, in varying degrees, that all taxpayers—or at least those in comparable economic or social situations—be treated the same.

Use tax A tax, adopted in tandem with the general sales tax, levied on goods brought into a jurisdiction from another jurisdiction where a sales tax is not levied or is levied at a lower rate. The use tax is designed to protect retailers in a taxing jurisdiction by discouraging consumers from making their purchases outside the jurisdiction simply to avoid its sales tax. Enforcement is difficult except on big-ticket items for which records of ownership are maintained by governments.

Use-value appraisal Also called *production-value appraisal,* an approach to property valuation that is based on the property's value given its current use and not its market value (highest and best use). State law typically allows this basis of appraisal for agricultural and open space land as a way of providing tax relief to farmers who own land on the fringe of an urban area where speculation by developers often increases land value well beyond what the land is worth for agricultural purposes.

User charge Levy assessed on consumers for the cost of providing a good or service. Under the authority of their proprietary powers, local governments assess user or service charges to recover a portion or the full cost of the good or service. Goods and services subject to a user charge share a common quality as private goods, those that could be produced by private businesses but for various reasons are provided by a local government.

Variable rate A two-part tariff in which users are charged a minimum rate for the capacity (or fixed) cost of access to the service and a variable rate based on the quantity of service used. Utility services typically use variable rates.

Vertical equity The distribution of the tax burden among taxpayers in different economic circumstances. Vertical equity considers both what constitutes different circumstances and the degree to which those differences are important in terms of the distribution of the tax burden.

Yield curve A graph that shows on the y-axis the return, or interest rate, of a security with the its different maturities displayed on the x-axis. Each type of security (municipal bonds, Treasury bills, CDs, etc.) has a distinctive yield curve. These curves are typically concave downward meaning that returns increase with increasing maturities but at a decreasing rate. An inverted yield curve is often a harbinger of a slowdown or even recession in the economy.

Zero-base budgeting (ZBB) A budget process that requires departments to prepare decision packages representing various service levels and to rank order them. Departmental rankings are then merged across the whole governmental unit to form a single, ranked list. Funding goes down the list until the money runs out.

Name index

Note: Information in notes is indicated by n.

Index

A Budgeting Guide for Local Government
Fourth Edition

Composition by
Kirie Samuels
for ICMA

Printing and binding by
Ecoprint
Silver Spring, Maryland